# REAL-TIME EMBEDDED COMPONENTS AND SYSTEMS

# REAL-TIME EMBEDDED COMPONENTS AND SYSTEMS

**SAM SIEWERT**

Da Vinci

**CHARLES RIVER MEDIA**
Boston, Massachusetts

Cover Design: Tyler Creative

CHARLES RIVER MEDIA
25 Thomson Place
Boston, Massachusetts 02210
617-757-7900
617-757-7969 (FAX)
crm.info@thomson.com
*www.charlesriver.com*

This book is printed on acid-free paper.

Sam Siewert. *Real-Time Embedded Components and Systems.*
ISBN: 1-58450-468-4

Library of Congress Cataloging-in-Publication Data
Siewert, Sam.
  Real-time embedded components and systems / Sam Siewert. -- 1st
ed.
    p. cm.
  Includes bibliographical references and index.
  ISBN 1-58450-468-4 (hardcover with CD : alk. paper)
  1. Embedded computer systems.  2. Real-time data processing.
I. Title.
TK7895.E42S54 2006
004.16--dc22
                                  2006009048

Printed in the United States of America
06 7 6 5 4 3 2 First Edition

I would like to dedicate this book to my two children,
Max and Lisa, who patiently understood when I had to work
on the text on evenings and weekends.

# Contents

# Preface

This book is intended to provide the practicing engineer with the necessary background to apply real-time theory to the design of embedded components and systems in order to successfully field a real-time embedded system. The book also is intended to provide a senior-year undergraduate or first-year graduate student in electrical engineering, computer science, or related field of study with a balance of fundamental theory, review of industry practice, and hands-on experience to prepare for a career in the real-time embedded system industries. Typical industries include aerospace, medical diagnostic and therapeutic systems, telecommunications, automotive, robotics, industrial process control, media systems, computer gaming, and electronic entertainment, as well as multimedia applications for general-purpose computing. Real-time systems have traditionally been fielded as hard real-time applications such as digital flight control systems, anti-lock braking systems, and missile guidance. More recently, however, intense interest in soft real-time systems has arisen due to the quickly growing market for real-time digital media services and systems.

The material in this book is based on a course offered in the Electrical and Computer Engineering Department at the University of Colorado since fall 2000 and follows a general organization that has proven to be very successful in this class: one-third theory, one-third practice, and one-third application. Students learn hard real-time theory and soft real-time concepts. Soft real time is not as well developed mathematically and not universally agreed upon yet as far as formal theory when compared to hard real time. Given balance of theory, practice, and application, you can learn fundamental concepts and go on to build a real-time embedded system of your own. Not all real-time systems must be embedded; however, this book focuses on embedded concepts for systems and components because the majority of real-time applications are embedded rather than general-purpose computing platforms.

The book is organized into three major parts: Part I, "Real-Time Embedded Theory," Part II, "Designing Real-Time Embedded Components," and Part III, "Putting It All Together." Chapter 2, "System Resources," and Chapter 3, "Processing," provide the bulk of the theory for real-time scheduling, although they also provide practical background on the design of real-time embedded systems. Chapter 7, "Soft Real-Time Services," discusses what soft real time is and why, how, and when soft real-time services are sufficient for applications. Chapter 9, "Debugging Components," discusses specialized test equipment, software, and methods used specifically for real-time embedded applications. Chapter 11, "High Availability and Reliability Design," provides specific methods for fault detection, isolation, and recovery, as well as methods to minimize probability and impact of failures. Chapter 12, "System Lifecycle," provides an overview of the process for developing a real-time embedded system. Chapter 12 does not provide a full treatment of software or systems engineering, but it does provide details specific to engineering real-time applications. This chapter is presented last to help you understand the process for hardware, firmware, and software development for systems built from components. Finally, the "Putting It All Together" section allows you to explore concepts at a much deeper level and gain hands-on experience. All the example systems can be built from inexpensive, off-the-shelf hardware using free software and firmware development tools.

The one-third theory, one-third practice, and one-third application formula for this book has been well tested and proven at the University of Colorado. This book is an excellent resource for the student as well as practicing engineer, especially engineers who may be making a career move from general-purpose computing applications to embedded systems and for those moving from best-effort applications to hard or soft real-time applications. Although not required, it will be helpful for you to be familiar with operating systems, microprocessor architecture, basic calculus, and common digital and analog circuit components.

# Acknowledgments

I would like to thank Kristy Klein, my fiancée at the time of writing this book, now hopefully my wife. I would also like to thank the innumerable people throughout my life who have taught me, including my academic advisors, my editors, my parents, and the many fine mentors I have worked with in the industry. I am particularly grateful to my father who proofread the very first manuscript. Last, but not least, I would like to thank the many students at the University of Colorado at Boulder and my teaching assistants who worked with early versions of this material contributed example code, and made many excellent suggestions for improvement. The teaching assistants who helped me and contributed to the success of the course over the past six years include: Colin Graham, Colette Wilklow, Chris Lee, Nishant Shah, Zachary Pfeffer, Daniel Walkes, Aman Bindra, Vikas Bhatia, and Muhammad Ahmad. Finally, I'd like to thank Wind River for generously supporting the course with the latest versions of their RTOS, tools, and real-time Linux® as the course has evolved.

# Part I

# Real-Time Embedded Theory

# 1 Introduction to Real-Time Embedded Systems

## In This Chapter

- Introduction
- A Brief History of Real-Time Systems
- A Brief History of Embedded Systems

## INTRODUCTION

The concept of *real-time* digital computing systems is an emergent concept compared to most engineering theory and practice. When requested to complete a task or provide a service in real-time, the common understanding is that this task must be done upon request and completed while the requester waits for the completion as an output response. If the response to the request is too slow, the requestor may consider lack of response a failure. The concept of real-time computing is really no different. Requests for real-time service on a digital computing platform are most often indicated by asynchronous interrupts. More specifically, inputs that constitute a real-time service request indicate a real-world event sensed by the system—for example, a new video frame has been digitized and placed in memory for processing. The computing platform must now process input related to the service request and produce an output response prior to a deadline measured relative to an event sensed earlier. The real-time digital computing system must produce a response upon request while the user and/or system wait. After the deadline established for the response, relative to the request time, the user gives up or the system fails to meet requirements if no response has been produced.

A common way to define *real time* as a noun is the time during which a process takes place or occurs. Used as an adjective, *real-time* relates to computer applications or processes that can respond with low bounded latency to user requests. One of the best and most accurate ways to define real time for computing systems is to clarify what is meant by correct real-time behavior. A correct real-time system must produce a functionally (algorithmically and mathematically) correct output response prior to a well-defined deadline relative to the request for a service.

The concept of *embedded systems* has a similar and related history to real-time systems and is mostly a narrowing of scope to preclude general-purpose desktop computer platforms that might be included in a real-time system. For example, the NASA shuttle mission control center includes a large number of commercial desktop workstations for processing of near real-time telemetry data. Often desktop real-time systems provide only soft real-time services or near real-time services rather than hard real-time services. Embedded systems typically provide hard real-time services or a mixture of hard and soft real-time services.

Again, a common-sense definition of embedding is helpful for understanding what is meant by a real-time embedded system. *Embedding* means to enclose or implant as essential or characteristic. From the viewpoint of computing systems, an *embedded system* is a special-purpose computer completely contained within the device it controls and not directly observable by the user of the system. An embedded system performs specific predefined services rather than user-specified functions and services as a general-purpose computer does.

The real-time embedded systems industry is full of specialized terminology that has developed as a subset of general computing systems terminology. To help you with that terminology, this book includes a glossary of common industry definitions. Although this book attempts to define specialized terminology in context, on occasion the glossary can help if you want to read the text out of order or when the contextual definition is not immediately clear.

## A BRIEF HISTORY OF REAL-TIME SYSTEMS

The origin of real time comes from the recent history of process control using digital computing platforms. In fact, an early definitive text on the concept was published in 1965 [Martin65]. The concept of real time is also rooted in computer simulation, where a simulation that runs at least as fast as the real-world physical process it models is said to run in real time. Many simulations must make a trade-off between running at or faster than real-time with less or more model fidelity.

The same is true for real-time graphical user interfaces (GUI), such as those provided by computer game engines. Not too much later than Martin's 1965 text on real-time systems, a definitive paper was published that set forth the foundation for a mathematical definition of hard real-time—"Scheduling Algorithms for Multiprogramming in a Hard-Real-Time Environment" [Liu73]. Liu and Layland also defined the concept of soft real-time in 1973, however there is still no universally accepted formal definition of soft real-time.

The concept of hard real-time systems became better understood based upon experience and problems noticed with fielded systems—one of the most famous examples early on was the Apollo 11 lunar module descent guidance overload. The Apollo 11 system suffered CPU resource overload that threatened to cause descent guidance services to miss deadlines and almost resulted in aborting the first landing on the moon. During descent of the lunar module and use of the radar system, astronaut Buzz Aldrin notes a computer guidance system alarm. As recounted in the book *Failure Is Not an Option* [Kranz00], Buzz radios, "Program alarm. It's a 1202." Eugene Kranz, the Mission Operations Director for Apollo 11, goes on to explain, "The alarm tells us that the computer is behind in its work. If the alarms continue, the guidance, navigation, and crew display updates will become unreliable. If the alarms are sustained, the computer could grind to a halt, possibly aborting the mission." Ultimately, based upon experience with this overload condition gained in simulation, the decision was to press on and ignore the alarm—as we all know, the Eagle did land and Neil Armstrong did later safely set foot on the Moon. How, in general, do you know that a system is overloaded with respect to CPU, memory, or IO resources? Clearly, it is beneficial to maintain some resource margin when the cost of failure is too high to be acceptable (as was the case with the lunar lander), but how much margin is enough? When is it safe to continue operation despite resource shortages? In some cases, the resource shortage might just be a temporary overload from which the system can recover and continue to provide service meeting design requirements.

Since Apollo 11, more interesting real-time problems observed in the field have shown real-time systems design to be even more complicated than simply ensuring margins. For example, the Mars Pathfinder spacecraft was nearly lost due to a real-time processing issue. The problem was not due to an overload, but rather a priority inversion causing a deadline to be missed despite having reasonable CPU margin. The Pathfinder priority inversion scenario is described in detail in Chapter 6, "Multi-Resource Services." As you'll see, ensuring safe, mutually exclusive access to shared memory can cause priority inversion. While safe access is required for functional correctness, meeting response deadlines is also a requirement for real-time systems. A real-time system must produce functionally correct answers on time, before deadlines for overall system correctness. Given some systems development experience, most engineers are familiar with how to design and test a system for correct function. Furthermore, most hardware engineers are familiar with methods to design digital logic timing and verify correctness. When hardware, firmware, and software are combined in a real-time embedded system, response timing must be designed and tested to ensure that the integrated system meets deadline requirements. This requires system-level design and test that goes beyond hardware or software methods typically used.

As history has shown, systems that were well tested still failed to provide responses by required deadlines. How do unexpected overloads or inversions happen? To answer these questions, some fundamental hard real-time theory must first be understood—this is the impetus for the "System Resources" chapter. By the end of this first section, you should be able to explain what happened in scenarios such as the Apollo 11 descent and the Mars Pathfinder deadline over-run and how to avoid such pitfalls.

# A BRIEF HISTORY OF EMBEDDED SYSTEMS

Embedding is a much older concept than real time. Embedded digital computing systems are often an essential part of any real-time embedded system and process sensed input to produce responses as output to actuators. The sensors and actuators are components providing IO and define the interface between an embedded system and the rest of the system or application. Left with this as the definition of an embedded digital computer, you could argue that a general-purpose workstation is an embedded system; after all, a mouse, keyboard, and video display provide sensor/actuator-driven IO between the digital computer and a user. However, to satisfy the definition of an embedded system better, we distinguish the types of services provided.

A general-purpose workstation provides a platform for unspecified, to-be-determined sets of services, whereas an embedded system provides a well-defined service or set of services such as anti-lock braking control. In general, providing general services is impractical for applications such as computation of $\pi$ to the $n$th digit, payroll, or office automation on an embedded system. Finally, the point of an embedded system is to cost-effectively provide a more limited set of services in a larger system, such as an automobile, aircraft, or telecommunications switching center.

## Real-Time Services

The concept of a real-time service is fundamental in real-time embedded systems. Conceptually, a *real-time service* provides a transformation of inputs to outputs in an embedded system to provide a function. For example, a service might provide thermal control for a subsystem by sensing temperature with thermistors (temperature sensitive resistors) to cool the subsystem with a fan or to heat it with electric coils. The service provided in this example is thermal management such that the subsystem temperature is maintained within a set range. Many real-time embedded services are digital control functions and are periodic in nature. An example of a real-time service that has a function other than digital control is digital media processing. A well-known real-time digital media processing application is the encoding of audio for transport over a network with playback (decoding) on a distant network node. When the record and playback services are run on two nodes and duplex transport is provided, the system provides voice communication services. In some sense, all computer applications are services, but real-time services must provide the function within time constraints that are defined by the application. In the case of digital control, the services must provide the function within time constraints required to maintain stability. In the case of voice services, the function must occur within time constraints so that the human ear is reasonably pleased by clear audio. The service itself is not a hardware, firmware, or software entity, but rather a conceptual state machine that transforms an input stream into an output stream with regular and reliable timing.

Listing 1.1 is a pseudocode outline of a basic service that polls an input interface for a specific input vector.

**LISTING 1.1**    Pseudocode for Basic Real-Time Service

```
void provide_service(void)
{
  if( initialize_service() == ERROR)
    exit(FAILURE_TO_INITIALIZE);
  else
    in_service = TRUE;
  while(in_service)
  {
    if(checkForEvent(EVENT_MASK) == TRUE)
    {
      read_input(input_buffer);
      output_buffer=do_service(input_buffer);
      write_output(output_buffer);
    }
  }
  shutdown_service();
}
```

This implementation is simple and lends itself well to a hardware state machine (shown in Figure 1.1). Implementing a service as a single looping state machine is often not a practical software implementation on a microprocessor when multiple services must share a single CPU. As more services are added, the loop must be maintained and all services are limited to a maximum rate established by the main loop period. This architecture for real-time services has historically been called the Main+ISR or Executive design when applied to software services running on a microcontroller or microprocessor. Chapter 2 will describe the Executive and Main+ISR system architectures in more detail. As the Executive approach is scaled, multiple services must check for events in a round-robin fashion. While one service is in the Execute state shown in Figure 1.1, the other(s) are not able to continue polling, which causes significant latency to be added to the sensing of the real-world events. So, Main+ISR works okay for systems with a few simple services that all operate at some basic period or multiple thereof in the main loop. For sys-

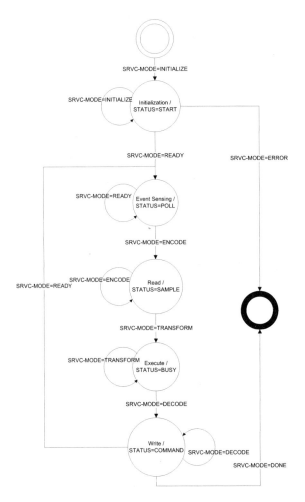

**FIGURE 1.1**   A simple polling state machine for real-time services.

tems concerned only with throughput, polling services are acceptable and perhaps even preferable, but for real-time services where event detection latency matters, multiple polling services do not scale well. For large numbers of services, this approach is not a good option without significant use of concurrent hardware state machines to assist main loop functions.

When a software implementation is used for multiple services on a single CPU, software polling is often replaced with hardware offload of the event detection and input encoding. The offload is most often done with an ADC (Analog to Digital Converter) and DMA (Direct Memory Access) engine that implements the Event Sensing state in Figure 1.1. This hardware state machine then asserts an interrupt input into the CPU, which in turn sets a flag used by a scheduling state machine to indicate that a software data processing service should be dispatched for execution. The following is a pseudocode outline of a basic event-driven software service:

```
void provide_service(void)
{
  if( initialize_service() == ERROR)
    exit(FAILURE_TO_INITIALIZE);
  else
    in_service = TRUE;
  while(in_service)
  {
    if(waitFor(service_request_event, timeout) != TIMEOUT)
    {
      read_input(input_buffer);
      output_buffer=do_service(input_buffer);
      write_output(output_buffer);
    }
      else post_timeout_error();
    post_service_aliveness(serviceIDSelf());
  }
  shutdown_service();
}
```

The preceding waitFor function is a state that the service sits in until a real-world event is sensed. When the event the service is tied to occurs, an interrupt service routine releases the software state machine so that it reads input, processes that input to transform it, and then writes the output to an actuation interface. Before entering the waitFor state, the software state machine first initializes itself by creating resources that it needs while in service. For example, the service may need to reserve working memory for the input buffer transformation. Assuming that initialization goes well, the service sets a flag indicating that it is entering the service loop, which is executed indefinitely until some outside agent terminates the service by setting the service flag to FALSE, causing the service loop to be exited. In the waitFor state, the service is idle until activated by a sensed event or by a timeout.

Timeouts are implemented using hardware interval timers that also assert interrupts to the multiservice CPU. If an interval timer expires, timeout conditions are handled by an error function because the service is normally expected to be released prior to the timeout. The events that activate the state machine are expected to occur on a regular interval or at least within some maximum period. If the service is activated from the waitFor state by an event, then the service reads input from the sensor interface (if necessary), processes that input, and produces output to an actuator interface. Whether the service is activated by a timeout or a real-world event, the service always checks in with the system health and status monitoring service by posting an aliveness indication. A separate service designed to watch all other services to ensure all services continue to operate on a maximum period can then handle cases where any of the services fail to continue operation.

The waitFor state is typically implemented by associating hardware interface interrupt assertion with software interrupt handling. If the service is implemented as a digital hardware Mealy/Moore SM (State Machine) rather than hardware SM + ISR + service loop, the SM would transition from the waitFor state to an input state based upon clocked combinational logic and the present input vector driven from a sensor ADC interface. The hardware state machine would then execute combinational logic and clock and latch flip-flop register inputs and outputs until an output vector is produced and ultimately causes actuation with a DAC. Ultimately, the state of the real world is polled by a hardware state machine, by a software state machine, or by a combination of both. Some combination of both is often the best trade-off and is one of the most popular approaches. Implementing service data in software provides flexibility so that modifications and upgrades can be made much more easily as compared to hardware modification.

Because a real-time service is triggered by a real-world event and produces a corresponding system response, how long this transformation of input to output takes is a key design issue. Given the broad definition of *service,* a real-time service may be implemented with hardware, firmware, and/or software components. In general, most services require an integration of components, including at least hardware and software. The real-world events are detected using sensors, often transducers and analog-to-digital converters, and are tied to a microprocessor interrupt with data, control, and status buffers. This sensor interface provides the input needed for service processing. The processing transforms the input data associated with the event into a response output. The response output is most often implemented as a digital-to-analog converter interface to an electromechanical actuator. The computed response is then output to the digital-to-analog interface to control some device situated in the real world. As noted, much of the real-time embedded theory today comes from digital control and process control where computing systems were embedded early on into vehicles and factories to provide automated control. Furthermore, digital control has a distinct advantage over analog because it can be programmed without hardware modification. An analog control system, or analog computer, requires rewiring and modification of inductors, capacitors, and resistors used in control circuitry.

Real-time digital control and process control services are periodic by nature. The system either polls sensors on a periodic basis, or the sensor components provide digitized data on a known sampling interval with an interrupt generated to the controller. The periodic services in digital control systems implement the control law of a digital control system. When a microprocessor is dedicated to only one service, the design and implementation of services is fairly simple. In this book, we will deal with systems that include many services, many sensor interfaces, many actuator interfaces, and one or more processors. Before delving into this complexity, let's review the elements of a service as shown in Figure 1.2.

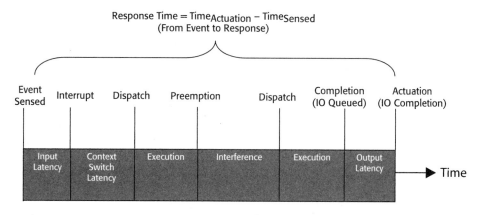

**FIGURE 1.2**   Real-time service timeline.

Figure 1.2 shows a typical service implemented with hardware IO components, including analog-to-digital converter interfaces to sensors (transducers) and digital-to-analog converter interfaces to actuators. The service processing is often implemented with a software component running as a thread of execution on a microprocessor. The service thread of execution may be preempted while executing by the arrival of interrupts from events and other services. You can also implement the service processing without software. The service may be implemented as a hardware state machine with dedicated hardware processing operating in parallel with other service processing. Implementing service processing in a software component has the advantage that the service may be updated and modified more easily. Often, after the processing or protocol related to a service is well known and stable, the processing can be accelerated with hardware state machines that either replace the software component completely in the extreme case, or most often, accelerate specific portions of the processing.

For example, a computer vision system that tracks an object in real-time may filter an image, segment it, find the centroid of a target image, and command an actuator to tilt and pan the camera to keep the target object in its field of view. The entire image processing may be completed 30 times per second from an input camera. The filtering step of processing can be as simple as applying a threshold to every pixel in a $640 \times 480$ image. However, applying the threshold operation with software can be time consuming, so it can be accelerated by offloading this step of the processing to a state machine that applies the threshold before the input interrupt is asserted. The segmentation and centroiding may be harder to offload because these algorithms are still being refined for the system. The service timeline for the hardware accelerated service processing is shown in Figure 1.3. In Figure 1.3, interference from other services is not shown, but would still be possible.

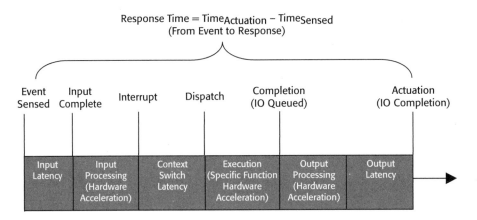

**FIGURE 1.3**    Real-time service timeline with hardware acceleration.

Ultimately, all real-time services may be hardware only or a mix of hardware and software processing in order to link events to actuations to monitor and control some aspect of an overall system. Finally, in both Figure 1.2 and Figure 1.3, response time is shown as being limited by the sum of the IO latency, context switch latency, execution time, and potential interference time. *Input latency* comes from the time it takes sensor inputs to be converted into digital form and transferred over an interface into working memory. *Context switch latency* comes from the time it takes code to acknowledge an interrupt indicating data is available, to save register values and stack for whatever program may already be executing (preemption), and to restore state if needed for the service that will process the newly available data. Execution ideally proceeds without interruption, but if the system provides multiple services, then the CPU resources may be shared and interference from other services will increase the response time. Finally, after a service produces digital output, there will be some latency in the transfer from working memory to device memory and potential DAC conversion for actuation output. In some systems, it is possible to overlap IO latency with execution time, especially execution of other services during IO latency for the current service that would otherwise leave the CPU under-used. Initially we will assume no overlap, but in Chapter 4, we'll discuss design and tuning methods to exploit IO-execution overlap.

In some cases, a real-time service might simply provide an IO transformation in real-time, such as a video encoder display system for a multimedia application. Nothing is being controlled per se as in a digital control application. However, such systems, referred to as *continuous media real-time applications*, definitely have all the characteristics of a real-time service. Continuous media services, like digital control, require periodic services—in the case of video, most often for frame rates of 30 or 60 frames per second. Similarly, digital audio continuous media systems require encoding, processing, and decoding of audio sound at kilohertz frequencies. In general, a real-time service may be depicted as a processing pipeline between a periodic source and sink as shown in Figure 1.4. Furthermore, the pipeline may involve several processors and more than one IO interface. The Figure 1.4 application simply provides video encoding, compression, transport of data over a network, decompression, and decoding for display. If the services on each node in the network do not provide real-time services, the overall quality of the video display at the pipeline sink may have undesirable qualities such as frame jitter and drop-outs.

Real-time continuous media services often include significant hardware acceleration. For example, the pipeline depicted in Figure 1.4 might include a compression and decompression state machine rather than performing compression and decompression in the software service on each node. Also, most continuous media processing systems include a data-plane and a control-plane for hardware and software components. The data-plane includes all elements in the real-time service pipeline, whereas the control-plane includes nonreal-time management of the pipeline through an API (Application Program Interface). A similar approach can be taken for the architecture of a digital control system that requires occasional management. In the case of the video pipeline shown in Figure 1.4, the control API might allow a user to increase or decrease the frame rate. The source might inherently be able to encode frames at 30 fps (frames per second), but the frames may be decimated and retimed to 24 fps.

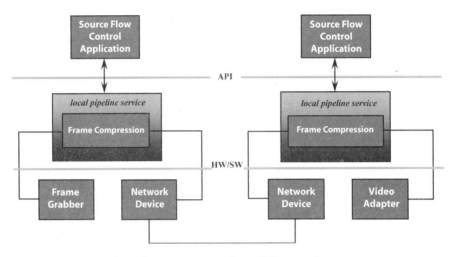

**FIGURE 1.4** Distributed continuous media real-time services.

So far, all the applications and service types considered have been periodic. One of the most common examples of a real-time service that is *not* periodic by nature is error-handling service. Normally a system does not have periodic or regular faults—if it does, the system most likely needs to be replaced! So, fault handling is often asynchronous. The timeline and characteristics of an asynchronous real-time service are however no different from those already studied. In Chapter 2, "System Resources," the characteristics of services will be investigated further so that different types of services can be better understood and designed for more optimal performance.

## Real-Time Standards

The POSIX (Portable Operating Systems Interface) group has established a number of standards related to real-time systems including the following:

**IEEE Std 2003.1b-2000:** Testing specification for POSIX part 1, including real-time extensions

**IEEE Std 1003.13-1998:** Real-time profile standard to address embedded real-time applications and smaller footprint devices

**IEEE Std 1003.1b-1993:** Real-time extension; now integrated into POSIX 1003.1

**IEEE Std 1003.1c-1995:** Threads; now integrated into POSIX 1003.1

**IEEE Std 1003.1d-1999:** Additional real-time extensions; now integrated into POSIX 1003.1-2001, which was later replaced by POSIX 1003.1-2003

**IEEE Std 1003.1j-2000:** Advanced real-time extensions; now integrated into POSIX 1003.1-2001, which was later replaced by POSIX 1003.1-2003

**IEEE Std 1003.1q-2000:** Tracing

The most significant standard for real-time systems from POSIX is 1003.1b, which specifies the API that most RTOS (Real-Time Operating Systems) and real-time Linux operating systems implement. The POSIX 1003.1b extensions include definitions of the following real-time operating system mechanisms:

- Priority Scheduling
- Real-Time Signals
- Clocks and Timers
- Semaphores
- Message Passing
- Shared Memory
- Asynchronous and Synchronous I/O
- Memory Locking

Some additional interesting real-time standards include the following:

- DO-178B, Software Considerations in Airborne Systems and Equipment Certification
- JSR-1—The Real-Time Specification for Java™
- The Object Management Group Real-Time CORBA 1.0 (for example, the TAO Common Object Request Broker Architecture)
- The IETF (Internet Engineering Task Force) RTP (Real-Time Transport Protocol) and RTCP (Real-Time Control Protocol) RFC 3550
- The IETF RTSP (Real-Time Streaming Protocol) RFC 2326
- ARINC-653, Aeronautical Radio, Incorporated Standards for partitioning computer resources in time and space

## SUMMARY

Now that you are armed with a basic definition of the concept of a real-time embedded system, we can proceed to delve into real-time theory and embedded resource management theory and practice. (A large number of specific terms and terminology are used in real-time embedded systems, so be sure to consult the complete glossary of commonly used terms at the end of this book.) This theory is the best place to start because it is fundamental. A good understanding of the theory is required before you can proceed with the more practical aspects of engineering components for design and implementation of a real-time embedded system.

ON THE CD

The Exercises, Labs, and the Example projects included with this text on the CD-ROM are intended to be entertaining as well as an informative and valuable experience—the best way to develop expertise with real-time embedded systems is to build and experiment with real systems. Although the Example systems can be built for a low cost, they provide a meaningful experience that can be transferred to more elaborate projects typical in industry. All the Example projects presented here include a list of components, list of services, and a basic outline for design and implementation. They have all been implemented successfully numerous times by students at the University of Colorado. For more challenge, you may want to combine elements and mix up services from one example with another; for example, it is possible to place an NTSC camera on the grappler of the robotic arm to recognize targets for pick-up with computer vision. A modification such as this to include a video stream is a nice fusion of continuous media and robotic applications that requires the application of digital control theory as well.

## EXERCISES

1. Provide examples of real-time embedded systems you are familiar with and describe how these systems meet the common definition of *real time* and *embedded*.
2. Find the Liu and Layland paper and read through section 3. Why do they assume that all requests for services are periodic? Why might this be a problem with a real application?
3. Define hard real-time services and soft real-time services and describe why and how they are different.

## CHAPTER REFERENCES

[Kranz00] Kranz, Gene, *Failure Is Not an Option*. Berkley Books, 2000.

[Liu73] Liu, C.L., and Layland, James W., "Scheduling Algorithms for Multiprogramming in a Hard-Real-Time Environment." *Journal of the Association for Computing Machinery*, Vol. 20, No. 1, (January 1973): pp. 46-61.

[Martin65] Martin, James, *Programming Real-Time Computer Systems*. Prentice-Hall, 1965.

# 2 System Resources

## In This Chapter

- Introduction
- Resource Analysis
- Real-Time Service Utility
- Scheduling Classes
- The Cyclic Executive
- Scheduler Concepts
- Real-Time Operating Systems
- Thread Safe Functions

## INTRODUCTION

Real-time embedded systems must provide deterministic behavior and often have more rigorous time- and safety-critical system requirements compared to general-purpose desktop computing systems. For example, a satellite real-time embedded system must survive launch and the space environment, must be very efficient in terms of power and mass, and must meet high reliability standards. Applications that provide a real-time service could in some cases be much simpler if they were not resource constrained by system requirements typical of an embedded environment. For example, a desktop multimedia application can provide MPEG playback services on a high-end PC with a high degree of quality without significant specialized hardware or software design; this type of scenario is "killing the problem with resources." The resources of a desktop system often include a high throughput CPU (GHz clock rate and billions of instructions per second), a high-bandwidth, low-latency bus (gigabit), a large-capacity memory system (gigabytes), and virtually unlimited public utility power. By comparison, an anti-lock braking system must run off the automobile's 12-volt DC power system, survive the under-hood thermal and vibration environment, and provide the braking control at a reasonable consumer cost. So for most real-time embedded systems, simply killing the problem with resources is not a valid option.

The engineer must instead carefully consider resource limitations, including power, mass, size, memory capacity, processing, and I/O bandwidth. Furthermore, complications of reliable operation in hazardous environments may require specialized resources such as error detecting and correcting memory systems. To successfully implement real-time services in a system providing embedded functions, resource analysis must be completed to ensure that these services are not only functionally correct, but that they produce output on time and with high reliability and availability. Part I of this book, "Real-Time Embedded Theory," provides a resource view of real-time embedded systems and methods to make optimal use of these resources. In Chapter 3, "Processing," we will focus on how to analyze CPU resources. In Chapter 4, "I/O Resources," resources will be characterized and methods of analysis presented. Chapter 5, "Memory," provides memory resource analysis methods. Chapter 6, "Multiresource Services," provides an overview of how these three basic resources related to workload throughput relate to more fundamental resources such as power, mass, and size. Chapters 2 through 6 provide the classic hard real-time view of resource sizing, margins, and deterministic system behavior. Chapter 7, "Soft Real-Time Services," completes the resource view by presenting the latest concepts for soft real-time resource management, where occasional service deadline misses and failure to maintain resource margins are allowed.

The three fundamental resources, CPU, memory, and I/O, are excellent places to start understanding the architecture of real-time embedded systems and how to meet design requirements and objectives. Furthermore, resource analysis is critical to the hardware, firmware, and software design in a real-time embedded system. Upon completion of the entire book, you will also understand all system resource issues, including cost, performance, power usage, thermal operating ranges, and reliability. Part II, "Designing Real-Time Embedded Components," provides a detailed look at the design of components, and Part III, "Putting It All Together," provides an overview of how to integrate these components into a system. However, the material in Part One is most critical, because a system designed around the wrong CPU core, insufficient memory, or I/O bandwidth, is sure to fail. From a real-time services perspective, insufficient memory, CPU, or I/O can make the entire project infeasible, failing to meet requirements. It is important to not only understand how to look at the three main resources individually, but also to consider multiresource issues, trade-offs, and how the main three interplay with other resources such as power.

Multiresource constraints such as power usage may result in less memory or a slower CPU clock rate, for example. In this sense, power constraints could in the end cause a problem with a design's capability to meet real-time deadlines.

## RESOURCE ANALYSIS

Looking more closely at some of the real-time service examples introduced in Chapter 1, there are common resources that must be sized and managed in any real-time embedded system including the following:

**Processing:** Any number of microprocessors or micro-controllers networked together

**Memory:** All storage elements in the system including volatile and non-volatile storage

**I/O:** Input and output that encodes sensed data and is used for decoding for actuation

In the upcoming three chapters, we will characterize and derive formal models for each of the key resources: processing, I/O, and memory. Here are brief outlines of how each key resource will be examined.

Traditionally the main focus of real-time resource analysis and theory has been centered around processing and how to schedule multiplexed execution of multiple services on a single processor. Scheduling resource usage requires the system software to make a decision to allocate a resource such as the CPU to a specific thread of execution. The mechanics of multiplexing the CPU by preempting a running thread, saving its state, and dispatching a new thread is called a *thread context switch*. Scheduling involves implementing a policy, whereas preemption and dispatch are context-switching mechanisms. When a CPU is multiplexed with an RTOS scheduler and context-switching mechanism, the system architect must determine whether the CPU resources are sufficient given the set of service threads to be executed and whether the services will be able to reliably complete execution prior to system required deadlines. The global demands upon the CPU must be determined. Furthermore, the reliability of the overall system hinges upon the repeatability of service execution prior to deadlines; ideally, every service request will behave so that meeting deadlines can be guaranteed. If deadlines can be guaranteed, then the system is safe. Because its behavior does not change over time in terms of ability to provide services by well-defined deadlines, the system is also considered deterministic. Before looking more closely at how to implement a deterministic system, a better understanding of system resources and what can make system response vary over time is required.

The main considerations include speed or instruction execution (clock rate), the efficiency of executing instructions (average Clocks Per Instruction [CPI]), algorithm complexity, and frequency of service requests. Chapter 3 provides a detailed examination of processing:

**Speed:** Clock Rate for Instruction Execution.

**Efficiency:** CPI or IPC (Instructions Per Clock); processing stalls due to hazards; for example, read data dependency, cache misses, and write buffer overflow stalls.

**Algorithm complexity:** $C_i$ = instruction count on service longest path for service $i$ and, ideally, is deterministic; if $C_i$ is not known, the worst case should be used–WCET (Worst-Case Execution Time) is the longest, most inefficiently executed path for service; WCET is one component of response time (as shown in Figures 1.2 and 1.3 in Chapter 1); other contributions to response-time come from input latency; dispatch latency; execution; interference by higher priority services and interrupts; and output latency.

**Service Frequency:** $T_i$ = Service Release Period.

Chapter 10, "Performance Tuning," provides tips for resolving execution efficiency issues. Execution efficiency is not a real-time requirement, but inefficient code can lead to large WCETs, missed deadlines, and difficult scheduling. So, understanding methods for tuning software performance can become important.

Input and output channels between processor cores and devices are one of the most important resources in real-time embedded systems and perhaps one of the most often overlooked as far as theory and analysis. In a real-time embedded system, low latency for I/O is fundamental. The response time of a service can be highly influenced by I/O latency as is evident in Figures 1.2 and 1.3 of Chapter 1. Many processor cores have the capability to continue processing instructions while I/O reads are pending or while I/O writes are draining out of buffers to devices. This decoupling helps efficiency tremendously, but when the service processing requires read data to continue or when write buffers become full, processing can stall; furthermore, no response is complete until writes actually drain to output device interfaces. So, key I/O parameters are latency, bandwidth, read/write queue depths, and coupling between I/O channels and the CPU. The coverage of I/O resource management in Chapter 4 includes the following:

- **Latency**
  - Arbitration latency for shared I/O interfaces
  - Read latency
  - Time for data transit from device to CPU core

- Registers, Tightly Coupled Memory (TCM), and L1 cache for zero wait-state single cycle access
- Bus interface read requests and completions: split transactions and delay
- Write latency
  - Time for data transit from CPU core to device
  - Posted writes prevent CPU stalls
  - Posted writes require bus interface queue
- **Bandwidth (BW)**
  - Average bytes or words transferred per unit time
  - BW says nothing about latency, so it is not a panacea for real-time systems
- **Queue depth**
  - Write buffer stalls will decrease efficiency when queues fill up
  - Read buffers—most often stalled by need for data to process
- **CPU coupling**
  - DMA channels help decouple the CPU from I/O
  - Programmed I/O strongly couples the CPU to I/O
  - Cycle stealing requires occasional interaction between the CPU and DMA engines

Memory resources are designed based upon cost, capacity, and access latency. Ideally all memory would be zero wait-state so that the processing elements in the system could access data in a single processing cycle. Due to cost, the memory is most often designed as a hierarchy with the fastest memory being the smallest due to high cost, and large capacity memory the largest and lowest cost per unit storage. Nonvolatile memory is most often the slowest access. The management, sizing, and allocation of memory for real-time embedded systems will be covered in detail in Chapter 5 and includes the following:

- Memory hierarchy from least to most latency
  - Level-1 cache
    - Single cycle access
    - Typically Harvard architecture—separate data and instruction caches
    - Locked for use as fast memory, unlocked for set-associative or direct mapped caches
  - Level-2 cache or TCM
    - Few or no wait-states (e.g., 2 cycle access)
    - Typically unified (contains both data and code)
    - Locked for use as TCM, unlocked to back L1 caches
- MMRs (Memory Mapped Registers)
- Main memory—SRAM, SDRAM, DDR (see Appendix A Glossary)
  - Processor bus interface and controller

- ■ Multicycle access latency on-chip
- ■ Many-cycle access latency off-chip
- ■ MMIO (Memory Mapped I/O) Devices
- ■ Nonvolatile memory like flash, EEPROM, and battery-backed SRAM
  - ■ Slowest read/write access, most often off-chip
  - ■ Requires algorithm for block erase: interrupt upon completion and poll for completion for flash and EEPROM
- ■ Total capacity for code, data, stack, and heap requires careful planning
- ■ Allocation of data, code, stack, heap to physical hierarchy will significantly affect performance

Traditionally, real-time theory and systems design have focused almost entirely on sharing CPU resources and, to a lesser extent, issues related to shared memory, I/O latency, I/O scheduling, and synchronization of services. To really understand the performance of a real-time embedded system and to properly size resources for the services to be supported, all three resources must be considered as well as interactions between them. A given system may experience problems meeting service deadlines because it is:

**CPU bound**: Insufficient execution cycles during release period and due to inefficiency in execution

**I/O bound:** Too much total I/O latency during the release period and/or poor scheduling of I/O during execution

**Memory bound:** Insufficient memory capacity or too much memory access latency during the release period

In fact, most modern microprocessors have MMIO (memory mapped I/O) architectures so that memory access latency and device I/O latency contribute together to response latency. Most often, many execution cycles can be overlapped with I/O and memory access time for better efficiency, but this requires careful scheduling of I/O during a service release. The concept of overlap and I/O scheduling is discussed in detail in Chapter 4, "I/O Resources."

This book provides a more balanced characterization of all three major resources. At a high level, a real-time embedded system can be characterized in terms of CPU, I/O, and memory resource margin maintained as depicted in Figure 2.1. The box at the origin in the figure depicts the region where a system would have high CPU, I/O, and memory margins—this is ideal, but perhaps not realistic due to cost, mass, power, and size constraints. The box in the top-right corner depicts the region where a system has very little resource margin.

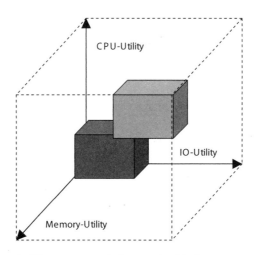

**FIGURE 2.1**  Real-time embedded system resource characterization.

Often the resource margin that a real-time embedded system is designed to maintain depends upon a number of higher-level design factors, including:

■  System cost
■  Reliability required (how often is the system allowed to fail if it is a soft-real-time system?)
■  Availability required (how often the system is expected to be out of service or in service?)
■  Risk of oversubscribing resources (how deterministic are resource demands?)
■  Impact of oversubscription (if resource margin is insufficient, what are the consequences?)

Unfortunately, prescribing general margins for any system with specific values is difficult. However, here are some basic guidelines for resource sizing and margin maintenance:

**CPU:**  The set of proposed services must be allocated to processors so that each processor in the system meets the Lehoczky, Shah, Ding theorem for feasibility. Normally, the CPU margin required is less than the RM LUB (Rate Monotonic Least Upper Bound) of approximately 30%. You'll see why this is in Chapter 3, "Processing." The amount of margin required depends upon the service parameters—mostly their relative release periods and how harmonic the periods are. Furthermore, for asymmetric MP (Multi-Processor) systems, scaling may be fairly linear if the loads on each processor are, in fact, independent. If services on different processors have dependencies and share resources such as memory or require message-based synchronization, however, the scalability is subject to Amdahl's law. Amdahl's law provides estimation for the speed-up provided by additional processors when dependencies exist between the processing on each processor. Potential speed-up is discussed further in the "Processing" section of this chapter as well.

**I/O:** Total I/O latency for a given service should never exceed the response deadline or the service release period (often the deadline and period are the same). You'll see that execution and I/O can be overlapped so that the response time is not the simple sum of I/O latency and execution time. In the worst case, the response time can be as is suggested by Figures 1.2 and 1.3 in Chapter 1. Overlapping I/O time with execution time is therefore a key concept for better performance. Overlap theory is presented in Chapter 4, "I/O Resources." Scheduling I/O so that it is overlaps is often called *I/O latency hiding*.

**Memory:** The total memory capacity should be sufficient for the worst-case static and dynamic memory requirements for all services. Furthermore, the memory access latency summed with the I/O latency should not exceed the service release period. Memory latency can be hidden by overlapping memory latency with careful instruction scheduling and use of cache to improve performance.

The largest challenge in real-time embedded systems is dealing with the trade-off between determinism and efficiency gained from less deterministic architectural features such as set-associative caches and overlapped I/O and execution. To be completely safe, the system must be shown to have deterministic timing and use of resources so that feasibility can be proven. For hard real-time systems where the consequences of failure are too severe to ever allow, the worst case must always be assumed. For soft real-time systems, a better trade-off can be made to get higher performance for lower cost, but with higher probability of occasional service failures. In the worst case, the response time equation is

$$\forall S_i, T_{response-i} \leq Deadline_i$$

$$T_{response-i} = T_{IO-Latency-i} + WCET_i + T_{Memory-Latency-i} + \sum_{j=1}^{i-1} T_{interference-j}$$

$$WCET \equiv Worst - Case - Execution - Time$$

$$\sum_{j=1}^{i-1} T_{interference-j} \equiv Total - Service_i - Preemption - Time \qquad (2.1)$$

All services $S_i$ in a hard real-time system must have response times less than their required deadline, and the response time must be assumed to be the sum of the total worst-case latency. Not all systems have true hard real-time requirements so that the absolute worst-case response needs to be assumed, but many do. Commercial aircraft flight control systems do need to make worst-case assumptions to be safe. However, worst-case assumptions need not be made for all services, just for those required to maintain controlled flight.

## REAL-TIME SERVICE UTILITY

To more formally describe various types of real-time services, the real-time research community devised the concept of a service utility function. The service utility function for a simple real-time service is depicted in Figure 2.2. The service is said to be released when the service is ready to start execution following a service request, most often initiated by an interrupt.

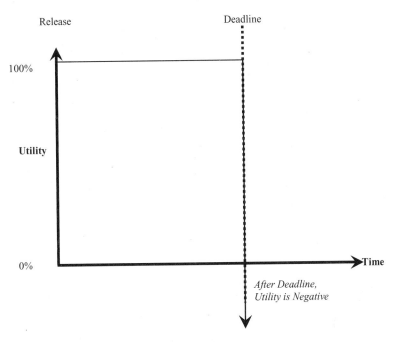

**FIGURE 2.2** Hard real-time service utility.

Notice that the utility of the service producing a response any time prior to the deadline relative to the request is full, and at the instant following the deadline, the utility not only becomes zero, but actually negative. The implication is that continuing processing of this service request after the deadline is not only futile, but may actually cause more harm to the system than simply discontinuing the service processing. A late response might actually be worse than no response.

More specifically, if an early response is also undesirable, as it would be in an isochronal service, then the utility is negative up to the deadline, full at the deadline, and negative again after the deadline as depicted in Figure 2.3. For an isochronal service, early completion of response processing requires the response to be held or buffered up to the deadline if it is computed early. The services depicted in Figures 2.2 and 2.3 are said to be hard real-time because the utility of a late response (or early in the case of isochronal) is not only zero, but also negative. A hard real-time system suffers significant harm from improperly timed responses. For example, an aircraft may lose control if the digital autopilot produces a late control surface actuation, or a satellite may be lost if a thrust is applied too long. Hard real-time services, isochronal or simple, require correct timing to avoid loss of life and/or assets. For digital control systems early responses can be just as destabilizing as late responses.

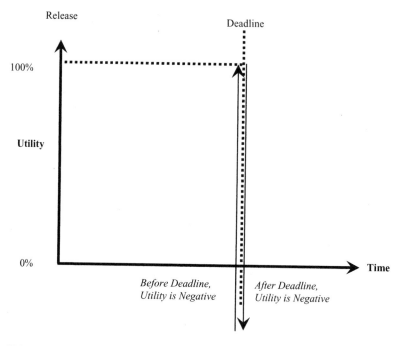

**FIGURE 2.3**  Isochronal service utility.

How does a hard real-time service compare to a typical nonreal-time application? Figure 2.4 shows a service that is considered to produce a response with best effort. Basically, the nonreal-time service has no real deadline because full utility is realized whenever a best effort application finally produces a result. Most desktop systems and even many embedded computing systems are designed to maximize overall throughput for a workload with no guarantee on response time, but with maximum efficiency in processing the workload. For example, on a desktop system, there is no limit on how much the CPU can be oversubscribed and how much I/O backlog may be generated. Memory is typically limited, but as CPU and I/O backlog increases, response times become longer. No guarantee on any particular response time can be made for best effort systems with backlogs. Some embedded systems, for example a storage system interface, also may have no real-time guarantees. For embedded systems that need no deadline guarantees, it makes sense that the design attempts to maximize throughput. A high throughput system may, in fact, have low latency in processing requests, but this still does not imply any sort of guarantee of response by a deadline relative to the request. As shown in Figure 2.4, full utility is assumed no matter when the response is generated.

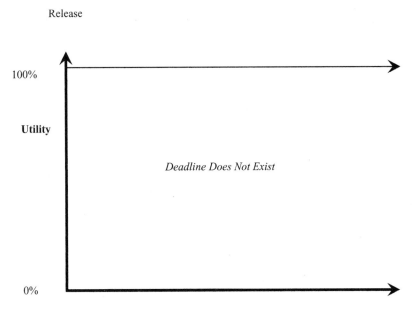

**FIGURE 2.4**  Best effort service utility.

The real-time research community agrees upon the definitions of hard real-time, isochronal, and best effort services. The exact definition of soft real-time services is, by contrast, somewhat unclear. One idea for the concept of soft real-time is similar to the idea of receiving partial credit for late homework because a service that produces a late response still provides some utility to the system. An alternative idea for the concept of soft real-time is also similar to a well-known homework policy in which some service drop-outs are acceptable. In this case, by analogy, no credit is given for late homework, but the student is allowed to drop their lowest score or scores. Either definition of soft real-time clearly falls between the extremes of the hard real-time and the best effort utility curves. Figure 2.5 depicts the soft real-time concept where some function greater than or equal to zero exists for soft real-time service responses after the response deadline—if the function is identically zero, a well-designed system will simply terminate the service after the deadline, and a service drop-out will occur. If some partial utility can be realized for a late response, a well-designed system may want to allow for some fixed amount of service overrun as shown in Figure 2.5.

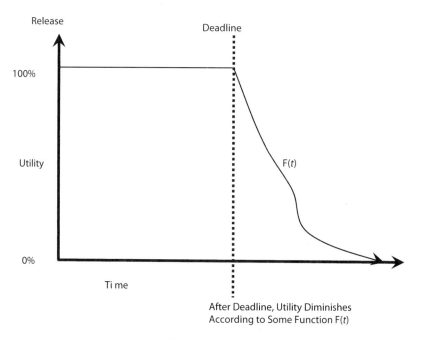

**FIGURE 2.5**    Soft real-time utility curve.

For continuous media applications (video and audio), most often there is no reason for producing late responses because they cause frame jitter. Often, it is best for these applications if the previous frame or sound-bite output is produced again and the late output dropped when the next frame is delivered on time. Of course, if multiple service drop-outs occur in a row, this leads to unacceptable quality of service. The advantage of a drop-out policy is that processing can be terminated as soon as it is determined that the current service in progress will miss its deadline, thereby freeing up CPU resources. By analogy, if an instructor gives zero credit for late homework (and no partial credit for partially completed work), a wise student will cease work on that homework as soon as they realize they can't finish and reallocate their time to homework for other classes. Other classes may have a different credit policy for accepting late work, but given that work on the futile homework has been dropped, the student may have plenty of time to finish other work on time.

A policy known as the *anytime algorithm* is analogous to receiving partial credit for partially completed homework and partial utility for a partially complete service. The concept of an anytime algorithm can only be implemented for services where iterative refinement is possible, that is, the algorithm produces an initial solution long before the deadline, but can produce a better solution (response) if allowed to continue processing up to the deadline for response. If the deadline is reached before the algorithm finds the optimal solution, then it simply responds with the best solution found so far. Anytime algorithms have been used most for robotic and AI (Artificial Intelligence) real-time applications where iterative refinement can be beneficial. For example, a robotic navigation system might include a path-planning search algorithm for the map it is building in memory. When the robot encounters an obstacle, it must decide whether to turn left or right. When not much of the environment is mapped, a simple random selection of left or right might be the best response possible. Later on, after more of the environment is mapped, the algorithm might need to run longer to find a path to its goal or at least one that gets the robot closer to its goal. Anytime algorithms are designed to be terminated at their deadlines and produce the best solution anytime, so by definition anytime services do not overrun deadlines, but rather provide some partial utility solution anytime following their release. The information derived during previous partial solutions may in fact be used in subsequent service releases; for example, in the robot path-planning scenario, paths and partial paths could be saved in memory for reuse when the robot returns to a location occupied previously. This is the concept of iterative refinement. The storage of intermediate results for iterative refinement requires additional memory resources (a dynamic programming method), but can lead to optimal solutions prior to the decision deadline, such as a robot that finds an optimal path more quickly and still avoids collisions and/or lengthy pauses to think! Why wouldn't the example robotic application simply halt when encountering an obstacle, run the search algorithm as long as it takes to find a solution, or determine that it has insufficient mapping or no possible path? This is possible, but may be undesirable if it is better that the robot not stand still too long because sometimes it may be better to do something rather than nothing.

By making a random choice, the robot might get lucky and map out more of the environment more quickly. Anytime algorithms are not always the best approach for services, but clearly they are another option for less deterministic services and avoiding overruns. If the robot simply ran until it determined the optimal answer each time, then this would constitute a best effort service rather than anytime. Figure 2.6 depicts an anytime real-time utility curve.

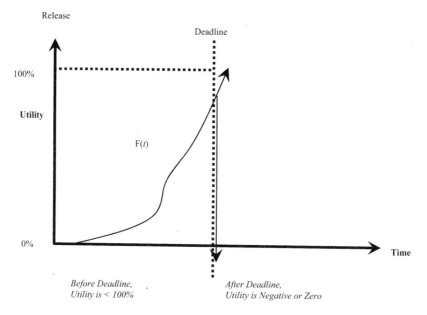

**FIGURE 2.6**  Anytime service utility.

Finally, services can be some combination of the previously explained service types: hard, isochronal, best-effort, soft, or anytime. For example, what about a soft isochronal service? An isochronal service can achieve partial utility for responses prior to the deadline, full utility at the deadline, and again partial utility after the deadline. For example, in a continuous media system, it may not be possible to hold early responses until the deadline, and it may also be beneficial to produce a late response—allow an overrun. In some sense, the idea of a hard isochronal service is hard to imagine, yet feedback digital control systems are a very important example of a hard isochronal application. That is, always producing the response exactly at the desired deadline relative to release. Isochronal systems are normally implemented with hold buffers and traditional hard real-time services, early service completions must be buffered, and CPU scheduling must ensure that late responses will never happen. So, a soft isochronal service would be far easier to implement because there is no need for early completion buffering and no need to detect and terminate services that overrun deadlines. Allowing indefinite overrun of any soft real-time service can ultimately be a problem. If overruns continue to occur and service releases start to overlap for the same service, the loading simply climbs higher and higher. How can such a system ever recover? Allowing indefinite overruns would be similar to the scenario where the overly conscientious student continues to work on more and more late homework, ultimately lowering grades in all courses to the point that total failure is the ultimate outcome. The example of a soft isochronal service is depicted in Figure 2.7.

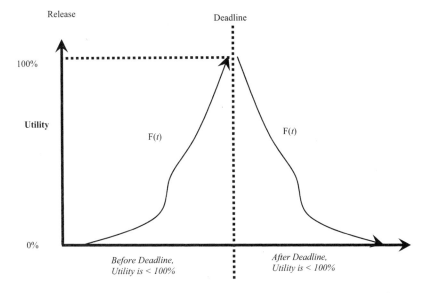

**FIGURE 2.7**  Soft isochronal service utility.

Clearly, an intelligent real-time agent would use a resource scheduling policy that leads to maximum utility in all responses for all services. For multiple services, the concept of maximizing total utility requires a normalization of utility scales. One possible way to normalize utility scales is to assign an importance factor to each service. Furthermore, in an ideal system, different policies would be applied for overruns based upon the known utility functions for each service and relative importance of each service. Using the student example again, the student being the ideal and ultimate scheduler in resource overload is smart enough to

1. Ensure sufficient margin for hard deadlines—attending classes where attendance is required.
2. Use a best-effort approach for extra-curricular activities.

3. Turn in late submissions for reduced credit in classes that allow this.
4. Apply the anytime policy for classes that do not accept late submissions, yet award partial credit.
5. Hold onto assignments completed early in classes where absent-minded professors might misplace an early submission.

Students are much smarter than most real-time embedded systems. It is likely that implementation of a resource-scheduling algorithm as intelligent and optimal as a student's is not practical for an embedded system. However, most real-time embedded systems do mix policies like the intelligent student did in the example, but most often only two at a time. One of the most frequently used mixes is a set of hard real-time services with some best-effort services. Guarantees for the hard real-time services are proven using methods discussed later in this chapter (Rate Monotonic Analysis), and best-effort services simply use all the left-over resource by executing in slack time.

The primary focus of this text is on understanding hard real-time, however, soft real-time and isochronal services are also covered. An examination of anytime services is not provided in this text. Anytime services are important to artificial intelligence and robotic systems where planning algorithms that are NP hard (Nondeterministic Polynomial bound on compute time) must be run in real-time. This is a very specialized form of real-time embedded system. Because soft real-time services are more generalized and less deterministic compared to hard real-time services, soft real-time is treated as an open issue in this text—a subject that is an open research area—whereas hard real-time is well understood and specific hard real-time policies can be proven optimal. The optimality will be demonstrated later in this chapter.

## SCHEDULING CLASSES

Scheduling services and their usage of resources can be accomplished by a large variety of methods. In this section, we consider scheduling system processors with work. In general, a system might have more than one processor (CPU), and any given processor might host one or more services. Allocating a CPU to each service provided by the system might be simplest from a scheduling viewpoint, but clearly, this would also be a costly solution. Furthermore, running services to completion ignoring all other requests on a first-come, first-served basis is also simple, but problems such as service starvation and missing deadlines can arise with this approach. To better understand real-time processor scheduling, you first need to review a taxonomy of all major scheduling policies that can be implemented as shown in Figure 2.8.

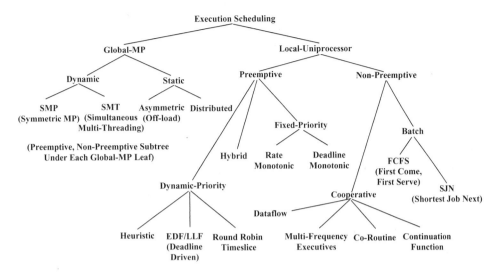

**FIGURE 2.8** Resource scheduling taxonomy.

ON THE CD

As is the case with most policies, no one policy is optimal for all system requirements, not even when all services must be hard real-time. The policies that can be made optimal and have traditionally been used for hard real-time systems are Rate Monotonic, Deadline Monotonic, and to a lesser extent, EDF/LLF. The first branch in the taxonomy is based upon hardware design; does the system contain a single CPU or multiple CPUs?

## Multiprocessor Systems

For multiprocessor systems, the first resource usage policy decision is whether each CPU will be used for a specific predetermined function (asymmetric, distributed) or whether workload will be assigned dynamically (symmetric). Most general-purpose MP (Multi-Processing) platforms provide SMP (Symmetric Multi-Processing) where the OS determines how to assign work to the set of available processors and most often attempts to balance the workload on all processors. An SMP OS is not simple to implement, and overhead for workload balancing can be high, so many embedded multiprocessor systems are asymmetric or distributed. Asymmetric multiprocessing is used frequently to take a service that was initially provided by software running on a general-purpose CPU and offload it to a hardware state-machine or tailored CPU to implement the service, therefore off-loading the more general purpose multiservice CPU. Distributed systems are typically asymmetric and communicate via message passing on a network rather than through shared memory, bus, or cross-bar. Other than the issue of load balancing, multiprocessor systems are most distinguished by their hardware architecture—shared memory, distributed message passing, or some hybrid of the two. The classic taxonomy for such systems includes SISD (Single Instruction, Single Data), SIMD (Single Instruction, Multi-Data), MISD (Multi-Instruction, Single Data), and MIMD (Multi-Instruction, Multi-Data). So, all the combinations of single or multiple instruction processing combined with single or multiple data paths are possible for MP architecture. Most embedded multiprocessor systems are multiple instruction and multiple data path hardware architectures that employ multiple CPUs for speed-up.

# THE CYCLIC EXECUTIVE

Many real-time systems, including complex, hard real-time, safety critical systems, provide real-time services using a *cyclic executive* architecture. Cyclic executives do not require an RTOS or generalized scheduling mechanism. A cyclic executive provides a loop control structure to explicitly interleave execution of more than one periodic process on a single CPU. The Cyclic Executive is often implemented as a main loop with an invariant loop body known as the cyclic schedule. A *cyclic schedule* includes function calls for each periodic service provided within the major period of the overall loop. The loop may include event polling to determine when to dispatch functions, and functions that need to be called at a higher frequency than the main loop will often be called multiple times within the loop. Likewise, functions implementing periodic services that need to be run at much lower frequency than the main loop may be called only on specific loop counts or only when polled events indicate a service request. For example, the NASA Space Shuttle flight software uses a cyclic executive design for the PASS (Primary Avionics Subsystem) and has provided decades of defect-free operation providing real-time control of a complex system [Carlow84].

The Space Shuttle PASS flight software includes the hard real-time safety critical GN&C (Guidance, Navigation, and Control) services that are dispatched by a cyclic executive from a dispatch table configured and selected based upon the current flight stage of the shuttle (ascent, on-orbit, re-entry). The highest frequency services maintain shuttle flight control and operate on a 40-millisecond period. As Carlow notes, "The high-frequency executive is scheduled at a relatively high priority to cycle at a 25 Hz rate and initiate all principal function processes directly related to vehicle flight control. Mid-frequency and low-frequency executives are scheduled at lower priorities. They initiate principal function processes, which operate at rates of 6.25 Hz down to 0.25 Hz." The scheduling of the GN&C executives is provided by the Process Management, which uses a multitasking priority queue structure and schedules the CPU in response to requests made through a service interface that defines event frequency and priority for service requests. This higher-level scheduler handles requests from the GN&C cyclic executive: SM (Systems Management), which monitors systems for faults; and VCO (Vehicle Checkout), which is used for preflight and on-orbit coast avionic systems testing. The GN&C cyclic executive is scheduled to run periodically at 25 Hz (40-millisecond period) and includes its own dispatch table to sequence GN&C services at the high, medium, and low frequencies previously described. The cyclic executive architecture has been an important and successful approach for hard real-time systems. Carlow explains the overall system: "[the flight software] architectures reflect a synchronous design approach within which the dispatching of each application process is timed to always occur at a specific point relative to the start of the overall system cycle or loop." Although the cyclic executive has been successful due to its simplicity and deterministic character, one of its drawbacks is the difficulty required to modify the cyclic schedule. For PASS, Carlow points out that, "A major benefit of this approach is repeatability; however, there is only limited flexibility to accommodate change."

The cyclic executive is often extended to handle asynchronous events with interrupts rather than relying only upon loop-based polling of inputs. This extension of the executive is called the Main+ISR design. As the name implies, this approach involves a main loop cyclic executive with the addition of ISRs (Interrupt Service Routines). The ISRs handle asynchronous events that interrupt the normal execution sequence of an embedded microprocessor. In the Main+ISR approach, the ISRs are best kept short and simple so they relay event data to the Main loop for handling. The Main+ISR approach has some advantage over the pure cyclic executive and polling for event input because it may reduce latency between event occurrence and handling. However, the Main+ISR approach has pitfalls as well. For example, if an input device malfunctions and raises interrupts at a much higher frequency than expected, significant interference to loop processing may be introduced. Although Main+ISR is more responsive to events as they occur, it may be less stable unless a concerted effort is made to protect the system for potential interrupt malfunctions related to interrupt source devices.

## SCHEDULER CONCEPTS

The design of a generalized RTOS scheduler for processor resources is covered well in most operating system texts. Here, we will briefly review some of the major concepts as they relate to real-time scheduling of the CPU resource. Real-time services may be implemented as threads of execution that have an execution context and are set into execution by a scheduler that determines which thread to dispatch. Dispatch is a basic mechanism to preempt the currently running thread, save its context, and restore the context of the thread to be run along with modification of the instruction pointer or program counter to start or resume execution of the new thread. The scheduler must implement the CPU sharing policy and the dispatcher must provide the context switch for each thread of execution. The dispatcher is required to save and restore all the state that each thread of execution uses including the following:

- Registers
- Stack
- Program counter
- Thread state

This would be a minimum execution context and is typical of real-time schedulers. By comparison, the Unix system executes threads in the context of a process and maintains a process descriptor for each thread. The process context includes much more additional state, such as I/O context, shared memory, and dynamic memory allocations. The thread state is one of the best ways to understand how a scheduler works. As illustrated in Table 2.1, thread states are based upon resources needed in the thread execution context.

**TABLE 2.1**    State Transition Table for a Thread of Execution

| Thread State | Description | Transition | Description |
|---|---|---|---|
| Ready | Thread is queued and ready to run, but has not been dispatched (given CPU) | Running | Thread selected for dispatch based upon scheduling policy |
| Running | Thread is executing on CPU | Pending | Thread needs another resource in addition to the CPU |
| | | Delayed | Wait requested by thread |
| | | Suspended | Thread raised unhandled exception during execution |
| | | Ready | Thread yields CPU |
| | | Non-Existent | Thread exits |
| Pending | Thread is waiting on a resource in addition to CPU | Ready | Additional resource has become available |
| | | Suspended | Pending thread is suspended by another thread |
| Delayed | Thread is waiting for delay period to end | Ready | Delay has expired |
| | | Suspended | Delayed thread is suspended by another thread |
| Suspended | Thread has raised unhandled exception or has been suspended by command from another thread | Ready | Suspension removed by another thread – thread activated |
| Non-Existent | Thread has not been created or allocated resources | Ready | Thread creation and activation |

*Dispatch policy*, how the scheduler decides which thread from the set of all those that are ready for dispatch, was the main differentiation in the taxonomy in Figure 2.8. As threads become ready to run, pointers to their context are normally placed on a ready queue by the scheduler for dispatch in the order determined by the scheduling policy. The scheduler must update the ready queue based upon new service request arrivals. The dispatcher will simply loop if the ready queue is empty. Note, however, that in VxWorks®, neither the scheduler nor the dispatcher shows up as a task. Also, unlike some operating systems, VxWorks does not include an idle task in the default configuration. In VxWorks, the scheduler and dispatcher are kernel context services rather than task context services. Preemptive schedulers are driven by interrupts and task calls into the kernel API. An interrupt or API call can cause the scheduler to switch context and to potentially dispatch a new thread or allow the same thread to continue execution. In VxWorks, an interrupt or an API call made by the currently running task are the only ways that the currently running task can be preempted. A fixed-priority preemptive scheduler simply dispatches threads from the ready queue based upon a priority they have been assigned at creation unless the application adjusts the priority at runtime. Most often, if two threads have the same priority, they are dispatched on a first-come, first-served basis. Almost all RTOSs include priority preemptive schedulers with support for the basic thread states outlined in Table 2.1.

One of the major drawbacks of a priority preemptive scheduling policy is the cost or overhead of the context switch that occurs on every interrupt. Systems such as Unix, which use a time-slice preemption scheme where an OS timer tick is generated every so many milliseconds by a programmable interval timer, have high overhead. By comparison, most RTOSs do not use a time-slice tick, and instead only reschedule when I/O generates an interrupt or when a thread makes a system call that results in yielding the CPU—a delay, exit, yield, call for an unavailable resource in addition to the CPU, or suspension due to exception. Otherwise, RTOS threads normally run to completion unless an event releases a thread (makes it ready) at higher priority than the presently executing thread.

Given an MP or uniprocessor hardware architecture, if more than one service can be requested on a given processor, the next branch in the taxonomy concerns whether requests will preempt services already in progress or queue and wait for services in progress to run to completion.

### Preemptive versus Nonpreemptive Schedulers

Nonpreemptive scheduling policy has existed for general-purpose computing from the beginning of computing systems. In general, this category can be subdivided into batch and cooperative processing. In batch systems, jobs that are submitted to a work queue are dequeued by the system OS and run to completion. The two most well known dequeue policies are FCFS (First Come First Served) and SJN (Shortest Job Next). The SJN policy has the advantage of completing the largest number of jobs per unit time, but long jobs may never be serviced, and furthermore, SJN requires an estimate of how long each job will require execution. Because real-time services are inherently characterized by producing a response relative to a request and deadline, neither nonpreemptive policy is of interest in this text.

All real-time services must provide a response relative to requests for the service (a release), and the response is most often constrained by a deadline. At the very least, because real-time systems are request oriented based upon real-world events, clearly these systems must support preemption or they must poll the real world on a regular basis and provide periodic service processing. Two nonpreemptive approaches are most often used in real-time systems: data flow and multifrequency executives. In a data flow, input interfaces are periodically checked, and when data is available, this data is processed and output is produced for consumption by the next service in the flow or terminated by producing a response. In data-flow processing, the inputs that start a flow are checked in a deterministic order most often, and flows are executed from start to finish or source to sink.

The best property of this type of scheduling policy is that it is fully deterministic—the order of execution in the service and between services (flows) is fully predictable. The disadvantage is that some flows may be known to require execution much more frequently than others—a modification to this scheme leads to a multifrequency executive (MFE). In the MFE, specific functions (data flows) are executed at a higher frequency than others. For example, a control system data flow may require execution 100 times per second for stable operation, whereas the guidance function may only require execution 1 time per second to direct the system to a target (hopefully without losing control!). Either approach may use asynchronous interrupts or may only poll input status registers; however, context switches beyond simple interrupt servicing are not done. That is, data flows are not switched prior to completion, and executive functions are not switched prior to completion; after a flow or executive function is dispatched (given the CPU), it runs to completion without significant preemption.

Preemptive service releases have an advantage in that the service can be designed much more independently than data flows or executives. Each service can assume that it will execute following release from an interrupt as if it is the only service on the CPU, except each service must be preemptable between release and completion (generation of response). The preemptability requires an operating system that will save and restore context for each executable service. Furthermore, each service must execute reentrant code if it is shared and must synchronize access to any globally shared resources. These requirements are true of any preemptive multiprogrammed system. The services are independent in the sense that no specific cooperation between services is required unless code or data is shared. Shared code or data simply requires reentrant code and shared data access synchronization. The services can be considered to be running asynchronously other than specific synchronization points for shared resource access. Thus, each service can be designed as a separate state machine rather than one state machine composed of many smaller state machines (as is typical of executives). Also, one flow of execution may, in fact, preempt another in cases where one service is more important than another (e.g., maybe one service has a shorter deadline or more negative impact if not completed by its deadline).

Because preemption opens up the possibility that more than one service might be ready to run, and there are fewer CPU resources than services ready to run, a dispatch decision must be made. One of the simplest dispatch policies is to give the CPU to the service assigned highest priority. These assigned priorities are never changed; they are fixed. To decide how to assign priorities, two common real-time policies are to assign highest priority to the service with the shortest release period (highest request frequency), which is known as RM (Rate Monotonic), and to assign the highest priority to the services with the shortest deadline relative to release, which is known as DM (Deadline Monotonic). Note that RM is identical to DM when the release period equals the deadline. As you will see in this chapter, the RM (and related DM) policy can be shown to provably meet system deadline requirements given deterministic release periods and service execution times. However, one major drawback is that fixed priorities do not guarantee maximum use of the CPU.

To attempt full usage of CPU resources and prove that services can meet deadlines, you are forced to consider preemptive dynamic priority policies. Two dynamic policies have been shown to have the capability to fully use CPU and guarantee deadlines assuming service execution times and request intervals are deterministic or bounded. Liu and Layland proposed Earliest Deadline First (EDF), along with RM, and showed them to be optimal—that is, policies that can schedule any set of services that can be scheduled (an exhaustive proof!). However, although RM is simpler, Liu and Layland also showed that RM fundamentally requires margin and less than full CPU use unless service requests are harmonic.

By comparison, in EDF, any time a new service request arrives (indicated by an interrupt asynchronous), the EDF scheduling policy adjusts all priorities so that the service with the earliest deadline is given highest priority. Ignoring the overhead of determining which service has the earliest impending deadline and ignoring overhead of priority reassignment, EDF can be shown to provide full use of the CPU where possible—even when requests intervals are not harmonic. The downside of EDF is that if request rates vary or execution times vary, the effect upon services is very hard to predict—which service will miss its deadline in an overload? Variations on EDF have been proposed that intend to improve the determinism of the system given variations, including Least Laxity First (LLF). The LLF policy assigns highest priority to the service that has the least difference between remaining execution time and its deadline—a measure of which service deadline is most pressing. The idea is that laxity may vary based upon execution rates, whereas the EDF assignment is not at all influenced by execution rate.

Given this overview of resource scheduling policies, you may wonder how these policies actually instantiate the various utility functions presented in the first section of this chapter. They don't, other than the hard real-time utility curve. If you can prove that with a policy and deterministic parameters that all services will complete prior to deadlines, the only utility curve this maps to is the hard real-time curve. Recall that the hard real-time utility curve provides full credit for any response delivered before the deadline relative to service request and no credit or negative credit for late response. The isochronal utility function can be implemented as a hard real-time service with early completions held until the response deadline. This approach can be used to implement both hard- and soft isochronal services. Policies and scheduling mechanisms for implementation of soft real-time utility and anytime services are open research areas.

## Preemptive Fixed Priority Scheduling Policy

Fixed priority preemptive policy is most widely used by real-time embedded systems employing an RTOS. Early on, most hard real-time systems used cyclic executives or multifrequency executives often found in systems such as the Space Shuttle guidance, navigation, and control primary avionics subsystem. The RTOS scheduling framework offers the same deterministic scheduling as the cyclic executive, but with far more flexibility in how services are defined and maintained. The principal reason for the pervasiveness of the RTOS in larger scale configurable real-time embedded systems is the fact that the policy has been proven optimal and a feasibility test exists, along with the ease of defining services as tasks rather than loop or interrupt contexts. The RM feasibility tests provide a method to prove that a given set of services (implemented as RTOS tasks) can be guaranteed to all meet their deadlines if the RM policy is used to assign priorities. For hard real-time systems where proof that services will not miss deadlines is desired, RM is an obvious choice. For example, RM is often used for commercial aircraft, for satellite systems, or any other system where failure to meet all deadlines can result in significant loss of life and/or assets. Finally, as you will see in this section, with an RM policy, you can predict and control exactly which services will miss deadlines in an overload scenario.

First, let's look at why the RM priority policy is optimal. Recall that the RM policy requires a framework where services are released asynchronously (typically via an interrupt) and placed on a ready queue indicating they need to run. A scheduler then dispatches each service based upon the highest priority task in the ready queue (all services are implemented as tasks and assumed to have unique priority). The service/task dispatched continues to run to completion unless an interrupt preempts the task presently executing. Following an interrupt, the scheduler reevaluates the ready queue and possibly dispatches a new task (a context switch) if a task of higher priority is added to the ready queue compared to that running prior to the interrupt. When a context switch occurs and a task/service is preempted prior to running to completion, this is called *interference*. In a fixed-priority preemptive system with only one service/task, interference is not possible. In a system with more than one service/task, any given task may be interfered with by all tasks that have been assigned higher priority.

With this fixed-priority preemptive framework, the scheduling problem must be further constrained to derive a formal mathematical model that proves deterministic behavior. Clearly it is impossible to prove deterministic behavior for a system that has nondeterministic inputs. Liu and Layland recognized this and proposed what they believed to be a reasonable set of assumptions and constraints on real systems to formulate a deterministic model. The assumptions and constraints are

**A1:** All services requested on periodic basis, the period is constant

**A2:** Completion-time < period

**A3:** Service requests are independent (no known phasing)

**A4:** Runtime is known and deterministic (WCET may be used)

**C1:** Deadline = period by definition

**C2:** Fixed-priority, preemptive, run-to-completion scheduling

**A5:** Critical instant—longest response time for a service occurs when all system services are requested simultaneously (maximum interference case for lowest priority service)

$A_1$ to $A_n$ are assumptions and $C_1$ to $C_n$ are constraints as presented by Liu and Layland in their paper.

Given the fixed-priority preemptive scheduling framework and assumptions described in the preceding list, we can now examine alternatives for assigning priorities and identify a policy that is optimal. Showing that the RM policy is optimal is most easily accomplished by inspecting a system with a small number of services.

An example with two services follows. Given services $S_1$ and $S_2$ with periods $T_1$ and $T_2$, execution times $C_1$ and $C_2$, and release periods $T_2 > T_1$, take, for example, $T_1 = 2$, $T_2 = 5$, $C_1 = 1$, $C_2 = 2$, and then if $prio(S_1) > prio(S_2)$, note Figure 2.9.

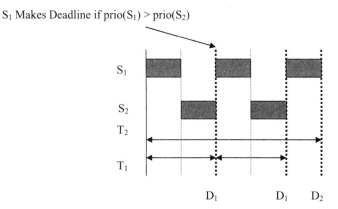

$S_1$ Makes Deadline if prio($S_1$) > prio($S_2$)

**FIGURE 2.9**    Example of RM priority assignment policy.

In this two-service example, the only other policy (swapping priorities from the preceding example) does not work. Given services $S_1$ and $S_2$ with periods $T_1$ and $T_2$ and $C_1$ and $C_2$ with $T_2 > T_1$, for example, $T_1 = 2$, $T_2 = 5$, $C_1 = 1$, $C_2 = 2$, and then if prio($S_2$) > prio($S_1$), note Figure 2.10.

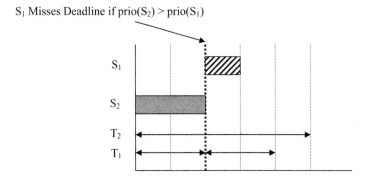

$S_1$ Misses Deadline if prio($S_2$) > prio($S_1$)

**FIGURE 2.10**    Example of nonoptimal priority assignment policy.

The conclusion that can be drawn is that for a two-service system, the RM policy is optimal, whereas the only alternative is not optimal because the alternative policy fails when a workable schedule does exist! The same argument can be posed for a three-service system, a four-service system, and finally an *N*-service system. In all cases, it can be shown that the RM policy is optimal. In Chapter 3, the Rate Monotonic Least Upper Bound (RM LUB) is derived and proven. Chapter 3 also provides system scheduling feasibility tests derived from RM theory that you can use to determine whether system CPU margin will be sufficient for a real-time safe operation.

## REAL-TIME OPERATING SYSTEMS

Many real-time embedded systems include an RTOS , which provides CPU scheduling, memory management, and driver interfaces for I/O in addition to boot or BSP (Board Support Package) firmware. In this text, example code included is based upon either the VxWorks RTOS from Wind River Systems or Linux. The VxWorks RTOS is available for academic licensing from Wind River through the University program free of charge (see Appendix C, "Wind River University Program Information"). Likewise, Linux is freely available in a number of distributions that can be tailored for embedded platforms (see Appendix C, "Real-Time Linux Distributions and Resources").

ON THE CD

Key features that an RTOS or an embedded real-time Linux distribution should have include the following:

- A fully preemptable kernel so that an interrupt or real-time task can preempt the kernel scheduler and kernel services with priority
- Low well bounded interrupt latency
- Low well bounded process, task, or thread context switch latency
- Capability to fully control all hardware resources and to override any built-in operating system resource management
- Execution tracing tools
- Cross-compiling, cross-debugging, and host-to-target interface tools to support code development on an embedded microprocessor
- Full support for POSIX 1003.1b synchronous and asynchronous intertask communication, control, and scheduling
- Priority inversion safe options for mutual exclusion semaphores (the mutual exclusion semaphore referred to in this text includes features that extend the early concepts for semaphores introduced by Dijkstra)
- Capability to lock memory address ranges into cache
- Capability to lock memory address ranges into working memory if virtual memory with paging is implemented
- High-precision timestamping, interval timers, and real-time clocks and virtual timers

The VxWorks, ThreadX, Nucleus, Micro-C-OS, RTEMS and many other available real-time operating systems provide the features in the preceding list. This has been the main selling point of the RTOS because it provides time-to-market acceleration compared to designing and coding a real-time executive from scratch, yet provides very direct and efficient interfacing between software applications and hardware platforms. Some RTOS options are proprietary and require licensing, and some, such as RTEMs or Micro-C-OS, require limited or no licensing, especially for academic or personal use only (a more complete list can be found in Appendix D, "RTOS Resources").

Linux was originally designed to be a multiuser operating system with memory protection, abstracted process domains, significantly automated resource management, and scalability for desktop and large clusters of general-purpose computing platforms. Embedding and adapting Linux for real-time requires distribution packaging, kernel patches, and the addition of support tools to provide the 11 key features listed previously. Several companies support real-time Linux distributions, including TimeSys Linux, FSM Labs Linux, Wind River Linux, Blue Cat Linux, Redhawk Linux, and many others (a more complete list can be found in Appendix C, "Real-Time Linux Distributions and Resources"). Real-time distributions of Linux require these patches:

- The Robust Mutex patch (*http://developer.osdl.org/dev/robustmutexes/*)
- Linux preemptable kernel patch (available from Monta Vista, TimeSys, FSM Labs)
- POSIX clocks and timers patches (*http://home.concepts-ict.nl/~rhdv/posix. html*, *http://sourceforge.net/projects/high-res-timers*)
- High-resolution timer patch (*http://www.cs.wisc.edu/paradyn/libhrtime/*)
- Linux Trace Toolkit (*http://www.opersys.com/LTT/*)
- Linux O(1) scheduler introduced in 2.6.x which provides an upper bound on scheduling dispatch independent of the number of processes active

Finally, the other option is to write your own resource-management kernel. In Chapter 10, "Performance Tuning," you'll see that although an RTOS provides a generic framework for resource management and multiservice applications, the cost of these generalized features is code footprint and overhead. So, in Chapter 8, "Embedded System Components," basic concepts for real-time kernel services are summarized. Understanding the basic mechanisms will be helpful to anyone considering development of a custom kernel. Building a custom resource-management kernel is not as daunting as it first may seem, but using a preexisting RTOS may also be an attractive option based upon complexity of services, portability requirements, time to market, and numerous system requirements. Because it is not clear whether use of an RTOS or development of a custom resource kernel is the better option, both approaches are discussed in this text.

In general, an RTOS provides a threading mechanism, in some cases referred to as a *task context*, which is the implementation of a service. A *service* is the theoretical concept of an execution context. The RTOS most often implements this as a thread of execution, with a well-known entry point into a code (text) segment, through a function, and a memory context for this thread of execution, which is called the *thread context*. In VxWorks, this is referred to as a task and the TCB (Task Control Block). In Linux, this is referred to as a process and a process descriptor. In the case of VxWorks, the context is fairly small, and in the case of a Linux process, the context is relatively complex, including I/O status, memory usage context, process state, execution stack, register state, and identifying data. In this book, *thread* will be used to describe the general implementation of a service (at the very least a thread of execution), *task* to describe an RTOS implementation, and *process* to describe the typical Linux implementation. Note that Linux FIFO threads are similar in many ways to a VxWorks task.

Typical RTOS CPU scheduling is fixed-priority preemptive, with the capability to modify priorities at runtime by applications, therefore also supporting dynamic-priority preemptive. Real-time response with bounded latency for any number of services requires preemption based upon interrupts. Systems where latency bounds are more relaxed might instead use polling for events and run threads to completion, increasing efficiency by avoiding disruptive asynchronous interrupt context switches. Remember, as presented in Chapter 1, we assume that response latency must be deterministic and that this is more important than throughput and overall efficiency. If you are designing an embedded system that doesn't really have real-time requirements, avoid asynchronous interrupts altogether. Dealing with asynchronous interrupts requires debugging in interrupt context and can add complexity that might be fully avoidable in a nonreal-time system. First, what really constitutes a real-time deadline requirement must be understood. By completion of Chapter 3, you should be able to clearly recognize whether a system requires priority preemptive scheduling or not. An RTOS provides priority preemptive scheduling as a mechanism that allows an application to implement a variety of scheduling policies:

- RM (Rate Monotonic) or DM (Deadline Monotonic), fixed priority
- EDF (Earliest Deadline First) or LLF (Least Laxity First), dynamic priority
- Simple run to completion cooperative tasking

These policies are a small subset of the larger taxonomy of scheduling policies presented previously (refer to Figure 2.8). In the case of simple run to completion cooperative tasking, the value of the RTOS is mostly the BSP, boot, driver, and memory management because the application really handles the scheduling. Given that bounded latency is most often a hard requirement in any real-time system, the focus is further limited to RM, EDF, and LLF. Ultimately, a real-time scheduler needs to support dispatch, execution context management, and preemption. In the simplest scenario, where services run to completion, but may be preempted by a higher priority service, the thread states are depicted in Figure 2.11.

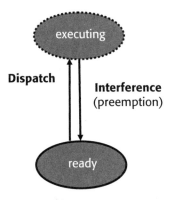

**FIGURE 2.11**  Basic dispatch and preemption states.

In the state transition diagram shown in Figure 2.11, we assume that a thread in execution never has to wait for any resources in addition to the CPU, that it never encounters an unrecoverable error, and there is never a need to delay execution. If this could be guaranteed, the scheduling for this type of system is fairly simple. All services can be implemented as threads, with a stack, a register state, and a thread state of executing or ready on a priority ordered queue. Most often, threads that implement services operate on memory or on an I/O interface. In this case, the memory or I/O is a secondary resource, which if shared or if significant latency is associated with use, may require the thread to wait and enter a pending state until this secondary resource becomes available. In Figure 2.12, we add a pending state, which a thread enters when a secondary resource is not immediately available during execution. When this secondary resource becomes available, for example when a device has data available, that resource can set a flag (semaphore), indicating availability to the scheduler to transition the pending thread back to the ready state.

In addition, if a thread may be arbitrarily delayed by a programmable amount of time, then it will need to enter a delayed state as shown in Figure 2.13. A delay is simply implemented by a hardware interval timer that provides an interrupt after a programmable number of CPU clock cycles or external oscillator cycles. When the timer is set, an interrupt handler for the expiration is installed so that the delay timeout results in restoration of the thread from delayed state back to ready state.

Finally, if a thread of execution encounters a nonrecoverable error, for example, division by zero in the code, then continuation could lead to significant system

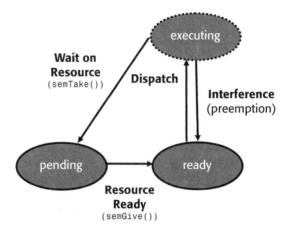

**FIGURE 2.12** Basic service states showing pending on secondary resource.

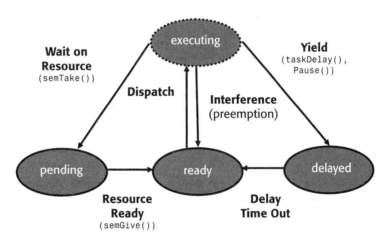

**FIGURE 2.13** Basic service states, including programmed delays.

endangerment. In the case of division by zero, this will cause an overflow result, which in turn might generate faulty command output to an actuator, such as a satellite thruster, which could cause loss of the asset. If the division by zero is handled by an exception handler that recalculates the result and therefore recovers within the service, continuation might be possible, but often recovery is not possible. Because the very next instruction might cause total system failure, a nonrecoverable exception should result in suspension of that thread. Figure 2.14 shows the addition of a suspended state. If a thread or task that is already in the delayed state

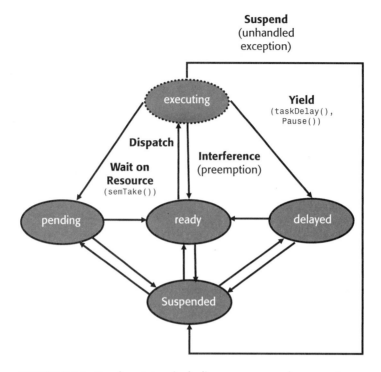

**FIGURE 2.14**   Service states, including programmed suspension or suspension due to exception.

can also be suspended by another task, as is the case with VxWorks, then additional states are possible in the suspended state, including delayed+suspended, pending+suspended, and simple suspended.

Although scheduling the CPU for multiple services with the implementation of threads, tasks, or processes is the main function of an RTOS, the RTOS also provides management of memory and I/O along with methods to synchronize and coordinate usage of these secondary resources along with the CPU. Secondary resources lead to the addition of the pending state if their availability at runtime can't be guaranteed in advance. Furthermore, if two threads must synchronize, one thread may have to enter the pending state to wait for another thread to execute up to the rendezvous point in its code. In Chapter 6, you'll see that this seemingly simple requirement imposed by secondary resources and the need for thread synchronization lead to significant complexity.

The RTOS provides I/O resource management through a driver interface, which includes common entry points for reading/writing data, opening/closing a session with a device by a thread, and configuring the I/O device. The coordination of access to devices by multiple threads and the synchronization of thread execution with device data availability are implemented through the pending state. In the simplest case, an Interrupt Service Routine (ISR) can indicate device data availability by setting a semaphore (flag), which allows the RTOS to transition the thread waiting for data to process from pending back to the ready state. Likewise, when a thread wants to write data to an I/O output buffer, if the buffer is currently full, the device can synchronize buffer availability with the thread again through an ISR and a binary semaphore. In Chapter 8, you'll see that all I/O and thread synchronization can be handled by ISRs and binary semaphores, but that alternative mechanisms such as message queues can also be used.

Memory in the simplest scenarios can be mapped and allocated once during boot of the system and never modified at runtime. This is the ideal scenario because the usage of memory is deterministic in space and time. Memory usage may vary, but the maximum used is predetermined, as is the time to claim, use, and release memory. In general, the use of the C library `malloc` is frowned upon in real-time embedded systems because this dynamic memory-management function provides allocation and deallocation of arbitrary segments of memory. Over time, if the segments truly are of arbitrary size, the allocation segments must be coalesced to avoid external fragmentation of memory as shown in Figure 2.15.

Likewise, if arbitrarily sized segments are mapped onto minimum size blocks of memory (e.g., 4 KB blocks), then allocation of a 1-byte buffer will require 4,096 bytes to be allocated with 4,095 bytes within this block wasted. This internal fragmentation is shown in Figure 2.16.

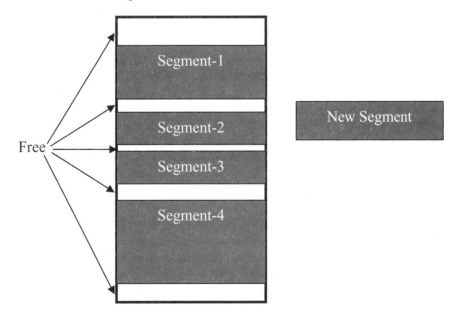

**FIGURE 2.15**  Memory fragmentation for data segments of arbitrary size.

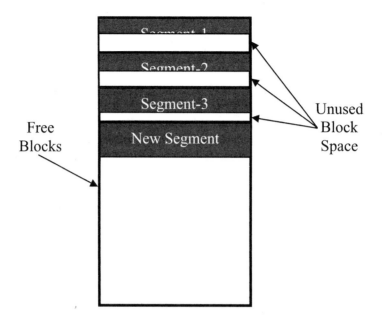

**FIGURE 2.16**   Internal block fragmentation for fixed-size dynamic allocation.

In many real-time embedded systems, a compromise for memory management can be reached whereby most working data segments are predetermined, and specific usage heaps (dynamically allocated blocks of memory) can be defined that have little to no external or internal fragmentation issues.

Overall, because an RTOS provides general mechanisms for CPU, memory, and I/O resource management, adopting an off-the-shelf RTOS such as VxWorks or embedded Linux is an attractive choice. However, if the resource usage and management requirements are well understood and simple, developing a custom resource kernel may be a good alternative.

## THREAD SAFE REENTRANT FUNCTIONS

When an RTOS scheduling mechanism is used, care must be taken to consider whether functions may be called by multiple thread contexts. Many real-time services may use common utility functions, and a single implementation of these common functions will save significant code space memory. However, if one function may be called by more than one thread and those threads are concurrently active, the shared function must be written to provide re-entrancy so that it is thread safe. Threads are considered concurrently active if more than one thread context is either executing or awaiting execution in the ready state in the dispatch queue. In this scenario, thread A might have called function F and could have been preempted before completing execution of F by thread B, which also calls function F. If F is a pure function that uses no global data and only operates on input parameters through stack, then this concurrent use is safe. However, if F uses any global data, this data may be corrupted and/or the function may produce incorrect results. For example, if F is a function that retrieves the current position of a satellite stored as a global state and returns a copy of that position to the caller, the state information could be corrupted, and inconsistent states could be returned to both callers. For this example, assume function F is defined as follows:

```
typedef struct position {double x, y, z;} POSITION;
POSITION satellite_pos = {0.0, 0.0, 0.0};
POSITION get_position(void)
{
    double alt, lat, long;

    read_altitude(&alt);
    read_latitude(&lat);
    read_longitude(&long);

    /* Multiple function calls are required to convert the geodetic
       navigational sensor state to a state in inertial coordinates
    */
    satellite_pos.x = update_x_position(alt, lat, long);
    satellite_pos.y = update_y_position(alt, lat, long);
    satellite_pos.z = update_z_position(alt, lat, long);
    return satellite_pos;
}
```

Now, if thread A has executed up to the point where it has completed its call to update_x_position, but not yet to the rest of get_position, and thread B preempts A, updating the position fully, thread A will be returned an inconsistent state. The state A returned will include a more recent value for x and older values for y and z because the alt, lat, and long variables are on the stack that is copied for each thread context. Thread B will be returned a consistent copy of the state updated from a set of sensor readings made in one call, but A will have the x value from B's call and will compute y and z from the alt, lat, long values on its stack sampled at an earlier time. The function as written here is not thread safe and is not re-entrant due to the global data, which is updated so that interrupts and preemption can cause partial update of the global data. VxWorks provides several mechanisms that can be used to make functions re-entrant. One strategy is to protect the global data from partial updates by preventing preemption for the update critical section using taskLock() and taskUnlock(). The solution to make this function thread safe using taskLock() and taskUnlock() is

```
typedef struct position {double x, y, z;} POSITION;
POSITION satellite_pos = {0.0, 0.0, 0.0};
POSITION get_position(void)
{
    double alt, lat, long;
    POSITION current_satellite_pos;

    read_altitude(&alt);
    read_latitude(&lat);
    read_longitude(&long);

    /* Multiple function calls are required to convert the geodetic
       navigational sensor state to a state in inertial coordinates

       The code between Lock and Unlock is the critical section.
    */
    taskLock();
    current_satellite_pos.x = update_x_position(alt, lat, long);
    current_satellite_pos.y = update_y_position(alt, lat, long);
    current_satellite_pos.z = update_z_position(alt, lat, long);
    satellite_pos = current_satellite_pos; /* assumes structure
assignment */
    taskUnlock();

    return current_satellite_pos;
}
```

The use of Lock and Unlock prevents the return of an inconsistent state to either function because it prevents preemption during the update of the local and global satellite position. The function is now thread safe, but potentially will cause a higher priority thread to wait upon a lower priority thread to complete this critical section of code. The VxWorks RTOS provides alternatives, including task variables (copies of globals maintained with task context), interrupt level Lock and Unlock, and an inversion-safe mutex. The simplest way to ensure thread safety is to avoid the use of global data and to implement only pure functions that use only local stack data; however, this may be impractical. Chapter 8 provides a more detailed discussion of methods to make common library functions thread safe.

## SUMMARY

A real-time embedded system should be analyzed to understand requirements and how they relate to system resources. The best place to start is with a solid understanding of CPU, memory, and I/O requirements so that hardware can be properly sized in terms of CPU clock rate (instructions per second), memory capacity, memory access latency, and I/O bandwidth and latency. After you size these basic three resources, determine resource margin requirements, and establish determinism and reliability requirements, then you can further refine the hardware design for the processing platform to determine power, mass, and size. In many cases, an RTOS provides a quick way to provide management of CPU, memory, and I/O along with basic firmware to boot the software services for an application. Even if an off-the-shelf RTOS is used, it is important to understand the common implementations of these resource management features along with theory on resource usage policy. In Chapter 3, the focus is CPU resource management; in Chapter 4, it's I/O interface management; in Chapter 5, memory management; and in Chapter 6 multiresource management. In general, for real-time embedded systems, service response latency is a primary consideration, and overall, the utility of the response over time should be well understood for the application being designed. Traditional hard real-time systems require response by deadline or the system is said to have failed. In Chapter 7, we consider soft real-time systems where occasional missed deadlines are allowed, and missed deadline handling and service recovery is designed into the system.

## EXERCISES

1.  Provide an example of a hard real-time service found in a commonly used embedded system and describe why this service utility fits the hard real-time utility curve.
2.  Provide an example of a hard real-time isochronal service found in a commonly used embedded system and describe why this service utility fits the isochronal real-time utility curve.
3.  Provide an example of a soft real-time service found in a commonly used embedded system and describe why this service utility fits the soft real-time utility curve.
4.  Implement a VxWorks task that is spawned at the lowest priority level possible and that calls semTake to enter the pending state, waiting for an event indicated by semGive. From the VxWorks shell, start this task and verify that it is in the pending state. Now, call a function that gives the

semaphore the task it is waiting on and verify that it completes execution and exits.

5. Implement a Linux process that is executed at the default priority for a user-level application and waits on a binary semaphore to be given by another application. Run this process and verify its state using the ps command to list its process descriptor. Now, run a separate process to give the semaphore causing the first process to continue execution and exit. Verify completion.

6. Read the Liu and Layland RMA paper (don't get hung up on math). Please summarize the paper's main points (at least three or more) in a short paragraph.

7. Write a paragraph comparing the RM and the Deadline Driven or EDF policies described in Liu and Layland in your own words and be complete, but keep it to one reasonably concise paragraph. Note that the Deadline Driver scheduling in Liu and Layland is now typically called a dynamic-priority EDF policy. In general, a number of policies that are deadline driven have evolved from the Deadline Driven scheduling Liu and Layland describe, including EDF and LLF. Give at least two specific differences.

8. Cross-compile code for VxWorks. Download the file two_tasks.c from the CD-ROM example code. Create a Tornado project that includes this file and download the file to a lab target. Using the *windshell*, use the function moduleShow to verify that the object code has been downloaded. Submit evidence that you have run moduleShow in your lab report (copy and paste into your report or do a Ctrl-Prnt Scrn). Next, still in the windshell, do an lkup "test_task" to verify that the function entry point for the two_tasks example has been dynamically linked into the kernel symbol table. Place evidence in your report. Note that typing help on a windshell command line will provide a summary of these basic commands. In addition, all commands can be looked up in the VxWorks API manual. Capture the output from the moduleShow command in the windshell and paste it into your lab write-up to prove that you've done this.

ON THE CD

9. Notice the two functions test_tasks1() and test_tasks2() in the two_tasks.c file. Describe what each of these functions does. Run each function in the windshell by typing the function name at the windshell prompt. Explain the difference in how synchronization of tasks is achieved in two different functions namely test_task1 and test_task2.

10. Run the WindView tool and capture output while the test_tasks program is running. Explain what you see—identify your tasks, where two tasks are running on the CPU and where they synchronize with semTake and semGive.

Provide a detailed explanation and annotate the trace directly by using Ctrl-Prnt Scrn and Ctrl-V to paste an image into your write-up and mark up the graphic directly. Describe the difference between `test_tasks1()` and `test_tasks2()` and how this is shown by the WindView output.

11. Now modify the two_tasks.c code so that you create a third task named `mytesttask` and write an entry point function that calls `pause()` and nothing else. Use the `i` command in the windshell and capture output to prove that you created this task. Does this task show execution on WindView? Why or why not?

12. For the next portion of the lab, you will experiment with creating a bootable project for the simulator. Create a bootable project based upon the Simulator BSP and configure a new kernel image so that it includes POSIX message queues. Build this kernel and launch the simulator with this image instead of the default image. Download an application project with the posix_mq.c CD-ROM code, and if you did the first part right, you will get no errors on download. Do `lkup "send"` and you should see the function entry points in the posix_mq.c module. Cut and past this output into your submission to show you did this.

**ON THE CD**

13. Set a breakpoint in function `sender` with the windshell command `b sender`. Now run `mq_demo` from the windshell. When the break point is hit, start a debug session using the Bug icon. Use the Debug menu, select Attach, and attach to the Sender task. You should see a debug window with the cursor sitting at the `sender` function entry point. Switch the View to Mixed Source and Disassembly and now count the number of instructions from the `sender` entry up to the call to `mq_open`. How many steps are there from a breakpoint set at this entry point until you enter `mq_open` using the single step into? Provide a capture showing the breakpoint output from your windshell.

## CHAPTER REFERENCES

[Briand99] Briand, Loïc, and Roy, Daniel, *Meeting Deadlines in Hard Real-Time Systems—The Rate Monotonic Approach.* IEEE Computer Society Press, 1999.

[Bovet00] Bovet, Daniel P., and Cesati, Marco. *Understanding the Linux Kernel.* O'Reilly, 2000.

[Burns91] Burns, A., "Scheduling Hard Real-Time Systems: A Review." *Software Engineering Journal,* (May 1991).

[Carlow84] Carlow, Gene D., "Architecture of the Space Shuttle Primary Avionics Software System," *Communications of the ACM.* Vol. 27, Number 9, (September 1984).

[Liu73] Liu, C., and Layland, J., "Scheduling Algorithms for Multiprogramming in a Hard Real-Time Environment." *Journal of Association for Computing Machinery*, Vol. 20, No. 1, (January 1973): pp. 46-61.

[Robbins96] Robbins, K. A., *Practical Unix Programming—A Guide to Concurrency, Communication, and Multithreading.* Prentice Hall, 1996.

[WRS99] Wind River Systems Inc., *VxWorks Programmer's Guide.* Wind River Systems, 1999.

# 3 Processing

## In This Chapter

- Introduction
- Preemptive Fixed-Priority Policy
- Feasibility
- Rate Monotonic Least Upper Bound (RM LUB)
- Necessary and Sufficient (N&S) Feasibility
- Deadline-Monotonic (DM) Policy
- Dynamic Priority Policies

## INTRODUCTION

Processing input data and producing output data for a system response in real time does not necessarily require large CPU resources, but rather careful use of CPU resources. Before considering how to make optimal use of CPU resources in a real-time embedded system, you must first better understand what is meant by processing in real time. The mantra of real-time system correctness is that the system must not only produce the required output response for a given input (functional correctness), but that it must do so in a timely manner (before a deadline). A *deadline* in a real-time system is a relative time after a service request by which time the system must produce a response. The relative deadline seems to be a simple concept, but a more formal specification of real-time services is helpful due to the many types of applications. For example, the processing in a voice or video real-time system is considered high quality if the service continuously provides output neither too early nor too late, without too much latency and without too much jitter between frames. Similarly, in digital control applications, the ideal system has a constant time delay between sensor sampling and actuator outputs. However, by comparison, a real-time service that monitors a satellite's health and status and initiates a safe recovery sequence when the satellite is in danger must enter the recovery as quickly as possible after the dangerous condition is detected. Digital control and continuous media (audio and video) are isochronal real-time services. Responses should not be generated too long after or too early after a service request. System health monitoring, however, is a simple real-time service where the system must produce a response (initiate the recovery sequence) no later than some deadline following the request.

# PREEMPTIVE FIXED-PRIORITY POLICY

Given that the RM priority assignment policy is optimal, as shown in the previous chapter, we now want to determine whether a proposed set of services is feasible. By feasible, we mean that the proposed set of services can be scheduled given a fixed and known amount of CPU resource. One such test is the RM LUB:

Liu and Layland proposed this simple feasibility test they call the RM Least Upper Bound (RM LUB). The RM LUB is defined as

$$U = \sum_{i=1}^{m} (C_i / T_i) \le m(2^{\frac{1}{m}} - 1)$$

**U:** Utility of the CPU resource achievable

**$C_i$:** Execution time of Service $i$

**m:** Total number of services in the system sharing common CPU resources

**$T_i$:** Release period of Service $i$

Without much closer inspection of how this RM LUB was derived, it is purely magical and must be accepted on faith.

Rather than just accept the RM LUB, we can instead examine the properties of a set of services and their feasibility and generalize this information: can we in general determine a feasibility test for a set of proposed services sharing a CPU according to RM policy?

To answer this question, we can simply diagram the timing for release, preemption, dispatch, and completion of a set of services from the critical instant and later. The critical instant assumes that in the worst case, all services might be requested at the same time. If we do attempt to understand a system by diagramming, for what period of time must the system be analyzed? If we analyze the scheduling with the RM policy for some arbitrary period, we may not observe the release and completion of all services in the proposed set. So, to observe all services, we at least need to diagram the service execution over a period equal to or greater than the largest period in the set of services. You'll see that if we really want to understand the use of the system, we actually must diagram the execution over the least common multiple of all periods for the proposed set of services, or *LSM* time. These concepts are best understood by taking a real example. Let's also see how this real example compares to the RM LUB.

For a system, can all Cs fit in the largest T over LCM (Least Common Multiple) time? Given Services $S_1$, $S_2$ with periods $T_1$ and $T_2$ and $C_1$ and $C_2$, assume $T_2 > T_1$, for example, $T_1 = 2$, $T_2 = 5$, $C_1 = 1$, $C_2 = 1$; and then if $\text{prio}(S_1) > \text{prio}(S_2)$, you can see that they can by inspecting a timing diagram as shown in Figure 3.1.

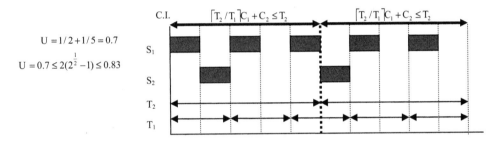

**FIGURE 3.1** Example of two-service feasibility testing by examination.

The actual utilization of 70% is lower than the RM LUB of 83.3%, and the system is feasible by inspection. So, the RM LUB appears to correctly predict feasibility for this case.

Why did Liu and Layland call the RM LUB a least upper bound? Let's inspect this bound a little more closely by looking at a case that increases utility, but remains feasible. Perhaps we can even exceed their RM LUB.

In this example, RM LUB is safely exceeded, given Services $S_1$, $S_2$ with periods $T_1$ and $T_2$ and $C_1$ and $C_2$; and assuming $T_2 = T_1$, for example, $T_1 = 2$, $T_2 = 5$, $C_1 = 1$, $C_2 = 2$; and then if $\text{prio}(S_1) > \text{prio}(S_2)$, note Figure 3.2.

By inspection, this two-service case with 90% utility is feasible, yet the utility exceeds the RM LUB. So, what good is the RM LUB? The RM LUB is a pessimistic feasibility test that will fail some proposed service sets that actually work, but it will never pass a set that doesn't work. A more formal way of describing the RM LUB is that it is a sufficient feasibility test, but not necessary.

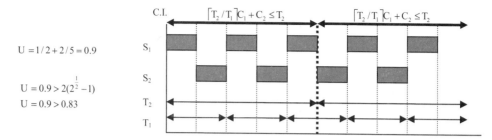

**FIGURE 3.2**   Example of two-service case exceeding RM LUB.

What exactly is meant by a sufficient condition or a necessary and sufficient condition? *Necessary, sufficient,* and *necessary and sufficient* have well-defined meaning in logic. As defined in Wikipedia, the free online encyclopedia, here are the standard definitions of all three:

**Necessary condition:** To say that A is *necessary* for B is to say that B *cannot* occur without A occurring, or that *whenever* (wherever, etc.) B occurs, so does A. Drinking water regularly is necessary for a human to stay alive. If A is a necessary condition for B, then the logical relation between them is expressed as "If B then A" or "B only if A" or "B → A."

**Sufficient condition:** To say that A is *sufficient* for B is to say precisely the converse: that A cannot occur without B, or whenever A occurs, B occurs. That there is a fire is sufficient for there being smoke. If A is a sufficient condition for B, then the logical relation between them is expressed as "If A then B" or "A only if B" or "A → B."

**Necessary and sufficient condition:** To say that A is necessary and sufficient for B is to say two things: 1) A is necessary for B and 2) A is sufficient for B. The logical relationship is therefore "A if and only if B". In general, to prove "P if Q", it is equivalent to proving both the statements "if P, then Q" and "if Q, then P."

For real-time scheduling feasibility tests, sufficient therefore means that passing the test guarantees that the proposed service set will not miss deadlines; however, failing a sufficient feasibility test does not imply that the proposed service set will miss deadlines. An N&S (Necessary and Sufficient) feasibility test is exact—if a service set passes the N&S feasibility test it will not miss deadlines, and if it fails to pass the N&S feasibility test, it is guaranteed to miss deadlines. Therefore, an N&S feasibility test is more exact compared to a sufficient feasibility test. The sufficient test is conservative and, in some scnearios, downright pessimistic. The RM LUB is useful, however, in that it provides a simple way to prove that a proposed service set is feasible. The sufficient RM LUB does not prove that a service set is infeasible—to do this, you must apply an N&S feasibility test. Presently, the RM LUB is the least complex feasibility test to apply. The RM LUB is O($n$) order $n$ complexity—requiring summation of service execution times and comparison to a simple expression that is a function of the number of services in the proposed set. By comparison, the only known N&S feasibility tests for the RM policy are $O(n^3)$—requiring iteration loops bounded by the number of services nested twice so that three nested loops must be executed (as shown in the "Feasibility" section of this chapter). If the feasibility test is performed once during design, then it makes sense to test the proposed service set with an N&S test. However, for quick calculations, "back of the envelope calculations," the RM LUB is still useful. In some cases, it also may be useful to perform a feasibility test in real time. In this case, the system providing real-time services might receive a request to suppport an additional service with known RM properties (period, execution time, and deadline) while presently running an existing service set—this is called *online* or *on-demand scheduling*—for this type of system, the feasibility test itself requires resources for evaluation—keeping the requirements of the feasibility test minimal may be advantageous. Either way, for online scheduling, the feasibility test is a service itself and requires resources like any other service.

Now that you understand how the RM LUB is useful, let's see how the RM LUB is derived. After understanding the RM LUB derivation, N&S feasibility algorithms are easier to understand as well. Finally, much like the demonstration that the RM policy is optimal with two services, it's easier to derive the RM LUB for two services (if you want to understand the full derivation of the RM LUB for an unlimited number of services, see Liu and Layland's paper [Liu73]).

## FEASIBILITY

Feasibility tests provide a binary result that indicates whether a set of services (threads or tasks) can be scheduled given their $C_i$, $T_i$, and $D_i$ specification. So the input is an array of service identifiers ($S_i$) and specifications for each, and the output is TRUE if the set can be safely scheduled so that none of the deadlines will be missed and FALSE if any one of the deadlines might be missed. There are two types of feasibility tests:

- Sufficient
- Necessary and Sufficient (N&S)

Sufficient feasibility tests will always fail a service set that is not real-time-safe (i.e., that can miss deadlines). However, a sufficient test will also fail a service set that is real-time-safe occasionally as well. Sufficient feasibility tests are not precise. The sufficient tests are conservative because they will never pass an unsafe set of services. N&S tests are precise. An N&S feasibility test will not pass a service set that is unsafe and likewise will not fail any test that is safe. The RM LUB is a sufficient test and therefore safe, but it will fail service sets that actually can be safely scheduled.

By comparison, the Scheduling Point and Completion tests for the RM policy are N&S and therefore precise. Examples showing the imprecise, but safe characteristic of the RM LUB are examined in the following section. It will also become clear that service sets with relatively harmonic periods can easily fail the sufficient RM LUB and be shown to be safe when analyzed—the more precise N&S feasibility tests will correctly predict such harmonic service sets as safe that may not pass the RM LUB. The N&S test will precisely identify the safe service set. The sufficient tests are yet another subset of the N&S safe subset as depicted in Figure 3.3.

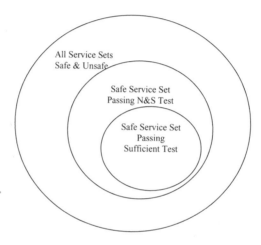

All Service Sets
Safe & Unsafe

Safe Service Set
Passing N&S Test

Safe Service Set
Passing
Sufficient Test

**FIGURE 3.3**   Relationship between sufficient and N&S feasibility tests.

## RATE MONOTONIC LEAST UPPER BOUND (RM LUB)

Taking the same two-service example shown earlier in Figure 3.2, we have the following set of proposed services. Given Services $S_1$, $S_2$ with periods $T_1$ and $T_2$ and execution times $C_1$ and $C_2$, assume that the services are released with $T_1 = 2$, $T_2 = 5$, execute deterministically with $C_1 = 1$, $C_2 = 2$, and are scheduled by the RM policy so that $prio(S_1) > prio(S_2)$. If this proposed system can be shown to be feasible so that it can be scheduled with the RM policy over the LCM (least common multiple) period derived from all proposed service periods, then the Lehoczky, Shah, and Ding theorem [Briand99] guarantees it real-time-safe. The theorem is based upon the fact that given the periodic releases of each service, the LCM schedule will simply repeat over and over as shown in Figure 3.4.

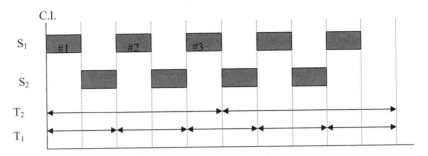

**FIGURE 3.4** Two-service examples used to derive RM LUB.

Note that there can be up to $\left\lceil \dfrac{T_2}{T_1} \right\rceil$ releases of $S_1$ during $T_2$ as indicated by the #1, #2, and #3 execution traces for $S_1$ in Figure 3.4. Furthermore, note that in this particular scenario, the utilization U is 90%.

The CI (Critical Instant) is a worst-case assumption that the demands upon the system might include simultaneous requests for service by all services in the system! This eliminates the complexity of assuming some sort of known relationship or phasing between service requests and makes the RM LUB a more general result.

Given this motivating two-service example, we can now devise a strategy to derive the RM LUB for any given set of services S for which each service $S_i$ has an arbitrary $C_i$, $T_i$. Taking this example, we examine two cases:

**Case 1:** $C_1$ short enough to fit all three releases in $T_2$ (fits $S_2$ critical time zone)

**Case 2:** $C_1$ too large to fit last release in $T_2$ (doesn't fit $S_2$ critical time zone)

Examine U in both cases to find common U upper bound. The critical time zone is depicted in Figure 3.5.

The $S_2$ critical time zone is best understood by considering the condition where $S_1$ releases occur the maximum number of times and for a duration that uses all possible time during $T_2$ without actually causing $S_2$ to miss its deadline. So, Case 1 where $S_1$ total resource required just fits the $S_2$ critical time zone $(T_2 - C_2)$ is shown in Figure 3.5.

In Case 1, all three $S_1$ releases requiring $C_1$ execution time fit in $T_2$ as shown in Figure 3.5. This is expressed by

$$C_1 \leq T_2 - T_1 \lfloor T_2 / T_1 \rfloor \qquad (3.1)$$

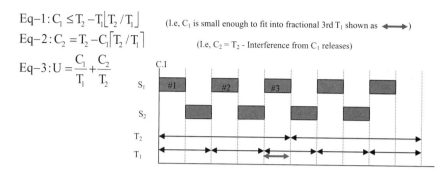

$$Eq\text{-}1: C_1 \le T_2 - T_1 \lfloor T_2 / T_1 \rfloor \qquad \text{(I.e, } C_1 \text{ is small enough to fit into fractional 3rd } T_1 \text{ shown as} \longleftrightarrow )$$

$$Eq\text{-}2: C_2 = T_2 - C_1 \lceil T_2 / T_1 \rceil \qquad \text{(I.e, } C_2 = T_2 \text{ - Interference from } C_1 \text{ releases)}$$

$$Eq\text{-}3: U = \frac{C_1}{T_1} + \frac{C_2}{T_2}$$

**FIGURE 3.5**  Example of critical time zone.

Note that the expression $\lfloor T_2 / T_1 \rfloor$ is the minimum number of times that $T_1$ occurs fully during $T_2$. The expression $T_2 - T_1 \lfloor T_2 / T_1 \rfloor$ is the fractional amount of time that the third occurrence of $T_1$ overlaps with $T_2$. Equation 3.2,

$$C_2 > T_2 - C_1 \lceil T_2 / T_1 \rceil \tag{3.2}$$

simply expresses the length of $C_2$ to be long enough to use all time not used by $S_1$—note that when the third release of $S_1$ just fits in the critical time zone shown in red, then $S_1$ occurs exactly $\lceil T_2 / T_1 \rceil$ times during $T_2$. From Figure 3.5 it should be clear that if $C_1$ was increased and $C_2$ held constant, the schedule would not be feasible; likewise if $C_2$ was increased and $C_1$ held constant, they just fit! It is also interesting to note that looking over LCM time, we do not have full utility, but rather 90%. Equation 3.3,

$$U = \frac{C_1}{T_1} + \frac{C_2}{T_2}, \tag{3.3}$$

defines the utility for the two services. At this point, let's plug the expression for $C_2$ in Equation 3.2 into Equation 3.3, which creates Equation 3.4:

$$U = \frac{C_1}{T_1} + \frac{\left[ T_2 - C_1 \lceil T_2 / T_1 \rceil \right]}{T_2}. \tag{3.4}$$

Now, simplify by the following algebraic steps:

$$U = \frac{C_1}{T_1} + \frac{T_2}{T_2} + \frac{\left[ -C_1 \lceil T_2 / T_1 \rceil \right]}{T_2} \quad \text{(pull out } T_2 \text{ term)}$$

$$U = \frac{C_1}{T_1} + 1 + \frac{\left[ -C_1 \lceil T_2 / T_1 \rceil \right]}{T_2} \quad \text{(note that } T_2 \text{ term is 1)}$$

$$U = 1 + C_1 \left[ \left( 1/T_1 \right) - \frac{\left\lceil T_2/T_1 \right\rceil}{T_2} \right]$$ (combine $C_1$ terms)

This gives you Equation 3.5:

$$U = 1 + C_1 \left[ \left( 1/T_1 \right) - \frac{\left\lceil T_2/T_1 \right\rceil}{T_2} \right] \qquad (3.5)$$

What is interesting about Equation 3.5 is that *U monotonically decreases with increasing $C_1$ when* $(T_2 > T_1)$. Recall that $T_2$ must be greater than $T_1$ given the RM priority policy assumed here. The term $\left[ (1/T_1) - \frac{\left\lceil T_2/T_1 \right\rceil}{T_2} \right]$ is always less than zero because $T_2$ is greater than $T_1$. This may not be immediately obvious, so let's analyze the characteristics of this expression a little closer. Say that we fix $T_1 = 1$ and be-cause $T_2$ must be greater than $T_1$, we let it be any value from $1 +$ to $\infty$. Note that when $T_2 = 1$, this is a degenerate case where the periods are equal—you'll find out later why this is something we never allow. If we plot the expression $\frac{\left\lceil T_2/T_1 \right\rceil}{T_2}$, you see that it is a periodic function that oscillates between 1 and 2 as we increase $T_2$, equaling 1 anytime $T_2$ is a multiple of $T_1$. By comparison, the term $(1/T_1)$ is con-stant and equal to 1 in this specific example (we could set $T_1$ to any constant value—try this and verify that the condition still holds true). Figure 3.6 shows the periodic relationship between $T_2$ and $T_1$ that guarantees that U monotonically de-creases with increasing $C_1$ when $(T_2 > T_1)$ for Case 1.

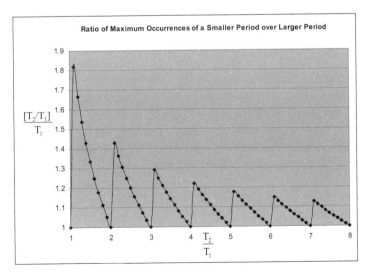

**FIGURE 3.6** Case 1 relationship of $T_2$ and $T_1$.

So, now that you understand the scenario where $C_1$ just fits into the critical time zone, let's look at Case 2.

In Case 2, the last release of $S_1$ does not fit into $T_2$, that is, $C_1$ spills over $T_2$ boundary on last release as shown in Figure 3.6. This spillover condition of the last release of $S_1$ during $T_2$ is expressed simply as Equation 3.6:

$$C_1 \geq T_2 - T_1 \lfloor T_2 / T_1 \rfloor. \tag{3.6}$$

Equation 3.6 is the same as Equation 3.1, but with the inequality flipped—when $S_1$'s $C_1$ is just a little too large to fit in the critical time zone shown in Figure 3.7.

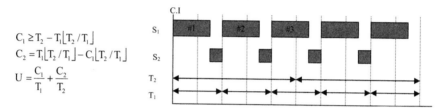

**FIGURE 3.7**   Case 2 overrun of critical time zone by $S_1$.

Even though $S_1$ overruns the critical time zone, some time remains for $S_2$, and we could find a value of $C_2$ for $S_2$ that still allows it to meet its deadline of $T_2$. To compute this smaller $C_2$, we first note that $S_1$ release #1 plus #2 in Figure 3.6 along with some fraction of #3 leave some amount of time left over for $S_2$. However, if we simply look at the first two occurrences of $T_1$ during $T_2$, leaving out the third release of $S_1$ during $T_2$, then we see that this time is the sum of all full occurrences of $T_1$ during $T_2$, which can be expressed as $T_1 \lfloor T_2 / T_1 \rfloor$. Furthermore, the amount of time that $S_1$ takes during this $T_1 \lfloor T_2 / T_1 \rfloor$ duration is exactly $C_1 \lfloor T_2 / T_1 \rfloor$. From these observations we derive Equation 3.7:

$$C_2 = T_1 \lfloor T_2 / T_1 \rfloor - C_1 \lfloor T_2 / T_1 \rfloor. \tag{3.7}$$

Substituting Equation 3.7 into the utility Equation 3.3 again as before, we get Equation 3.8:

$$U = \frac{C_1}{T_1} + \frac{[T_1 \lfloor T_2 / T_1 \rfloor - C_1 \lfloor T_2 / T_1 \rfloor]}{T_2}. \tag{3.8}$$

Now simplifying by the following algebraic steps:

$$U = (T_1 / T_2)\lfloor T_2 / T_1 \rfloor + \frac{C_1}{T_1} + \frac{\left[-C_1\lfloor T_2 / T_1 \rfloor\right]}{T_2} \quad \text{(separating terms)}$$

$$U = (T_1 / T_2)\lfloor T_2 / T_1 \rfloor + C_1\left[(1 / T_1) - (1 / T_2)\lfloor T_2 / T_1 \rfloor\right] \quad \text{(pulling out common}$$
$C_1$ term).

This gives us Equation 3.9:

$$U = (T_1 / T_2)\lfloor T_2 / T_1 \rfloor + C_1\left[(1 / T_1) - (1 / T_2)\lfloor T_2 / T_1 \rfloor\right]. \quad (3.9)$$

What is interesting about Equation 3.9 is that *U monotonically increases with increasing $C_1$ when* $(T_2 > T_1)$. Recall again that $T_2$ must be greater than $T_1$ given the RM priority policy assumed here. The term $(1 / T_2)\lfloor T_2 / T_1 \rfloor$ is always smaller than $(1 / T_1)$ because $T_2$ is greater than $T_1$. As before, this may not be immediately obvious, so let's analyze the characteristics of this expression a little closer—once again, we fix $T_1 = 1$ and because $T_2$ must be greater than $T_1$, we let it be any value from $1+$ to $\infty$. Now if we plot this again, you see that $(1 / T_2)\lfloor T_2 / T_1 \rfloor$ is less than 1 in all cases and therefore also less than $(1 / T_1)$ as can be seen in Figure 3.8.

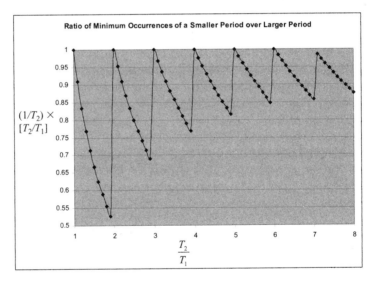

**FIGURE 3.8** Case 2 relationship of $T_2$ and $T_1$.

So, now you also understand the scenario where $C_1$ just overruns the critical time zone. The key concept is that in Case 1, we have the maximum number of occurrences of $S_1$ during $T_2$, and, in Case 2, we have the minimum.

If we now examine the utility functions for both Case 1 and Case 2:

$$U = 1 + C_1 \left[ (1/T_1) - \frac{\lceil T_2/T_1 \rceil}{T_2} \right] (3.5)$$

$$U = (T_1/T_2) \lfloor T_2/T_1 \rfloor + C_1 \left[ (1/T_1) - (1/T_2) \lfloor T_2/T_1 \rfloor \right] (3.9)$$

Let's plot the two utility functions on the same graph setting $T_1 = 1$, $T_2 = 1 +$ to $\infty$, and $C_1 = 0$ to $T_1$.

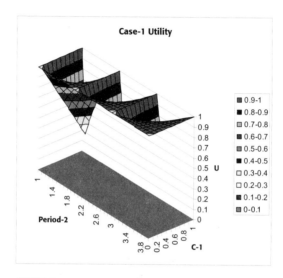

**FIGURE 3.9**    Case 1 utility with varying $T_2$ and $C_1$.

When $C_1 = 0$, this is not particularly interesting because this means that $S_2$ is the only service that requires CPU resource—likewise, when $C_1 = T_2$, then this is also not so interesting because it means that $S_1$ uses all the CPU resource and never allows $S_2$ to run. Looking at the utility plot for Equation 3.5 in Figure 3.9 and Equation 3.9 in Figure 3.10, you can clearly see the periodicity of utility where maximum utility is achieved when $T_1$ and $T_2$ are harmonic.

What we really want to know is where the utility is equal for both cases so that we can determine utility independent of whether $C_1$ exceeds or is less than the critical time zone. This is most easily determined by subtracting Figure 3.9 and Figure 3.10 data to find where the two function differences are zero. Figure 3.11 shows that the two function differences are zero on a diagonal when $T_2$ is varied from 1 times to 2 times $T_1$, and $C_1$ is varied from zero to $T_1$.

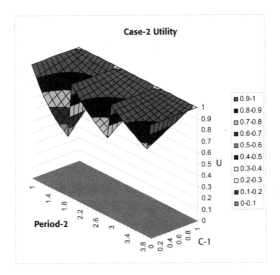

**FIGURE 3.10**    Case 2 utility with varying $T_2$ and $C_1$.

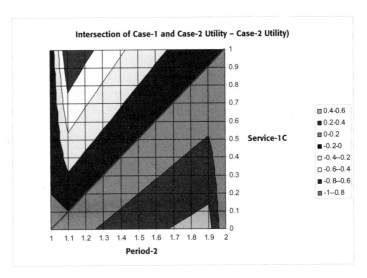

**FIGURE 3.11**    Intersection of Case 1 and Case 2 utility curves.

Finally, if we then plot the diagonal of either utility curve (from Equation 3.5 or Equation 3.9) as shown in Figure 3.12, we see that identical curves that clearly have a minimum near 83% utility.

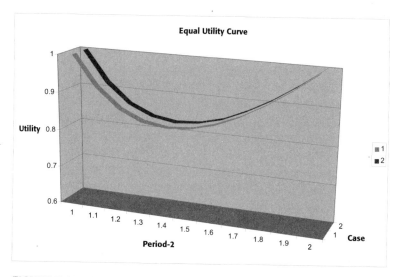

**FIGURE 3.12** Two-service utility minimum for both cases.

Recall that Liu and Layland claim the least upper bound for safe utility given any arbitrary set of services (any relation between periods and any relation between critical time zones) is defined as: $U = \sum_{i=1}^{m}(C_i / T_i) \le m(2^{\frac{1}{m}} - 1)$. For two services, $m(2^{\frac{1}{m}} - 1) = 0.83!$

We have now empirically determined that there is a minimum safe bound on utility for any given set of services, but in doing so, we can also clearly see that this bound can be exceeded safely for specific $T_1$, $T_2$, and $C_1$ relations.

For completeness, let's now finish the two service RM LUB proof mathematically. We'll argue that the two cases are valid only when they intersect, and given the two sets of equations this can only occur when $C_1$ is equal for both cases:

$$C_1 = T_2 - T_1 \lfloor T_2 / T_1 \rfloor$$
$$C_2 = T_2 - C_1 \lceil T_2 / T_1 \rceil$$
$$U = \frac{C_1}{T_1} + \frac{C_2}{T_2}$$

Now, plug $C_1$ and $C_2$ simultaneously into the utility equation to get Equation 3.10:

$$U = \frac{T_2 - T_1 \lfloor T_2 / T_1 \rfloor}{T_1} + \frac{T_2 - C_1 \lceil T_2 / T_1 \rceil}{T_2}$$

$$U = \frac{T_2 - T_1 \lfloor T_2 / T_1 \rfloor}{T_1} + \frac{T_2 - (T_2 - T_1 \lfloor T_2 / T_1 \rfloor) \lceil T_2 / T_1 \rceil}{T_2}$$

$$U = \frac{T_2 - T_1 \lfloor T_2 / T_1 \rfloor}{T_1} + \frac{T_2 - T_2 \lceil T_2 / T_1 \rceil + T_1 \lfloor T_2 / T_1 \rfloor \lceil T_2 / T_1 \rceil}{T_2}$$

$$U = (T_2 / T_1) - \lfloor T_2 / T_1 \rfloor + 1 - \lceil T_2 / T_1 \rceil + (T_1 / T_2) \lfloor T_2 / T_1 \rfloor \lceil T_2 / T_1 \rceil$$

$$U = 1 - \lceil T_2 / T_1 \rceil + (T_1 / T_2) \lfloor T_2 / T_1 \rfloor \lceil T_2 / T_1 \rceil + (T_2 / T_1) - \lfloor T_2 / T_1 \rfloor$$

$$U = 1 - (T_1 / T_2) \left( (T_2 / T_1) \lceil T_2 / T_1 \rceil - \lfloor T_2 / T_1 \rfloor \lceil T_2 / T_1 \rceil - (T_2 / T_1)^2 + (T_2 / T_1) \lfloor T_2 / T_1 \rfloor \right)$$

$$U = 1 - (T_1 / T_2) \left[ \lceil T_2 / T_1 \rceil - (T_2 / T_1) \right] \left[ (T_2 / T_1) - \lfloor T_2 / T_1 \rfloor \right] \qquad (3.10)$$

Now, let whole integer number of interferences of $S_1$ to $S_2$ over $T_2$ be $I = \lfloor T_2 / T_1 \rfloor$ and the fractional interference be $f = (T_2 / T_1) - \lfloor T_2 / T_1 \rfloor$. From this, we can derive a simple expression for utility:

$$U = 1 - \left( \frac{f(1-f)}{(T_2 / T_1)} \right) \qquad (3.11)$$

The derivation for Equation 3.11 is based upon substitution of I and $f$ into Equation 3.10 as follows:

$$U = 1 - (T_1 / T_2) \left[ \lceil T_2 / T_1 \rceil - (T_2 / T_1) \right] \left[ (T_2 / T_1) - \lfloor T_2 / T_1 \rfloor \right]$$

$$U = 1 - (T_1 / T_2) \left[ 1 + \lfloor T_2 / T_1 \rfloor - (T_2 / T_1) \right] \left[ (T_2 / T_1) - \lfloor T_2 / T_1 \rfloor \right] \text{ based on ceiling}$$
(N.d) = 1 + floor(N.d)

$$U = 1 - (T_1 / T_2) \left[ 1 - \left( (T_2 / T_1) - \lfloor T_2 / T_1 \rfloor \right) \right] \left[ (T_2 / T_1) - \lfloor T_2 / T_1 \rfloor \right]$$

$$U = 1 - (T_1 / T_2)(1 - f)(f)$$

$$U = 1 - \left( \frac{f(1-f)}{(T_2 / T_1)} \right)$$

By adding and subtracting the same denominator term to Equation 3.11, we can get:

$$U = 1 - \left( \frac{f(1-f)}{\lfloor T_2/T_1 \rfloor + (T_2/T_1) - \lfloor T_2/T_1 \rfloor} \right)$$

$$U = 1 - \left( \frac{f(1-f)}{(1+f)} \right)$$

The smallest I possible is 1, and the LUB for U occurs when I is minimized, so we substitute 1 for I to get:

$$U = 1 - \left( \frac{(f - f^2)}{(1+f)} \right)$$

Now taking the derivative of U w.r.t. $f$, and solving for the extreme, we get:

$$\partial U / \partial f = \frac{(1+f)(1-2f) - (f-f^2)(1)}{(1+f)^2} = 0$$

Solving for $f$, we get:

$$f = \left( 2^{1/2} - 1 \right)$$

And, plugging $f$ back into U, we get:

$$U = 2 \left( 2^{1/2} - 1 \right)$$

The RM LUB of $m(2^{\frac{1}{m}} - 1)$ is $2 \left( 2^{1/2} - 1 \right)$ for $m = 2$, which is true for the two-service case—Q.E.D.

Having derived the RM LUB by inspection and by mathematical manipulation, we learned that the pessimism of the RM LUB that leads to low utility for real-time safety is based upon a bound that works for all possible combinations of $T_1$ and $T_2$. Specifically, the RM LUB is pessimistic for cases where $T_1$ and $T_2$ are harmonic—in these cases, you can safely achieve 100% utility! In many cases, as shown by demonstration in Figure 3.5 and the Lehoczky, Shah, Ding theorem, you can also safely use a CPU at levels below 100% but above the RM LUB. The RM LUB still has value because it's a simple and quick feasibility check that is sufficient. Going through the derivation, it should now be evident that in many cases, safely using 100% of the CPU resource is not possible with fixed-priority preemptive scheduling and the RM policy. In the next section, the Lehoczky, Shah, Ding theorem is presented and provides a necessary and sufficient feasibility test for RM policy.

# NECESSARY AND SUFFICIENT (N&S) FEASIBILITY

Two algorithms for determination of N&S feasibility testing with RM policy are easily employed:

- Scheduling Point Test
- Completion Time Test

To always achieve 100% utility for any given service set, you must use a more complicated policy with dynamic priorities. You can achieve 100% utility for fixed-priority preemptive services, but only if their relative periods are harmonic. Note also that RM theory does not account for I/O latency. The implicit assumption is that I/O latency is either insignificant or known deterministic values that can be considered separately from execution and interference time. In the upcoming "Deadline-Monotonic Policy" section, you'll see that it's straightforward to slightly modify RM policy and feasibility tests to account for a deadline shorter than the release period, therefore allowing for additional output latency. Input latency can be similarly dealt with, if it's a constant latency, by considering the effective release of the service to occur when the associated interrupt is asserted rather than the real-world event. Because the actual time from effective release to effective release is no different than from event to event, the effective period of the service is unchanged due to input latency. As long as the additional latency shown in Figure 3.13 is acceptable and does not destabilize the service, it can be ignored. However, if the input latency varies, this causes period jitter. In cases where period jitter exists, you simply assume the worst-case frequency or shortest period possible.

## Scheduling Point Test

Recall that by the Lehoczky, Shah, Ding theorem, if a set of services can be shown to meet all deadlines form the critical instant up to the longest deadline of all tasks in the set, then the set is feasible. Recall the critical instant assumption from Liu and Layland's paper, which states that in the worst case, all services might be requested at the same point in time. Based upon this common set of assumptions, Lehoczky, Shah, and Ding introduced an iterative test for this theorem called the Scheduling Point Test:

$$\forall i, 1 \leq i \leq n, \min \sum_{j=1}^{i} C_j \left\lceil \frac{(l)\,T_k}{T_j} \right\rceil \leq (l)\,T_k$$

$$(k,l) \in R_i$$

$$R_i = \left\{ (k,l) \,\middle|\, 1 \leq k \leq i, l = 1, ..., \left\lfloor \frac{T_i}{T_k} \right\rfloor \right\}$$

- Where $n$ is the number of tasks in the set $S_i$ to $S_n$, where $S_1$ has higher priority than $S_{2,}$ and $S_n$ has higher priority than $S_{n>1.}$
- $j$ identifies $S_j$, a service in the set between $S_1$ and $S_{n.}$
- $k$ identifies $S_k$, a service whose $l$ periods must be analyzed.
- $l$ represents the number of periods of $S_k$ to be analyzed.
- $\left\lceil \frac{(l)T_k}{T_j} \right\rceil$ represents the number of times $S_j$ executes within l periods of $S_k$.
- $\lceil T_2 / T_1 \rceil$ is the time required by $S_j$ to execute within l periods of $S_k$—if the sum of these times for the set of tasks is smaller than l periods of $S_k$, then the service set is feasible.

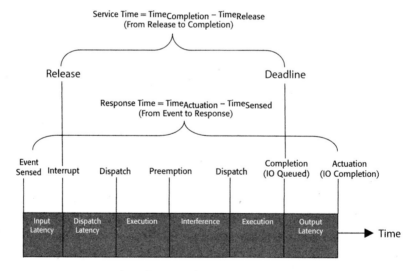

**FIGURE 3.13**   Service effective release and deadline.

ON THE CD

The C code algorithm is included with test code on the CD-ROM for the Scheduling Point Test. Note that the algorithm assumes arrays are sorted according to the RM policy where `period[0]` is the highest priority and shortest period.

## Completion Time Test

The Completion Time Test is presented as an alternative to the Scheduling Point Test [Briand99]:

$$a_n(t) = \sum_{j=1}^{n} \left\lceil \frac{t}{T_j} \right\rceil C_j$$

- $\left\lceil \frac{t}{T_j} \right\rceil$ is the number of executions of $S_j$ at time $t$.

- $\left\lceil \frac{t}{T_j} \right\rceil C_j$ is the demand of $S_j$ in time at t.

- $a_n(t)$ is the total cumulative demand from the n tasks up to time $t$.

Passing this test requires proving that $a_n(t)$ is less than or equal to the deadline for $S_n$, which proves that $S_n$ is feasible. Proving this same property for all S from $S_1$ to $S_n$ proves that the service set is feasible.

The C code algorithm for the completion time test can be found on the CD-ROM and assumes arrays are sorted according to the RM policy where `period[0]` is the highest priority and shortest period.

ON THE CD

# DEADLINE-MONOTONIC POLICY

Deadline-monotonic (DM) policy is very similar to RM except that highest priority is assigned to the service with the shortest deadline. The DM policy is a fixed-priority policy (be sure not to confuse this with EDF where priority is assigned dynamically with highest priority assigned to the active service with the nearest or earliest deadline at any given point in time). The DM policy eliminates the original RM assumption that service period must equal service deadline and allows RM theory to be applied for scenarios even when deadline is less than period. This is useful for dealing with significant output latency. The DM policy can be shown to be an optimal fixed-priority assignment policy like RM policy because $D_i$ and $T_i$ differ only by a constant value, and $D_i \leq T_i$. The DM policy feasibility tests are most easily implemented as iterative tests like Scheduling Point and the Completion Time Test for RM policy. This policy and associated feasibility tests were first introduced by Alan Burns and Neil Audsley [Audsley93]. The sufficient feasibility test they first introduced is simple and intuitive:

$$\forall i : 1 \leq i \leq n : \frac{C_i}{D_i} + \frac{I_i}{D_i} \leq 1.0 \tag{3.12}$$

$C_i$ is the execution time for service $i$, and $I_i$ is the interference time service $i$ experiences over its deadline $D_i$ time period since the time of request for service.

Equation 3.12 states that for all services from 1 to $n$, if the deadline interval is long enough to contain the service execution time interval plus all interfering execution time intervals, then the service is feasible. If all services are feasible, then the system is feasible (real-time safe).

Interference to Service $S_i$ is due to preemption by all higher priority services $S_1$ to $S_{i-1}$, and the total interference time is the number of releases of $S_j$ over the deadline interval $D_i$. The number of $S_i$ interferences is then multiplied by execution time $C_j$ and summed for all $S_j$. Note that $S_j$ always has higher priority than $S_i$.

$$I_i = \sum_{j=1}^{i-1} \left\lceil \frac{D_i}{T_j} \right\rceil C_j \qquad (3.13)$$

$\left\lceil \frac{D_i}{T_j} \right\rceil$ is the worst-case number of releases of $S_j$ over the deadline interval for $S_i$. Because the interference is the worst-case number of releases, interference is over-accounted for—the last interference may be only partial. So, there will be $\left\lfloor \frac{D_i}{T_j} \right\rfloor$ full interferences and some partial interference from the last additional interference. So, we can better account for the partial interference with

$$I_i = \sum_{j=1}^{i-1} \left[ \left[ \left\lfloor \frac{D_i - D_j}{T_j} \right\rfloor + 1 \right] C_j + \left[ \left\lceil \frac{D_i}{T_j} \right\rceil - \left[ \left\lfloor \frac{D_i - D_j}{T_j} \right\rfloor + 1 \right] \right] \times \mathrm{Min}\left[ C_j, D_i - \left\lfloor \frac{D_i}{T_j} \right\rfloor T_j \right] \right] \quad (3.14)$$

$\left[ \left\lfloor \frac{D_i - D_j}{T_j} \right\rfloor + 1 \right] C_j$ is the full interference time, $\left[ \left\lceil \frac{D_i}{T_j} \right\rceil - \left[ \left\lfloor \frac{D_i - D_j}{T_j} \right\rfloor + 1 \right] \right] = 0$ if no partial interference and 1 if there is, and $\mathrm{Min}\left[ C_j, D_i - \left\lfloor \frac{D_i}{T_j} \right\rfloor T_j \right]$ is the partial interference time if it exists.

However, even Equation 3.14 does not exactly account for partial interference. So, both Equations 3.13 and 3.14 combined with Equation 3.12 are only sufficient feasibility tests.

A slightly different approach to dealing with $T_i \neq D_i$ is to simply assume that $S_i$ has a shorter period than it really does until $T_i = D_i$. This approach is a variation of period transform that would affect overall utilization, but allows the RM policy and feasibility approaches to be applied without modification, including the N&S Completion Time Test and/or Scheduling Point Test. In general, period transform is used to increase the frequency of a periodic service to raise its RM priority, often by dividing the implementation of the service into multiple parts. Because output latencies typically are not a huge portion of response time, period transform is a practical way to force real-world problems into the RM framework—deriving a DM N&S feasibility test would be another option. However, the N&S DM feasibility test is complex, so unless there is a huge output latency, period transform is the best approach due to the large body of well-understood RM theory.

An alternative to RM or DM are the dynamic priority polices derived from the deadline-driven dynamic priority approach first presented by Liu and Layland. In the next section, we'll explore the advantages and disadvantages of dynamic priorities compared to static. Today, for hard real-time systems that must provide deterministic responses to service requests, fixed-priority RM policy remains the most widely used and universally accepted theory.

## DYNAMIC PRIORITY POLICIES

Priority preemptive dynamic priority systems can be thought of as a more complex class of priority preemptive where priorities are adjusted by the scheduler every time a new service is released and ready to run. The concept was first formally introduced by Liu and Layland [Liu73] with their description of deadline-driven scheduling policy. The policy Liu and Layland specified in their paper later became known as an EDF (Earliest Deadline First) dynamic priority policy. The policy is called EDF because the scheduler gives highest priority to the service that has the soonest deadline whenever a dispatch decision is made. This also means that anytime an additional thread is placed on the ready queue, the EDF scheduler must reevaluate all dispatch priorities because the newly added thread may not have a deadline later than all the existing threads on the ready queue. Basically, the EDF scheduler must be able to insert the new thread into the queue based upon time to its deadline relative to the time to deadline for all other threads—the insertion has a complexity that is of the order $n - O(n)$, where $n$ is the number of threads on the queue. By comparison a fixed priority policy scheduler can be implemented with complexity that is $O(1)$, or constant time using priority queues. Liu and Layland proved that the potential utility for EDF is full and that deadlines can be guaranteed with EDF. This is an incredible result when compared to fixed-priority RM policy. Essentially no margin is required for real-time safety. Is this really true? If so, then why wouldn't EDF be the only policy ever used for real-time systems? Figure 3.14 shows a scenario where the fixed-priority RM policy fails, and EDF succeeds. Furthermore, it shows that a related dynamic priority policy, LLF (Least Laxity First), also succeeds where RM fails.

Like EDF, LLF is a dynamic-priority policy where services on the ready queue are assigned higher priority if their laxity is the least. *Laxity* is the time difference between their deadline and remaining computation time. This requires the scheduler to know all outstanding service request times, their deadlines, the current time, and remaining computation time for all services, and to reassign priorities to all services on every preemption. Estimating remaining computation time for each service can be difficult and typically requires a worst-case approximation. Like EDF, LLF can also schedule 100% of the CPU for schedules that can't be scheduled by the static RM policy.

| Example 1 | T1 | 2 | C1 | 1 | U1 | 0.5 | LCM = | 70 |
|---|---|---|---|---|---|---|---|---|
| | T2 | 5 | C2 | 1 | U2 | 0.2 | | |
| | T3 | 7 | C3 | 2 | U3 | 0.285714 | Utot = | 0.985714 |

| RM Schedule | | | | | | | | | | |
|---|---|---|---|---|---|---|---|---|---|---|
| S1 | | | | | | | ???????? | | | |
| S2 | | | | | | ???????? | | | | |
| S3 | | | | | | | LATE | | | |
| EDF Schedule | | | | | | | | | | |
| S1 | | | | | | | | | | |
| S2 | | | | | | | | | | |
| S3 | | | | | | | | | | |
| TTD | | | | | | | | | | |
| S1 | 2 | X | 2 | X | 2 | X | 2 | X | 2 | X |
| S2 | 5 | 4 | X | X | X | 5 | 4 | 3 | X | X |
| S3 | 7 | 6 | 5 | 4 | 3 | 2 | X | 7 | 6 | 5 |
| LLF Schedule | | | | | | | | | | |
| S1 | | | | | | | | | | |
| S2 | | | | | | | | | | |
| S3 | | | | | | | | | | |
| Laxity | | | | | | | | | | |
| S1 | 1 | X | 1 | X | 1 | X | 1 | X | 1 | X |
| S2 | 4 | 3 | X | X | X | 4 | 3 | 2 | X | X |
| S3 | 5 | 4 | 3 | 2 | 2 | 1 | X | 5 | 4 | 3 |

**FIGURE 3.14** RM policy overload scenario.

Intuitively, it's hard to believe that the use of any resource can be safe with no margin at all. Even the slightest miscalculation on resources required can cause an overload (overuse of resources). This is a likely scenario given that determining the actual execution time that all services will require is not easy unless very pessimistic worst-case times are assumed. So, it becomes interesting to consider what happens to threads or services in an overload scenario for a given policy. For EDF, overload leads to nondeterministic failure—that is, it's very hard to predict exactly which and how many services will miss their deadlines in an overload. It depends upon the state of the relative priorities during the overload, which in turn depends upon the order of time to deadline times for all services ready to run.

By comparison, for fixed-priority polices such as RM, in an overload, all services of lower priority than the service that is overrunning may miss their deadline, yet all services of higher priority are guaranteed not to be affected as shown in Figure 3.15.

For EDF an overrun by any service may cause all other services on the ready queue to miss their deadlines; a new service added to the queue, therefore adjusting priorities for all, will not preempt the overrunning service. The overrunning service has a time to deadline that is negative because it has passed, so it continues to be the highest priority service and continues to cause others to wait and potentially miss deadlines. In an overrun scenario, common policy is to terminate the release of a service that has overrun. This causes a service dropout. However, simply detecting overrun and terminating the overrunning service takes some

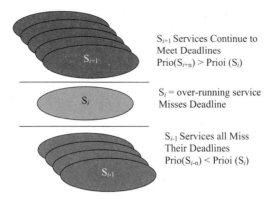

**FIGURE 3.15**   RM policy overload scenario.

CPU resource, which without any margin means that some other service will miss its deadline—with overrun control EDF becomes much more well behaved in an overload scenario—the services with the soonest deadlines will then clearly be the ones to lose out. However, determining which services this will be in advance—based upon the dynamics of releases relative to each other—is still difficult. Figure 3.16 graphically depicts the potentially cascading EDF overload failure scenario—all services queued while the overrunning service executes potentially miss their deadlines, and the next service is likely to overrun as well causing a cascading failure. Probably the best option for an EDF overload is to dump all services in the queue—this at least would be more deterministic.

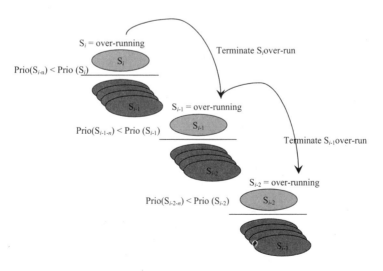

**FIGURE 3.16**   EDF policy cascading failure overload scenario.

Variations of EDF exist where a different policy is encoded into the deadline-driven, dynamic-priority framework (defined originally by Liu and Layland). One of the more interesting variations is LLF. In LLF, highest priority is assigned to the service that has the least difference between its remaining execution time and its upcoming deadline. Laxity is the time difference between their deadline and remaining computation time for a service. Determining the least laxity service requires the scheduler to know all outstanding service request times, their deadlines, the current time, and remaining computation time for all services. After all this is known, the scheduler must then reassign priorities to all services on every event that adds another service to the ready queue. Estimating remaining computation time for each service can be difficult and typically requires a worst-case approximation. The LLF policy encodes the concept of imminence, which intuitively makes sense—every student knows that they should work on the homework where they have the most to do and which is due soonest first—unless of course that particular homework is not worth much credit.

In some sense, all priority encoding policies, dynamic or static, miss the point—what we really want to do is encode which service is most important and make sure that it gets the resources it needs first. We want an intelligent scheduler, like a student who takes into consideration laxity, impact of missing a deadline for a given assignment, cost of dropping one or more, and then intelligently determines how to spend resources for maximum benefit. This concept is an open research area in soft real-time systems and has been investigated by a number of researchers [Brandt99]. In fact, since the landmark Liu and Layland formalization of RM and deadline-driven scheduling, most of the processor resource research has been oriented to one of four things:

■  Generalization and reducing constraints for RM application
■  Solving problems related to RM application for real systems
■  Devising alternative policies for deadline-driven scheduling
■  Devising new soft real-time policies to reduce margin required in RM policy

In Chapter 7, "Soft Real-Time Services," we will explore some of the methods that have been proposed to adapt RM and deadline-driven policies to situations where an occasional service dropout or overrun is acceptable. Soft real-time methods for handling missed deadlines will be more closely examined along with more in-depth coverage of EDF and LLF scheduling.

## SUMMARY

Fixed-priority preemptive scheduling with a RM priority assignment policy (shortest period has highest priority) is most often used and advised for hard real-time systems. Hard real-time systems by definition must have deadline guarantees because the consequences of a missed deadline are total system failure, significant loss of assets, and possible loss of human life. All service sets run as threads of execution should be tested with a sufficient or better yet N&S feasibility test before being fielded for hard real-time operation. Passing an N&S feasibility test guarantees a service set will meet its deadlines as long as $C_i$, $T_i$, and $D_i$ were properly specified and are deterministic or worst case. For quick analysis, a sufficient test such as the RM LUB may be useful. The potential disharmony in period is the reason that the RM LUB is less than full utility for two or more services. Services that have harmonic periods can be safely scheduled with utility exceeding the RM LUB despite failing to pass this test and will pass an N&S test. In general, dynamic priority policies such as EDF and LLF are not considered safe for hard real-time systems due to their difficult-to-predict deadline overrun characteristics. Dynamic priority policies do work well for soft real-time applications, such as game engines, video, audio, and multimedia applications, where an occasional service dropout is acceptable.

## EXERCISES

1. Code the sufficient RM scheduling feasibility test (Liu and Layland paper, p.9, Theorem 5) for the following ANSI C function prototype:

```
int RM_sufficient(
int Ntasks,
int *tid,
unsigned long int *T,
unsigned long int *C,
unsigned long int *D);
```

   Ntasks is the number of tasks in the task set, tid is an array of unique task Ids, T is an array of the release periods, C is an array of the computation times, D is an array of the deadlines (T must equal D for each tid in RM). Finally, the function should simply return 1 if the system can be scheduled, and 0 if it can't.

2. Code the Completion Time Test (found earlier in this chapter) for the following ANSI C function prototype:

```
int Sched_completion(
int Ntasks,
int *tid,
unsigned long int *T,
unsigned long int *C,
unsigned long int *D);
```

   Parameters are defined again as in #1. Assume that T must equal D in all cases.

3. Describe in your own words what the difference is between a *sufficient* and a *necessary and sufficient* scheduling feasibility test.

4. Why is the sufficient RM LUB so pessimistic?

5. If EDF can be shown to meet deadlines and potentially has 100% CPU resource utilization, then why is it not typically the hard real-time policy of choice? What are the drawbacks to using EDF compared to RM/DM? In an overload situation, how will EDF fail?

6. Code a function to compute the Fibonacci sequence to any number of terms. The sequence is 0, 1, 1, 2, 3, 5, 8, 13, 21, 34, 55, 89, . . . The Fibonacci sequence or Fibonacci numbers begin with 0 and 1. The next term is then the sum of the two previous terms. (Do not be concerned if your Fibonacci number overflows an unsigned 32-bit integer, just let it overflow).

7. Now, determine how many terms in the sequence correspond to 10 milliseconds of computation on a lab target PC (the answer may vary depending upon the specific target used). The easiest way to do this is to use WindView to measure the CPU time taken by a task calling your function with a large value. See how long that takes and then scale up or down the number as needed to achieve 10 milliseconds of computation. Repeat this to determine how many terms are required for 20 milliseconds of computation using WindView.

8. Given a task set with two tasks calling your Fibonacci sequence, one with $N$ terms for 10 milliseconds of execution and the other for 20 milliseconds, is the system feasible if the 10 millisecond task is released every 20 milliseconds and the 20 millisecond task every 50 milliseconds? ($T_1 = 20$ msec, $T_2 = 50$ msec, $C_1 = 10$ msec, $C_2 = 20$ msec, and all $D_i$'s = $T_i$'s). Base your answer upon the Lehoczky, Shah, and Ding Theorem.

9. Run the preceding system and show evidence that it works or explain why it won't.

# CHAPTER REFERENCES

[Audsley93] Audsley, N., A. Burns, and A. Wellings, "Deadline Monotonic Scheduling Theory and Application." *Control Engineering Practice*, Vol. 1: (1993): pp. 71-78, 1993.

[Brandt99] Brandt, Scott, "Soft Real-Time Processing with Dynamic Quality of Service Level Resource Management." Ph.D. Dissertation, Department of Computer Science, University of Colorado, 1999.

[Briand99] Briand, Loïc and Daniel Roy, "Meeting Deadlines in Hard Real-Time Systems." IEEE Computer Society, 1999, pp. 28-31.

[Liu73] Liu, C., and J. Layland, "Scheduling Algorithms for Multiprogramming in a Hard Real-Time Environment." *Journal of the Association for Computing Machinery*, Vol. 20, No. 1, (January 1973): pp. 46-61.

# 4  I/O Resources

## In This Chapter

- Introduction
- Worst-Case Execution Time
- Intermediate I/O
- Execution Efficiency
- I/O Architecture

## INTRODUCTION

The input and output to a service shown previously in Figure 3.13 of Chapter 3 requires I/O to/from a device such as a sensor or actuator (encoder or decoder). This I/O is part of the response time, and as shown in Chapter 3, it simply adds to response latency, but does not affect the service execution or interference time during the response. Most services, unless they are trivial, involve some intermediate I/O after the initial sensor input and before the final posting of output data to a write buffer. This intermediate I/O is most often MMR (Memory Mapped Register) or memory device I/O. If this intermediate I/O has single core cycle latency, zero wait-state, then it has no additional impact on the service response time. However, if the intermediate I/O stalls the CPU core, then this increases the response time while the CPU processing pipeline is stalled. Rather than considering this intermediate

I/O as device I/O, it is more easily modeled as an execution efficiency. Device I/O latency is hundreds, thousands, and even millions of core cycles. By comparison, intermediate I/O latency is typically tens or hundreds of core cycles—if more latency than this is possible, then the core hardware design should be reworked.

## WORST-CASE EXECUTION TIME

Ideally the execution time for a service release would be deterministic. For simple microprocessor architectures, this may be true. The Intel® 8088 and the Motorola® 68000, for example, have no CPU pipeline, no cache, and given memory that has no wait-states, you can take a block of code and count the instructions from start to finish. Furthermore, for these architectures, the number of CPU cycles required to execute each instruction is known—some instructions may take more cycles than others, but all are known numbers. So, the total number of CPU clock cycles required to execute a block of code can be calculated. To compute deterministic execution time for a service, the following system characteristics are necessary:

- Exact number of instructions executed from service release input up to response output.
- The exact number of CPU clock cycles for each instruction is known.
- The number of CPU clock cycles for a given instruction is constant.

Let's assume that the second and third characteristics are true, providing deterministic hardware. The same set of instructions always requires the same number of CPU clocks to execute. This alone does not guarantee deterministic execution time because an algorithm may be data driven. The number of loop iterations or the depth of recursion of the algorithm may be a function of the inputs to the algorithm. For data-driven algorithms, the path length, or total instruction count, is a function of the input. Most algorithms are data driven. Any block of code that contains decision constructs such as "if" statements or "case" statements will execute a different path based upon the outcome of the "if" expression or the "case" statement. For simple data-driven algorithms and code blocks, you can simply count instructions in all paths and compare to determine the longest path. This appears simple enough for a small block of code and simple algorithm, but what about an application that performs a complex service? For example, assume a service needs to find the root of a function where the function is not simple. In the case of finding a root for a function that is determined by integrating sensor rates over time, the function is data driven and not known a-priori. Say you want to predict when a rolling satellite will be brought to rest via deceleration using a thruster—that is, when the thrust function (and therefore acceleration) causes the velocity function to reach zero. The thrust function is often known for a particular type of thruster. One method to find the root of any function is to iterate, bisecting an interval to define $x$ and feeding the bisection value into $F(x) = 0$ to test how close the current guess for $x$ is to zero. If the guess is higher, then a lesser or greater subinterval will be selected for the next iteration. If $F(x)$ is a continuous function, then with successive iterations, the interval will become diminishingly small and the bisection of that interval, or $x$, will come closer and closer to the true value of $x$ where $F(x)$ is zero. How many iterations will this take? The answer depends upon the following requirements:

■ Accuracy of $x$ needed
■ Complexity of the function $F(x)$
■ The initial interval

Finally, some functions may actually have more than one solution as well. Many numerical methods are similar to finding roots by bisection in that they require a total path length that varies with the input. For such algorithms, you need to place an upper bound on the path length to define WCET (Worst-Case Execution Time).

Assuming an upper bound on the algorithmic path length and deterministic hardware, then the WCET is safe as an input to an RM (Rate Monotonic) feasibility test. A service release that requires less than the maximum path length simply enjoys more than necessary resource margin. With the evolution of CPU hardware design, most microprocessors have evolved to maximize throughput and provide better overall efficiency by employing acceleration to the most commonly executed instruction sequences and data references. This is typified by the RISC (Reduced Instruction Set Computer) with instruction pipelining and use of memory caches. As CPU core clock rates increased, memory access latency for comparably scaled capacity has generally not kept pace. So, most RISC pipelined architectures make use of cache, a small zero wait-state (single CPU cycle access latency) memory. Unfortunately, cache is too small to hold many applications. So, set associative memories are used to temporarily hold main memory data—when the cache holds data for an address referenced by a program, this is a hit, and the single cycle access to data and/or code allows the CPU pipeline to fetch an instruction or load data into a register in a single cycle. A cache miss, however, stalls the pipeline. Furthermore, I/O from MMRs (Memory Mapped Registers) may require more than a single CPU core cycle and will likewise stall the CPU pipeline if the data is needed for the next instruction. Detecting potential stalls and avoiding them is an art that can increase execution efficiency overall for a CPU—for example, instructions that cause an MMR read can be executed out of order so that the instruction requiring the read data is executed as late as possible, delaying the potential pipeline stall.

The point of pipelining, described in detail in the next section, is to increase overall execution efficiency. However, as is evident from the examples of cache misses and MMR latencies that may cause a data dependency stall, pipelines will stall, and this is a function of the instruction and data stream. The efficiency is therefore data and code driven and not deterministic. So, execution efficiency will vary, even for the same block of code, because cache contents may not only be a function of the current thread of execution, but also of the previous threads that executed in the past. In summary, WCET is a function of the longest path length and the efficiency in executing that path. Equation 4.1 describes WCET:

$$WCET = \left[ CPI_{worst-case} \times Longest - Path - Instruction - Count \right] \times Clock - Period \qquad (4.1)$$

The CPI is a figure that describes efficiency in pipelined execution as the number of Clocks Per Instruction on average that are required to execute each instruction in a block of code. In the next two sections, "Increasing Efficiency" and "Overlapping Execution with I/O," we discuss how best- and worst-case CPI can be determined or at least approximated well. The longest path instruction count must be determined by inspection, formal software engineering proof, or by actual instruction count traces in a simulator or with the target CPU architecture. Warning—most CPU core documentation states a CPI that is best case rather than worst case.

For full determinism in WCET for hard real-time systems, you must guarantee the following:

- All memory access is to known latency memory, including locked cache or main memory with zero or bounded wait-states.
- Unlocked cache hits are not expected in unlocked cache because the hit rate is not deterministic.
- Overlap of CPU and device I/O is not expected nor required to meet deadlines.
- All other pipeline hazards in addition to cache misses and device I/O read/write stalls are lumped into CPI and taken as worst case (e.g. branch-density × branch penalty).
- Longest path is known, and instruction count for it is known.

For soft real-time systems, you can allow occasional service drop-outs or limited overruns and therefore use ACET (Average-Case Execution Time). The ACET can be estimated from the following information:

- Expected L1 and L2 cache hit/miss ratio and cache miss penalty.
- Expected overlap of CPU and device I/O required to meet deadlines.
- All other pipeline hazards are typically secondary and can be ignored like branch misprediction.
- Average length path is known, and the instruction count for it is known.

In summary, you have the following two equations:

$$WCET = Memory - Latency + Device - IO - Latency +$$
$$[Longest - Path - Inst - Count \times CPI_{Effective}]$$

$$ACET = [Expected - Cache - Miss - Rate \times Miss - Penalty] + [NOA \times IO - Latency] + \quad (4.2)$$
$$[Expected - Path - Inst - Count \times CPI_{Effective}]$$

In these equations, the effective CPI accounts for secondary pipeline hazards such as branch mispredictions. The term NOA (Non-Overlap Allowed) is 1.0 if IO time is not overlapped with processing at all.

## INTERMEDIATE I/O

In a nonpreemptive run-to-completion system with a pipelined CPU, six key related equations describe CPU-I/O overlap. Note that the I/O described here is device I/O that occurs during the service execution, rather than the initial I/O, which releases the service in the first place. In some sense, the device I/O occurring during service execution can be considered micro-I/O and usually consists of MMR access rather than block-oriented DMA (Direct Memory Access) I/O. Although this intermediate I/O is much lower latency than the initial block I/O latency, it reduces the execution efficiency significantly. Ideally, with careful generation of machine code (compiler optimizations), careful hardware design for pipeline instruction reordering, and careful service design, you can minimize the loss of efficiency due to micro-I/O. First, you must understand what it means to overlap I/O with CPU.

Consider the following overlap *definitions*:

- ICT = Instruction Count Time (Time to execute a block of instructions with no stalls = CPU Cycles × CPU Clock Period)
- IOT = Bus Interface I/O Time (Bus I/O Cycles × Bus Clock Period)
- OR = Overlap Required—percentage of CPU cycles that must be concurrent with I/O cycles
- NOA = Non-Overlap Allowable for $S_i$ to meet $D_i$—percentage of CPU cycles that can be in addition to I/O cycle time without missing service deadline
- $D_i$ = Deadline for Service $S_i$ relative to release (interrupt initiating execution)
- CPI = Clocks Per Instruction for a block of instructions

The characteristics of overlapping I/O cycles with CPU cycles for a service $S_i$ are summarized as follows by the five possible *overlap conditions* for CPU time and I/O time relative to $S_i$ deadline $D_i$:

1. $D_i \geq$ IOT is required; otherwise, if $D_i <$ IOT, $S_i$ is *I/O-Bound*.
2. $D_i \geq$ ICT is required; otherwise, if $D_i <$ ICT, $S_i$ is *CPU-Bound*.
3. $D_i \geq$ (IOT + ICT) requires no overlap of IOT with ICT.
4. If $D_i <$ (IOT + ICT) where ($D_i \geq$ IOT and $D_i \geq$ ICT), overlap of IOT with ICT is required.
5. If $D_i <$ (IOT + ICT) where ($D_i <$ IOT or $D_i <$ ICT), deadline $D_i$ can't be met regardless of overlap.

For all five overlap conditions listed here, ICT > 0 and IOT > 0 must be true. If ICT and IOT are zero, no service is required. If ICT or IOT alone is zero, then no overlap is possible. When IOT = O, this is an ideal service with no intermediate IO.

From these observations about overlap in a nonpreemptive system, we can deduce the following axioms:

$$CPI_{worst-case} = (ICT + IOT) / ICT \qquad (4.3)$$

$$CPI_{best-case} = (max(ICT, IOT)) / ICT \qquad (4.4)$$

$$CPI_{required} = D_i / ICT \qquad (4.5)$$

$$OR = 1 - [(D_i - IOT) / ICT] \qquad (4.6)$$

$$CPI_{required} = [ICT(1 - OR) + IOT] / ICT \qquad (4.7)$$

$$NOA = (D_i - IOT) / ICT \qquad (4.8)$$

$$OR + NOA = 1 \text{ (by definition)} \qquad (4.9)$$

Equations 4.7 and 4.8 provide a cross-check. Equation 4.7 should always match equation 4.5 as long as condition 4 or 3 is true. Equation 4.9 should always be 1.0 by definition—whatever isn't overlapped must be allowable, or it would be required. When no overlapping of core device I/O cycles is possible with core CPU cycles, then the following condition must hold for a service to guarantee a deadline:

$$\left[Bus - IO - Cycles \times Core - to - Bus - Factor\right] + Core - Cycles < WCET_i < D_i \qquad (4.10)$$

The WCET must be less than the service's deadline because we have not considered interference in this CPU-I/O overlap analysis. Recall that interference time must be added to release I/O latency and WCET:

$$\forall S_i, T_{response-i} \leq Deadline_i$$

$$T_{response-i} = T_{IO-Latency-i} + WCET_i + T_{Memory-Latency-i} + \sum_{j=1}^{i-1} T_{int\,erference-j} \qquad (4.11)$$

The WCET deduced from Equation 4.10 must therefore be an input into the normal RM feasibility analysis that models interference. The Core-to-Bus-Factor term is ideally 1. This is a zero wait-state case where the processor clock rate and bus transaction rate are perfectly matched. Most often, a read or write will require multiple core cycles.

The overlap required (OR) is indicative of how critical execution efficiency is to a service's capability to meet deadlines. If OR is high, then the capability to meet deadlines requires high efficiency, and deadline overruns are likely when the pipeline stalls. In a soft real-time system, it may be reasonable to count on an OR of 10 to 30%, which can be achieved through compiler optimizations (code scheduling), hand optimizations (use of prefetching), and hardware pipeline hazard handling. Note that the ICT and IOT in Figure 4.1 are shown in nanoseconds as an example for a typical 100 MHz to 1 GHz CPU core executing a typical block of code of 100 to 6,000 instructions with a $CPI_{effective} = 1.0$. It is not possible to have OR > 1.0, so the cases where OR is greater than 1.0 are not feasible.

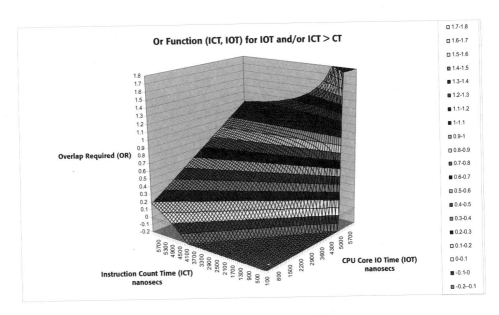

**FIGURE 4.1** CPU-10 overlap required for given ICT and IOT.

## EXECUTION EFFICIENCY

When WCET is too worst case, a well tuned and pipelined CPU architecture increases instruction throughput per unit time and significantly reduces the probability of WCET occurances. In other words, a pipelined CPU reduces the overall CPI required to execute a block of code. In some cases, IPC (Instructions Per

Clock), which is the inverse of CPI, is used as a figure of merit to describe the over-all possible throughput of a pipelined CPU. A CPU with better throughput has a lower CPI and a higher IPC. In this text, we will use only CPI noting that:

$$CPI = \frac{1}{IPC}$$

The point of pipelined hardware architecture is to ensure that an instruction is completed every clock for all instructions in the ISA (Instruction Set Architecture). Normally CPI is 1.0 or less overall in modern pipelined systems. Figure 4.2 shows a simple CPU pipeline and its stage overlap such that one instruction is completed (retired) every CPU clock.

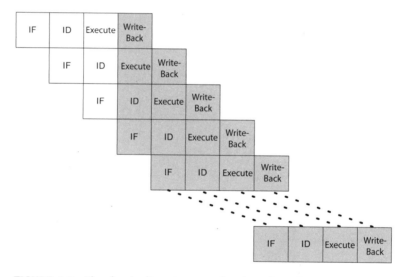

**FIGURE 4.2**   Simple pipeline stage overlap (Depth = 4).

In Figure 4.2, the stages are Instruction Fetch (IF), Instruction Decode (ID), Execute, and register Write-Back. This example pipeline is four stage, so for the pipeline to reach steady-state operation and a CPI of 1.0, it requires four CPU cycles until a Write-Back occurs on every IF. At this point, as long as the stage overlapping can continue, one instruction is completed every CPU clock.

Pipeline design requires minimization of hazards, so the pipeline must stall the one-cycle Write-Backs to produce correct results. The strategies for pipeline design are well described by computer architecture texts [Hennessy03], but are summa-rized here for convenience. Hazards that may stall the pipeline and increase CPI include the following:

- Instruction and data cache misses, requiring a high latency cache load from main memory
- High latency device reads or writes, requiring the pipeline to wait for completion
- Code branches—change in locality of execution and data reference

The instruction and data cache misses can be reduced by increasing cache size, keeping a separate data and instruction cache (Harvard architecture), and allowing the pipeline to execute instructions out of order so that something continues to execute while a cache miss is being handled. The hazard can't be eliminated unless all code and data can be locked into a Level-1 cache (Level-1 cache is single cycle access to the core by definition).

The high latency device read/write hazard is very typical in embedded systems where device interfaces to sensors and actuators are controlled and monitored via MMRs. When these devices and their registers are written or read, this can stall the pipeline while the read or write completes. A split-transaction bus interface to device MMRs can greatly reduce the pipeline hazard by allowing reads to be posted and the pipeline to continue until the read completion is really needed—likewise a split transaction bus allows writes to be posted to a bus interface queue in a single cycle. When a write is posted, the pipeline goes on assuming the MMR write will ultimately complete, but that other instructions in the pipeline do not necessarily need this to complete before they execute.

Finally, code branching hazards can be reduced by branch prediction and speculative execution of both branches—even with branch prediction and speculative execution, a misprediction typically requires some stall cycles to recover.

By far, the pipeline hazards that contribute most to lowering CPI are cache misses and core bus interface I/O latency (e.g., MMR access). Branch mispredictions and other pipeline hazards often result in stalls of much shorter duration (by orders of magnitude) compared to cache misses and device I/O. The indeterminism of cache misses can be greatly reduced by locking code in instruction cache and locking data in data cache. A Level-1 instruction and data cache is often too small to lock down all code and all data required, but some architectures include a Level-2 cache, which is much larger and can also be locked. Level-2 cache usually has 2-cycle or more, but less than 10-cycle access time—locking code and data into L2 cache is much like having a 1 or more wait-state memory. Low wait-state memory is often referred to as a TCM (Tightly Coupled Memory). This is ideal for a real-time embedded system because it eliminates much of the nondeterminism of cache hit/miss ratios that are data-stream and instruction-stream driven. An L2 cache is often unified (holds instructions and data) and 256 KB, 512 KB, or more in size. So, you should lock all real-time service code and data into L1 or L2 caches, most often L2, leaving L1 to increase efficiency with dynamic loading. All best effort service code and data segments can be kept in main memory because dead-lines and determinism are not an issue, and any unlocked L1 or L2 cache increases the execution efficiency of these main-memory-based best effort services.

Eliminating nondeterminism of device I/O latency and pipeline hazards is very difficult. When instructions are allowed to execute while a write is draining to a device, this is called *weakly consistent*. This is okay in many circumstances, but not when the write must occur before other instructions not yet executed for correct-ness. Posting writes is also ultimately limited by the posted write bus interface queue depth—when the queue is full, subsequent writes must stall the CPU until the queue is drained by at least one pending write. Likewise, for split-transaction reads, when an instruction actually uses data from the earlier executed read in-struction, then the pipeline must stall until the read completes. Otherwise the de-pendent instruction would execute with stale data, and the execution would be errant. A stall where the pipeline must wait for a read completion is called a *data-dependency stall*. When split-transaction reads are scheduled with a register as a destination, this can create another hazard called register pressure—the register awaiting read completion is tied up and can't be used at all by other instructions until the read completes even though they are not dependent upon the read. You can reduce register pressure by adding a lot of general-purpose registers (most pipelined RISC architectures have dozens and dozens of them) as well as by pro-viding an option to read data from devices into cache. Reading from a memory-mapped device into cache is normally done with a cache prefetch instruction. In the worst case, we must assume that all device I/O during execution of a service stalls the pipeline so that

$$\text{WCET} = \left[ (\text{CPI}_{best=case} \times Longest-Path-Instruction-Count) + Stall-Cycles \right] \times Clock-Period$$

If you can keep the stall cycles to a deterministic minimum by locking code into L2 cache (or L1 if possible) and by reducing device I/O stall cycles, then WCET can be reduced. Cache locking helps immensely and is fully deterministic.

# I/O ARCHITECTURE

In this chapter, I/O has been examined as a resource in terms of latency (time) and bandwidth (bytes/second). The view has been from the perspective of a single processor core and I/O between that processor core and peripherals. The emer-gence of advanced ASIC architectures, such as SoC (System-on-a-Chip), has brought about embedded single-chip system designs that integrate multiple processors with many peripherals in more complex interconnections than BIU (Bus Interface Unit) designs. Figure 4.3 provides an overview of the many interconnection networks that can be used on chip and between multichip or even multisubsystem designs, including traditional bus architectures.

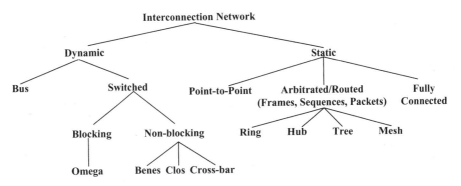

**FIGURE 4.3** A taxonomy of interconnection networks.

The cross-bar interconnection fully connects all processing and I/O components without any blocking. The cross-bar is said to be dynamic because a matrix of switches must be set to create a pathway between two end-points as shown in Figure 4.4. The number of switches required is a quadratic function of the number of end-points such that $N$ points can be connected by $N^2$ switches—this is a costly interconnection. Blocking occurs when the connection between two end-points prevents the simultaneous connection between two others due to common pathways that can't be used simultaneously. The bus interconnection, like a cross-bar, is dynamic, but is fully blocking because it must be time multiplexed and allows no more than two end-points within the entire system to be connected at once.

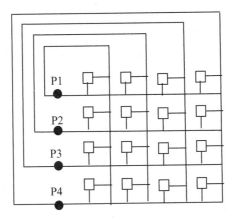

**FIGURE 4.4** Cross-bar interconnection network.

A nonblocking interconnection such as the cross-bar provides low-latency communication between two end-points by providing a dedicated nonblocking circuit. By comparison, an end-point communicating over a bus must request access for the bus, be granted the bus by a controller, address another end-point on the bus, transfer data, and relinquish the bus. If the bus is busy, the bus controller makes the requestor wait in a request queue. This bus arbitration time greatly increases I/O latency. Interconnection hardware components will be discussed in greater detail in Chapter 8, "Embedded System Components."

## SUMMARY

The overall response time of a service includes input, intermediate I/O, and output latency. The input and output latencies can most often be determined and added to the overall response time. Intermediate I/O is more complex because intermediate I/O includes register, memory bus, and, in general, interconnection network latencies that will stall an individual processor's execution. The stall time reduces execution efficiency for each processor, and unless these stall cycles can be used for other work, increases WCET for the service.

## EXERCISES

1. If a processor has a cache hit rate of 99.5% and a cache miss penalty of 160 core processor cycles, what will the average CPI be for 1,000 instructions?
2. If a system must complete frame processing so that 100,000 frames are completed per second and the instruction count per frame processed is 2,120 instructions on a 1-GHz processor core, what is the CPI required for this system? What is the overlap between instructions and I/O time if the intermediate I/O time is 4.5 microseconds?
3. Read the Sha, Rajkumar, et al. paper, "Priority Inheritance Protocols: An Approach to Real-Time Synchronization." Write a brief summary noting at least three key concepts from this paper.
4. Review the CD-ROM code for heap_mq.c and posix_mq.c. Write a brief paragraph describing how these two message queue applications are similar and how they are different. Make sure you not only read the code, but that you build it, load it, and execute it to make sure you understand how both applications work.
5. Write VxWorks code that spawns two tasks: A and B. A should initialize and enter a while(1) loop in which it does a semGive on a global binary semaphore S1 and then does a semTake on a different global binary sema-

phore S2. B should initialize and enter a `while(1)` loop in which it does a `semTake` of S1, delays 1 second, and then does a `semGive` of S2. Test your code on a target or VxSim and turn in all source with evidence that it works correctly (e.g., show counters that increment in windshell dump).

6. Now run the code from the previous exercise and analyze a WindView trace for it. Capture the WindView trace and add annotations by hand that clearly show `semGive` and `semTake` events, the execution time, and delay time. Note any unexpected aspects of the trace.

7. Use `taskSwitchHookAdd` and `taskSwitchHookDelete` to add some of your own code to the wind kernel context switch sequence and prove it works by increasing a global counter for each preempt/dispatch context switch and timestamping a global with the last preempt/dispatch time with the x86 PIT (programmable interval timer)—see the CD-ROM sample PIT code. The VxWorks `tickGet()` call can also be used to sample relative times, but is only accurate to the tick resolution (1 millisecond assuming `sysClkRateSet(1000)`). Make an On/Off wrapper function for your add and delete so that you can turn on your switch hook easily from a `windsh` command line and look at the values of your two globals. Turn in your code and windshell output showing that it works.

ON THE CD

8. Modify your hook so that it will compute separate preempt and dispatch counts for a specific task ID or set of task IDs (up to 10) and the last preempt and dispatch times for all tasks you are monitoring. Run your code from Exercise 4 and monitor it by calling your On/Off wrapper before running your test tasks. What are your counts and last times and how do they compare with WindView analysis?

9. Use your program to analyze the number of `tNetTask` dispatches/preemptions and modify the code to track the average time between dispatch and preemption. Write a program to gather stats on `tNetTask` for 30 seconds. What is the number of dispatches/preemptions? What is the average dispatch time?

## CHAPTER REFERENCES

[Almasi89] Almasi, George, and Allan Gottlieb, *Highly Parallel Computing*. The Benjamin/Cummings Publishing Company, 1989.

[Hennessy03] Patterson, David, and John Hennessy, *Computer Architecture: A Quantitative Approach*, 3rd ed. Morgan Kaufmann Publishers, 2003.

[Patterson94] Hennessy, John and David Patterson, *Computer Organization and Design: The Hardware/Software Interface*. Morgan Kaufmann Publishers, 1994.

# 5 Memory

## INTRODUCTION

In the previous chapter, memory was analyzed from the perspective of latency, and, in this sense, was treated like most any other I/O device. For a real-time embedded system, this is a useful way to view memory although it's very atypical compared to general-purpose computing. In general, memory is typically viewed as a logical address space for software to use as a temporary store for intermediate results while processing input data to produce output data. The physical address space is a hardware view where memory devices of various type and latency are either mapped into address space through chip selects and buses or are hidden as caches for mapped devices. Most often an MMU (Memory Management Unit) provides the logical-to-physical address mapping (often one-to-one for embedded systems) and provides address range and memory access attribute checking. For example, some memory segments may have attributes set so they are read only. Typically, all code is placed in read-only attribute memory segments. Memory-Mapped I/O (MMIO) address space most often has a non-cacheable attribute set to prevent output data from being cached and never actually written to a device. From a higher level software viewpoint, where memory is viewed as a global store and an interface to MMIO, it's often useful to set up shared memory segments useable by more than one service. When memory is shared by more than one service, care must be taken to prevent inconsistent memory updates and reads. From a resource perspective, total memory capacity, memory access latency, and memory interface bandwidth must be sufficient to meet requirements.

## PHYSICAL HIERARCHY

The physical memory hierarchy for an embedded processor can vary significantly based upon hardware architecture. However, most often, a Harvard architecture is used, which has evolved from GPCs (general-purpose computers) and is often employed by embedded systems as well. The typical Harvard architecture with separate L1 (Level-1) instruction and data caches, but with unified L2 (Level-2) cache and either on-chip SRAM or external DDR (Dynamic Data RAM) is shown in Figure 5.1.

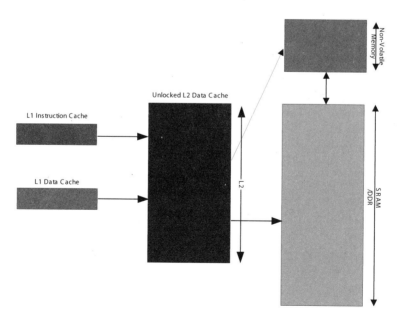

**FIGURE 5.1**   Harvard architecture physical memory hierarchy.

From the software viewpoint, memory is a global resource in a single address space with all other MMIO devices as shown in Figure 5.2.

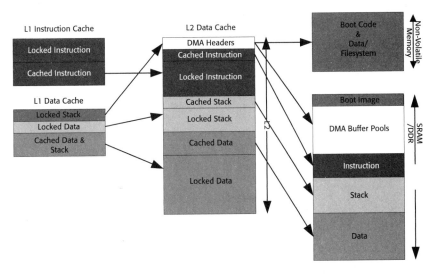

**FIGURE 5.2**  Logical partitioning and segmenting of physical memory hierarchy by firmware.

Memory system design has been most influenced by GPC architecture and goals to maximize throughput, but not necessarily to minimize the latency for any single memory access or operation. The multilevel cached memory hierarchy for GPC platforms now often includes Harvard L1 and unified L2 caches on-chip with off-chip L3 unified cache. The caches for GPCs are most often set associative with aging bits for each cache set (line) so that the LRU (Least Recently Used) sets are replaced when a cache line must be loaded. An $N$-way set-associative cache can load an address reference into any $N$ ways in the cache allowing for the LRU line to be replaced. The LRU replacement policy, or approximation thereof, leads to a high cache hit to miss ratio so that a processor most often finds data in cache and does not have to suffer the penalty of a cache miss. The set-associative cache is a compromise between a direct-mapped and a fully associative cache. In a direct-mapped cache, each address can be loaded into one and only one cache line making the replacement policy simple, yet often causing cache thrashing. *Thrashing* occurs when two addresses are referenced and keep knocking each other out of cache, greatly decreasing cache efficiency. Ideally, a cache memory would be so flexible that the LRU set (line) for the entire cache would be replaced each time, minimizing the likelihood of thrashing. Cost of fully associative array memory prevents this as does the cost of so many aging bits, and most caches are four-way or eight-way set associative with 2 or 3 aging bits for LRU. Figure 5.3 shows a direct-mapped cache where a main memory that is four times the size of the cache memory has memory sets (collections of four or more 32-bit byte addressable words), which can only be loaded into one cache set.

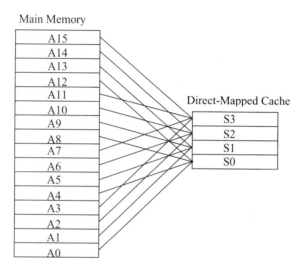

**FIGURE 5.3**   Direct mapping of memory to cache lines (sets).

By comparison, Figure 5.4 shows a two-way set-associative cache for a main memory four times the size of the cache. Each line can be loaded into one of four locations in the cache. The addition of 2 bits to record how recently each line was accessed relative to the other three in the set allows the cache controller to replace lines that are LRU. The LRU policy assumes that lines that have not been accessed recently are less likely to be accessed again anytime soon. This has been shown to be true for most code where execution has locality of reference where data is used within small address ranges (often in loops) distributed throughout memory for general-purpose programs.

For real-time embedded systems, the unpredictability of cache hits/misses is a problem. It makes it very difficult to estimate WCET (Worst-Case Execution Time). In the extreme case, it's really only safe to assume that every cache access could incur the miss penalty. For this reason, for hard real-time systems, it's perhaps advisable not to use cache. However, this would greatly reduce throughput to obtain deterministic execution. So, rather than including multilevel caches, many real-time embedded systems instead make investment in TCM (Tightly Coupled Memory), which is single-cycle access for the processor, yet has no cache functionality.

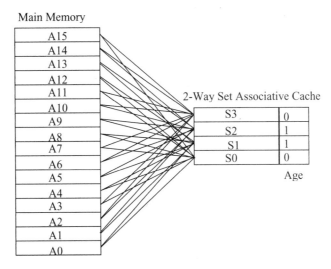

**FIGURE 5.4**   Two-way set-associative mapping of memory to cache lines (sets).

Furthermore, TCM is often dual ported so that service data (or context) can be loaded via DMA and read/written at the same time. Some GPC processors include L1 or L2 caches that have the capability to lock ways so that the cache can be turned into this type of TCM for embedded applications.

The realization that GPC cache architecture is not always beneficial to real-time embedded systems, especially hard real-time systems, has lead to the emergence of the software-managed cache. Furthermore, compared to GPCs, where it is very difficult to predict the care with which code will be written, embedded code is often carefully analyzed and optimized so that data access is carefully planned. A software-managed cache uses application-specific logic to schedule loading of a TCM with service execution context by DMA from a larger, higher latency external memory. Hardware cost of a GPC cache architecture is avoided and the management of execution context tailored for the real-time services—the scheduling of DMAs and the worst-case delay for completing a TCM load—must of course still be carefully considered.

## CAPACITY AND ALLOCATION

The most basic resource concern associated with memory should always be total capacity needed. Many algorithms include space and time trade-offs and services often need significant data context for processing. Keep in mind that cache does not contribute to total capacity because it stores only copies of data rather than unique data. This is another downside to cache for embedded systems where capacity is often limited. Furthermore, latency for access to memory devices should be considered carefully because high latency access can significantly increase WCET and cause problems meeting real-time deadlines. So, data sets accessed with high frequency should of course be stored in the lowest latency memory.

## SHARED MEMORY

Often two services find it useful share a memory data segment or code segment. In the case of a shared data segment, the read/write access to this shared memory must be guaranteed to be consistent so that one service in the middle of a write is not preempted by another, which could then read partially updated data. For example, a satellite system might sample sensors and store the satellite state vector in a shared memory segment. The satellite state vector would typically include 3 double precision numbers with the X, Y, Z location relative to the center of Earth, 3 double precision numbers for the velocity, and 3 more double precision numbers with the acceleration relative to Earth. Overall, this state would likely have 9 double precision numbers that can't be updated in a single CPU cycle. Furthermore, the state vector might also contain the attitude, attitude rate, and attitude acceleration—up to 18 numbers! Clearly it would be possible for a service updating this state to be preempted via an interrupt causing a context switch to another service that uses the state. Using a partially updated state would likely result in control being issued based upon corrupt state information and might even cause loss of the satellite.

   To safely allow for shared memory data, the mutual exclusion semaphore was introduced [Tannenbaum87]. The mutex semaphore protects a critical section of code that is executed to access the shared memory resource. In VxWorks, two functions support this: semTake(Semid) and semGive(Semid). The semTake(Semid) blocks the calling service if Semid=0 and allows it to continue execution if Semid=1. The semGive(Semid) increments Semid by 1, leaving it at 1 if it is already 1. When the semGive(Semid) causes Semid to go from 0 to 1, any services blocked earlier by a call to semTake(Semid) when Semid was 0, now unblocks one of the waiting services. Typically the waiting services are unblocked in first-in, first-out order. By surrounding the code that writes and/or reads the shared memory with semTake(Semid) and semGive(Semid) using a common Semid, the updates and reads are guaranteed to be mutually exclusive. The critical sections are shown in Table 5.1.

**TABLE 5.1**   The Mutex Semaphore Protects Critical Code

| Update-Code | Read-Code |
|---|---|
| ... | ... |
| `semTake(Semid);` | `semTake(Semid);` |
| `X = getX();` | `control(X, Y, Z);` |
| `Y = getY();` | `semGive(Semid);` |
| `Z = getZ();` | ... |
| `semGive(Semid);` | ... |
| ... | ... |

Clearly if the Update-Code was interrupted and preempted by the Read-Code at line 4 for example, then the `control(X, Y, Z)` function would be using the new X and possibly an incorrect and definitely old Y and Z. However, the `semTake(Semid)` and `semGive(Semid)` guarantee that the Read-Code can't preempt the Update-Code no matter what the RM policies are. How does it do this? The `semTake(Semid)` is a TSL instruction (Test and Set-Lock). In a single cycle, supported by hardware, the Semid memory location is first tested to see if it is 0 or 1. If 1, set to 0, and execution continues; if Semid is 0 on the test, the value of Semid is unchanged, and the next instruction is a branch to a wait-queue and CPU yield. Whenever a service does a `semGive(Semid)`, the wait-queue is checked and the first waiting service is unblocked. The unblocking is achieved by dequeuing the waiting service from the wait-queue and then placing it on the ready-queue for execution inside the critical section at its normal priority.

## ECC MEMORY

For safety-critical real-time embedded systems, it is imperative that data corruption is detected and ideally corrected in real time if possible. This can be accomplished by using ECC (Error Correcting Circuitry) memory interfaces. An ECC memory interface can detect and correct SBEs (Single Bit Errors) and also can detect MBEs (Multi-Bit Errors), but can not correct MBEs. The encoding for the extended parity bits for ECC is based upon the Hamming code. When data is written to memory, parity bits are calculated according to a Hamming encoding and added to a memory word extension (an additional 8 bits for a 32-bit word). When data is read out, check bits are computed by the ECC logic. These check bits, called the *syndrome*, encode read data errors as follows:

1. If Check-Bits = 0 AND parity-encoded word = 0 => NO ERRORS
2. If Check-Bits != 0 AND parity-encoded word = 1 => SBE, CAN CORRECT

3. If Check-Bits != 0 AND parity-encoded word = 0 => MBE DETECTED, HALT
4. If Check-Bits = 0 AND parity-encoded word = 1 => parity ERROR, CAN CORRECT

On MBEs, the processor normally halts because the next instruction executed with unknown corrupted data could cause a fatal error. By halting, the CPU will go through a hardware watch-dog timer reset and safe recovery instead.

For a correctable SBE, the CPU raises a nonmaskable interrupt that software should handle by acknowledging and then reading the address of the SBE location, and finally writing the corrected data back to the memory location from the read register. The ECC automatically corrects data as it is read from memory into registers, but most often it's up to the software to write the corrected data in the register back to the corrupted memory location. In some implementations hardware may also automate the write-back of corrected data.

To understand how Hamming encoding works to compute extended parity and a syndrome capable of SBE detection/correction and MBE detection, it is best to learn by example. Figure 5.5 shows a Hamming encoding for an 8-bit word with 4 parity bits and an overall word parity-bit shown as pW.

| | | 0 | 1 | 2 | 3 | 4 | 5 | 6 | 7 | 8 | 9 | 10 | 11 | 12 |
|---|---|---|---|---|---|---|---|---|---|---|---|---|---|---|
| | | pW | p01 | p02 | d01 | p03 | d02 | d03 | d04 | p04 | d05 | d06 | d07 | d08 |
| | D | X | X | X | 1 | X | 1 | 0 | 0 | X | 0 | 1 | 0 | 0 |
| | p01 | | 0 | | 1 | | 1 | | 0 | | 0 | | 0 | |
| | p02 | | | 0 | 1 | | | 0 | 0 | | | 1 | 0 | |
| | p03 | | | | | 1 | 1 | 0 | 0 | | | | | 0 |
| | p04 | | | | | | | | | 1 | 0 | 1 | 0 | 0 |
| | p05 | | | | | | | | | | | | | |
| | p06 | | | | | | | | | | | | | |
| | ED | 1 | 0 | 0 | 1 | 1 | 1 | 0 | 0 | 1 | 0 | 1 | 0 | 0 |

| | | | 0 | 1 | 2 | 3 | 4 | 5 | 6 | 7 | 8 | 9 | 10 | 11 | 12 |
|---|---|---|---|---|---|---|---|---|---|---|---|---|---|---|---|
| | | | pW | p01 | p02 | d01 | p03 | d02 | d03 | d04 | p04 | d05 | d06 | d07 | d08 |
| SYN | ED | | 1 | 0 | 0 | 1 | 1 | 1 | 0 | 0 | 1 | 0 | 1 | 0 | 0 |
| | c01 | 0 | | 0 | | 1 | | 1 | | 0 | | 0 | | 0 | |
| | c02 | 0 | | | 0 | 1 | | | 0 | 0 | 0 | 1 | | | |
| | c03 | 0 | | | | | 1 | 1 | 0 | 0 | | | | | 0 |
| | c04 | 0 | | | | | | | | | 1 | 0 | 1 | 0 | 0 |
| | c05 | X | | | | | | | | | | | | | |
| | c06 | X | | | | | | | | | | | | | |
| | pW | 0 | | | | | | | | | | | | | |
| | CD | | 1 | 0 | 0 | 1 | 1 | 1 | 0 | 0 | 1 | 0 | 1 | 0 | 0 |

**FIGURE 5.5** Hamming encoding for 8-bit word with no error in computed syndrome.

In Figure 5.5, the ED (Encoded Data) is the same as the CD (Corrected Data). Furthermore, the check bits are zero and pW, parity for the ED, remains zero as well. Figure 5.6 shows a more interesting scenario where bit-5, which is data bit d02, is flipped. This could occur due to an environmental hazard such as EMI (Electromagnetic Interference) or charged particle radiation. When this occurs, because it's an SBE, the Hamming syndrome (check bits) detects and corrects this error as shown in Figure 5.6.

| | | 0 | 1 | 2 | 3 | 4 | 5 | 6 | 7 | 8 | 9 | 10 | 11 | 12 |
|---|---|---|---|---|---|---|---|---|---|---|---|---|---|---|
| | | pW | p01 | p02 | d01 | p03 | d02 | d03 | d04 | p04 | d05 | d06 | d07 | d08 |
| | D | X | X | X | 1 | X | 1 | 0 | 0 | X | 0 | 1 | 0 | 0 |
| | p01 | | 0 | | 1 | | 1 | | 0 | | 0 | | 0 | |
| | p02 | | | 0 | 1 | | | 0 | 0 | | 0 | 1 | | |
| | p03 | | | | | 1 | 1 | 0 | 0 | | | | | 0 |
| | p04 | | | | | | | | | 1 | 0 | 1 | 0 | 0 |
| | p05 | | | | | | | | | | | | | |
| | p06 | | | | | | | | | | | | | |
| | ED | 1 | 0 | 0 | 1 | 1 | 1 | 0 | 0 | 1 | 0 | 1 | 0 | 0 |

| | | 0 | 1 | 2 | 3 | 4 | 5 | 6 | 7 | 8 | 9 | 10 | 11 | 12 |
|---|---|---|---|---|---|---|---|---|---|---|---|---|---|---|
| | | pW | p01 | p02 | d01 | p03 | d02 | d03 | d04 | p04 | d05 | d06 | d07 | d08 |
| SYN | ED | 1 | 0 | 0 | 1 | 1 | 1 | 0 | 0 | 1 | 0 | 1 | 0 | 0 |
| c01 | 0 | | 0 | | 1 | | 1 | | 0 | | 0 | | 0 | |
| c02 | 0 | | | 0 | 1 | | | 0 | 0 | | 0 | 1 | | |
| c03 | 0 | | | | | 1 | 1 | 0 | 0 | | | | | 0 |
| c04 | 0 | | | | | | | | | 1 | 0 | 1 | 0 | 0 |
| c05 | X | | | | | | | | | | | | | |
| c06 | X | | | | | | | | | | | | | |
| pW | 1 | | | | | | | | | | | | | |
| | CD | 1 | 0 | 0 | 1 | 1 | 1 | 0 | 0 | 1 | 0 | 1 | 0 | 0 |
| SBE Correction | | | | | | | | | | | | | | |

**FIGURE 5.6**   Hamming syndrome catches and corrects an SBE.

In the Figure 5.6 example, the syndrome computed is nonzero and the pW=1, which is the case for a correctable SBE. Notice that the syndrome value of binary 1010 encodes the errant bit position for bit-5, which is data bit d02. Figure 5.7 illustrates an MBE scenario.

Note that the syndrome is nonzero, but the pW=0, meaning that an uncorrectable MBE has occurred. Figure 5.8 shows a scenario where the ED parity is corrupted.

In this case, the syndrome is zero and pW=1 indicating a parity error on the overall encoded data word. This is a correctable SBE. Similarly, it's possible that one of the Hamming extended parity bits could be flipped as a detectable and correctable SBE as shown in Figure 5.9.

| | | 0 | 1 | 2 | 3 | 4 | 5 | 6 | 7 | 8 | 9 | 10 | 11 | 12 |
|---|---|---|---|---|---|---|---|---|---|---|---|---|---|---|
| | | pW | p01 | p02 | d01 | p03 | d02 | d03 | d04 | p04 | d05 | d06 | d07 | d08 |
| | D | X | X | X | 1 | X | 1 | 0 | 0 | X | 0 | 1 | 0 | 0 |
| | p01 | | 0 | | 1 | | 1 | | 0 | | 0 | | 0 | |
| | p02 | | | 0 | 1 | | | 0 | 0 | | 0 | 1 | | |
| | p03 | | | | | 1 | 1 | 0 | 0 | | | | | 0 |
| | p04 | | | | | | | | | 1 | 0 | 1 | 0 | 0 |
| | p05 | | | | | | | | | | | | | |
| | p06 | | | | | | | | | | | | | |
| | ED | 1 | 0 | 0 | 1 | 1 | 1 | 0 | 0 | 1 | 0 | 1 | 0 | 0 |

| | | 0 | 1 | 2 | 3 | 4 | 5 | 6 | 7 | 8 | 9 | 10 | 11 | 12 |
|---|---|---|---|---|---|---|---|---|---|---|---|---|---|---|
| | | pW | p01 | p02 | d01 | p03 | d02 | d03 | d04 | p04 | d05 | d06 | d07 | d08 |
| SYN | ED | 1 | 0 | 0 | 1 | 1 | 0 | 0 | 0 | 1 | 1 | 1 | 0 | 0 |
| c01 | 0 | | 0 | | 1 | | 0 | | 0 | | 0 | | 0 | |
| c02 | 0 | | | 0 | 1 | | | 0 | 0 | | 1 | 1 | | |
| c03 | 0 | | | | | 1 | 0 | 0 | 0 | | | | | 0 |
| c04 | 0 | | | | | | | | | 1 | 1 | 1 | 0 | 0 |
| c05 | X | | | | | | | | | | | | | |
| c06 | X | | | | | | | | | | | | | |
| pW | 0 | | | | | | | | | | | | | |
| | CD | ? | ? | ? | ? | ? | ? | ? | ? | ? | ? | ? | ? | ? |
| MBE | | | | | | | | | | | | | | |

**FIGURE 5.7**   Hamming syndrome catches MBE, but can't correct the data.

| | | 0 | 1 | 2 | 3 | 4 | 5 | 6 | 7 | 8 | 9 | 10 | 11 | 12 |
|---|---|---|---|---|---|---|---|---|---|---|---|---|---|---|
| | | pW | p01 | p02 | d01 | p03 | d02 | d03 | d04 | p04 | d05 | d06 | d07 | d08 |
| | D | X | X | X | 1 | X | 1 | 0 | 0 | X | 0 | 1 | 0 | 0 |
| | p01 | | 0 | | 1 | | 1 | | 0 | | 0 | | 0 | |
| | p02 | | | 0 | 1 | | | 0 | 0 | | 0 | 1 | | |
| | p03 | | | | | 1 | 1 | 0 | 0 | | | | | 0 |
| | p04 | | | | | | | | | 1 | 0 | 1 | 0 | 0 |
| | p05 | | | | | | | | | | | | | |
| | p06 | | | | | | | | | | | | | |
| | ED | 1 | 0 | 0 | 1 | 1 | 1 | 0 | 0 | 1 | 0 | 1 | 0 | 0 |

| | | 0 | 1 | 2 | 3 | 4 | 5 | 6 | 7 | 8 | 9 | 10 | 11 | 12 |
|---|---|---|---|---|---|---|---|---|---|---|---|---|---|---|
| | | pW | p01 | p02 | d01 | p03 | d02 | d03 | d04 | p04 | d05 | d06 | d07 | d08 |
| SYN | ED | 0 | 0 | 0 | 1 | 1 | 1 | 0 | 0 | 1 | 0 | 1 | 0 | 0 |
| c01 | 0 | | 0 | | 1 | | 1 | | 0 | | 0 | | 0 | |
| c02 | 0 | | | 0 | 1 | | | 0 | 0 | 0 | 1 | | | |
| c03 | 0 | | | | | 1 | 1 | 0 | 0 | | | | | 0 |
| c04 | 0 | | | | | | | | | 1 | 0 | 1 | 0 | 0 |
| c05 | X | | | | | | | | | | | | | |
| c06 | X | | | | | | | | | | | | | |
| pW | 0 | | | | | | | | | | | | | |
| | CD | 1 | 0 | 0 | 1 | 1 | 1 | 0 | 0 | 1 | 0 | 1 | 0 | 0 |
| SBE CORRECTION | | | | | | | | | | | | | | |

**FIGURE 5.8**   Hamming syndrome catches and corrects pW SBE.

| | | 0 | 1 | 2 | 3 | 4 | 5 | 6 | 7 | 8 | 9 | 10 | 11 | 12 |
|---|---|---|---|---|---|---|---|---|---|---|---|---|---|---|
| | | pW | p01 | p02 | d01 | p03 | d02 | d03 | d04 | p04 | d05 | d06 | d07 | d08 |
| | D | X | X | X | 1 | X | 1 | 0 | 0 | X | 0 | 1 | 0 | 0 |
| | p01 | | 0 | | 1 | | 1 | | 0 | | 0 | | 0 | |
| | p02 | | | 0 | 1 | | | 0 | 0 | | 0 | 1 | | |
| | p03 | | | | | 1 | 1 | 0 | 0 | | | | | 0 |
| | p04 | | | | | | | | | 1 | 0 | 1 | 0 | 0 |
| | p05 | | | | | | | | | | | | | |
| | p06 | | | | | | | | | | | | | |
| | ED | 1 | 0 | 0 | 1 | 1 | 1 | 0 | 0 | 1 | 0 | 1 | 0 | 0 |

| | | 0 | 1 | 2 | 3 | 4 | 5 | 6 | 7 | 8 | 9 | 10 | 11 | 12 |
|---|---|---|---|---|---|---|---|---|---|---|---|---|---|---|
| | | pW | p01 | p02 | d01 | p03 | d02 | d03 | d04 | p04 | d05 | d06 | d07 | d08 |
| SYN | ED | 1 | 0 | 0 | 1 | 1 | 1 | 0 | 0 | 1 | 0 | 1 | 0 | 0 |
| c01 | 0 | | 0 | | 1 | | 1 | | 0 | | 0 | | 0 | |
| c02 | 0 | | | 0 | 1 | | | 0 | 0 | 0 | 1 | | | |
| c03 | 0 | | | | | 1 | 1 | 0 | 0 | | | | | 0 |
| c04 | 0 | | | | | | | | | 1 | 0 | 1 | 0 | 0 |
| c05 | X | | | | | | | | | | | | | |
| c06 | X | | | | | | | | | | | | | |
| pW | 0 | | | | | | | | | | | | | |
| | CD | 1 | 0 | 0 | 1 | 1 | 1 | 0 | 0 | 1 | 0 | 1 | 0 | 0 |
| SEE CORRECTION | | | | | | | | | | | | | | |

**FIGURE 5.9**  Hamming syndrome catches and corrects corrupt parity bit SBE.

This covers all the basic correctable SBE possibilities as well as showing how an uncorrectable MBE is detected. Overall, the Hamming encoding provides perfect detection of SBEs and MBEs, unlike a single parity bit for a word, which can detect all SBEs, but can only detect MBEs where an odd number of bits are flipped. In this sense, a single parity bit is an imperfect detector and also offers no correction because it does not encode the location of SBEs.

## FLASH FILESYSTEMS

Flash technology has mostly replaced the use of EEPROM (Electronically Erasable Programmable Read-Only Memory) as the primary updateable and nonvolatile memory used for embedded systems. Usage of EEPROM continues for low-cost, low-capacity NVRAM (Non-Volatile RAM) system requirements, but most often Flash memory technology is used for boot code storage and for storage of non-volatile files. Flash filesystems emerged not long after Flash devices. Flash offers in-circuit read, write, erase, lock, and unlock operations on sectors. The erase and lock operations operate on the entire sector, most often 128 KB in size. Read and write operations can be a byte, word, or block. The most prevalent Flash technology is

NAND (Not AND) Flash, where the memory device locations are erased to all 1s, and writes are the NAND of the write data and the current memory contents. Data can only be written to erased locations with all 1s unless it is unchanged, and sectors can typically be erased 100,000 times or more before they are expected to fail as read-only memory.

Based upon the characteristics of Flash, it's clear that minimizing sector erases will maximize Flash part lifetime. Furthermore, if sectors are erased at an even pace over the entire capacity, then the full capacity will be available for the overall expected lifetime. This can be done fairly easily for usages such as boot code and boot code updates. Each update simply moves the new write data above the previously written data and sectors are erased as needed. When the top of Flash is encountered, the new data wraps back to the beginning sector. This causes even wear because all sectors are erased in order over time. Filesystems are more difficult to implement with wear leveling because arbitrarily sized files and a multiplicity of them leads to fragmentation of the Flash memory. The key to wear leveling for a Flash filesystem is to map filesystem blocks to sectors so that the same sector rotation and even number of erases can be maintained as was done for the single file boot code update scheme. A scenario for mapping 2 files each with two 512-byte LBAs (Logical Block Addresses) and a Flash device with 2 sectors, each sector 2,048 bytes in size (for simplicity of the example) shows that 16 LBA updates can be accommodated for 5 sector erases. This scenario is shown in Figure 5.10 for 16 updates and total of 5 sector

| Sector Erased (S0, S1) | 0,0 | 1,1 | 1,1 | 1,1 | 1,1 | 2,1 | 2,1 | |
|---|---|---|---|---|---|---|---|---|
| **S1** | | | | | | | | |
| PB7 | FREE | FREE | FREE | LB3 | LB3 | LB3 | LB3 | |
| PB6 | FREE | FREE | LB2 | LB2 | INVLD | INVLD | INVLD | |
| PB5 | FREE | LB3 | LB3 | INVLD | INVLD | INVLD | INVLD | |
| PB4 | FREE | LB2 | INVLD | INVLD | INVLD | INVLD | INVLD | |
| **S0** | | | | | | | | |
| PB3 | FREE | FREE | FREE | LB1 | LB1 | FREE | LB1 | |
| PB2 | FREE | FREE | LB0 | LB0 | INVLD | FREE | FREE | |
| PB1 | FREE | LB1 | LB1 | INVLD | FREE | FREE | LB2 | |
| PB0 | FREE | LB0 | INVLD | INVLD | INVLD | FREE | LB0 | UPDATES |
| FS LBs Updated | | 0,1,2,3 | 0,2 | 1,3 | 0,2 | 0,2 | 0,2 | 10 |
| FS LBs Cached | | | | | 0,2 | 0,2 | | |
| Sector LBs Buffered | | | | | 1 | | | |

| Sectors Erased (S0, S1) | 2,1 | 2,1 | 2,2 | 2,2 | 2,2 | 2,2 | 3,2 | 3,2 | |
|---|---|---|---|---|---|---|---|---|---|
| **S1** | | | | | | | | | |
| | LB3 | INVLD | FREE | FREE | LB2 | LB2 | LB2 | LB2 | |
| | INVLD | INVLD | FREE | FREE | LB0 | LB0 | LB0 | LB0 | |
| | INVLD | INVLD | FREE | LB3 | LB3 | INVLD | INVLD | INVLD | |
| | INVLD | INVLD | FREE | LB1 | LB1 | INVLD | INVLD | INVLD | |
| **S0** | | | | | | | | | |
| | LB1 | INVLD | INVLD | INVLD | INVLD | INVLD | FREE | FREE | |
| | FREE | FREE | FREE | FREE | FREE | FREE | FREE | FREE | |
| | LB2 | LB2 | LB2 | LB2 | INVLD | INVLD | FREE | LB3 | |
| | LB0 | LB0 | LB0 | LB0 | INVLD | INVLD | FREE | LB1 | UPDATES |
| FS LBs Updated | 0,2 | 1,3 | 1,3 | 1,3 | 0,2 | 1,3 | 1,3 | 1,3 | 6 |
| FS LBs Cached | | 1,3 | 1,3 | | | 1,3 | 1,3 | | |
| Sector LBs Buffered | | | | | | | | | |

**FIGURE 5.10** Simple Flash wear leveling example.

erases (3 for Sector 0 and 2 for Section 1). Continuing this pattern 32 updates can be completed for 10 sector erases (5 for section 0 and 5 for sector 1). In general approximately 6 times more updates than evenly distributed erases.

With wear leveling, Flash is expected to wear evenly so that the overall lifetime is the sum of the erase limits for all the sectors rather than the limit on one, yielding a lifetime with millions of erases and orders of magnitude more file updates than this. Wear leveling is fundamental to making filesystem usage with Flash practical.

## SUMMARY

Memory resource capacity, access latency, and overall access bandwidth should be considered when analyzing or designing a real-time embedded memory system. Although most GPC architectures are concerned principally with memory throughput and capacity, real-time embedded systems are comparatively more cost sensitive and often are designed for less throughput, but with more deterministic and lower worst-case access latency.

## EXERCISES

1. Describe why a multilevel cache architecture might not be ideal for a hard real-time embedded system.
2. Write VxWorks code that starts two tasks, one that writes one of two phrases alternatively to a shared memory buffer, including 1) "The quick brown fox jumps over the lazy dog" and 2) "All good dogs go to heaven." When it's done, have it call TaskDelay(143). Now add a second task that reads the phrases and prints them out. Make the reader task higher priority than the writer and have it call TaskDelay(37). How many times does the reader task print out the correct phrases before they become jumbled?
3. Fix the problem in #2 using semTake() and semGive in VxWorks to protect the readers/writers critical section.
4. Develop an example of a 32-bit Hamming encoded word (39 bits total) and show a correctable SBE scenario.
5. For the preceding problem, now show an uncorrectable MBE scenario.

## CHAPTER REFERENCES

[Mano91] Mano, Morris M., *Digital Design*, 2nd ed. Prentice-Hall, 1991.

[Tannenbaum87] Tannenbaum, Andrew S., *Operating Systems: Design and Implementation*. Prentice-Hall, 1987.

# 6 Multiresource Services

## In This Chapter

- Introduction
- Blocking
- Deadlock and Livelock
- Critical Sections to Protect Shared Resources
- Priority Inversion
- Power Management and Processor Clock Modulation

## INTRODUCTION

Ideally, the service response as illustrated in Figure 3.13 of Chapter 3 is based upon input latency, acquiring the CPU resource, interference, and output latency only. However, many services need more resources than just the CPU to execute. For example, many services may need mutually exclusive access to shared memory resources or a shared intermediate I/O resource. If this resource is not in use by another service, this presents no problem. However, if a service is released and pre-empts another running service based upon RM policy, only to find that it lacks a resource held by another service, then it is blocked. When a service is blocked, it must yield the CPU despite the RM policy. We hope that the preempted service that holds the additional resource will complete its mutually exclusive use of that resource, at which time, the high-priority service will unblock, potentially preempt other services, and continue execution. However, as you'll see in this chapter, blocking may not be temporary if conditions are sufficient for deadlock or priority inversion.

## BLOCKING

Blocking occurs anytime a service can be dispatched by the CPU, but isn't because it is lacking some other resource such as access to a shared memory critical section or access to a bus. When blocking has a known latency, it could simply be added into response time, accounted for, and therefore would not adversely affect RM analysis, although it would complicate it. The bigger concern is unbounded blocking, where the amount of time a service will be blocked awaiting a resource is indefinite or at least hard to calculate. Three phenomena related to resource sharing can cause this: deadlock, livelock, and unbounded priority inversion. Deadlock and livelock are always unbounded by definition. Priority inversion can be temporary, but under certain conditions, priority inversion can be indefinite.

Blocking can be extremely dangerous because it can cause a very underutilized system to miss deadlines. This is counter intuitive—how can a system with only 5% CPU loading miss deadlines? If a service is blocked for an indefinite time, then the CPU is yielded for an indefinite time, leaving plenty of CPU margin, but the service fails to produce a response by its deadline.

## DEADLOCK AND LIVELOCK

In Figure 6.1, service $S_1$ needs resources A and C, $S_2$ needs A and B, and $S_3$ needs B and C. If $S_1$ acquires A, then $S_2$ acquires B, then $S_3$ acquires C followed by requests by each for their other required resource, a circular wait evolves as shown in Figure 6.1. *Circular wait*, also known as the deadly embrace, causes indefinite deadlock. No progress can be made by Services 1, 2, or 3 in Figure 6.1 unless resources held by each are released. Deadlock can be prevented by making sure the circular wait scenario is impossible. It can be detected if each service is designed to post a keep-alive as discussed in Chapter 11, "High Availability and Reliability Design." When the keep-alive is not posted due to the deadlock, then a supervisory service can restart the deadlocked service. However, it's possible that when deadlock is detected and services are restarted, that they could simply reenter the deadlock over and over. This variant is called *livelock* and also prevents progress completely despite detection and breaking of the deadlock.

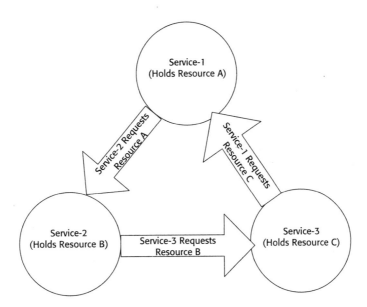

**FIGURE 6.1**    Shared resource deadlock (circular wait).

One solution to prevent livelock following deadlock detection and restarting is to include a random back-off time on restart for each service that was involved—this ensures that one beats the other two to the resource subset needed and completes acquisition allowing each service the same opportunity in turn.

What if the supervisor service is involved in the deadlock? In this case, a hardware timer known as a watch-dog timer is used to require the supervisor service to reset a countdown timer periodically. If the supervisor service becomes deadlocked and can't reset the watch-dog timer countdown, then the watch-dog timer expires and resets the entire system with a hardware reset. This causes the firmware to reboot the system in hopes that the supervisor deadlock will not evolve again. These strategies will be discussed in more detail in Chapter 11, which covers high availability and high reliability design methods.

Even with random back-off, the amount of time that a service will fail to make progress is hard to predict and will likely cause a deadline to be missed, even when the CPU is not highly loaded. The best solution is to eliminate the conditions necessary for circular wait. One method of avoidance is to require a total order on the locking of all resources that can be simultaneously acquired. In general, deadlock conditions should be avoided, but detection and recovery schemes are advisable as well. Further discussion on this topic of avoidance versus detection and recovery can be found in current research [Minoura82], [Reveliotis00].

## CRITICAL SECTIONS TO PROTECT SHARED RESOURCES

Shared memory is often used in embedded systems to share data between two ser-vices. The alternative is to pass messages between services, but often even messages are passed by synchronizing access to a shared buffer. Different choices for service to service communication will be examined more closely in Chapter 8, "Embedded System Components." When shared memory is used, because real-time systems allow for event-driven preemption of services by higher priority service releases at any time, shared resources such as shared memory must be protected to ensure mutually exclusive access. So, if one service is updating a shared memory location (writing), it must fully complete the update before another service is allowed to preempt the writer and read the same location as described already in Chapter 4. If this *mutex* (mutually exclusive access) to the update/read data is not enforced, then the reader might read a partially updated message. If the code for each service that either updates or reads the shared data is surrounded with a semTake() and semGive() (in VxWorks for example), then the update and read will be uninter-rupted despite the preemptive nature of the RTOS scheduling. The first caller to semTake() will enter the critical update section, but the second caller will be blocked and not allowed to enter the partially updated data, causing the original service in the critical section to always fully update or read the data. When the cur-rent user of the critical section calls semGive() upon leaving the critical section, the service blocked on the semTake() is then allowed to continue safely into the critical section. The need and use of semaphores to protect such shared resources is a well-understood concept in multithreaded operating systems.

## PRIORITY INVERSION

*Priority inversion* is simply defined as any time that a high priority service has to wait while a lower priority service runs—this can occur in any blocking scenario. We're most concerned about unbounded priority inversion. If the inversion is bounded, then this can be lumped into the response latency and accounted for so that the RM analysis is still possible. The use of any *mutex* (mutual exclusion) sem-aphore can cause a temporary inversion while a higher priority service is blocked to allow a lower priority service to complete a shared memory read or update in its entirety. As long as the lower priority service executes for a critical section WCET, the inversion is known to last no longer than the lower priority service's WCET for the critical section.

What causes unbounded priority inversion? Three conditions are necessary for unbounded inversion:

- Three or more services with unique priority in the system—High (**H**), Medium (**M**), Low (**L**) priority sets of services.
- At least two services of different priority share a resource with mutex protection—one or more high and one or more low involved.
- One or more services not involved in the mutex has priority between the two involved in the mutex.

Essentially, a member of the **H** priority service set catches an **L** priority service in the critical section and is blocked on the `semTake(semid)`. While the **L** priority service executes in the critical section, one or more **M** priority services interfere with the **L** priority service's progress for an indefinite amount of time; the **H** priority service must continue to wait not only for the **L** priority service to finish the critical section, but for the duration of all interference to the **L** priority service. How long will this interference go on? This would be hard to put an upper bound on—clearly it could be longer than the deadline for the **H** priority service.

Figure 6.2 depicts a shared memory usage scenario for a spacecraft system that has two services using or calculating navigational data providing the vehicle's position and attitude in inertial space; one service is a low priority thread of execution that periodically points an instrument based upon position and attitude at a target planet to look for a landing site. A second service, running a high priority, is using basic navigational sensor readings and computed trajectory information to update the best estimate of the current navigational state. In Figure 6.2, a set of **M** priority services {**M**} that are unrelated to the shared memory data critical section can cause **H** to block for as long as **M** services continue to preempt the **L** service stuck in the critical section.

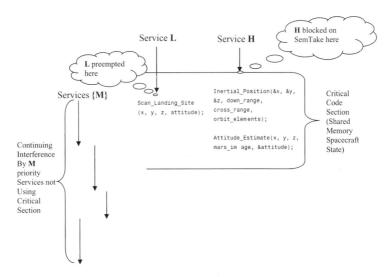

**FIGURE 6.2**  Unbounded priority inversion scenario.

## Unbounded Priority Inversion Solutions

One of the first solutions to unbounded priority inversion is to use task or interrupt locking (VxWorks `intLock()` and `intUnlock()` or task Lock () and task Unlock ()) to prevent preemptions in critical sections completely, which operates in the same way as a priority ceiling protocol. Priority inheritance was introduced as a more optimal method that limits the amplication of priority in a critical section only to the level required to bound inversions. By comparison, interrupt locking and priority ceiling essentially disable all preemption for the duration of the critical section, but very effectively bound the inversion. To describe better what is meant by priority inheritence, you must understand the basic strategy to avoid indefinite interference while a low priority task is in a critical section. Basically, the **H** priority service gives its priority temporarily to the **L** priority service so that it will not be preempted by the **M** priority services while finishing up the critical section—normally the **L** priority service restores the priority loaned to it as soon as it leaves the critical section. The priority of the **L** service is temporarily amplified to the **H** priority to prevent the unbounded inversion. One downside to priority inheritance is that it can chain. When **H** blocks, it is possible that shortly after **H** loans its priority to **L**, another **H**+$n$ priority service will block on the same semaphore, therefore requiring a new inheritance of **H**+$n$ by **L** so that **H**+$n$ is not blocked by services of priority **H**+1 to **H**+$n$–1 interfering with **L**, which has priority **H**. The chaining is complex, so it would be easier to simply give **L** a priority that is so high that chaining is not necessary. This idea became the priority ceiling emulation protocol (also known as highest locker). The priority ceiling protocol is more exacting and was first described in terms of Ada language server and client tasks [Goodenough88]. With priority ceiling emulation protocol, when the inversion occurs, **L** is temporarily loaned the highest priority possible, ensuring that it completes the critical section with one priority amplification. However, the ceiling protocol is not ideal because it amplifies the priority of **L** higher than it really needs to be. This overamplification could cause other problems such as significant interference to high-frequency, high-priority services.

A further refinement of priority ceiling is the least-locker protocol. In least-locker, the priority of **L** is amplified to the highest priority of all those services that can potentially request access to the critical section. The only downside to least-locker is that it requires the programmer to indicate to the operating system what the least-locker priority should be. Any mistake in specification of the least-locker priority may cause unbounded inversion. In theory, the programmer should know very well what services can enter a given critical section and therefore also know the correct least-locker priority.

The problem of priority inversion became famous with the Mars Pathfinder spacecraft. The Pathfinder spacecraft was on final approach to Mars and would need to complete a critical engine burn to capture into a Martian orbit within a few days after a cruise trajectory lasting many months. The mission engineers readied the craft by enabling new services. Services such as meteorological processing from instruments were designed to help determine the insertion orbit around Mars because one of the objectives of the mission was to land the Sojourner rover on the surface in a location free of dangerous dust storms. When the new services were activated during this critical final approach, the Pathfinder began to reboot when one of the highest priority services failed to service the hardware watch-dog timer. Discussed in more detail in Chapter 11, watch-dog timers are used to ensure that software continues to sanely execute. If the countdown watch-dog timer is not reset periodically by the highest priority periodic service, the system is wired to reset and reboot to recover from software failures such as deadlock or livelock. Furthermore, most systems will reboot in an attempt to recover several times, and if this repeats more than three times, the system will safe itself, expecting operator intervention to fix the recurring software problem.

It was not immediately evident to the mission engineers why Pathfinder was rebooting other than it was caused by failure to reset the watch-dog timer. Based upon phenomena studied in this chapter alone, reasons for a watch-dog timeout could include the following:

- Deadlock or livelock preventing the watch-dog reset service from executing
- Loss of software sanity due to programming errors such as a bad pointer, an improperly handled processor exception, such as divide by zero, or a bus error
- Overload due to miscalculation of WCETs for the final approach service set
- A hardware malfunction of the watch-dog timer or associated circuitry
- A multibit error in memory due to space radiation causing a bit upset

Most often, the reason for reset is stored in a nonvolatile memory that is persistent through a watch-dog reset so that exceptions due to programming errors, memory bit upsets, and hardware malfunctions would be apparent as the reason for reset and/or through anomalies in system health and status telemetry.

After analysis on the ground using a test-bed with identical hardware and data playback along with analysis of code, it was determined that Pathfinder might be suffering from priority inversion. Ideally, a theory like this would be validated first on the ground in the test-bed by recreating conditions to verify that the suspected bug could cause the observed behavior. Priority inversion was suspected because a message-passing method in the VxWorks RTOS used by firmware developers was found to ultimately use shared memory with an option bit for priority, FCFS (First Come First Served), or inversion safe policy for the critical section protecting the shared memory section. In the end, the theory proved correct, and the mission was saved and became a huge success. This story has helped underscore the importance of understanding multiresource interactions in embedded systems as well as design for field debugging. Prior to the Pathfinder incident, the problem of priority inversion was mostly viewed as an esoteric possibility rather than a likely failure scenario. The unbounded inversion on Pathfinder resulted from shared data used by **H**, **M**, and **L** priority services that were made active by mission controllers during final approach.

## POWER MANAGEMENT AND PROCESSOR CLOCK MODULATION

Power and layout considerations for embedded hardware often drives real-time embedded systems to designs with less memory and lower speed processor clocks. The power consumed by an embedded processor is determined by switching power, short-circuit current, and current leakage within the logic circuit design. The power equations summarizing and used to model the power used by an ASIC (Application Specific Integrated Circuit) design are

- $P_{average} = P_{switching} + P_{short\text{-}circuit} + P_{leakage}$
- $P_{switching} = (S_{probability})(C_L)(V_{supply})^2(f_{clk})$—due to capacitor charge/discharge for switching
- $P_{short\text{-}circuit} = t(S_{probability})(V_{supply})(I_{short}$ —due to current flow when gates switch

The terms in the preceding equations are defined as follows:

- $P_{leakage}$ is the power loss based upon threshold voltage.
- $S_{probability}$ is the probability that gates will switch, or a fraction of gate switches on average.
- $C_L$ is load capacitance.
- $I_{short}$ is short circuit current.
- $f_{clk}$ is the CPU clock frequency.

The easiest parameters to control are the $V_{supply}$ and the processor clock frequency to reduce power consumption.

Furthermore, the more power put in, the more heat generated. Often real-time embedded systems must operate with high reliability and at low cost so that active cooling is not practical. Consider an embedded satellite control system—a fan is not even feasible for cooling because the electronics will operate in a vacuum. Often passive thermal conduction and radiation are used to control temperatures for embedded systems. More recently, some embedded systems have been designed with processor clock modulation so that $V_{supply}$ can be reduced along with CPU clock rate under the control of firmware when it's entering less busy modes of operation or when the system is overheating.

## SUMMARY

Real-time embedded systems are most often designed according to hardware power, mass, layout, and cost constraints, which in turn define the processor, I/O, and memory resources available for use by firmware and software. Analysis of a single resource such as CPU, memory, or I/O alone is well understood for real-time embedded systems—the subject of Chapters 3, 4, and 5. The analysis of multiresource usage, such as CPU and memory, has more recently been examined. The case of multiple services sharing memory and CPU lead to the understanding that deadlock, livelock, and priority inversion could interfere with a service's capability to execute and complete prior to a deadline—even when there is more than sufficient CPU resource. The complexity of multiple resource usage by a set of services can lead to scenarios where a system otherwise determined to be hard real-time safe, can still fail.

## EXERCISES

1. Implement the RM LUB feasibility test presented in an Excel spreadsheet. Verify CPU scheduling feasibility by hand drawing timing diagrams and using the spreadsheet. Example: $T_1=3$, $T_2=5$, $T_3=15$, $C_1=1$, $C_2=2$, $C_3=3$. What is the LCM of the periods and total utility? Does the example work? Does it pass the RM LUB feasibility test? Why or why not?
2. Given that EDF can provide 100% CPU utilization and provides a deadline guarantee, why isn't EDF always used instead of fixed priority RMA?
3. Using the same example from #1 ($T_1=3$, $T_2=5$, $T_3=15$, $C_1=1$, $C_2=2$, $C_3=3$), does the system work with the EDF policy? How about LLF? Do EDF and LLF result in the same or a different scheduling?
4. Examine the example code `deadlock.c` for Linux from the CD-ROM, which demonstrates deadlock and fix it.
5. Examine the example code `prio_invert.c` from the CD-ROM, which demonstrates priority inversion and use WindView to show that without the priority inheritance protocol, the inversion occurs; also show that with the priority inheritance protocol, the problem is corrected.

ON THE CD

ON THE CD

## CHAPTER REFERENCES

[Goodenough88] Goodenough, John, and Lui Sha, "The Priority Ceiling Protocol: A Method for Minimizing the Blocking of High-Priority Ada Tasks." CMU/SEI-88-SR-4 Special Report.

[Minoura82] Minoura, Toshimi, "Deadlock Avoidance Revisited." *Journal of the ACM*, 29(4), (October 1982): pp. 1032-1048.

[Reveliotis00] Reveliotis, S. A., "An Analytical Investigation of the Deadlock Avoidance vs. Detection and Recovery Problem in Buffer-Space Allocation of Flexibly Automated Production Systems." Technical Report, Georgia Tech, 2000.

[Shah90] Shah, Lui, Rangunthan Rajkumar, and John P. Lehoczky, "Priority Inheritance Protocols: An Approach to Real-Time Synchronization." *IEEE Transaction on Computers*, Vol. 39, No. 9, (September 1990).

[Vahalia96] Vahalia, Uresh, *Unix Internals; The New Frontiers.* Prentice-Hall, Inc., 1996.

# 7 Soft Real-Time Services

## In This Chapter

■ Introduction
■ Missed Deadlines
■ Quality of Service
■ Alternatives to Rate Monotonic Policy
■ Mixed Hard and Soft Real-Time Services

## INTRODUCTION

Soft real time is a simple concept, defined by the utility curve presented in Chapter 2, "System Resources." The complexity of soft real-time systems arises from how to handle resource overload scenarios. By definition, soft real-time systems are not designed to guarantee service in worst-case usage scenarios. So, for example, back-to-back cache misses causing a service execution efficiency to be much lower than expected, might cause that service's deadline or another lower priority service's deadline to be overrun. How long should any service be allowed to run past its deadline if at all? How will the quality of the services be impacted by an overrun or by a recovery method that might terminate the release of an overrunning service? This chapter provides some guidance on how to handle these soft real-time scenarios and, in addition, explains why soft real-time methods can work well for some services sets.

## MISSED DEADLINES

Missed deadlines can be handled in a number of ways:

- Termination of the overrunning service as soon as the deadline is passed
- Allowing an overrunning service to continue running past a deadline for a limited duration
- Allowing an overrunning service to run past a deadline indefinitely

Terminating the overrunning scenario as soon as the deadline is passed is known as a *service drop-out*. The outputs from the service are not produced, and the computations completed up to that point are abandoned. For example, an MPEG decoder service would discontinue the decoding and not produce an output frame for display. The observable result of this handling is a decrease in quality of service. A frame drop-out results in a potentially displeasing video quality for a user. If drop-outs rarely occur back to back and rarely in general, this might be acceptable quality. If soft real-time service overruns are handled with termination and drop-outs, the expected frequency of drop-outs and reduction in quality of service should be computed.

The advantage of service drop-outs is that the impact of the overrunning service is isolated to that service alone—other higher priority and lower priority services will not be adversely impacted as long as the overrun can be quickly detected and handled. For an RM policy, the failure mode is limited to the single overrunning service (refer to Figure 3.15 of Chapter 3). Quick overrun detection and handling always results in some residual interference to other services and could cause additional services to also miss their deadlines—a cascading failure. If some resource margin is maintained for drop-out handling, this impact can still be isolated to the single overrunning service.

Allowing a service to continue an overrun beyond the specified deadline is risky because the overrun causes unaccounted-for interference to other services. Allowing such a service to overrun indefinitely could cause all other services to fail of lesser priority in an RM policy system. For this reason, it's most often advisable to handle overruns with termination and limited service drop-outs. Deterministic behavior in a failure scenario is the next best thing compared to deterministic behavior that guarantees success. Dynamic priority services are more susceptible to cascading failures (refer to Figure 3.16 in Chapter 3) and therefore also more risky as far as impact of an overrun and time for the system to recover. Cascading failures make the computation of drop-out impact on quality of service harder to estimate.

## QUALITY OF SERVICE

Quality of service (QoS) for a real-time system can be quantified based upon the frequency that services produce an incorrect result or a late result compared to how often they function correctly. A real-time system is said to be correct only if it produces correct results on time. In Chapter 11, "High Availability and Reliability Design," the classic design methods and definitions of availability and reliability will be examined. The QoS concept is certainly related. The traditional definition of availability of a service is defined as

- Availability = MTBF / (MTBF + MTTR)
- MTBF = Mean Time Between Failures
- MTTR = Mean Time to Recovery

If a service has higher availability, does it also have higher quality? From the viewpoint of service drop-outs, measured in terms of frames delivered, for example, for a video decoder, then higher availability does mean fewer service drop-outs over a given period of time. This formulation for QoS can be expressed as:

- QoS = 1 – (Drop-outs / Deliveries)
- Where QoS =1 is full quality and 0 is no quality of service

So, in this example, availability and QoS are directly related to the degree that number of drop-outs will be directly proportional to availability. However, delivering decoded frames for display is an isochronal process (defined in Chapter 2). Presenting frames for display too early causes frame jitter and lower QoS with no service drop-outs and 100% availability. Systems providing isochronal services and output most often use a DM (Deadline Monotonic) policy and buffer and hold outputs that are completed prior to the isochronal deadline to avoid jitter. The measure of QoS is application specific. For example, isochronal networks often define QoS as the degree to which packets transported approximate a constant bit-rate dedicated circuit. To understand QoS well, the specific application domain for a service must be well understood. In the remaining sections of this chapter, soft real-time methods that can be used to establish QoS for an application are reviewed.

## ALTERNATIVES TO RATE MONOTONIC POLICY

The RM policy can lead to pessimistic maintenance of high resource margins for sets of services that are not harmonic (described in Chapter 3, "Processing").

Furthermore, RM policy makes restrictive assumptions such as T=D. Because QoS is a bit harder to nail down categorically, designers of soft real-time systems should consider alternatives to RM policy that might better fit their application-specific measures of QoS. For example, in Figure 7.1, the RM policy would cause a deadline overrun and a service drop-out decreasing QoS, but it's evident that EDF or LLF dynamic priority policies will result in higher QoS because both avoid the overrun and subsequent service drop out.

| Example 2 | T1 | 2 | C1 | 1 | U1 | 0.5 | LCM = | 70 |
|-----------|----|----|----|----|----|-----|-------|-----|
| | T2 | 5 | C2 | 1 | U2 | 0.2 | | |
| | T3 | 7 | C3 | 1 | U3 | 0.142857 | | |
| | T4 | 13 | C4 | 2 | U4 | 0.153846 | Utot = | 0.996703 |

RM Schedule

| | | | | | | | | | | |
|---|---|---|---|---|---|---|---|---|---|---|
| S1 | | | | | | | | | | |
| S2 | | | | | | | | | ??????? | |
| S3 | | | | | | | | | | |
| S4 | | | | | | | | | | FAILURE |

EDF Schedule

| | | | | | | | | | |
|---|---|---|---|---|---|---|---|---|---|
| S1 | | | | | | | | | |
| S2 | | | | | | | | | |
| S3 | | | | | | | | | |
| S4 | | | | | | | | | |

TTD

| | | | | | | | | | | | | | |
|----|----|---|----|----|---|---|---|---|---|---|---|---|---|
| S1 | 2 | X | 2 | X | 2 | X | 2 | X | 2 | X | 2 | X | 2 | X |
| S2 | 5 | 4 | X | X | X | 5 | X | X | X | X | 5 | 4 | 3 | 2 |
| S3 | 7 | 6 | 5 | 4 | X | X | X | 7 | 6 | 5 | 4 | 3 | X | X |
| S4 | 13 | 12 | 11 | 10 | 9 | 8 | 7 | 6 | 5 | 4 | X | X | X | X |

LLF Schedule

| | | | | | | | | | |
|---|---|---|---|---|---|---|---|---|---|
| S1 | | | | | | | | | |
| S2 | | | | | | | | | |
| S3 | | | | | | | | | |
| S4 | | | | | | | | | |

Laxity

| | | | | | | | | | | | | | |
|----|----|----|---|---|---|---|---|---|---|---|---|---|---|
| S1 | 1 | X | 1 | X | 1 | X | 1 | X | 1 | X | 1 | X | 1 | X |
| S2 | 4 | 3 | X | X | X | 4 | X | X | X | X | 4 | 3 | 2 | 1 |
| S3 | 5 | 4 | 3 | 2 | X | X | X | 5 | 4 | 3 | X | X | X | X |
| S4 | 11 | 10 | 9 | 8 | 7 | 6 | 5 | 4 | 4 | 3 | 2 | 1 | X | X |

**FIGURE 7.1**   Highly loaded system—RM deadline overrun.

The EDF and LLF policies are not always better from a QoS viewpoint. Figure 7.2 shows how EDF, LLF, and RM all perform equally well for a given service scenario. From a practical viewpoint, the decision to be made on scheduling policy should be a balance between the impact on QoS by the more adaptive EDF and LLF policies compared to the more predictable failure modes and deterministic behavior of RM in an overload situation. This may be difficult to compute and might be best evaluated by trying all three policies with extensive testing.

In cases where EDF, LLF, and RM perform equally well in a nonoverload scenario, RM might be a better choice because the impact of a failure is simpler to contain; that is, there is less likelihood of cascading service drop-outs given upper bounds on overrun detection and handling.

As shown in Figure 7.3, it's well worth noting that systems designed to have harmonic service request periods do equally well with EDF, LLF, and RM. Designing systems to be harmonic can greatly simplify real-time scheduling.

| Example 3 | T1 | 3 | C1 | 1 | U1 | 0.33 | LCM = | 15 |
|---|---|---|---|---|---|---|---|---|
|  | T2 | 5 | C2 | 2 | U2 | 0.4 |  |  |
|  | T3 | 15 | C3 | 3 | U3 | 0.2 | Utot = | 0.93 |

RMS chedule
S1
S2
S3

EDF Schedule
S1
S2
S3

TTD
| S1 | 3 | X | X | 3 | X | X | 3 | X | X | 3 | X | X | 3 | X | X |
|---|---|---|---|---|---|---|---|---|---|---|---|---|---|---|---|
| S2 | 5 | 4 | 3 | X | X | 5 | 4 | 3 | X | X | 5 | 4 | X | X | X |
| S3 | 15 | 14 | 13 | 12 | 11 | 10 | 9 | 8 | 7 | 6 | 5 | 4 | 3 | 2 | X |

LLF Schedule
S1
S2
S3

Laxity
| S1 | 2 | X | X | 2 | X | X | 2 | X | X | 2 | X | X | 2 | X | X |
|---|---|---|---|---|---|---|---|---|---|---|---|---|---|---|---|
| S2 | 3 | 2 | 2 | X | X | 3 | 3 | 2 | X | X | 3 | 3 | X | X | X |
| S3 | 12 | 11 | 10 | 9 | 8 | 8 | 7 | 6 | 5 | 5 | 4 | 3 | 3 | 2 | X |

**FIGURE 7.2**   Three policies and three common schedules.

| Example 4 | T1 | 2 | C1 | 1 | U1 | 0.5 | LCM = | 16 |
|---|---|---|---|---|---|---|---|---|
|  | T2 | 4 | C2 | 1 | U2 | 0.25 |  |  |
|  | T3 | 16 | C3 | 4 | U3 | 0.25 | Utot = | 1 |

RMS chedule
S1
S2
S3

EDF Schedule
S1
S2
S3

TTD
| S1 | 2 | X | 2 | X | 2 | X | 2 | X | 2 | X | 2 | X | 2 | X | 2 | X |
|---|---|---|---|---|---|---|---|---|---|---|---|---|---|---|---|---|
| S2 | 4 | 3 | X | X | 4 | 3 | X | X | 4 | 3 | X | X | 4 | 3 | X | X |
| S3 | 16 | 15 | 14 | 13 | 12 | 11 | 10 | 9 | 8 | 7 | 6 | 5 | 4 | 3 | 2 | 1 |

LLF Schedule
S1
S2
S3

Laxity
| S1 | 1 | X | 1 | X | 1 | X | 1 | X | 1 | X | 1 | X | 1 | X | 1 | X |
|---|---|---|---|---|---|---|---|---|---|---|---|---|---|---|---|---|
| S2 | 3 | 2 | X | X | 3 | 2 | X | X | 3 | 2 | X | X | 3 | 2 | X | X |
| S3 | 12 | 11 | 10 | 9 | 9 | 8 | 7 | 6 | 6 | 5 | 4 | 3 | 3 | 2 | 1 | 0 |

**FIGURE 7.3**   Full utility from a harmonic schedule.

Figure 7.4 shows yet another example of a harmonic schedule where policy is inconsequential.

For isochronal services, DM policy can have advantage by relaxing T=D. This allows for analysis of systems where services can complete early to buffer and hold outputs to reduce presentation jitter and thereby increase QoS. Figure 7.5 shows a scenario where the DM policy succeeds when the RM would fail due to requirements where D can be greater or less than the release period T.

**Example 5**

| | | | | | | | | |
|---|---|---|---|---|---|---|---|---|
| T1 | 2 | C1 | 1 | U1 | 0.5 | LCM = | 10 | |
| T2 | 5 | C2 | 2 | U2 | 0.4 | | | |
| T3 | 10 | C3 | 1 | U3 | 0.1 | Utot = | 1 | |

**RM S chedule**
S1
S2
S3

**E DF S chedule**
S1
S2
S3

**TTD**

| | | | | | | | | | |
|---|---|---|---|---|---|---|---|---|---|
| S1 | 2 | X | 2 | X | 2 | X | 2 | X | 2 | X |
| S2 | 5 | 4 | 3 | 2 | X | 5 | 4 | 3 | X | X |
| S3 | 10 | 9 | 8 | 7 | 6 | 5 | 4 | 3 | 2 | 1 |

**LLF S chedule**
S1
S2
S3

**Laxity**

| | | | | | | | | | |
|---|---|---|---|---|---|---|---|---|---|
| S1 | 1 | X | 1 | X | 1 | X | 1 | X | 1 | X |
| S2 | 3 | 2 | 2 | 1 | X | 3 | 3 | 2 | X | X |
| S3 | 9 | 8 | 7 | 6 | 5 | 4 | 3 | 2 | 1 | 0 |

**FIGURE 7.4** A harmonic service set.

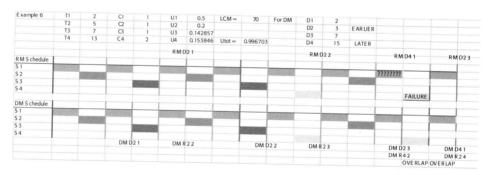

**Example 6**

| | | | | | | | | | |
|---|---|---|---|---|---|---|---|---|---|
| T1 | 2 | C1 | 1 | U1 | 0.5 | LCM = | 70 | For DM | D1 | 2 |
| T2 | 5 | C2 | 1 | U2 | 0.2 | | | | D2 | 3 | EARLIER |
| T3 | 7 | C3 | 1 | U3 | 0.142857 | | | | D3 | 7 |
| T4 | 13 | C4 | 2 | U4 | 0.153846 | Utot = | 0.996703 | | D4 | 15 | LATER |

**FIGURE 7.5** DM can work where RM fails.

# MIXED HARD AND SOFT REAL-TIME SERVICES

Many systems include services that are hard real time, soft real time, and best effort. For example, a computer vision system on an assembly line may have hard real-time services where missing a deadline would cause shutdown of the process being controlled. Likewise, operators may want to occasionally monitor what the computer vision systems "sees." The video for monitoring should have good QoS so that a human monitor can assess how well the system is working, whether lighting is sufficient, and whether frame rates appear reasonable. Finally, in the same system, operators may occasionally want to dump maintenance data and have no real requirements for how fast this is done—it can be done in the background whenever spare cycles are available.

The mixing of hard, soft, and best effort can be done by admitting the services into multiple periodic servers for each. The hard real-time services can be scheduled within a time period (epoch) during which the CPU is dedicated only to hard real-time services (all others are preempted). Another approach is to period transform all the hard real-time services so that they have priorities that encode their importance. Either way, we ensure that the hard real-time services will preempt all soft services and best effort services on a deterministic and periodic basis.

Best-effort services can always be handled by simply scheduling all these services at the lowest priority and at an equal priority among them. At lowest priority, best-effort services become slack time stealers that execute only when no real-time (hard or soft) services are requesting processor resources.

## SUMMARY

Soft real-time services assume that some service releases will fail to meet deadline requirements. Careful consideration should be given to how service deadline overruns will be handled and how this will impact QoS.

## EXERCISES

ON THE CD

1. Review `posix_clock.c` and `posix_rt_timers.c` contained on the CD-ROM. Write a brief paragraph describing how these two modules work and what features of the POSIX 1003.1b real-time extensions they demonstrate. Make sure you not only read the code, but that you build it, load it, and execute it to make sure you understand how both applications work.

ON THE CD

2. Build, load, and analyze the CD-ROM `ittimer_test.c` module for VxWorks and describe how it works. Specifically what states does the `itimer_test()` task context transition between if it's spawned in a task context using `sp itimer_test()`.

ON THE CD

3. Build, load, and run the CD-ROM `posix_sw_wd.c` software watch-dog monitor code and describe how it executes. Provide evidence for your description with supporting WindView traces.

## CHAPTER REFERENCES

[WRS99] *VxWorks Reference Manual 5.4*, available online as "windman" or hard copy, as Edition 1. WRS, 1999.

[WRS99] *VxWorks Programmer's Guide 5.4*, Edition 1. WRS, 1999.

# Part

# Designing Real-Time Embedded Components

# 8 Embedded System Components

## In This Chapter

- Introduction
- Hardware Components
- Firmware Components
- RTOS System Software Mechanisms
- Software Application Components

## INTRODUCTION

System design can be approached in a bottom-up or a top-down fashion. The *bottom-up approach* consists of determining the fundamental components that go into a system. The *top-down approach* is a hierarchical breakdown of the system into subsystems and then into components. The top-down approach can be viewed as a concrete breakdown of the system into smaller parts as suggested here, but often an abstract top-down approach is useful where the system is broken down by service and function. This functional top-down approach is described in Chapter 12, "System Lifecycle." In this chapter, we first examine common components of a real-time embedded system in the concrete sense going from the overall system down to components. Familiarity of the components can assist the designer in making more optimal system design decisions. The design of a real-time embedded system can be viewed as a hierarchy of subsystems as depicted in Figure 8.1 for a real-time stereo-vision tracking system.

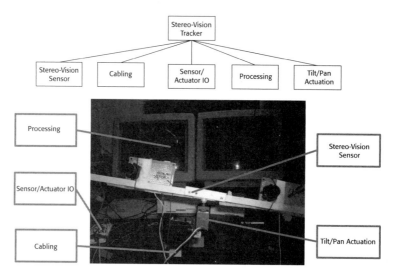

**FIGURE 8.1** Subsystems in a stereo-vision tracking system.

The stereo-vision tracking system has a simple goal—keep a bright object in the field of view of both cameras even if the object moves and estimate the distance from the camera assembly to the object. A more functional service view of the same stereo-vision tracking system would look much different. This is depicted by the hierarchy for the same system shown in Figure 8.2.

**FIGURE 8.2** Services in a stereo-vision tracking system.

The stereo-vision tracking system is an example design that is examined in more detail in Chapter 15, "Computer Vision Applications."

# HARDWARE COMPONENTS

The hardware components of a real-time embedded system include a wide range of mechanical and electrical components. For example, in the stereo-vision tracking system we have:

- Structural and mechanical—camera assembly
- Electro-mechanical actuators—tilt and pan servos
- Electro-mechanical sensors (transducers)—none, but servo position sensors could be added
- Optical sensors—NTSC cameras
- Cabling—power, NTSC signal, RS232, CAT-5 twisted pairs
- Digital state-machines, microcontrollers, and microprocessors—x86 microprocessor, PIC microcontroller
- Analog frontend (sensor) and backend (actuator) circuits—NTSC, TTL pulse-width modulation
- Networks or bus interfaces—RS232 serial, Ethernet, PCI
- Thermal management—CPU fans

Typically, additional test equipment hardware may also be required, including monitors, development computing environment, oscilloscope, digital multimeter, and a logic analyzer. This is not part of the system, however, although the test equipment is required to fully implement and verify its proper implementation and operation.

In the following sections, basic hardware components such as those used in the stereo-vision tracking system are described.

## Sensors

*Sensors* are devices that respond to physical stimulus (light, heat, pressure, stress/strain, acceleration, magnetism) by transforming the associated energy into electrical energy or by modifying the electrical properties in a circuit. For example, a camera is a sensor that converts photon energy into electrical charge that represents the photon flux for each picture element in an array. A thermistor is a resistor circuit where the resistance of the thermistor changes with temperature and therefore so does the circuit current at a given voltage and voltage drop across the load. A sensor assembly may also interface this analog frontend to a digital encoding interface. Analog to digital converters (ADCs) are used to sample and hold charge, thereby converting the analog circuit current/voltage into a digital value. For example, an 8-bit ADC will encode a sensor circuit operational voltage range into 256 levels. Without encoding, sensors are useful in analog control systems, but for use in digital control systems, encoding is critical. Real-time embedded systems therefore require digital encoding of all sensor input with the exception of subsystems, which are all analog.

The sensor AFE (analog frontend) involves physics that are very particular to the environmental phenomena being sensed and the method for generating measurable changes in an analog circuit based upon physical stimulus. Many sensors are electro-mechanical devices where mechanical stimulus such as stress/strain, the force per unit area and resulting deformation, or motion causes a change in analog circuit voltage/current. Resistance in many materials is a function of stress, strain, and/or temperature; thus these mechanical properties can be measured using the right material as a resistor in a circuit in the AFE. Motion can be sensed also with a variation of resistance through potentiometers, where resistance is modified by mechanically varying the resistive path in a circuit. A simple example is the use of a multi-turn potentiometer to modify resistance in a circuit with rotation. The sensor couples a physical phenomenon to an electrical one. This coupling may be more erudite as is the case with an optical encoder that uses periodic interruption of an opto-coupler (LED and photodiode) in a circuit through mechanical mechanisms such as a filter wheel. In this case the opto-coupler interruptions are counted to estimate rotation.

The sensor always includes the AFE, but may also include the analog-to-digital encoding as well. In the case of an NTSC (National Television Standards Committee) camera, the camera outputs an analog signal that encodes photo intensity in an image field of view in an analog raster output. The NTSC analog signal can be further encoded from the NTSC signal into a digital image, which is an array of alpha-RGB (Red, Green, Blue) pixels that indicate luminance and chrominance of subareas of the camera's field of view—picture element or pixel alpha-RGB values encoded using an ADC (Analog-to-Digital Converter). This is the approach taken in the stereo-vision example. An alternative might employ a CCD (Charge Coupled Device) camera, which provides a more direct encoding of photo-intensity (photon flux) in terms of electrical charge. The range of methods used by sensors to encode the wide range of physical phenomena and associated energy into electrical energy is too broad to comprehensively discuss in this text. The key concept however is that all sensors do convert physical stimulus into electrical outputs that affect an analog circuit, which in turn can be encoded into a digital input using an ADC. The ADC implementation has significant impact on the encoding capability, including the following:

- Sampling frequency
- Sample accuracy
- Input range

The ADC takes an analog input (voltage and current for a given sensor resistence) and converts it into a digital word, most often from 8 bit to 16 bit. Change in sensor resistence is ultimately measured by change in voltage drop over the circuit. The ADC requires a reference voltage, $V_{ref,}$ and normally encodes all inputs into a range of values from zero to $\frac{V_{ref}}{(2^n)}$, sothat for a 5V reference, a typical 16-bit ADC can encode the voltage in an AFE into increments representing a change of 0.0763 millivolts with an input range of 0 to 5V for the AFE signal. The resolution can clearly be increased by reducing the reference voltage, $V_{ref}$; however, this is at the cost of constraining the input range. This trade-off drives the selection of how many bits the ADC provides in the encoding—to accommodate large input ranges and high resolution, the ADC must have more bits for the encoding. The final question is how fast can the AFE be sampled? This depends upon the type of ADC:

**Flash:**  Using comparators, 1 per voltage step, and resistors

**Successive approximation:**  Comparators and counting logic

The flash ADC conversion speed is the sum of the comparator delays and logic delay—typically flash ADCs are the fastest variety. The successive approximation ADC uses comparators to determine first whether the input is greater than half the reference, then to determine whether it's greater than one quarter, and so on until the LSB (Least Significant Bit) comparison is made and the signal level has been approximated successively to the bit accuracy of the ADC—this takes as many clock cycles as the ADC has bits. One more issue with any ADC is how the input signal is sampled—if it changes significantly during the ADC process, then the results will not be accurate, so ADCs must sample and hold the input. The sample and hold time will add latency and thus reduce the maximum inter-sample frequency. Furthermore, the ADC may automatically sample and provide an interrupt or FIFO input to a state-machine or microprocessor, or the ADC may require commands to sample the input and then convert it. For high-rate encoding such as video, a dedicated hardware state-machine typically provides the ADC control and stores encoded data in a FIFO for transfer to a microprocessor via DMA. Methods for transferring encoded data are discussed in more detail in the "Firmware Components" section.

## Actuators

Fundamentally, an *actuator* is a transducer that converts electrical energy into some other form such as sound, motion, heat, or electromagnetism. The simplest form of actuation is switching. The relay provides a mechanism that can be actuated to open or close a switch on command from a digital I/O interface. This on/off control does not provide continuous output or simple variation of output amplitude over time. A *servomechanism*, or *servo*, is an actuator that converts electrical energy into mechanical rotation using a motor and a control interface. Heating elements that are nothing more than resistors can be modulated to provide heat for a system that requires minimum operating temperatures and to provide cooling using fans, louvers, or some other form of conductive, convective, or radiative cooling. Digital values are decoded into analog signals through an analog backend (ABE) for actuation so that a digitally encoded value drives the voltage in the ABE circuit. This is most often done using either PWM (Pulse Width Modulation) or a DAC (Digital-to-Analog converter) so that the amplitude in the ABE can be driven by a stream of digital encoded outputs. With PWM, a periodic digital pulse (TTL logic level, for example) is driven out with a duty cycle that is proportional to the desired amplitude of the signal at a given point in time. The DAC provides the proportional output automatically based upon the last commanded digital output rather than decoding using a digital duty cycle. Much like ADC sensor interfaces, DAC actuator interfaces should be characterized by

- Type of actuation—on/off or DAC/PWM modulated
- Speed of actuation
- Accuracy of modulation

Most often for accurate high-rate actuators, a DAC is required rather than relays or PWM. For audio output, PCM (Pulse Code Modulation) is used for input sampling and driving an output DAC for duration and at variable output levels.

Actuators can be very unstable and suffer over-shoot or failure to settle without careful design and potential feedback from sensors. For example, a scanning mirror can be used to move an optical field of view very accurately by deflecting a pick-off mirror on an optical path through a small angle. An electromechanical mechanism known as a voice-coil flexure can be driven by a DAC so that electromagnetic coils are used to deflect a mirror on a rubber flexure to the left or right—furthermore, the mirror can be restored to a previous position by allowing the flexure to spring back, dampened by the electromagnetic coils. Some of the high-rate feedback control for such an actuator might be implemented as a traditional analog control circuit rather than relying upon the digital real-time embedded system to provide such control.

## I/O Interfaces

The I/O, in general, to and from a real-time embedded system can be classified first as either analog or digital. In the case of analog I/O, as seen in the previous section, an ADC is required to encode analog inputs and a DAC, PWM, or relay interface is required to decode digital outputs when analog I/O is interfaced to a real-time embedded system. Many embedded systems may actually be subsystems in a much larger system and therefore may not actually have direct analog I/O—instead, many real-time embedded systems have digital I/O only or in addition to analog I/O. Either way, at some point, all I/O becomes digital once encoded or prior to decode. So, prior to the ABE or after the AFE, the embedded system simply sees digital I/O. The form of the digital I/O can vary significantly and can be characterized as:

■  Word-at-a-time I/O
■  Block I/O

Furthermore, the method of interfacing word or block I/O can be

■  MMIO
■  Port I/O

In the case of word I/O, a simple set of registers defines the interface to the AFE/ABE and provides status, data, and control for encode/decode. A single word is written to an ABE for output to a data register, the output is started by setting control bits, and the output status is monitored using the status register. Likewise, for an AFE interface, status can be polled to determine when new encoded data is available, and samples can be commanded through control and monitored via status. The word I/O interfaces require significant interaction with the real-time embedded system and are not very efficient, but do provide simple low rate I/O interfaces. These interfaces require programmed I/O where a CPU is involved in each input and output for all phases of the read/write, status monitoring, and control. This is often not desirable for higher-rate interfaces where even powerful CPUs would spend way too many cycles on programmed I/O and not enough on processing to provide services. So, most high-rate interfaces have a block I/O interface where a state-machine or DMA engine provides command and control of the word encoding/decoding and less frequently interrupts the CPU when significantly large blocks of data have been encoded/decoded—typically 1,024-, 2,048-, or 4,096-byte blocks.

Processor cores traditionally have provided I/O through dedicated pins from the CPU to other devices called *I/O ports*. An alternative is to save on off-chip interface pins by mapping MMIO onto existing address and data lines in/out of the CPU so that I/O causes devices to be read or written in the same address space as memory devices. Many processors, such as the Intel x86, provide both port I/O and MMIO. When devices are memory mapped, care must be taken to ensure that the MMU (Memory Management Unit) is aware that particular address ranges are being used for device I/O so that output data is not cached, writes are fully drained to the device rather than buffered, and the address range is allowed to be accessed without exception. Memory locations can be cached, and often it isn't necessary for the CPU to wait for writes to be updated in actual memory devices after writes have been queued; for device I/O, all writes should be fully drained and not cached so that actuation is reliable. If, for example, an output to a DAC was cached for later write-back and this output was driving speaker output, this would cause playback drop-out.

Figure 8.3 shows the components of the stereo-vision sensor subsystem for the stereo-vision tracker. This sensor device consists of two NTSC cameras and two PCI (Peripheral Component Interconnect) frame grabbers, which use the Bt 878 encoder chip to acquire and encode the NTSC camera output. The data acquisition is composed of an NTSC signal-encoding interface, a PCI bus data I/O DMA channel, and a programmable DMA engine. The encoding is performed at 30 frames per second for a selection of video encoding formats, including the maximum resolution of 640 × 480, 32-bit pixels where each pixel is composed of an 8-bit intensity, alpha, and three 8-bit fields encoding RGB. The AFE for an NTSC encoder uses a PLL (Phase Lock Loop) to synchronize with the NTSC signal to sample and digitize the signal to form a YCrCb (Y = luminance, CrCb = red and blue chrominance). The color NTSC signal format was an enhancement to the original grayscale television signal format. The basic NTSC signal format includes 525 horizontal traces to illuminate a phosphor screen with 262.5 even scan lines and 262.5 odd with blanking time for signal retracing. The intensity of the tracing beam is modulated during the even/odd interlaced line tracing so that each pixel is illuminated for 125 nanoseconds for 427 pixels/line and 10 microseconds of blanking between lines yielding a scan line time of 63.6 microseconds. The NTSC camera produces a signal conforming to this NTSC standard for direct input into a

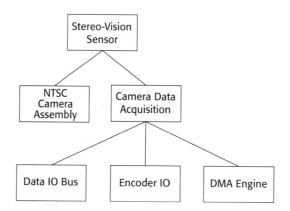

**FIGURE 8.3**    NTSC vision subsystem in stereo-vision tracking system.

standard television monitor. The interlacing of horizontal scan lines, that is, tracing odd lines followed by even line tracing each frame, reduces flicker at the NTSC frame rate of approximately 30 fps (29.97 actual). The AFE PLL synchronizes with the scan line by detecting the NTSC sync and blanking levels and then programs the ADCs to sample the signal for each pixel to encode YCrCb. The YCrCb data is latched into an internal FIFO memory, and a synchronized DMA engine drains the FIFO with PCI bus transfers from the encoder to host system memory. The YCrCb format for NTSC was chosen so that grayscale televisions can display color NTSC signals by simply using the luminance portion of the signal alone. Most encoders support automatic conversion from YCrCb into alpha-RGB using linear scaling formulas based upon characteristics of human vision:

$$R = Y + Cr$$
$$G = Y - 0.51 \times Cr - 0.186 \times Cb$$
$$B = Y + Cb$$

The relationship between the YCrCb and RGB signals are

$$Y = 0.3R + 0.59G + 0.11B$$
$$Cr = R - Y = R - (0.3R + 0.59G + 0.11B)$$
$$Cb = B - Y = B - (0.3R + 0.59G + 0.11B)$$

The DMA engine is a simple processor with an RISC instruction set that provides control over the encoding as well as the PCI DMA transfer and generation of host interrupts. So, for example, using the Bt 878, microcode can be written to encode the 525 NTSC input even and odd lines with 427 pixels each into a range of formats (e.g., 320 × 240 alpha-RGB or 80 × 60 grayscale) based upon the ADC sampling rates with instructions to transfer the encoded data and to generate an interrupt at the completion of each frame encoded and transferred over PCI. The 320 × 240 alpha-RGB frames (307,200 bytes/frame) are transferred by the DMA engine using multiple PCI bus bursts, typically 512 bytes to 4 KB each. This is typical of a high-rate block transfer I/O interface for a high data rate sensor. In this example, two encoders are bursting video data on the PCI bus simultaneously to two different DMA buffers in two different host memory address ranges.

The stereo-vision tracker also incorporates a low-rate actuation I/O interface to enable the system to tilt and pan the stereo-vision sensor (cameras and baseline mount) to follow a bright target that may be moving to keep the target in both camera fields of view. Figure 8.4 describes the components making up this low-rate actuation subsystem.

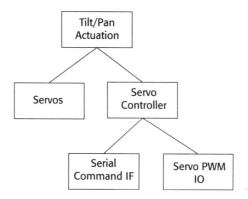

**FIGURE 8.4** Tilt/pan servo subsystem in stereo-vision tracking system.

The tilt/pan actuation subsystem uses two servos to provide the tilt and pan rotational degrees of freedom. The servos are commanded with a TTL PWM signal (Servo PWM I/O) generated by a microcontroller (Servo Controller). The specific signal generated, and thus position of the servo, can be commanded by a microprocessor through a multidrop serial interface (Serial Command IF). The serial command interface is simple and only allows the microprocessor to write out command data 1 byte at a time. This is a typical low-rate interface.

## Processor Complex

Almost all modern real-time embedded systems include a general-purpose CPU to process firmware/software to provide updatable and flexible services by processing and linking sensor inputs to actuator outputs. If the services that a real-time embedded system must provide are so well known that they can be fully committed to a hardware state machine, then perhaps a processor complex (or set of interconnected CPUs) is not needed. Most often, services are expected to change over time, are not well enough specified initially, or are too complex to consider hardware-only implementations. The processor complex may be composed of the following:

- A single CPU with port I/O and bus interface MMIO
- Multiple CPUs on an internal bus with port/MMIO
- Multiple CPUs with an interconnection network and port/MMIO

In the case of our working stereo-vision system example, a main x86 CPU provides a platform for image processing to compute the centroid of the target object as seen by the left and right cameras and encoded using the Bt 878 PCI-bus NTSC encoder subsystem. The servo control is achieved using the Servo Controller, a Microchip PIC, which commands multiple servos to tilt/pan the camera assembly using TTL logic level PWM based upon a serial byte stream command to the controller. Figure 8.5 shows the subsystems (Servo Control and Image Processing) that compose the overall stereo-vision system processing to provide the tracking and ranging services. The Servo Control subsystem uses a digital control law based upon calculated centroid inputs to tilt/pan the stereo-vision sensors in real time to keep the target in the field of view and produces a series of servo commands as output. The Image Processing subsystem uses alpha-RGB video frames at a maximum rate of 30 fps to compute the centroid of the target as seen by each camera and the range to the target based upon a triangulation calculation.

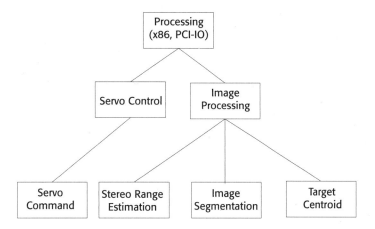

**FIGURE 8.5** Processing subsystem in stereo-vision tracking system.

## Processor and I/O Interconnection

For multi-CPU real-time embedded systems, an interconnection network is required to enable I/O and processing to be distributed. The interconnection network can be

- Simple bus or backplane (e.g., PCI or VME)
- On-chip local bus with BIU to backplane I/O bus
- A cross-bar on-chip interconnection between CPUs
- An off-board network—e.g., firewire, USB, Ethernet

Figure 8.6 shows a taxonomy of interconnection strategies that can be used to integrate CPUs and I/O interfaces in an embedded system.

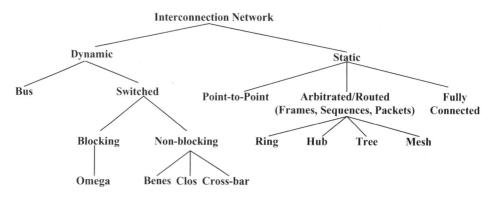

**FIGURE 8.6** Taxonomy of processor-I/O interconnection strategies.

Most embedded systems are integrated with either a scalable bus architecture like PCI, point-to-point serial links, or networks.

## Bus Interconnection

Many different bus architectures have been used and are being used for embedded systems. To better understand integration of processing and I/O with a bus interconnection, this chapter examines the VME (Versa Module Extension) bus and the PCI (Peripheral Component Interconnect) bus. The VME bus has historically been a popular and simple bus architecture used with embedded systems; by contrast, PCI is an emergent bus architecture that offers traditional parallel bus integration as well as high-speed serial interconnection with PCI Express.

The PCI bus, introduced as a replacement for the ISA (Industry Standard Architecture) bus prevalent in the desktop PC domain, has evolved and become a popular I/O-to-processor complex integration method in embedded systems. A goal of the first PCI standard, 2.1, was to provide a bus where I/O adapters could be interfaced to processor complexes with plug-and-play integration. Plug and play provides a standard for PCI controllers (masters) to probe the bus and find devices after they have been added without any modification to the master interface. The PCI bus was designed to integrate with the legacy ISA bus through an interface called the South Bus. The main PCI controller interface was called the North Bus. At the time that PCI was first introduced, many embedded systems were integrated using the VME bus. Building a real-time embedded system based upon bus integration allows system designers to decompose the system into subsystems with interface and processor boards that can be designed, built, and tested as units and later integrated on a standard interconnection. Both VME and PCI provide this modularity compared to custom backplane or on-board integration. The bus integration also provides a fast signal interface compared to packet or frame transmission networks (this has started to change recently as you'll see later). Table 8.1 briefly summarizes and compares features of VME-32 and PCI 2.x.

**TABLE 8.1**  Comparison of PCI and VME Buses

| Feature | VME Bus | PCI 2.x Bus |
|---|---|---|
| Bus Transfers | Asynchronous 20 MHz | Synch Clock 33/66 MHz |
| Target Addressing | 32-, 24-, or 16-bit address (A32, A24, A16) | Multiplexed 32/64-bit Address/Data Bus |
| Data Transfer | 32-, 24-, or 16-bit separate Data Bus | Multiplexed with 32-bit Address Bus |
| Data Transfer Types | Word or Block Transfer limited to a specific block size (e.g. 512 bytes) | Burst Transfer Always with Min and Max Length |
| Device Interrupt Mechanism | Daisy-Chained Prio Interrupts | 4 Shared Interrupt Lines: A-D Routed to Programmable Interrupt Controller |
| Interrupt Vectoring | Interrupt Data Cycle following Interrupt Level | Map A-D onto Processor vector, e.g. onto IRQ 0...15 on x86 with directo IRQ to vector mapping |
| Bus Access Arbitration for multiple initiators (masters) | No Arbitration, Firmware or custom controller must ensure mutex access | Built-in Hidden Arbitration |
| Device addressing | Custom-designed MMIO | Plug and Play Configuration Space allows firmware to set an MMIO or IO base address at run time |
| Expansion and form factors | Custom Bus Integration on 6U boards with 3U/6U D-shell form factor | No custom expansion, but many standard form factors: Compact PCI, PC/104+, PMC, and standard PC 2.x |
| Faster options | VME-64+ | PCI-X 1.0a, 2.0, and PCI-Express |

The features of PCI that have made it successful and a popular integration bus are burst transfer (most I/O has become high rate and is most efficient with block transfer), built-in arbitration, and plug-and-play configuration. The two most commonly used form factors for real-time embedded systems are Compact PCI (D-shell backplane connector) and PC/104+ (a stackable small board form factor). The PCI bus has also been very popular as a chipset interconnection on single-board embedded systems. One reason for the popularity of PCI as a chip interconnection on board is the definition of PCI bridges, which allow for bus-to-bus PCI integration. The PCI 2.x standard provides 32-bit 33-MHz bus cycles and up to 64-bit at 66 MHz for updated 2.x, yielding bandwidth of 128 million bytes per second to 512 million bytes per second. The effective bandwidth given arbitration, addressing, and device response latency overhead will be significantly reduced by bus transaction protocol overhead, but still on the order of 100 to 500 million bytes per second. For the stereo-vision example, which transfers 2 streams of 32-bit alpha-RGB 320 × 240 frames 30 times per second, it requires 18,432,000 bytes per second, or approximately 20% of the available PCI 2.1 effective bandwidth (assuming effective bandwidth is 100 million bytes per second). A single, full-resolution encoding (525 × 427) video stream would require 26,901,000 bytes per second, or about 27% of PCI 2.1 effective bandwidth.

The chipset used for video encoding in the stereo-vision example is the Bt878, now also updated as the Cirrus Stream Machine, and works by fetching DMA RISC engine code from host memory, so some additional PCI transfers are initiated by the chip to fetch code as well as transfer of frame data to the host memory. The stereo-vision systems implemented at the University of Colorado using PCI 2.1 have had no problem making use of PCI 2.1 for this application with a 320 × 240 30 fps alpha-RGB encoding. Many embedded applications have more than enough bandwidth available from PCI 2.x. One final important feature of PCI is that initiators can configure targets for a maximum and minimum burst length. The minimum serves as a method to reduce overhead so that targets can't transfer small blocks that would incur high overhead for each bus arbitration and address cycle compared to fewer larger block transfers. The maximum prevents a target from overusing the bus and provides some fairness in bus arbitration for multitarget systems.

The commercial computing market, specifically high-speed networking, graphics, and databases, have pushed PCI to evolve into a very high bandwidth interconnection. The AGP (Accelerated Graphics Port) standard was developed as a specific single-target expansion for PCI to accommodate high bandwidth RAM-DAC (RAM Digital-to-Analog Converters) used to drive monitors with high-fidelity graphics. Following PCI 2.x, the PCI-X 1.0a and PCI-X 2.0 standards were developed for networking and database host bus adapters and provide 64-bit 133 MHz and up to 64-bit 266/533 MHz bandwidth. The theoretical limit of the PCI bus signaling is 533 MHz. At this speed, the problem of skew between the address/data lines is significant and requires careful layout of the bus traces and advanced signaling techniques that make PCI-X 2.0 expensive and difficult to implement, especially for buses that accommodate more than one target and initiator. The development of Gigabit Ethernet at 1 G and 10 G rates (where G = gigabit/sec) has helped drive the demand for high-rate PCI. The PCI-X 1.0a standard, at 64-bit 133 MHz (just over 1 GB/sec), has made it popular for gigabit Ethernet network interfaces. To support 10 G Ethernet, PCI-Express was developed, which has a drastically different signaling and physical layer than PCI or PCI-X. PCI-Express provides high speed 2.5 G serial byte lanes that can be ganged up. With the introduction of PCI-X, the standard introduced an important new concept—split transactions.

In PCI 2.x, when a device has high response latency, the bus delays until the target device responds. With the delay policy, having even one slow target on the bus decreases performance for all targets and initiators on the bus. Split transactions eliminate this delay by providing buffer queues for writes to the bus so that they can be posted by an initiator and drained to a slow target over the bus when it's ready. The initiator is not delayed in this case as long as the write buffer queue is not exhausted before the data is drained to the target. Likewise, on reads, split transaction allows the initiator to post a read request to the bus, which initiates the target read, and if the target is slow, allows the target to negotiate for completion in a later transaction—the bus is freed in the meantime for other transactions. Both PCI-X and PCI-Express are split-transaction bus standards—this greatly improves the effective bandwidth because it does not allow the bus to be held for arbitrarily long delay periods. However, there is, of course, still arbitration and addressing overhead.

## High-Speed Serial Interconnection

As traditional backplane buses have become problematic as far as laying out signal traces and dealing with high-speed signaling and skew (rates above 100 MHz), several new high-speed serial interconnection standards were introduced:

- Universal Serial Bus
- Firewire
- PCI-Express
- Gigabit Ethernet

All four serial/network interconnections can be used for real-time embedded systems and provide an attractive alternative to bus integration. A full discussion of all the high-rate serial protocols is beyond the scope of this text.

The wide adoption of PCI for real-time embedded systems in the past and key features of PCI-Express make it an interconnection for scaling existing systems that is becoming popular. PCI-Express can be routed on a board, on a backplane, and even out of a box on a cable for short distances. Furthermore, it's composed of serial byte lanes operating at 2.5 G for each lane with the capability to gang up lanes in x1, x2, x4, x8, and x16 configurations. The stated design goal of PCI-E (PCI-Express) is to maximize the bandwidth per pin on the interconnection. Each PCI-E byte lane is full duplex, allowing concurrent transmit and receive at 2.5 G. Given these characteristics, we can compare the PCI 2.x, PCI-X, and PCI-E standards as far as bandwidth per pin:

**PCI-E:**  $[(2.5 \text{ G/s/dir} \times 8\text{b/dir}) \times (1\text{B/8b})]/40 \text{ pins} = 100 \text{ MB/s/pin}$

**PCI 2.x:**  $[(32\text{b} \times 33 \text{ MHz}) \times (1\text{B/8b})]/84 \text{ pins} = 1.58 \text{ MB/s/pin}$

**PCI-X 2.0 266:**  $[(64\text{b} \times 266 \text{ MHz}) \times (1\text{B/8b})]/150 \text{ pins} = 7.09 \text{ MB/s/pin}$

PCI-E clearly has the advantage from the perspective of interconnection layout and cabling over PCI 2.x and PCI-X. The complication is that serial byte lane transmission requires significant digital signal processing on each byte lane. Like fiber channel and gigabit Ethernet, PCI-E uses an 8b/10b encoding scheme with a link layer and network layered architecture to achieve 2.5 G transfer rates. Given the demands of gigabit transport, the cost of this digital signal processing and network stack implementation has actually become more feasible than the cost of traditional bus high-speed layout. Furthermore, the ability to use high-speed serial interconnection on-chip, on-board, and off-board makes these standards more attractive than traditional bus architectures. Finally, PCI-E has been designed to be compatible with PCI 2.x and PCI-X from the firmware viewpoint, despite a radically different data transport method. The PCI-E standard supports the same plug-and-play configuration, burst transfers, interrupts, and all basic features of PCI 2.x.

The PCI-E interconnection provides byte lane interconnection with a network layered architecture as shown in Figure 8.7.

The PCI-E standard not only provides significantly more bandwidth compared to PCI 2.x and PCI-X, it also provides some features to support real-time continuous media with isochronal channels. The isochronal channels provide bandwidth and latency performance guarantees for transport. The advent of PCI-E, USB, Firewire, and Gigabit Ethernet has provided an alternative interconnection architecture for real-time embedded systems. These new high-speed serial interconnections likely will be designed into many future real-time embedded systems.

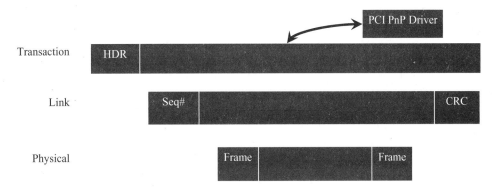

**FIGURE 8.7** PCI-Express byte lane network architecture.

## Low-Speed Serial Interconnection

Many real-time embedded systems not only include high-rate I/O for services such as video or network transport, but also include low-rate command/response or monitoring interfaces. For example, in our stereo-vision system, the servos are commanded through a low-rate multidrop RS232 interface. The Microchip PIC (Programmable Integrated Circuit) has a TTL logic level digital serial interface that can be interfaced to the higher voltage RS232 serial interface. The servos in the stereo-vision application can tilt/pan through wide angles quickly, but only have an accuracy of several degrees, so the command rate required to track a quickly moving object at a distance of 10 feet or more is on the order of 1 to 100s of milliseconds. The command protocol used on the PIC is a simple byte stream command format with opcode bytes and operand bytes. To command a given servo to a new position simply requires sending a PIC address (because the serial interconnection is multidrop), a servo address and opcode byte, followed by a servo position operand. A command therefore requires 4 bytes, and at a 1 millisecond rate, this is only 4,000 bytes/second. Clearly PCI, USB, Firewire, or any of the previously presented high-rate interconnection architectures are not warranted for this type of interface.

The RS232, common serial, point-to-point data transmission has been used in real-time embedded systems since the advent of the industry and remains a common low-rate and debug interface. The RS232 link normally tops out around 115,200 bits/second (about 12 KB/sec) and is not capable of long-distance transmission due to line noise at the 12-volt signaling levels it uses. Other options have evolved that provide similar low- to medium-rate transmission with longer distance, multidrop, and higher bit rates. These options are widely used in real-time embedded systems:

**RS422:** A differential +/− 5v serial link capable of 1 MB/sec and distances up to 1 km

**Multidrop RS232, RS422:**  Adding a protocol to address targets on a common link with capability to forward

**I2C:**  A medium-speed digital interconnection typically used on-board to interconnect chips such as EEPROM to a processor

**SPI:**  A digital serial protocol capable of medium rates

A full discussion of all the low- to medium-rate serial protocols is beyond the scope of this text.

## Interconnection Systems

Having discussed the components that can be used to interconnect devices with processors in a real-time embedded system, let's briefly discuss how these components might be arranged in an interconnection architecture. Real-time embedded system architectures and design will be discussed more fully in Chapter 12, but an overview will help summarize the possibilities. Two architectures are most common. The first is the hierarchical network interconnecting a main processor complex with a number of microcontrollers. This architecture has been most popular in robotics and also for aerospace applications where many sensors and actuators are distributed in a large system, yet processing and services provide system-level functions. For example, a robotic arm that has 5 degrees of freedom (base, shoulder, elbow, wrist, and claw) with torque control so that it can handle massive objects, might include a microcontroller to provide control for each joint motor. The 5 microcontrollers, one at each joint, can interface locally to the actuation motor with a DAC and provide closed-loop feedback control based upon local position and stress/strain sensors to provide smooth rotation even when the arm is handling objects with significant mass. Providing the local control reduces the amount of cabling back to the main processor. The DAC and the sensor interface cabling is routed to the microcontroller, which is physically integrated local to each joint (or control point). The microcontroller has more than sufficient capability to provide the torque control and closed-loop monitoring. Now, the 5 microcontrollers can be interfaced via a low- to medium-rate serial interconnection back to the main processor complex for commands and to provide status—the main processor complex runs complex services such as path planning, possibly camera-based object recognition, a user interface, and system health and status monitoring. In fact, the robotics community likens this hierarchical approach to the human body, which includes local reflex control as well as centralized processing in the brain—e.g., Rodney Brooks' subsumption architecture.

The alternative to the hierarchical interconnection is a centralized processor complex integrated on a high-rate interconnection such as PCI, with many I/O device interfaces also integrated on PCI. This architecture has an advantage in that all processing can be done in a single processor complex—the distributed processing of the hierarchical architecture requires different development, debug, and test methods compared to the processor complex—often the processor complex is a microprocessor with an RTOS, and the microcontrollers are simple Main+ISR applications. The downside to the centralized processing is that most often all I/O cabling must come from the common central processing enclosure and be routed to sensors and actuators distributed throughout the system. Deciding which type of architecture makes most sense is often driven by the system requirements for actuators and sensors—the number, how distributed they are, how much latency in sensor/actuator activation is allowable, and, of course, cost and complexity.

## Memory Subsystems

Real-time embedded systems require nonvolatile data storage to boot the system and to start services. After a power-on reset, the processors in the processor complex each vector to a hardware-defined starting address to execute code. This starting address, typically a high address such as 0xFFE0_0000, is designed to map a nonvolatile storage device, such as EEPROM or Flash memory, so that boot code can be stored permanently at this address and executed following a reset to initialize the system. The boot code initializes all basic interfaces and normally loads a basic RTOS so that application services can be loaded and run. The code (often called text segment), data (initialized, uninitialized, and read only), heap, and stack segments must be created in a working memory by firmware. Figure 8.8 shows a typical memory map for an embedded system.

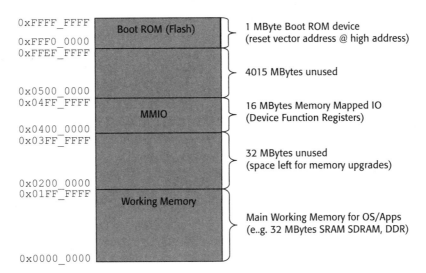

**FIGURE 8.8** Common memory map for an embedded system.

The memory map is really a logical view of memory from the viewpoint of address space through which firmware and software can access devices. From a hardware viewpoint, memory is better described as a hierarchy of storage devices:

■ Registers (CPU and memory mapped for device control)
■ Cache
■ Working Memory
■ Extended Memory

Figure 8.9 shows a typical memory hierarchy for an embedded system.

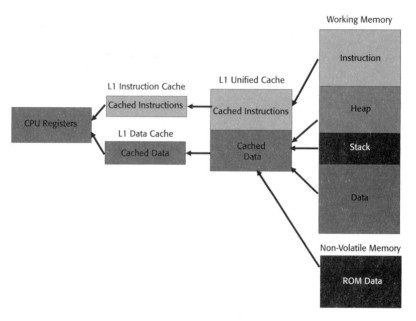

**FIGURE 8.9** Common physical memory hierarchy for an embedded system.

## FIRMWARE COMPONENTS

Some components can only be realized in hardware, but many can be implemented with software or firmware (noting that software interfacing directly to hardware is typically called firmware). Furthermore, if the real-time embedded system has any software-based services or even just management, firmware is needed to interface hardware resources to software applications.

## Boot Code

The universal definition of *firmware* is code or software that runs out of a non-volatile device to make hardware resources available for the rest of the application software. Firmware providing this function is normally referred to in general as *board support package* (BSP) firmware because traditionally, this firmware has initialized and made available all on-board resources for a processor complex to software applications. Before the resources have been fully initialized, the firmware boots the board by executing code out of a nonvolatile device so that one or more basic interfaces is made operable and the system can now download additional application software. For example, the BSP boot firmware might initialize an Ethernet interface and provide TFTP download of application code for execution.

## Device Drivers

Device interface drivers are most often considered firmware because they directly interface to hardware resources and make those resources available to higher-level software applications. The architecture of a device driver interface is depicted in Figure 8.10 and includes both a HW bottom half interface and a SW top half interface.

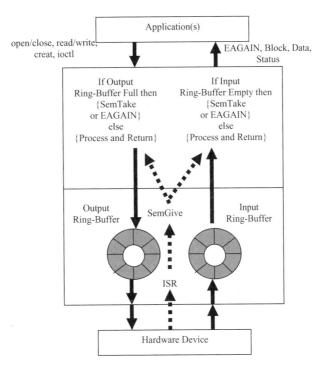

**FIGURE 8.10**  Device driver firmware interface.

## Operating System Services

Not all real-time embedded systems require an operating system as discussed in Chapter 3. Most RTOS implementations do, however, provide a layer of software that acts a single interface for all applications to gain access to system resources. Furthermore, most real-time systems incorporate an RTOS, which provides a framework for resource management and for scheduling processor resources with an RM policy. The RTOS also provides commonly needed services and libraries used by application services. The most fundamental services and mechanisms provided include the following:

- Priority preemptive scheduler for threads
- Thread control block management
- Inter-thread synchronization and communication (e.g., semaphores and message queues)
- Basic I/O for system debug and bring-up (e.g., serial, Ethernet, LED)
- ISR (Interrupt Service Routine) installation on interrupt vectors
- Transition from boot to operational state
- Timers for delays and blocked thread timeouts
- Drivers for basic hardware devices (serial, Ethernet, timers, nonvolatile memory)

Extended services beyond these may be provided to assist development and debug of a system:

- Cross debug agent
- Interactive shell to view control blocks and system context
- Capability to dynamically load and execute code object files
- Interface to resource analysis tools (e.g., WindView)

## RTOS SYSTEM SOFTWARE MECHANISMS

An RTOS does not need to provide the same wealth of system services as a full multiuser operating system such as Linux. The understanding is that the RTOS user prefers simpler mechanisms and is willing to take on more responsibility in the application to explicitly manage resources. For this reason, it is important that programmers working with an RTOS code with extra precaution to avoid time-wasting debug sessions. Some good coding practices that are even more important with an RTOS compared to Windows® or Linux include the following:

- Always check return codes for an RTOS API function call.
- Be aware of stack sizes for each task created and stack usage by local C variables and parameters passed to ensure that stack overruns are not causing problems.
- Use tools such as the Tornado™ browser and WindView™ to ensure that you have not overloaded the CPU.
- VxWorks compiled with the MMU Basic only has memory protection for the kernel code, so check array bounds extra carefully to ensure that wild writes are not destabilizing code.
- Do not use `printf` in time-critical code because it introduces blocking that will significantly change timing (instead use `logMsg()` calls).
- Be careful only to use API calls that are documented as okay to use in interrupt handlers in your kernel and ISR code (for example, you can't receive a message in an ISR, but you can send one).
- Set priorities of tasks according to RM theory and demote standard VxWorks services if required.
- Write shutdown functions for tasks that release all resources that tasks create and use.

Following the preceding precautions will make writing RTOS code easier. The standard RTOS mechanisms are designed to make mutithreaded real-time applications simpler. Multiple threads need methods for sharing resources, sharing data, synchronizing, keeping track of time, and receiving notification of asynchronous events. The CD-ROM includes numerous examples of using basic mechanisms in the VxWorks RTOS.

ON THE CD

## Message Queues

The VxWorks RTOS supports both POSIX and native message queue mechanisms. Message queues are used to synchronize tasks and to pass data between them. The enqueue and dequeue operations are thread safe (a partial write or read is not possible).

Both types of message queues can be read and written in blocking or non-blocking modes. For blocking modes, when a task does a read on an empty message queue, it blocks until a message is enqueued by another task allowing it to read and continue. Likewise when a task tries to write a full message queue in blocking mode, it is blocked until the queue has room for the new message. It is wise to set a timeout upper bound rather than using WAIT_FOREVER so that indefinite blocking will not occur and errors in synchronization and resource management will be detected through timeouts rather than failure to make progress.

For nonblocking message queues, when a task does a read on an empty queue, it will be returned the error code EAGAIN, indicating that no messages were available to read and that the task should try again later. Likewise, for a nonblocking message queue, a task will get the same EAGAIN error code if it tries to write to a full queue. This indicates that the writer should try again later, perhaps allowing a read of that queue to create space.

The POSIX message queues include a feature to enqueue messages with a priority level and to read the priority when messages are dequeued. Higher priority messages are always dequeued first. This essentially allows a sender to put an important message onto the head of the queue. Example code for usage of message queues in VxWorks can be found on the CD-ROM in the VxWorks-Examples directory. The posix_mq.c shows basic features of POSIX message queues, including priorities. The heap_mq.c file shows how pointers to heap allocated buffers can be used with message queues for zero copy buffers. For the heap message queue, the sender must always allocate and set the pointer before sending it, and the receiver should determine when it is safe to deallocate the buffer. Message queue sends can be called in ISR context, but receive can never be called in ISR context, only in task context.

ON THE CD

## Binary Semaphores

The binary semaphore is the simplest and most often used mechanism in the RTOS. The semGive() function is often used in ISR context to unblock a service handling task when data becomes available as indicated by a hardware interrupt. The semTake() call is most often used by tasks to wait for a server request (new data available) or to synchronize with another task. The two_tasks.c code on the CD-ROM provides an example of tasks that synchronize each other using a binary semaphore. Care should be taken to set the binary semaphore initial state (FULL or EMPTY), and the protocol for unblocking must be selected. Protocols for unblocking include SEM_Q_FIFO and SEM_Q_PRIORITY. For SEM_Q_FIFO, if multiple tasks block on the same semaphore, then they are unblocked in the order that they originally arrived and blocked. If instead SEM_Q_PRIORITY is used, then the highest priority task will be unblocked first. The FIFO protocol ensures fairness, and the PRIORITY protocol helps minimize potential priority inversion. Finally in cases where multiple tasks may be blocked and if all blocking tasks should be released at the same time, the semFlush() function provides this feature.

## Mutex Semaphores

Mutex semaphores are tracked by task and include protocol for unblocking tasks waiting to enter critical sections protected by the mutual exclusion semTake() and semGive(). A mutual exclusion semaphore uses the same take and give calls, but is created with semMCreate() in VxWorks. For mutex semaphores, three unblocking protocols can be specified:

**PRIORITY:** Unblocks highest priority task first.

**FIFO:** Unblocks in the same order tasks arrived in for fairness.

**INVERSION_SAFE:** Implements priority inheritance described in Chapter 6.

Mutex semaphores should be used to implement re-entrant functions when these functions need to access global resources. Initial conditions are important and most often mutex semaphores are initially set full to allow initial access to critical sections. The prio_invert.c code shows an example of using an inversion-safe mutex semaphore in VxWorks.

ON THE CD

## Software Virtual Timers

Most embedded hardware systems include several hardware interval timers. A PIT (Programmable Interval Timer) can be set so that it will generate an interrupt on a periodic basis, often 1, 10, or 100 milliseconds. The ISR handling the hardware PIT interrupt (IRQ0 on the x86 architecture) updates virtual timers, which keep track of the interrupt count (called *ticks* in VxWorks). All taskDelay() calls, timeouts specified, and calls to tickGet() are driven by the PIT interrupt rate. If the basic rate is set to 1 millisecond with sysClkRateSet(1000), then timing accuracy for delays and timeouts will be within 2 milliseconds. It is possible to have just missed a tick expiration when a timer is first set and also possible to overrun at least one tick before a timeout handler is invoked. The PIT can be set to raise timer interrupts more frequently than 1000x per second, but this starts to require significant CPU time to maintain virtual time at high rates. The CD-ROM includes three examples to demonstrate the use of virtual time, including itimer_test.c, posix_clock.c, and posix_rt_timers.c.

ON THE CD

## Software Signals

Software signals can be thought of as the software equivalent of an interrupt. They are the main mechanism providing asynchronous handling of events in task context. A task can set itself up to catch signals thrown by other tasks or by ISRs. The CD-ROM includes rt_signal_test.c, which demonstrates the use of POSIX real-time signals. These signals queue, unlike most signals, which prevents loss of signals if a signal is thrown while the catching task is in the process of handling a previously thrown signal.

ON THE CD

# SOFTWARE APPLICATION COMPONENTS

Software components represent the most easily updated and flexible implementation of services in a real-time embedded system. The service state machine can be coded in an RTOS framework readily using tasks and task synchronization mechanisms, including binary semaphores, mutex semaphores, message queues, ring buffers, and ISRs.

## Application Services

*Application services* are software images loaded after boot and after some form of RTOS is functional to provide specific services. These services are simply software implementations of service state machines and execute code within the context of a task.

Services must often be synchronized with each other or ISRs. This is normally accomplished with a binary semaphore. The binary semaphore blocks the calling task until the semaphore is given by an ISR or another task. So, if a task calls sem-Take(S) where S=0, the task is blocked and enters a pending state until another task or ISR uses semGive(S) to set S=1. When S is set, then all tasks blocked (in a queue) are unblocked in queue order one at a time based upon creation with the SEM_Q_FIFO option. Some RTOS frameworks, such as VxWorks, provide a sem-Flush(S), which unblocks all tasks presently blocked on S no matter how many have queued on S. The following example, "two tasks," provides a simple instructive example of the use of a binary semaphore by two service tasks in the VxWorks RTOS framework. The two tasks C code is

```
#include "vxWorks.h"
#include "semLib.h"
#include "sysLib.h"

SEM_ID synch_sem;
int abort_test = FALSE;
int take_cnt = 0;
int give_cnt = 0;

void task_a(void)
{
  int cnt = 0;
  while(!abort_test)
  {
    taskDelay(1000);
    for(cnt=0;cnt < 10000000;cnt++);
```

```
      semGive(synch_sem);
      give_cnt++;
   }
}

void task_b(void)
{
   int cnt = 0;
   while(!abort_test)
   {
      for(cnt=0;cnt < 10000000;cnt++);
      take_cnt++;
      semTake(synch_sem, WAIT_FOREVER);
      taskDelay(1000);
   }
}

void test_tasks(void)
{
   sysClkRateSet(1000);
   synch_sem = semBCreate(SEM_Q_FIFO, SEM_FULL);
   /* receiver runs at a higher priority than the sender */
   if(taskSpawn("task_a", 10, 0, 4000, task_a, 0, 0, 0, 0, 0, 0, 0, 0,
0, 0) == ERROR)
   {
      printf("Task A task spawn failed\n");
   }
   else
      printf("Task A task spawned\n");
   if(taskSpawn("task b", 11, 0, 4000, task_b, 0, 0, 0, 0, 0, 0, 0, 0,
0, 0) == ERROR)
   {
      printf("Task B task spawn failed\n");
   }
   else
      printf("Task B task spawned\n");
}
```

The test_tasks function spawns task A and task B with entry points task_a() and
task_b(). Task A is assigned priority 10, which is higher than Task B priority 11. The
semaphore synch_sem is initially set full (=1). When Task A is spawned, it will preempt
Task B, but will delay for 1 second (1,000 ticks), and then execute a loop and give
synch_sem. Because Task A yields the CPU initially, Task B will execute despite being

lower priority and will execute its loop and take synch_sem. On the first execution of Task B, the take will be successful, and Task B will then delay for 1 second—the state of synch_sem will be empty (=0) at this point. Following the take by Task B, Task A will have come out of delay and will preempt B whether it's done with its delay and busy or not—at this point Task A will give synch_sem, and this strict alternation will continue. The initial condition of synch_sem (full=1 or empty=0) is critical as well as the relative priorities of Task A and Task B. It is possible for the two tasks to deadlock if the initial conditions are different. The example will always alternate as it's provided here, but if Task A, the giver, did not yield the CPU with a task delay call and was assigned higher priority, it's possible that Task B would never run because it can't preempt Task A. This system as presented here will not deadlock either because circular wait is not possible given the priorities and the initial conditions.

## Reentrant Application Libraries

Code shared by multiple threads of execution, as is often the case with application code, must be reentrant. Reentrant code is able to be interrupted and preempted in the execution context of one thread and then executed in the context of a new thread without side effects that would cause either thread to suffer functional bugs. So, reentrant code must carefully handle global resources and protect them so that they are mutually exclusively used by multiple threads. The following are the four main methods to ensure that global data is either protected or converted into task specific context data:

- Protection of data with use of intLock() and intUnlock() to ensure that preemption around global data accesses is impossible at the ISR and task level.
- Protection of data with use of taskLock() and taskUnlock() to ensure that preemption around global data accesses is impossible at the task level.
- Elimination of global data with task variables so that data is no longer shared but owned by a task context and stored in the TCB (Task Control Block).
- Protection of global data with use of semMCreate() to establish a mutex semaphore and semTake() and semGive() to wrap the critical sections where global data is manipulated with multiple instructions that could otherwise be interrupted or preempted.
- Use of stack data only (C parameters and function locals) so that each calling task has its own copy of the data.

Any of these global data elimination or protection methods will make functions thread safe so that they are re-entrant and can be used by multiple concurrently active threads. One of the best and simplest ways to make a function thread safe is to recall that global data can be eliminated by making use of stack only. In C, local variables and parameters are maintained in stack memory. Every VxWorks task must specify stack space when taskSpawn() is called. Insufficient stack space and declaration of large arrays as C locals can introduce bugs. However, stack only variables in functions implements a pure function that is thread safe.

## Communicating and Synchronized Applications

Application code normally requires multiple services to synchronize and to share data or global resources. As discussed in the previous chapter, a region of memory can be shared by two tasks and updated or read in a critical section using a mutex semaphore—the mutex semaphore guarantees mutually exclusive access to the shared memory by one task at a time in spite of the possibility of preemption of one task by another. A higher level abstraction of this is the message queue (see Figure 8.11). The message queue provides a buffer shared by two tasks and allows each task to atomically enqueue or dequeue a message buffer. The atomic enqueue and dequeue operations are implemented using a critical section.

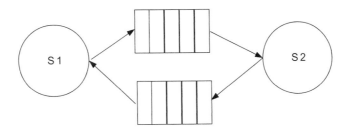

**FIGURE 8.11**   Message queue communication between tasks.

A critical section simply requires that other tasks (services) are not able to preempt $S_1$ or $S_2$ while they are in the middle of copying a message from their local memory into the global message queue buffer. The underlying implementation can use mutex semaphores to prevent more than one task from entering the critical section. Other methods that can be used include taskLock, taskUnlock, whereby the scheduler is actually disabled around the critical section (no preemption is possible at all!). Finally, it's also possible to use intLock, intUnlock to mask out interrupts entirely in a critical section—recall that preemption occurs through an interrupt or an RTOS system call (a yield inside a critical section is an error). The taskLock approach works, but prevents all scheduling during the critical section and therefore has negative impact on the RM policy. Likewise, the intLock approach works as well because it disables scheduling changes in addition to masking interrupts and potentially missing events associated with those interrupts. The user of the message queue, however, does not need to be concerned with the implementation, but rather that the enqueue and dequeue are atomic (nonpreemptable). The implementation of the message queue should ideally not disable scheduling and should prevent unbounded priority inversion.

The message queue, once created, has simple semantics for the enqueue and dequeue that can be either BLOCKING or NONBLOCKING. The message queue is created with a fixed message size, a maximum queue length, and BLOCKING or NONBLOCKING semantics. When the queue is created BLOCKING, writers to a full queue will be blocked when they try to enqueue a message. Likewise, readers will be blocked when they try to dequeue a message from an empty queue. With the alternative NONBLOCKING semantics, the writer to a full queue will simply be returned an error code, EAGAIN, indicating that the enqueue was not successful. Likewise, the reader of an empty queue will be returned EAGAIN indicating that there was nothing to dequeue. A service using the message queue in a NON-BLOCKING mode may want to do other work and attempt to enqueue or dequeue again at a later time. The BLOCKING semantics are used when the service has nothing else worthwhile to do if it can't enqueue or dequeue successfully.

One downside of message queues is that they require a copy of the S1 local buffer in the global message queue buffer—this is not so efficient. A variant use of message queues that improves efficiency is the heap message queue. In this case, pointers are sent as messages rather than data. The pointers are set to point to a buffer allocated by the sender and the pointer received is used to access and process the buffer—the receiver normally frees the buffer. It is key that the sender allocate the buffer and the receiver deallocate to avoid exhaustion of the associated buffer heap (a pool of reusable buffers). Figure 8.12 shows a heap message queue. The heap message queue avoids the copy otherwise required, which takes considerable CPU time and wastes memory due to double-buffering of the same data.

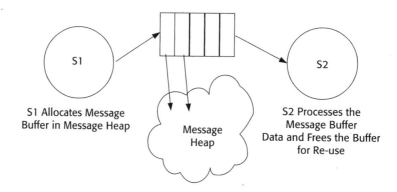

**FIGURE 8.12**  Heap-based message queue communication between tasks.

Because the buffer heap associated with the message queue is typically much larger than the queue depth (size), normally the queue will become filled with pointers and block writers before the heap is exhausted. As long as the sender always allocates heap and the receiver always deallocates, the heap message queue works safely and much more efficiently.

## SUMMARY

A real-time embedded system is composed of hardware, firmware, and software components. Services can be implemented in hardware, firmware, or software, or some combination of the three. Component design should be completed so that components can be tested as individual units and then integrated into a larger system design.

## EXERCISES

1. Read the following chapters in *PCI System Architecture* by Anderson and Shanley: 1, 2, 17, 18, and 19. This should give you a good overview of the PCI design and how to write code to probe for PCI devices and configure them. You'll also find Sections 3.1 to 3.3 and Section 3.9 of Chapter 3 from the *VxWorks Programmer's Guide* useful.

2. Write a VxWorks ISR that calls tickAnnounce every tick and does a semGive on a global binary semaphore every $N$ ticks of the system clock, where $N$ is a global variable so that the semGive frequency is adjustable via the shell. Now, write a VxWorks task that does a semTake and immediately updates a global counter to record virtual ticks. Write a driver program to test both the ISR and task and provide output, which provides evidence that you got it working. So, for example, if you adjust $N$ to 1000, on our system, your count should increase by one every second. Note that you are replacing the VxWorks virtual timer ISR, so you must call tickAnnounce so the kernel can still keep track of time!

3. Now write an abstracted top-half for your driver which includes all the standard driver entry points (open, read, write, and close) and blocks a calling task on a read until $N$ ticks have elapsed, at which time, it stuffs the read buffer with a time structure, including seconds and milliseconds. Write a test driver that opens the abstracted device and reads from it in a loop printing the time in seconds and milliseconds—provide evidence this is working. A write to your driver should allow for a reset of the virtual time value maintained by your driver (i.e., writing anything resets it to zero).

4. Write a PCI device probing function that can be used to find devices on PCI bus 0 and determines vendor ID. Use your code to find the Cirrus logic PCI video adapters and the Intel North-Bridge (NB) chip-set in the lab and provide evidence that your code works (These devices will be found on every target—some targets may have additional devices as well.)
5. Write a PCI probing function to determine the configuration of the NB, including latency timing and the arbitration control. Finally, determine whether the NB will allow memory access by masters other than the main CPU. Demonstrate that your probe works and describe your probe output. Finally, describe how the NB/SB interface in PCI allows for shared interrupts (PCI and IRQ).

## CHAPTER REFERENCES

[Shanley99] Shanley, Tom, and Don Anderson, *PCI System Architecture,* 4th ed. Addison-Wesley, 1999.

# 9 Debugging Components

## INTRODUCTION

Debug ideally includes hardware and software support in the form of monitoring and control so that errant conditions can be reproduced and analyzed so corrective action can be taken to eliminate bugs. Corrections can be made with software or hardware modification to eliminate the errant behavior detected by a debug monitor. A debug monitor is any code or hardware state machine or interface that allows the user to observe errant, unexpected deviations from designed behavior. To detect and define a bug, the system designer must first have a clear concept of correct behavior from a design specification. In this chapter, common debug software and hardware mechanisms, both built-in to the system and external, are reviewed. It would be impossible to include a comprehensive review in one chapter, so the goal of this chapter is to arm you with knowledge so that at the very least, you'll know what questions to ask and how to further research debug methods.

## EXCEPTIONS

Code is often developed as a set of functions to be called by other code modules or applications in a larger system. When code is designed for use by others, it's important to program defensively so that a function does not assume that it will be passed only expected arguments. Likewise, for applications calling library functions that are perhaps linked in as object code and not verified at the source level, it's possible that this code might perform an illegal instruction, attempt to decode a bad address, overflow its stack, or any number of other errant behaviors. In general, mature code bases will not suffer from such shortcomings, but during development, integration, and test, it may be useful to use exception handling and program asserts to isolate errant functions and code blocks.

One of the simplest and most common mistakes that can cause almost every microprocessor to generate an exception is to divide-by-zero. Division by zero causes an overflow and an undefined arithmetic result. In VxWorks, the kernel includes default exception handling, which suspends the task that caused the exception and prints out debug information to assist with locating the cause of the exception.

For example, the following code will cause the divide-by-zero exception on the VxWorks simulator and if compiled and run on Linux. Nobody would ever write code this obviously wrong; however, if the denominator is computed and data driven, division by zero might not be so obvious. For the purpose of understanding how exceptions work, it's also one of the easiest to force on all processors.

```
#include "stdio.h"

int diverror(void)
{
    return 1/0;
}
```

Run on the VxWorks simulator, the output to the windshell indicates that the task just spawned caused an exception and the suspended task ID noted along with the program counter and the target status register.

```
-> sp diverror
task spawned: id = 10f0f60, name = s1u1
value = 17764192 = 0x10f0f60
->
Exception number 0: Task: 0x10f0f60 (s1u1)
```

```
Divide Error
Program Counter:            0x00f45368
Status Register:            0x00010246


408a0b   _vxTaskEntry    +47 : _diverror (0, 0, 0, 0, 0, 0, 0, 0, 0, 0)
```

Probing a little deeper with the Tornado tools, dumping the task states in the windshell reveals that the created task from the sp command has been put into the suspended state by the VxWorks scheduler:

```
-> i
  NAME          ENTRY        TID    PRI   STATUS        PC         SP

tExcTask      _excTask     1108de0   0 PEND          408358   1108ce0
tLogTask      _logTask     11032b0   0 PEND          408358   11031b0
tWdbTask      _wdbTask     10fe668   3 READY         408358   10fe518
s1u1          _diverror    10f0f60 100 SUSPEND       f45368   10f0ed8
value = 0 = 0x0
```

Dumping exception debug information to the windshell or console along with suspension of the offending task is the default handling of a microprocessor exception for VxWorks. This is often sufficient during development; however, an application might want to supply specific exception handling. The VxWorks kernel therefore includes a callback that can be registered with the kernel so that the application can provide custom handling or recovery from exceptions. The divide-by-zero code is now modified to include an exception hook:

```
#include "stdio.h"
#include "excLib.h"

void myExcHook(int taskID, int excVec, void *excStackFrame)
{
    logMsg("Exception Trap for task 0x%x, excVec=0x%x\n", taskID,
excVec);
}
int diverror(void)
{
    excHookAdd(myExcHook);
    return 1/0;
}
```

The added application-specific handler is called in addition to the default handling. The setout utility is used to ensure that the handler logMsg is output to the windshell.

```
-> setout
Original setup: sin=3, sout=3, serr=3
All being remapped to your virtual terminal...
You should see this message now!!!
0x10f92b8 (t1): You should also see this logMsg
value = 32 = 0x20 = ' ' = __major_os_version__ + 0x1c
-> testExc
choose an exception [b=bus error, d=divide by zero]:
Generating divide by zero exception


Exception number 0: Task: 0x10f92b8 (t2)


Divide Error
Program Counter:            0x00f4510e
Status Register:            0x00010206

408a0b   _vxTaskEntry   +47 : 423df8 (110e450, 0, 0, 0, 0, 0, 0, 0, 0,
0)
423e51   _wdbFuncCallLibInit+ad : _testExc (0, 0, 0, 0, 0, 0, 0, 0, 0,
0)
f452eb   _testExc       +f3 : _diverror (0)
0x10f92b8 (t2): Trapped an Exception for task 0x10f92b8
value = 0 = 0x0


-> i
  NAME        ENTRY        TID    PRI   STATUS      PC        SP

tExcTask    _excTask     1108de0  0 PEND        408358    1108ce0
tLogTask    _logTask     11032b0  0 PEND        408358    11031b0
tWdbTask    _wdbTask     10fe668  3 READY       408358    10fe518
t2          0x423df8     10f92b8  4 SUSPEND     f4510e    10f91c0
value = 0 = 0x0
```

Similarly in Linux, if the same code with divide by zero is executed, the process is terminated and a core is dumped to the file system for debug. Before looking into Linux, first run the same example code and now generate a bus error. After this second run, the task listing using the i command shows that the task for the divide-by-zero run and the task for the bus error are both now in a suspended state.

```
-> testExc
choose an exception [b=bus error, d=divide by zero]:
Generating bus error segfault exception

Exception number 0: Task: 0x10f0f60 (t3)

General Protection Fault
Program Counter:          0x00f4512d
Status Register:          0x00010206

408a0b    _vxTaskEntry    +47 : 423df8 (110d948, 0, 0, 0, 0, 0, 0, 0, 0,
0)
423e51    _wdbFuncCallLibInit+ad : _testExc (0, 0, 0, 0, 0, 0, 0, 0, 0,
0)
f452cf    _testExc        +d7 : _buserror (ffffffff)
0x10f0f60 (t3): Trapped an Exception for task 0x10f0f60
value = 0 = 0x0
-> i
  NAME          ENTRY         TID    PRI    STATUS      PC        SP

tExcTask     _excTask       1108de0    0 PEND          408358    1108ce0
tLogTask     _logTask       11032b0    0 PEND          408358    11031b0
tWdbTask     _wdbTask       10fe668    3 READY         408358    10fe518
t2           0x423df8       10f92b8    4 SUSPEND       f4510e    10f91c0
t3           0x423df8       10f0f60    4 SUSPEND       f4512d    10f0e88
value = 0 = 0x0
```

The default handling in Linux or VxWorks is essentially the same if an exception is raised by errant code executing in a task or Linux process context. The default exception handling is much more drastic for code executing in VxWorks kernel or ISR context. In VxWorks, the default handling reboots the target. Looking now at output on the simulator console, the default VxWorks exception handler also provides indication of the exception here as well.

```
        VxWorks

Copyright 1984-2002  Wind River Systems, Inc.

         CPU: VxSim for Windows
   Runtime Name: VxWorks
Runtime Version: 5.5
   BSP version: 1.2/1
        Created: Jul 20 2002, 19:23:59
```

```
        WDB Comm Type: WDB_COMM_PIPE
                WDB: Ready.


Exception !
 Vector 0 : Divide Error          Program Counter : 0x00f4510e
 Status Register : 0x00010206
Exception !
 Vector 13 : General Protection Fault          Program Counter :
0x00f4512d
 Status Register : 0x00010206
```

On Linux, the same code causes a core dump when the shell is configured to allow this.

To ensure that core dumps are allowed, use the built-in shell command unlimit after compiling the example exception-generating code provided on the CD-ROM.

```
[siewerts@localhost ex]$ tcsh
[siewerts@localhost ~/ex]$ gcc -g gen_exception.c -o genexc
[siewerts@localhost ~/ex]$ unlimit
```

Now, run the genexc executable to generate a segmentation fault by dereferencing a bad pointer:

```
[siewerts@localhost ~/ex]$ ./genexc
choose an exception [b=bus error, d=divide by zero]:b
Generating bus error segfault exception
Segmentation fault (core dumped)


On a Linux system, the core file dumped can be loaded and debugged with
gdb. This allows for examination of the stack trace and identifies the
offending line of C code: [siewerts@localhost ~/ex]$ gdb genexc
core.13472
GNU gdb Red Hat Linux (5.2.1-4)
Copyright 2002 Free Software Foundation, Inc.
GDB is free software, covered by the GNU General Public License, and
you are
welcome to change it and/or distribute copies of it under certain
conditions.
Type "show copying" to see the conditions.
There is absolutely no warranty for GDB.  Type "show warranty" for
details.
This GDB was configured as "i386-redhat-linux"...
Core was generated by `./genexc'.
```

```
Program terminated with signal 11, Segmentation fault.
Reading symbols from /lib/i686/libc.so.6...done.
Loaded symbols for /lib/i686/libc.so.6
Reading symbols from /lib/ld-linux.so.2...done.
Loaded symbols for /lib/ld-linux.so.2
#0  0x0804837f in buserror (badPtr=0xffffffff) at gen_exception.c:38
38          someData = *badPtr;
(gdb) bt
#0  0x0804837f in buserror (badPtr=0xffffffff) at gen_exception.c:38
#1  0x080483d8 in main () at gen_exception.c:56
#2  0x420158d4 in __libc_start_main () from /lib/i686/libc.so.6
(gdb)
```

Run the code again and this time generate the divide-by-zero exception. Now load the core file dumped for the divide-by-zero exception generator, and, once again, the stack trace and offending line of code can be examined with gdb.

```
[siewerts@localhost ~/ex]$ ./genexc
choose and exception [b=bus error, d=divide by zero]:d
Generating divide by zero exception
Floating exception (core dumped)
[siewerts@localhost ~/ex]$

siewerts@localhost ~/ex]$ gdb genexc core.13473
GNU gdb Red Hat Linux (5.2.1-4)
Copyright 2002 Free Software Foundation, Inc.
GDB is free software, covered by the GNU General Public License, and
you are
welcome to change it and/or distribute copies of it under certain
conditions.
Type "show copying" to see the conditions.
There is absolutely no warranty for GDB.  Type "show warranty" for
details.
This GDB was configured as "i386-redhat-linux"...
Core was generated by `./genexc'.
Program terminated with signal 8, Arithmetic exception.
Reading symbols from /lib/i686/libc.so.6...done.
Loaded symbols for /lib/i686/libc.so.6
Reading symbols from /lib/ld-linux.so.2...done.
Loaded symbols for /lib/ld-linux.so.2
#0  0x08048368 in diverror (arg=0) at gen_exception.c:31
31          someNum = 1/arg;
(gdb)
```

So, both Linux and VxWorks provide stack trace information and the location in code where the exception is raised. When an exception occurs, it's easiest to single-step debug the code to determine why the code is causing the exception. In the Tornado environment, this is most easily done using the Cross Wind debug tool as shown in Figure 9.1. The "Single Step Debugging" section of this chapter will cover exactly how to start and use the single-step debugger in Tornado.

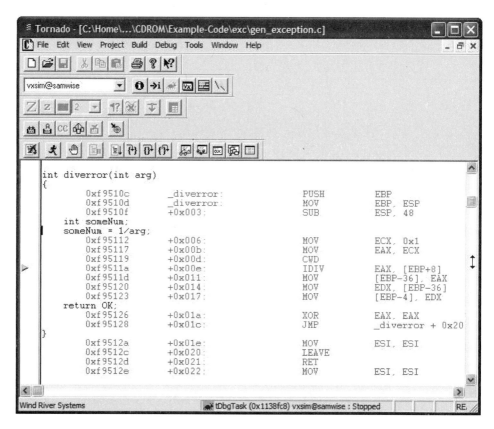

**FIGURE 9.1** Using Tornado Cross Wind to Analyze Exception.

Likewise, in Linux, a graphical single-step debugger will make it easier to determine why code is raising an exception. Numerous graphical debuggers are available for Linux and most run on top of the gdb command-line debugger. Figure 9.2 shows usage of the KDE environment Kdbg graphical debugger.

Again, the "Single-Step Debugging" section of this chapter covers exactly how to start and use the single-step debugger in the Linux KDE environment.

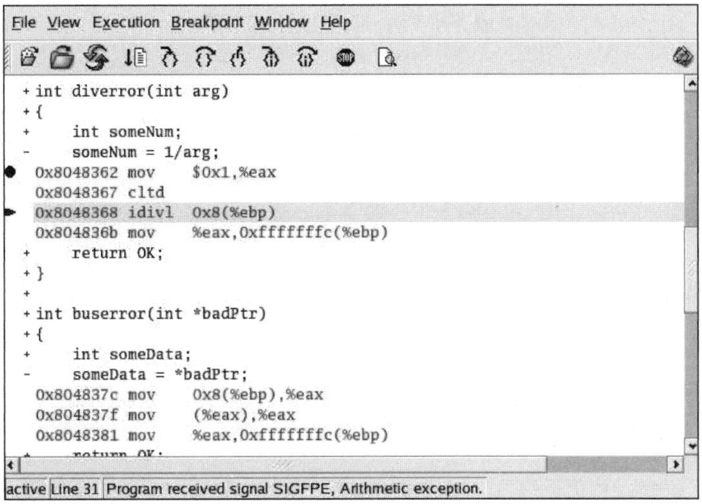

**FIGURE 9.2** Using KDE Development Kdbg to Analyze an Exception.

## ASSERT

Preventing exceptions rather than handling them is more proactive. Certainly code can check for conditions that would cause an exception and verify arguments to avoid the possibility of task suspension or target reboot. The standard method for this type of defensive programming is to include assert checks in code to isolate errant conditions for debug. In C code, pointers are often passed to functions for efficiency. A caller of a function might not pass a valid pointer, and this can cause an exception or errant behavior in the called function that can be difficult to trace back to the bad pointer. The following code demonstrates this with a very simple example that first passes printAddr a valid pointer and then passes a NULL pointer:

```c
#include "stdio.h"
#include "stdlib.h"
#include "assert.h"

char validPtr[] = "some string";
char *invalidPtr = (char *)0;

void printAddr(void *ptr)
{
    /* will assert and exit program here if pointer is NULL */
    assert((int)ptr);
```

```
    printf("ptr = 0x%08x\n", ptr);
}

int main(void)
{
    printAddr(validPtr);
    printAddr(invalidPtr);

    return OK;
}
```

Running the preceding code on a VxWorks target or VxSim produces the following output:

```
ptr = 0x00f453ac
Assertion failed: (int)ptr, file C:/Home/Sam/Book/CDROM/Example-
Code/assert.c, line 11
```

Use of assert checking in code makes the error in the calling arguments obvious and avoids confusion. Without the assert check on the pointer parameter, it might seem that there is an error in the function called when it finally attempts to dereference or otherwise use the pointer, which would most likely cause an exception. The assert check is also supported in Linux.

## CHECKING RETURN CODES

Any RTOS such as VxWorks provides a significant API with mechanisms for task control, inter-task communication, synchronization, memory management, and device interfacing. Calls into the API can fail for numerous reasons:

- Failure to meet preconditions by the application (e.g., semTake when semaphore has not been created).
- Kernel resources have been exhausted.
- A bad pointer or argument is passed by the application.
- A timeout occurs on a blocking call.

For this reason, application code should always check return codes and handle failures with warnings logged or sent to console or assert. Not checking return codes often leads to difficult-to-figure-out failures beyond the initial obvious API call failure.

In VxWorks the task variable errno always indicates the last error encountered during an API call. A call to perror() in VxWorks will also print more useful debug information when an API call returns a bad code.

## SINGLE-STEP DEBUGGING

Single-step debugging is often the most powerful way to analyze and understand both software algorithmic errors, hardware/software interfaces errors, and sometimes even hardware design flaws. Single-step debugging can be done at three different levels in most embedded systems:

- Task- or process-level debugging
- System- or kernel-level debugging
- Processor-level debugging

Most application developers are accustomed to task- or process-level debugging. In this case, a process or task is started in VxWorks or Linux and most often a breakpoint is set for the entry point of the task or process. This method allows the user to debug only one thread of execution at a time. Often, this is sufficient control because either the application being debugged is signally threaded, or if multithreaded, then other threads in the overall application will most often block awaiting synchronizing events (e.g., a semaphore or message) before proceeding. Debugging asynchronous multithreaded applications is much more difficult and requires either system- or kernel-level debugging or processor level using TAP (Test Access Port) hardware tools.

Task-level debugging in VxWorks is simple. Command-line debugging can be performed directly within the windshell. Graphical debugging can be performed using the Tornado tool known as Cross Wind, and then accessed and controlled through a source viewer that displays C code, assembly, or a mixed mode. For embedded systems, debugging is described as cross-debugging because the host system on which the debug interface runs does not have to be the same architecture as the target system being debugged. On the other hand, it certainly can be the same, which might be the case for an embedded Linux system or an embedded VxWorks system running on Intel architecture. Furthermore, the embedded system may not have sufficient I/O interfaces for effective debug. A cross debugging system runs a debug agent on the embedded target and debug source viewing, and command and control is done on a host system. For Tornado, the host tool is Cross Wind and the debug agent is WDB (Wind Debug). The debug agent accepts commands and replies with current target state information when requested.

One of the most basic features of any debugger is the capability to set breakpoints and to run or single step between them. There are two ways that breakpoints are most often implemented:

■ Hardware breakpoints
■ Software breakpoints

Hardware breakpoints require that the processor include a breakpoint address register, a comparator that determines whether the IP (Instruction Pointer) or PC (Program Counter) matches the requested break address, and a mechanism to raise a debug exception. The debug exception causes a halt in the normal thread of execution, and the debug agent installs a handler so that the user can examine the state of the target at the point of this exception. One important and notable characteristic of hardware breakpoints is that the number is limited to the number of comparator registers provided by the specific processor architecture. Often the limit is only two or at most a half dozen, but it's definitely limited by hardware supporting resources. A significant advantage of hardware breakpoints is that they do not modify the code being debugged at all and are reliable even if memory is modified or errantly corrupted. A processor reset or power cycle is most often the only way they can be cleared.

Software breakpoints are unlimited in number. They are implemented by inserting an instruction into the code segment of the thread of execution being debugged. They modify the code, but only by inserting a single instruction to raise a debug exception at each requested breakpoint. After the debug exception is raised, the debug agent handling of the exception is identical. When the debug agent steps beyond the current breakpoint it must restore the original code it replaced with the debug exception instruction. Software breakpoints have the disadvantage that they can and mostly likely will be lost every time code is reloaded, if memory is errantly corrupted, and when a processor is reset.

Most software debug agents, such as WDB and the GNU debug agent, use software breakpoints due to their flexibility and unlimited number. For task-level debug, the host Cross Wind debug tool requests the WDB debug agent to set a breakpoint in a code segment for a specific task. This allows the debug agent to handle the debug exception and to compare the current task context to the task  being debugged and to suspend that task. Run the example code sequencer that creates two tasks that run and can be calibrated to run for 10 to 20 milliseconds on any target system, and the sequencer releases serviceF10 ever 20 milliseconds and serviceF20 every 50 milliseconds. This uses 90% of the processor cycles while it runs. After the two tasks are running, their state can be observed with the i command to dump all task control blocks.

```
-> i
  NAME          ENTRY         TID      PRI   STATUS       PC         SP

tExcTask        _excTask      1158de0    0  PEND         408358     1158ce0
tLogTask        _logTask      11532b0    0  PEND         408358     11531b0
tWdbTask        _wdbTask      114e668    3  READY        408358     114e518
t1              0x423df8      11492b8    4  DELAY        408358     11491d8
serviceF10      _fib10        1140f60   21  PEND         408358     1140e74
serviceF20      _fib20        113bc08   22  PEND         408358     113bb1c
value = 0 = 0x0
```

The t1 task is the sequencer and most often will be observed in delay between releases of serviceF10 and serviceF20. The two services will most often be observed as pending while they wait for release. The i command is implemented by a request to the tWdbTask (the target agent), so it will be observed as ready (running in VxWorks) because it has to be running to make the observation. Now, start the Cross Wind debugger (usually by clicking on a bug icon), select Attach, and then select serviceF10 and use the i command to dump the TCBs (Task Control Blocks) again. Figure 9.3 shows the Cross Wind debugger now attached to serviceF10.

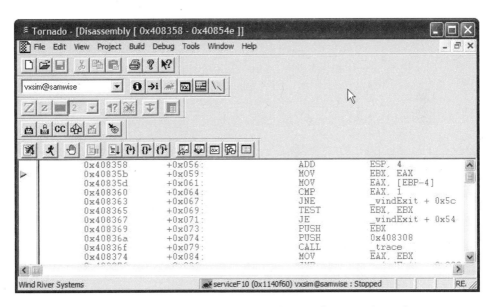

**FIGURE 9.3**   Cross Wind debugger attached asynchronously to running task.

```
-> i
  NAME          ENTRY         TID     PRI   STATUS      PC        SP

tExcTask      _excTask      1158de0   0 PEND        408358   1158ce0
tLogTask      _logTask      11532b0   0 PEND        408358   11531b0
tWdbTask      _wdbTask      114e668   3 READY       408358   114e518
t1            0x423df8      11492b8   4 DELAY       408358   11491d8
serviceF10    _fib10        1140f60  21 SUSPEND     408358   1140e74
serviceF20    _fib20        113bc08  22 PEND        408358   113bb1c
value = 0 = 0x0
```

The serviceF10 task has been suspended by the WDB debug agent. Now the debug agent can be queried for any information on the state of this task and code executing in the context of this task that the user wants to see. It can be single-stepped from this point as well. When this is done, most often the running task is caught by the attach somewhere in kernel code, and if the user does not have full kernel source, a disassembly is displayed along with a single-step prompt.

Asynchronously attaching and single stepping a running task is often not helpful to the user debugging the code being scheduled by the kernel and which calls into the kernel API. Instead of attaching to a running task, now start the same sequencer from the debugger (first stop the debugger and restart the target or simulator to shut down the running tasks). Now, restart the debugger after the target or simulator is running again and from the Debug menu, select Run. Start Sequencer from the Run dialog box and select Break at Entry. Note that arguments to the function entry point can also be passed in from the debugger tool if needed. At the windshell, output will indicate that the task has been started and that it has hit a breakpoint immediately on entry.

```
->
Break at 0x00f940e7: _Sequencer + 0x3         Task: 0x11492b8 (tDbgTask)

-> i
  NAME          ENTRY         TID     PRI   STATUS      PC        SP

tExcTask      _excTask      1158de0    0 PEND       408358   1158ce0
tLogTask      _logTask      11532b0    0 PEND       408358   11531b0
tWdbTask      _wdbTask      114e668    3 READY      408358   114e518
tDbgTask      _Sequencer    11492b8  100 SUSPEND     f940e7   1149244
value = 0 = 0x0
```

Note the debug agent wrapper task tDbgTask with the entry point started from the debugger is in the suspend state. At the same time, a viewer window with a source-level debug prompt appears in Tornado as shown in Figure 9.4.

**FIGURE 9.4** Cross Wind source-level debugging.

In general, a C compiler generates numerous machine code instructions for each line of C code, and the source-level debugger can view the current IP (Instruction Pointer) location in a mixed C source and disassembled view as shown in Figure 9.5. This view can be very useful if the C compiler is generating bad code (not likely, but possible) or if it's generating inefficient code (more likely).

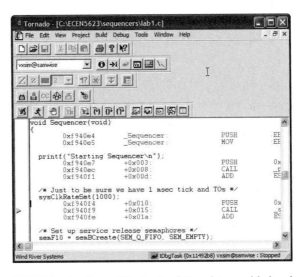

**FIGURE 9.5** Cross Wind mixed C and Assembly level debugging.

Process-level debug in Linux is often the equivalent of task-level debug in VxWorks. A Linux process can be multithreaded with POSIX threads, for example, in which case the pthread is the equivalent of the VxWorks task. One advantage of embedding Linux is that many of the application algorithms can be developed and debugged on the host Linux system without cross debugging. Cross debugging is only required when the bug is related to how the code specifically executes on the target system. Figure 9.6 shows the use of Kdbg to debug the multithreaded priority inversion demo code found on the CD-ROM.

ON THE CD

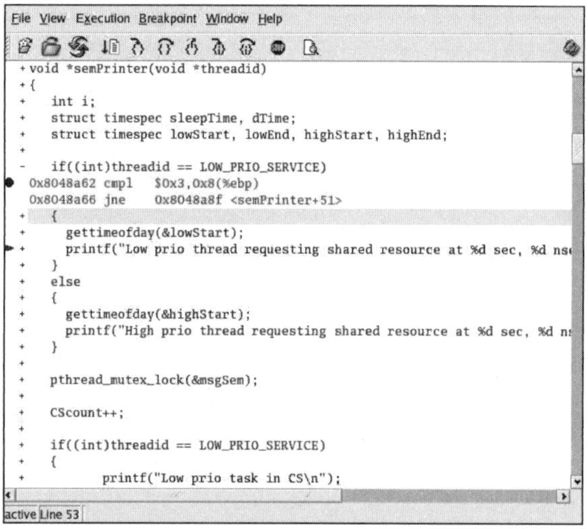

**FIGURE 9.6**  Kdbg mixed C and Assembly source-level debugging.

The example pthread code can be built using gcc linking in the pthread library and using the -g option to include debug symbols.

```
[siewerts@localhost ~/ex]$ gcc -g pthread.c -lpthread -o pthread
```

The Kdbg application can load the pthread executable and will find the C source based upon the ELF (Executable and Linking Format) information, which includes all symbols as well as the source code path.

If an embedded Linux application needs to be debugged, it can be remotely debugged with gdb by connecting to gdb remotely over a serial or TCP connection over Ethernet. To use gdb remotely, you must link debugging stubs with your embedded application and then use gdb target remote /dev/ttyS0, for example, to connect over serial to the embedded application for debug.

System- or kernel-level debugging rather than attaching to a single task or process is tricky because both the Linux and the VxWorks systems rely upon basic services (or daemons in Linux) to maintain communication with the user. For example, in VxWorks, the WDB and shell tasks must run along with the net task to maintain communication between the Tornado host tools and the target. Similarly, Linux communicates through shells or a windowing system. In VxWorks, system-level debug requires a special kernel build and the use of a polling driver interface for communication. Likewise, Linux requires use of kdb the kernel debugger. The advantage of system-level debug is that it allows for single stepping of the entire kernel and all applications scheduled by it. System- or kernel-level debugging is most often used by Linux driver, kernel module, and kernel featuredevelopers.

Instead of system-level debug, a hardware debug method can be used to single step the entire processor rather than using the system-debug software method. This has an advantage in that no services are needed from the software because communication is provided by hardware. The JTAG (Joint Test Application Group) IEEE standard has evolved to include debug functionality through the TAP (Test Access Port). A *JTAG* is a device that interfaces to a host via parallel port, USB, or Ethernet to command and control the TAP hardware that allows for processor single stepping, register loads and dumps, memory loads and dumps, and even download of programs for services such as flashing images into nonvolatile memory. Figure 9.7 shows the Wind River VisionCLICK JTAG debugger running on a laptop connected to a PowerPC evaluation board with a parallel port host interface and a JTAG BDM (Background Debug Mode) connection to the PowerPC TAP.

**FIGURE 9.7** Typical JTAG debugger setup.

The JTAG standard includes external clocking of the device under test (most often the processor for debug), the capability to clock test data in or out of the TAP, and reset control. The TAP provides basic decoding of address, data, and control so that any addressable memory within the processor can be read or written. A JTAG debugger can be used, including extended versions of gdb, so that code segments loaded via JTAG into memory of nonvolatile memory can be single stepped. Although JTAG debugging requires additional hardware tools, it has powerful capability. For example, code can be boot-strapped onto a system that has no current boot code. Bringing up new hardware and downloading, testing, and flashing initial boot code that runs from a system reset vector is a firmware development task. By definition, firmware is software that runs out of nonvolatile memory, most often to boot a device and make it useable by higher-level software, often loaded by the firmware. The JTAG requires no target software support and provides an interface so that initial boot-strap code can be loaded, debugged, and eventually programmed into a nonvolatile boot memory device. After the platform has been boot-strapped with JTAG, a more traditional debug agent such as WDB can be used instead for system-level or task-level debug.

## KERNEL SCHEDULER TRACES

Kernel scheduler tracing is a critical debug method for real-time systems. Real-time services run either as ISRs or as priority preemptive scheduled tasks. In VxWorks, this is the default scheduling mechanism for all tasks. In Linux, the POSIX thread FIFO scheduling policy must be used for system scope threads. Process scope POSIX threads are only run when the process that owns them is run. System scope POSIX threads, such as VxWorks tasks, are run according to preemptive priorities by the kernel. The kernel itself must also be preemptable for deterministic real-time scheduling. The Linux kernel can be patched to make it preemptable like the VxWorks Wind kernel. Given a preemptable priority-driven multiservice system as just described, RM theory and policy can be used to assign priorities to services and to determine whether the system is feasible. A system is feasible if none of the services will miss their required deadlines. Theory is an excellent starting point, but the theoretical feasibility of a system should be verified and any deadline misses observed must be debugged.

The Tornado/VxWorks development framework includes a tool called WindView that provides an event trace of all tasks (services) and ISRs (services) in the system along with synchronous and asynchronous events. A semaphore give and take is shown as a synchronous event on the context trace along with asynchronous events such as interrupts, exceptions, and timeouts. Figure 9.8 shows a WindView trace for an NTSC video capture driver, which transports frames to an external viewing application over TCP.

In Figure 9.8, the 1 millisecond interval timer interrupt can be seen as INT0. Exactly 33 of these occur between the two starts of the tBtvid task releases. The

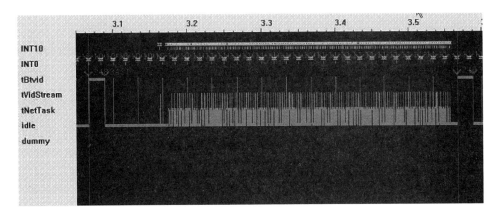

**FIGURE 9.8**    WindView trace for video capture and transport.

video encoder frame rate for this trace was 30 fps. The INT10 interrupt is associated with the tNetTask and is the Network Interface Card (NIC) DMA completion interrupt. The bulk of the service activity between frame acquisitions are releases of the streaming task and the TCP/IP network task. Idle time indicates that the processor is not fully utilized, and in a WindView trace, this is time that the Wind kernel dispatcher was spinning and waiting for something to dispatch from the ready queue by priority. Figure 9.9 shows two synthetic load services (each service computes the Fibonacci sequence): $S_1$ runs for 10 msec every 20 msecs, and $S_2$ runs for 20 msecs every 50 msecs.

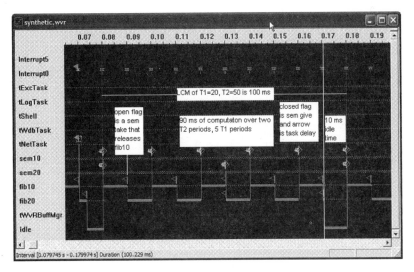

**FIGURE 9.9**    WindView trace for synthetic service loading.

On this trace, the semaphores used to sequence and release the two services, fib10 and fib20, can be seen along with two sequencers, sem10 and sem20, which simply delay and give semaphores to release fib10 and fib20. The task delays are indicated by the right-pointing arrows and the hashed trace. The solid traces for fib10 and fib20 are processor execution time, and the dotted trace indicates time where some other task or interrupt is running, or idle time. This particular two-service scenario uses 90% of the available processor cycles over a 100 msec period. The 100 msec period is the LCM (Least Common Multiple) of the two release periods $T_1$=20 and $T_2$=50 msecs. The expected execution times are $C_1$=10 msecs and $C_2$=20 msecs for $S_1$ and $S_2$. From this trace, it's clear that the releases of the services are well synchronized, and the execution times are accurate and as expected. Time-stamping on the trace is done using architecture-specific hardware timers, such as the interval timer, or on the Pentium®, the TSC (Time Stamp Counter), which is as accurate as the processor cycle rate. In general, timestamping is accurate to a microsecond or less when supported by a hardware timestamp driver.

Scheduler traces of tasks and kernel events such as WindView are clearly very illuminating when debugging real-time systems. Situations like services overrunning deadlines are made obvious and allow the debugger to zero in on problematic sequences and perhaps better synchronize services. WindView can also be very helpful when services simply run too long and must be tuned to improve efficiency. The runtime of each release can be clearly observed. Using a function call, wvEvent, in application code, the trace can be further annotated with the chevron indicators and counts shown previously in Figure 9.8. These application event indicators can be used for events such as frame counts or anything that is useful for tracing application-level events. Although WindView is clearly useful, a frequent concern is how intrusive all this tracing is to the execution of application services.

WindView is a tracing mechanism that involves software in-circuit rather than hardware in-circuit to collect the trace data. SWIC (Software In-Circuit) methods are advantageous because they don't require electrical probing like Logic Analyzers (LAs), no built-in logic on processor chips, and can be added to systems in the field and even remotely accessed. The author worked on a project where operators of a space telescope have the option of turning on WindView collection and dumping a trace back to Earth over the NASA Deep Space Network—hopefully this will never be needed. To understand how intrusive SWIC methods such as WindView are, you need to understand the event instrumentation and the trace output. The least intrusive way to collect trace data is to buffer the trace records in memory (typically bit-encoded 32-bit words or cache-line-sized records). Most processors have posted write-buffer interfaces to memory that have significant throughput bandwidth. Looking more closely at the traces in Figures 9.8 and 9.9 earlier in the chapter, it's clear that events occur at the rate of milliseconds on the 200 MHz processor the traces were taken on. In general, if the trace is of events that occur every 1 million or more processor cycles as they do here, and the trace writes to memory take one write-back cycle, the trace output loading on the processor is very low. The instrumentation to detect events in the Wind kernel requires built-in logic in the kernel itself. The instrumentation requires logical tests. Overall, each event trace point might take 10 to 100 processor cycles every 1 million cycles—a very low additional loading to the processor for tracing. For low load tracing, it's critical that the trace be buffered to memory. After collecting trace data, the full trace should be dumped only after all collection is done and during nonreal-time operation or slowly during slack time. Dumping a trace buffer can be very intrusive and significant care should be taken on how and when this is done. In all traces shown in this chapter, dumping was done after collection by my request using the WindView host tools.

Building trace instrumentation into the Wind kernel is simple. The Tornado configuration tool can be used to specify how the WindView instrumentation is built into the VxWorks kernel, where and how much trace data is buffered, and how timestamping is done. Figure 9.10 shows usage of the Tornado kernel configuration tool and specifically WindView instrumentation, download, and timestamping options for the VxWorks build.

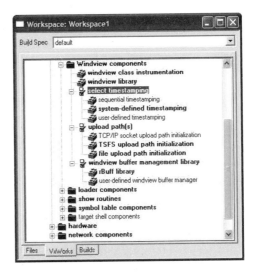

**FIGURE 9.10**    Adding WindView kernel instrumentation.

Linux can be traced using a tool called the Linux Trace Toolkit, which is very similar to WindView. The operation is a bit different, but the end result is the same: a SWIC trace of kernel and system events, including application services. Like VxWorks, to use LTT, you must patch and build a custom Linux kernel with

LTT instrumentation. The details of LTT usage are well covered by the maintainers of LTT and by *Linux Device Drivers* [Corbet05] and *Building Embedded Linux Systems* [Yaghmour03]. Note that SWIC tracing can be easily built into most any system by placing memory writes with efficient encoded trace records into the kernel scheduler. Much of the work is related to dumping the trace buffer and post processing it for analysis. Often placing the instrumentation in the kernel is very straightforward.

# TEST ACCESS PORTS

The IEEE 1149.1 standard for JTAG was originally designed for boundary scan to ensure that devices on a digital electronic board assembly were all properly connected. Designed primarily for factory verification, the interface includes test data in and test data out signals so that bit sequences can be shifted into and out of a chain of devices under test. An expected test data output sequence can be verified for a test data input sequence. The interface also includes a clock input and reset. Eventually, microprocessor and firmware developers determined that JTAG could be extended with the TAP interface. The TAP allows a JTAG to send bit patterns through the scan chain and also allows the JTAG user to command a processor, single step it, load registers and memory, download code, and dump registers and memory out so that commands and data can be sent to the device under test. A processor with a TAP can be fully clocked and controlled by a JTAG device, which allows the user to boot-strap it into operation right out of the hardware reset logic.

From the basic JTAG functionality, external control of microprocessors for firmware development has continued to evolve. Multiprocessor systems on a single chip can also be controlled by a single JTAG when they are placed on a common boundary scan chain. The TAP allows for selection of one of the processors with bypass logic in the chain so that processors not under JTAG control can forward commands and data. More on-chip features to support JTAG have evolved and are often referred to as on-chip debug, yet the basic command and control of these additional features is still through the basic JTAG signal interface. Before JTAG, firmware was developed for new hardware systems with a "burn and learn" approach where EEPROM devices were externally programmed and socketed into the new system to provide nonvolatile boot code to execute from the processor reset vector. Typically, the EEPROM was programmed to first initialize a serial port to write out some confirming "hello world" data, blink an LED, and initialize basic components such as memory. If the EEPROM program didn't work, the firmware programmer would try again, repeating the process until progress was made.

After a PROM program was developed for a new processor board, most often the program was provided as a PROM monitor to make things easier for software developers. PROM monitors would provide basic code download features, memory dumps, disassembly of code segments, and diagnostic tests for hardware components on the system board. The PROM monitor was a common starting point for developing more sophisticated boot code and firmware to provide platform services for software.

Today, most systems are boot-strapped with JTAG rather than "burn and learn" or PROM monitors. The capability of JTAG and on-chip debug has progressed so much that, for example, the entire Tornado/VxWorks tool system can be run over JTAG, including WindView. This allows firmware and software developers to bring up new hardware systems rapidly, most often the same day that hardware arrives back from fabrication. The history of this evolution from burn and learn to PROM monitors to use of JTAG and more advanced on-chip debug is summarized well by Craig A. Haller of Macraigor Systems [Zen]:

> First there was the "crash and burn" method of debugging. . . . After some time, the idea of a hardware single step was implemented. . . . At some point in history, someone (and after reading this I will get lots of email claiming credit) had the idea of a debugger monitor (aka ROM monitor). . . . Similar in concept to the ROM emulator, the next major breakthrough in debugging was the user friendly in-circuit emulator (ICE). . . . The latest addition to the debugger arsenal is on-chip debugging (OCD). . . . Some processors enhance their OCD with other resources truly creating complete on-chip debuggers. IBM's 4xx PowerPC family of embedded processors have a seven wire interface ("RISCTrace") in addition to the OCD ("RISCWatch") that allow for a complete trace of the processor's execution.

The OCD that Craig Haller describes is a combination of JTAG with a trace port, which approximates the capability of an ICE. The ICE traditionally included a chip bond-out interface so that the ICE could monitor all pin I/O signals to the DUT (Device Under Test). This was more valuable when most processors interfaced to memory to fetch code and update data without cache, on-chip memory, on-chip busses, and in the case of SoC (System-on-a-Chip), even multiple processor cores on chip. Monitoring external signals when all of the action is on chip makes no sense. So, the ICE has become less widely used and methods of OCD (On-Chip Debug) are expanding to include not only JTAG and trace, but even on-chip ILAs (Internal Logic Analyzers) and signal probe muxes such as the Xilinx Chip Scope monitor. Given the trends with larger and larger levels of integration on a single chip with SoC designs, OCD will continue to expand.

## TRACE PORTS

Simpler microcontrollers and older microprocessors often were integrated into a system using an ICE (In-Circuit Emulator). An ICE includes an interface that is interposed between a processor and the system board and can monitor and control all input and output signals to and from the device. The ICE can therefore track the state of the device under test as long as no internal memory devices other than registers are loaded and stored to an externally visible memory. When on-chip cache emerged as a processor feature, this made a true ICE difficult to implement. Then the ICE had no idea what was being loaded from cache and written back to cache on-chip and could easily lose track of the internal state of the processor being emulated. The emulation provided not only all the features of JTAG TAP, but also full-speed state tracing so that bugs that were only observable running at full speed, and not seen when single stepping, could be understood. This type of hardware or software bug, often due to timing issues or race conditions in code that is not well synchronized, is known as a *Heisenbug*. The name indicates that like the Heisenburg Uncertainty Principle, where a particle's position and momentum can't be simultaneously observed, a Heisenbug can't be single stepped and the faulty logic observed simultaneously. This type of bug is observable only under full-speed conditions and is difficult to isolate and reproduce in a single-step debug mode. An ICE can be invaluable for understanding and correcting a Heisenbug.

Trace ports have emerged as a solution for the cost and complexity of ICE implementation and the ability to debug full-speed execution of software with no intrusion at the software level. WindView is also an approach, but does involve intrusion at the software level. Trace ports use internal hardware monitors to output internal state information on a limited number of dedicated I/O pins from a processor to an external trace acquisition device. For example, the IP can be output from the processor core onto 32 output pins every cycle so that the thread of execution can be traced while a system runs full speed. The trace analysis is done offline after the fact, but collection must occur at the same speed as the execution, and therefore external trace acquisition requires test equipment such as a Logic Analyzer or specialized digital signal capture device. For a full picture of what code is doing in a full-speed trace, the IP must be captured along with data address and data value vectors on the interface unit between the processor core and the memory system, including cache. This is a significant number of output pins. Most often, trace ports abbreviate information to reduce trace port pin count. For example, a trace port might include the IP only (no data or address information) and furthermore compress the IP output to 8 bits. The 32-bit IP can be compressed down to 8 bits by including built-in trace logic that outputs only relative offsets from an initial four-cycle output of the IP at the start of the trace. Most often, code branches locally in loops or in decision logic rather than making absolute 32-bit address branches. If the code does take a 32-bit address branch, then the internal logic can indicate this so that the external trace capture system can obtain the new IP over five or more core cycles.

Trace ports can be invaluable for difficult bugs observable only at full-speed operation. However, a trace port is expensive, complicated, and not easy to decode and use because it requires external logic analysis equipment. As a result, internal trace buffers are being designed into most processor cores today. The internal trace buffer stores a limited number of internal state vectors, including IP, address, and data vectors, by a hardware collection state machine into a buffer that can be dumped. Trace buffers or trace registers (often the buffer is seen as a single register that can be read repeatedly to dump the full contents) are typically set up to continuously trace and stop trace on exception or on a software assert. This allows the debugger to capture data up to a crash point for a bug that is only observable during extended runtimes at full speed. This post-mortem debug tool allows a system that crashed to be analyzed to determine what led to the crash. For extensive debug, some trace buffers are essentially built-in LAs that allow software to program them to collect a range of internally traceable data, including bus cycle data, the IP, address, data vector, and register data, to emulate the capability that hardware/software debuggers had when all these signals could be externally probed with an LA.

## POWER-ON SELF TEST AND DIAGNOSTICS

An important part of the boot firmware is the ability to test all hardware interfaces to the processor. Boot code can implement a series of diagnostic tests after a power on reset based on a nonvolatile configuration and indicate how far it has advanced in the testing since reset through LEDs, tones, or a record in nonvolatile memory. This process is called POST (Power-On Self Tests) and provides a method for debugging boot failures. If the POST codes are well known, then a hardware failure can be diagnosed and fixed easily. For example, if the POST code indicates that all interfaces are okay, but that memory tests failed, then replacing memory is likely to fix the problem. POST codes are also often output on a bus to memory or an external device, so probing an external bus allows you to capture POST codes and diagnose problems even when the external devices on that bus are not operating correctly. The x86 PC BIOS (Basic Input Output System) has a rich history of POST and POST code output to well-known devices and interfaces so that configuration and external device failures can be readily diagnosed and fixed [POST]. A career can be made writing and understanding BIOS firmware and, for that matter, firmware on any system. A significant part of a firmware engineer's job is simply getting a processor up and cycling monitor and diagnostic code safely so that the system can be more easily used by application programmers.

Describing how diagnostics can be written in general is difficult because the range of peripheral devices a processor might interface to is endless. However, all processors interface to memory, either internal on-chip or external off-chip memory. So, every firmware engineer should be familiar with memory testing. Memory tests include the following:

- Walking 1s test to verify processor to memory data bus interface
- Memory address bus verification
- ECC (Error Correction Circuitry) initialization and test
- Device pattern testing

The walking 1s test ensures that memory devices have been properly wired to the processor bus interface. Byte lanes for wide memory buses could be swapped, and shorts, open circuits, noise, or signal skew could all cause data to be corrupted on the memory interface. A walking 1s test should simply write data to memory with words or arrays of words that match the width of the memory data bus. A memory bus is often 128 bits or wider. Most architectures support load/store multiple or load/store string instructions that allow multiple registers to be written to the bus or read from the bus for aligned data structures. On the PowerPC G4, load/store string instructions can be used to write 128 bits to memory on a 128-bit memory bus with walking 1s to ensure that the interface is fully functional. Memory data buses wider than a single 32 bit will have a bus interface that may coalesce multiple writes to adjacent word addresses, but using the multiword instructions helps ensure that the test uses the full bus width.

ON THE CD
The following code included on the CD-ROM uses structure assignment in C to coax the compiler into generating load/store string instructions with the proper gcc C compiler directives.

```
#include "stdio.h"
#include "assert.h"

/* 4 x 32-bit unsigned words = 128-bit */
typedef struct multiword_s
{
    unsigned int word[4];
} multiword_t;

/* these declarations should be aligned on 128-bit boundary */
const multiword_t test_zero = {{0x0,0x0,0x0,0x0}};
volatile multiword_t test_pattern = {{0x0,0x0,0x0,0x0}};
volatile multiword_t test_location = {{0x0,0x0,0x0,0x0}};
```

```
void assign_multi(void)
{
    test_location = test_pattern;
}


void test_multi(void)
{
    register int i, j;

    for(i=0;i<4;i++)
    {
        test_pattern = test_zero;

        for(j=0;j<32;j++)
        {
            /* walk the 1 up the bits in 128-bit aligned structure */
            test_pattern.word[i] = (0x1 << j);

            /* structure assignment */
            assign_multi();

            /* assert if stored data does not have a bit set */
            assert(test_location.word[i]);

        }
    }
}


int main(void)
{
    test_multi();
}
```

Compiling this code on a Darwin OS PowerPC G4 Macintosh with no particular compiler directives, the assign_multi function code does not use load/store string instructions.

```
Sam-Siewerts-Computer:~ samsiewert$ gcc mw.c -o mw
Sam-Siewerts-Computer:~ samsiewert$ otool -v -t mw > mw.out
```

The otool is a binary utility for Darwin OS that will disassemble object code. The disassembled code for mw.c reveals that the compiler does not normally generate load/store string instructions. The load/store multiple instructions (stmw and

lmw) are used to push and pop the stack. The 128-bit structure assignment load/
store instructions are indicated in bold type.

```
_assign_multi:
00002a70    stmw    r30,0xfff8(r1)
00002a74    stwu    r1,0xffd0(r1)
00002a78    or      r30,r1,r1
00002a7c    mfspr   r0,lr
00002a80    bcl     20,31,0x2a84
00002a84    mfspr   r8,lr
00002a88    mtspr   lr,r0
00002a8c    addis   r9,r8,0x0
00002a90    addi    r9,r9,0x5ac
00002a94    addis   r2,r8,0x0
00002a98    addi    r2,r2,0x59c
00002a9c    lwz     r0,0x0(r2)
00002aa0    lwz     r11,0x4(r2)
00002aa4    lwz     r10,0x8(r2)
00002aa8    lwz     r2,0xc(r2)
00002aac    stw     r0,0x0(r9)
00002ab0    stw     r11,0x4(r9)
00002ab4    stw     r10,0x8(r9)
00002ab8    stw     r2,0xc(r9)
00002abc    lwz     r1,0x0(r1)
00002ac0    lmw     r30,0xfff8(r1)
00002ac4    blr
```

Modifying the compile line a bit to request level-2 optimization and to allow
load/store string code generation and disassembling again the same structure
assignment in C now is done with one lswi and one stswi in place of the four lwz
(load word and zero) and four stw (store word) instructions.

```
Sam-Siewerts-Computer:~ samsiewert$ gcc -O2 -mstring mw.c -o mw
Sam-Siewerts-Computer:~ samsiewert$ otool -v -t mw > mw.out

_assign_multi:
00002b24    mfspr   r0,lr
00002b28    bcl     20,31,0x2b2c
00002b2c    mfspr   r10,lr
00002b30    mtspr   lr,r0
00002b34    addis   r9,r10,0x0
00002b38    addis   r2,r10,0x0
```

```
00002b3c    addi    r9,r9,0x504
00002b40    addi    r2,r2,0x4f4
00002b44    lswi    r5,r2,16
00002b48    stswi    r5,r9,16
00002b4c    blr
```

Instead of coaxing the compiler into the load/store string instructions, the assembly could be written and called from the C. The most important point, however, is that the memory test should test the full bus width and not just one word at a time. The mw.c code has debug output that can be turned on by passing –DDEBUG on the compile line so that the walking 1s test patterns can be observed, and the 128-bit alignment of the multiword structures can be verified. Note that the addresses of the structures are all multiples of 0x10, 16 bytes, or 128 bits. By default, most compilers align structures unless specifically directed not to, but it's still a good idea to verify this. Some of the walking 1s output has been abbreviated here:

```
addr(test_zero) = 0x00002ff0
addr(test_pattern) = 0x00003020
addr(test_location) = 0x00003030


i=0, j=0   mword = 0x00000000000000000000000000000001
i=0, j=1   mword = 0x00000000000000000000000000000002
i=0, j=2   mword = 0x00000000000000000000000000000004
i=0, j=3   mword = 0x00000000000000000000000000000008
...
i=0, j=31  mword = 0x00000000000000000000000080000000

i=1, j=0   mword = 0x00000000000000000000000100000000
i=1, j=1   mword = 0x00000000000000000000000200000000
i=1, j=2   mword = 0x00000000000000000000000400000000
i=1, j=3   mword = 0x00000000000000000000000800000000
...
i=1, j=31  mword = 0x00000000000000008000000000000000

i=2, j=0   mword = 0x00000000000000010000000000000000
i=2, j=1   mword = 0x00000000000000020000000000000000
i=2, j=2   mword = 0x00000000000000040000000000000000
i=2, j=3   mword = 0x00000000000000080000000000000000
...
i=2, j=31  mword = 0x00000000800000000000000000000000
```

```
i=3, j=0   mword = 0x00000001000000000000000000000000
i=3, j=1   mword = 0x00000002000000000000000000000000
i=3, j=2   mword = 0x00000004000000000000000000000000
i=3, j=3   mword = 0x00000008000000000000000000000000
...
i=3, j=31  mword = 0x80000000000000000000000000000000
```

The memory address bus can be tested by storing and retrieving patterns to addresses that are powers of two [Barr99]. By addressing with powers of two, the address tested walks 1s on the address lines. Furthermore, addresses might be aliased either due to a mistake or on purpose if not fully decoded. For example, the same 32-MB memory can be addressed in the range from 0x00000000 to 0x001FFFFFF (0x002000000 bytes) and then again from 0x002000000 to 0x003FFFFFF, and so on. This could be an address decoding error if it's intended that the memory only be mapped once in the first 32 MB of the address space and not aliased at other multiples of 0x002000000. This would happen if the address decoding only included 26 bits rather than 32 bits. Most often a pattern of alternating 1s and 0s is used (0xAA or 0x55) for each byte to ensure that bits can be set to 0 and 1 at all locations. The pattern and antipatterns are operated on bitwise and combined to quickly verify data written and read back. This pattern and antipattern test can be written and read back over the entire memory range for a full device test.

## EXTERNAL TEST EQUIPMENT

Use of external test equipment for debug can be expensive, but also can save countless hours localizing a hardware/software interface bug that might be very difficult to isolate otherwise. Historically, the most common external test equipment used for verifying hardware/software systems included an oscilloscope and a Logic Analyzer. The oscilloscope is used mostly to isolate signaling issues with the hardware, to verify signals, and to tune output signals. The oscilloscope is most useful to the hardware engineer, but from a systems viewpoint, it's valuable in embedded systems for verifying the outermost extents of the system from sensor inputs (analog) to actuator outputs (analog or PWM signals). Figure 9.11 shows the interface between a VxWorks embedded processor system, which captures frames from an NTSC camera, runs an image-processing service that determines where a visual target is in the camera's FOV (Field of View), and then commands tilt/pan servos to center the object in the camera's FOV. The MSO (Mixed Signal Oscilloscope) shown can probe 2 analog and 16 digital sources. Here the MSO is used to examine an NTSC output and verify the 30 fps output rate of the camera.

Examining the NTSC Signal for Thumbnail Camera
(Analog/Digital interface between Processor and Sensor/Actuator Subsystem)

**FIGURE 9.11**  System interfaces for an embedded system.

Likewise, a relatively inexpensive MSO can be used for low-speed, limited-width digital logic analysis as well. Logic analyzers have an advantage over oscilloscopes in that they can observe 16, 32, or more signals at the same time, but only at well-defined logic levels such as TTL ($V_{threshold} = 1.4V$) and CMOS ($V_{threshold} = 2.5V$). The oscilloscope can be used to look at the same channels and to see their analog nature, including noise, rise time, fall time, and overshoot. The MSO has an advantage in that it can display LA output and one or more oscilloscope changes on the same view, allowing for logic analysis with probing of the same signals to examine analog signal issues that might be affecting digital logic.

Using the MSO to analyze an NTSC signal at milliseconds of resolution, the odd and even line raster periods can be seen at half the frame period (frame rate is 30 fps). Figure 9.12 shows the odd and even raster output signals measured with the MSO from a composite output CCTV (Closed Circuit Television) camera. NTSC is interlaced 2:1, so the field rate is 60 fps. The composite signal output from the NTSC camera combines luminance and chrominance. The signal changes based upon the scene that the camera views, but the basic period does not.

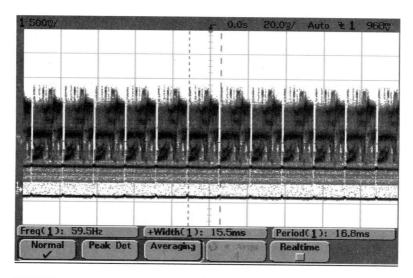

**FIGURE 9.12**  NTSC composite signal odd and even scan lines.

Using the MSO to go to a microsecond resolution, now the individual scan lines within an odd/even raster can be detected. The CCTV cameras have 510 horizontal pixels and 492 vertical pixels, so 246 odd lines are digitized and then 246 even lines. Each line therefore has a period of 67.75 microseconds in theory based upon the frame rate. Figure 9.13 shows each scan line as having a period of 61.7 microseconds. However, the simple calculation does not take into account vertical

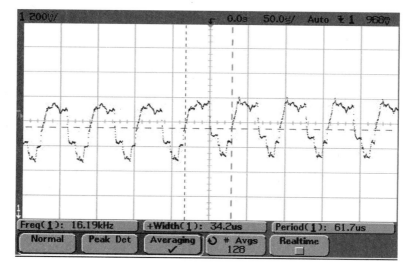

**FIGURE 9.13**  NTSC composite signal individual scan lines.

blank lines (where closed caption is inserted into the NTSC signal) or the latency between the odd and even scans. The measured period for a single scan line is less than the theoretical upper bound on the scan line period and therefore makes sense.

The MSO can also be used to analyze the tilt/pan servo control channels. A hobby servo is not rigorously standardized, but in general the servo circuit and gearing is designed to be controlled by a PWM output with a separation between peaks of 20 to 80 milliseconds and a pulse width that varies between 2 milliseconds and 1 millisecond with servo center near 1.5 milliseconds. Servo characteristics can vary, so each new hobby servo should be individually characterized and the PWM output signal tuned to it for the best results. The spacing between the pulses allows hobby radios to multiplex multiple servo signals into one PWM output, so the receiver can demultiplex to allow for four or more channels on a single RC (Radio Control) frequency. For the applications of hobby servos presented in this book, only one signal is carried on each PWM signal, so the spacing between pulses can vary significantly and has no effect. The pulse width sets the servo position. Figure 9.14 shows an MSO measurement of the PWM signal generated by the NCD 209 2 channel servo control chip.

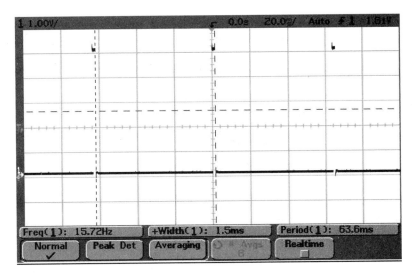

**FIGURE 9.14** NCD 209 servo controller default PWM output.

Note that the pulse width for the servo centering (the default output) is 1.5 milliseconds as expected and that the spacing between pulses is 63 milliseconds.

For the most part, oscilloscopes are used to verify signals and to tune generated output signals, to look for noise issues, crosstalk, or other signal integrity problems in embedded system interfaces to sensors and actuators. Logic analyzers on the other hand are most often used in the digital domain depicted earlier in Figure 9.11. An LA (Logic Analyzer) can be used to debug logic after analog signals have been digitized or before digital signals are output to drive DACs or PWM actuators like servos. Likewise, an LA can be used to debug internal digital logic on a processor board or even to trace events on digital software/hardware interfaces such as buses or GPIO (General Purpose I/O) where the signal level is a common logic level. Probing high-speed logic signals such as those found on a DDR memory bus can be difficult due to speed, skew issues, and complexity in decoding the logic. Probing low-speed logic such as GPIO or simpler memory interfaces such as SRAM is much simpler. High-speed specialized buses such as PCI are often most easily traced using a bus analyzer that is specifically designed to capture and analyze logic signals only on one bus interface. Because the trend in embedded systems is to move external memory on-chip, the most useful probing is GPIO or using external bus analyzers such as a PCI analyzer.

With a bus analyzer or LA used to capture GPIO output, software can be instrumented to emit trace information to the external bus or GPIO pins for analysis. However, given enough memory for a software trace buffer, it's not clear how this is more advantageous than the SWIC WindView style of tracing. In fact, Wind River often describes WindView as a software LA. A write to an external bus or GPIO memory-mapped address can be just as intrusive or more intrusive than posting a write to on-chip or external memory. However, oscilliscopes and LAs continue to be useful in general for diagnosing hardware problems and for tracing software that is not instrumented and software/hardware interactions.

## APPLICATION-LEVEL DEBUGGING

Application-level debugging can be done by single stepping a thread or using WindView. However, for multithread applications, single stepping is sometimes not as useful when the interaction between threads is the problem being examined. WindView is helpful, but only shows kernel events unless it's further instrumented by the addition of wvEvent() calls in the application being debugged. However, wvEvent() has only limited information associated with it, so often programmers resort to printf calls so they can output state information to a console in string format. This can sometimes work okay, but often causes new bugs and can be misleading because printf calls significantly change execution timing. This occurs mostly because printf requires a large amount of code from the C library to execute and also requires potential blocking while data is output to console devices. In VxWorks, printf should also not be called from ISR or kernel context. The better way to debug with output to a console is using logMsg. Logging simply causes a message to be queued that points to a message buffer. The actual string output is completed by a logging service rather than in the calling context. This allows the console I/O to be decoupled from the calling thread of execution, and the caller is only slowed down for the duration of an in-memory write and message enqueue. Furthermore, the priority of the logging service (task) can be controlled and therefore interference to real-time services by `logMsg` debug output is also controlled better than inline `printf` calls.

## SUMMARY

Debugging the software/hardware interface, applications, and complex multiservice interactions can be difficult. Poorly synchronized services can suffer from race conditions. Likewise, poorly designed hardware/software interfaces that do not include synchronizing mechanisms can also have race conditions. In general, separate services should synchronize through semaphores or message queues if they need to interact, and likewise software should synchronize with hardware through interrupts, polling status registers, or through control interfaces. Simple functional software errors can be easily caught through use of parameter checking and assert calls. Hardware diagnostics and POST run by boot firmware can make hardware failures easier to isolate. Good practices can prevent many bugs before they become difficult to diagnose. However, many bugs related to software/hardware integration will still arise; when they do, knowledge of debug monitors, trace, and external test equipment is invaluable.

## EXERCISES

1. Use an oscilloscope to characterize a common sensor or actuator interface. Specifically, use a hobby servo controller such as the NCD 209 and characterize the PWM for a given hobby servo and its limits of operation.
2. Use WindView to analyze the synthetic loading example included on the CD-ROM. By default, it includes two services that use 90% of the processor cycles. Modify this example to create an overload by increasing $S_2$ runtime to 30 milliseconds. Use a WindView trace to prove that this overloads the processor.

ON THE CD

3. Download and set up LTT on a Linux system. Take a trace and explain what you observe.

## CHAPTER REFERENCES

[Barr99] Barr, M., *Programming Embedded Systems in C and C++*. O'Reilly, 1999.

[Corbet05] Corbet, J., A. Rubini, and G. Kroah-Hartman, *Linux Device Drivers.* O'Reilly, 2005.

[GDB] *http://www.gnu.org/software/gdb/documentation/*

[LTT] *http://www.opersys.com/LTT/*

[POST] *http://bioscentral.com/*

[PowerPC] *PowerPC Microprocessor Family: The Programming Environments for 32-bit Microprocessors.* Motorola MPCFPE32B/AD Rev. 1, 1997.

[Yaghmour03] Yaghmour, K., *Building Embedded Linux Systems.* O'Reilly, 2003.

[Zen] *http://www.macraigor.com/zenofbdm.pdf*

# 10 Performance Tuning

## In This Chapter

- Introduction
- Basic Concepts of Drill-Down Tuning
- Hardware-Supported Profiling and Tracing
- Building Performance Monitoring into Software
- Path Length, Efficiency, and Calling Frequency
- Fundamental Optimizations

## INTRODUCTION

The art of performance tuning a system or application is a huge topic that can't be covered completely in this chapter. The chapter covers basic methods and provides enough knowledge for you to pursue a more in-depth understanding of performance tuning on your own with further study. Performance tuning is critical to real-time embedded systems when services are missing deadlines. Otherwise, efficient, high performance execution of services is not necessary, although it can help the designer to save cost, reduce power, and simplify thermal cooling for systems. Fundamentally, a real-time system is operating correctly when it produces the required output (functions) and produces them by a specific deadline relative to request. Early in a project, system designers must size processing based upon understanding of the complexity of service algorithms. After algorithms are implemented and the system is running, services may take longer to run than expected and overrun deadlines. When this happens, there are several options:

- Reduce the complexity of the algorithm
- Reduce the frequency of services
- Increase the execution efficiency of the algorithms with tuning
- Increase the processor throughput by upgrading hardware to run with a faster clock, more bandwidth, more memory, and less latency

From the standpoint of real-time correctness, any of these options is acceptable. Reducing the complexity of the algorithms for services may be an option, but might degrade the overall system quality. For example, software codecs (compression and decompression protocol for a data stream) can provide high rates of compression at the cost of higher algorithmic complexity. If the compression or decompression can't keep up with the desired frame rate, the options include a lower performance codec that is simpler and can be executed at the desired frame rate, or a lower frame rate. The simpler codec that provides less compression will require transport with higher bandwidth.

Often the options of reducing performance (e.g., lower frame rate) or of obtaining more resources (e.g., more bandwidth or increasing processor cycle rate) are not feasible or will not meet the system requirements. An alternative to more resources or performance reduction is performance tuning to optimize the efficiency of service execution. This is easily said and hard to do. Ideally, a system design should not count heavily upon performance tuning to make it feasible, but tuning can save a project that would otherwise not work. From an RM perspective, tuning is just reducing WCET for a software service. Another option is to offload a service or specific functions that the service performs to hardware state machines. Offloading functions can increase overall system concurrency and provide significant speed-up. (Portions of the material on performance tuning presented in this chapter was first published on the IBM developerWorks Web site, © IBM developerWorks. Reprinted with permission.)

## BASIC CONCEPTS OF DRILL-DOWN TUNING

The performance of firmware and software must be tuned to a workload. A *workload* is a sequence of service requests, commands, I/Os, or other quantifiable transactions that exercise the software. Workloads most often are produced by workload generators rather than real-world service provision. Good workloads capture the essential features of real-world workloads and allow for replay or generation of the service requests at a maximum rate so that bottlenecks can be identified in systems. Most workload-generation tools are application- or service domain-specific, for example, compiler benchmarks or I/O subsystem workloads generated by IOmeter, a commonly used disk I/O workload generator.

Characteristics of code segments that most affect performance include the following:

■ Segment path length (instruction count)
■ Segment execution efficiency (cycle count for a given path)
■ Segment calling frequency (in hertz)
■ Execution context (critical path, or error path)

The critical path includes code executed at high frequency for performance evaluation workloads and benchmarks. This is often a small portion of the overall code implemented and may also often fit into L1 instruction or L2 unified cache.

Interrupt-based profiling is the best place to start analyzing software services and deadline overruns. Interrupt profiling requires that the system be run with a well-defined test workload, ideally a workload that stresses the services and is causing deadline overruns. The interrupt profiler samples the IP (Instruction Pointer) or LR (Link Register) to determine location in code on a periodic basis. The LR is used in many architectures because it contains a return from interrupt address, and the samples of where the code was in execution are taken by interrupt. Observing the IP in the sample interrupt routine is of little use for profiling. Often a 1-millisecond sample rate is used. The workload should be repetitive at some frequency; for example, a video frame rate of a specific resolution, a data request rate for a specific transfer size, a digital control loop sensor sample, and control law output rate, or any workload that generates uniform periodic service requests. Multiple workloads can be analyzed, but while profiling, one workload should be run at a time. Mixed workloads are much harder to profile and understand. While a uniform workload is being run, the profiler samples the execution locations, and with asynchronous sampling relative to the workload period (this is important), the profile begins to stabilize and show where in the code most of the time is spent for the given workload.

Where time is spent, which service and function the IP or LR is observed in most often, is a function of three characteristics of the services:

■ Frequency of service execution (or function execution)
■ Instruction count or path length for each service release (or function)
■ Efficiency of code execution in each service release (or function)

Note that the profiling can be mapped to services (tasks), to functions, to lines of C code, or even to individual machine code instructions. Figure 10.1 shows how a profile collected at the level of hits observed at a 32-bit code address can be mined to understand where time is being spent from a very high level down to a machine code instruction.

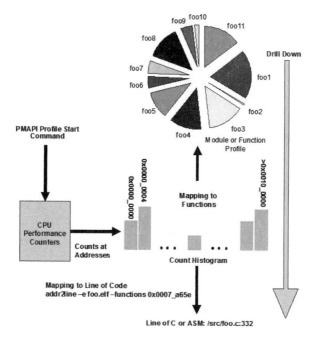

**FIGURE 10.1** Performance profile data mining (hotspot drill-down) concept.

As mentioned in the introduction, frequency and instruction count reduction can solve the performance problem, but at the cost of overall system performance. Ideally, the goal is to identify inefficient code, or *hotspots* as they are often called, and to make modifications so those code blocks execute more efficiently. A cycle-based profile, where periodic sampling of the IP or LR is used, does identify hotspots in general and sets up more detailed analysis for why those code blocks are hot—frequency of execution, number of instructions in the block, or poor execution efficiency. Poor execution efficiency can be the result of stalling a processor pipeline, missing cache, blocking reads from slow devices, misaligned data structures, nonoptimal code generation from a compiler, bad coding practices, inefficient bus usage, and unnecessary computation.

One approach to tuning is to go through code from start to finish and look for efficiency issues, correct them, and try running again. This is tedious. It can work, but the time required, the slow pay-off, and the large number of code changes required all contribute to risk with this approach. A better approach is to identify the hotspots, narrowing the scope of code changes significantly, and then examine this subset of the code for potential optimization. Combined with profiling and hotspot identification, optimization now has a feedback loop so that the value of optimizations can be measured as code is modified. The feedback approach reduces risk (modifying any working code always runs the risk of introducing a bug or destabilizing the code base) and provides focus for the effort. For any tedious effort, it's also affirming to measure progress, and rerunning the profile and observing that less time is spent in a routine after an optimization is welcome feedback. It should be noted that high-level performance measures often show no apparent improvement for localized optimizations. An optimization may lead to a hurry up and wait scenario for that particular function or service where a bottleneck elsewhere in the system masks the improvement.

The overall process being proposed is called *drill-down*. First, hotspots are identified without regard to why they are hot, and then closer analysis determines why specific sections of service code or the system are rate limiting. This initial level of analysis is important because it can help drive focus on the truly rate-limiting software blocks. If the software is not the rate-limiting bottleneck in the system, then profiling will still help, but will result in arriving at blocking locations more quickly. If the bottlenecks are related to I/O latencies, this will still show up as a hotspot, but the optimization required may require code redesign or system redesign. For example, status registers that are read and respond slowly to the read request will stall execution if the read data is used right away. Reading hardware status into a cached state long before the data must be processed reduces stall time. Ideally, the hardware/software interface would be modified to reduce the read latency in addition. Many system-level design improvements can be made to avoid I/O bottlenecks. For example, fast-access TCM is used so that the impact of cache misses (the miss penalty) is minimized or, in some cases, for single-cycle access memory, eliminated.

Adjusting hardware resources may often be impossible, especially during the hardware/software integration phase of a project. If you need more single-cycle on-chip memory, a huge cost and time investment is necessary to adjust this resource. Instead, if you can modify firmware and software to minimize the loss of performance through a bottleneck, you might reach improvement without hardware changes. System architects should ideally determine what their bottleneck will be and then plan for scalability. Firmware and software engineers with tuning tools and some hardware support built in to their systems can ensure that maximum performance is achieved for any given set of hardware resource constraints. The rest of this chapter discusses common built-in CPU performance measurement hardware features and how you can use them to tune firmware and software for optimal performance. Simple interrupt-based profiling will help, but the ability to separate hotspots out based upon frequency, instruction count, and execution efficiency requires some built-in hardware assist. The good news is that almost all modern processor cores now include PMUs (Performance Monitoring Units) or performance counters that can provide even better vision into performance issues than interrupt-based profiles.

Ideally, after a workload set is identified and performance optimizations are being considered for inclusion in a code base, ongoing performance regression testing should be in place. Performance regression testing should provide simple high-level metrics to evaluate current performance in terms of MIPs, FLOPs, transactions or I/Os per second. Also, some level of profiling should be included, perhaps supported by performance counters. The generation of this data should be automatic and be able to be correlated to specific code changes over time. In the worst case, this can allow for backing out code optimizations that did not work and for quick identification of code changes or added features that adversely affect performance.

## HARDWARE-SUPPORTED PROFILING AND TRACING

Some basic methods for building performance monitoring capability into the hardware include:

- Performance event counters (PMU)
- Execution trace port (branch encoded)
- Trace register buffer (branch encoded)
- Cycle and interval counters for timestamping

We now focus on built-in event counters and how they can be used to profile firmware and software to isolate execution efficiency hotspots. Tracing is advised after hotspots are located. In general, *tracing* provides shorter-duration visibility into the function of the CPU and firmware, but can be cycle-accurate and provides a view of the exact order of events within a CPU pipeline. Trace is often invaluable for dealing with esoteric timing issues and hardware or software interaction bugs, and you can also use it to better understand performance bottlenecks. A profile provides information that is much like an initial medical diagnosis. The profile answers the question, where does it hurt? By comparison, although a profile can't tell the tuner anything about latency, a trace provides a precise measure of latency. Profiling supported by performance counters can not only indicate where time is spent, but also hotspots where cache is most often missed or code locations where the processor pipeline is most often stalled. A trace is needed to determine stall duration and to analyze the timing at a stall hotspot.

Understanding latency for I/O and memory access can enable better overlap of processing with I/O. One of the most common optimizations is to queue work and start I/O early so that the CPU is kept as busy as possible. So, although profiling is the most popular approach to tuning, tracing features should still be designed into the hardware for debug and performance tuning as well.

Many (although not all) common CPU architectures include trace ports or the option to include a trace port. The IBM and AMCC PowerPC 4xx CPUs, Xilinx® Virtex® II Pro, ARM® Embedded Trace Macrocell, and Tensilica® are among the chips that fall into this category. The 4xx series of processors has included a branch-encoded trace port for many years. The branch-encoded trace port makes a nice compromise between visibility into the core and pin-count coming off-chip to enable tracing. Because the trace is encoded, it isn't cycle-accurate, but is accurate enough for hardware or software debugging and for performance optimization. Given modern EDA (Electronic Design Automation) tools, ASIC design verification has advanced to the point where all significant hardware issues can be discovered during simulation and synthesis. SoC (System-on-a-Chip) designs make post-silicon verification difficult if not impossible, because buses and CPU cores may have few or no signals that come off-chip. For hardware issues that might arise with internal on-chip interfaces, the only option is to use built-in logic analyzer functions, such as those provided by the Virtex Chip-Scope. This type of cycle-accurate trace is most often far more accurate than is necessary for tuning the performance of firmware or software.

Encoded-branch trace, as provided by the IBM and AMCC PowerPC 4xx, requires only eight I/O pins per traceable core. The encoding is based upon trace output that provides information on a core-cycle basis on interrupt vectors, relative branches taken, and the occasional absolute branch taken. Most branches and vectors that the program counter follows are easily encoded into 8 bits. Typical processors might have at most 16 interrupt vectors, requiring only 4 bits to encode the interrupt source. Furthermore, relative branches for loops, C switch blocks, and if blocks typically span short address ranges that might require 1 or 2 bytes to encode. Finally, the occasional long branch to an absolute 32-bit address requires 4 bytes. So, overall, encoded output is typically 1 to 5 bytes for each branch point in code. Given that most code has a branch density of 1 in 10 instructions or less, the encoded output, which can take up to 5 cycles to output an absolute branch, is still very accurate from a software execution order and timing perspective.

The program counter is assumed to linearly progress between branch points. So, the branch trace is easily correlated to C or assembly source code after it's acquired through a logic analyzer or acquisition tool such as RISCTrace, developed by IBM for debug. Due to the high rate of acquisition, which is nearly the cycle rate of the CPU, the trace window for a trace port is limited. For example, even a 64-MB trace buffer would capture approximately 16 million branch points or about 200 million instructions. At a clock rate of 1 GHz, that's only one fifth of a second of code execution. This information is invaluable for hardware and software debugging and timing issues, as well as direct measurement of latencies. However, most applications and services provide a large number of software operations per second over long periods of time. For visibility into higher-level software performance, profiling provides information that is much easier to use than the information tracing provides. After a profile is understood, trace can provide an invaluable level of drill-down to understand poorly performing sections of code.

Performance counters first appeared in the IBM PowerPC architecture in a patent approved in 1994. Since then, the manufacturers of almost all other processor architectures have licensed or invented similar features. The Intel PMU is a well-known example in wide use, perhaps most often used by PC game developers. The basic idea is simple. Instead of directly tracing code execution on a CPU, a built-in state machine is programmed to assert an interrupt periodically so that an ISR can sample the state of the CPU, including the current address of the program counter. Sampling the program counter address is the simplest form of performance monitoring and produces a histogram of the addresses where the program counter was found when sampled. This histogram can be mapped to C functions and therefore provides a profile indicating the functions in which the program counter is found most often.

This indicates calling frequency, size of a function (larger functions have larger address bins), and number of cycles that are spent in each function. With 32-bit word-sized address bins, the profile can provide this information down to the instruction level and therefore by line of C code. Most performance counter state machines also include event detection for CPU core events, including cache misses, data dependency pipeline stalls, branch mispredictions, write-back queue stalls, and instruction and cycle counts.

These events, like periodic cycle-based sampling, can also be programmed to assert an interrupt for ISR sampling of current program counter and related event counts. This event profile can indicate address ranges (modules, functions, lines of code) that have hotspots. As stated earlier, a hotspot is a code location where significant time is spent or where code is executing poorly. For example, if a particular function causes a cache miss counter to fire the sampling interrupt frequently, this indicates that the function should be examined for data and instruction cache inefficiencies. Finally, from these same event counts it is also possible to compute metrics such as CPI for each function with simple instrumentation added to function entry and exit points. This use of counters with inline code to sample those counters (instrumentation) is a hybrid approach between tracing and profiling, often referred to as *event tracing*. The performance counters require a hardware cell built into the CPU core, but also require some firmware and software support to produce a profile or event trace. If the cost, complexity, or schedule prevents inclusion of hardware support for performance monitoring, pure software methods can be used instead.

# BUILDING PERFORMANCE MONITORING INTO SOFTWARE

Most of the basic methods for building performance monitoring capability into a system require firmware and software support:

- Performance counter API (hardware supported)
- Direct code instrumentation to sample cycle and event counters for trace (hardware supported)
- Steady-state asynchronous sampling of counters through interrupts (hardware supported)
- Software event logging to memory buffer (software only, but hardware time-stamp improves quality)
- Function or block entry/exit tracing to a memory buffer (software only, with post-build modification of binary executables)

Software event logging is a pure software in-circuit approach for performance monitoring that requires no special hardware support. Most embedded operating system kernels provide an event logging method and analysis tools, such as the WindView and Linux Trace Toolkit event analyzers. At first, this approach might seem really intrusive compared to the hardware-supported methods. However, modern architectures such as the PowerPC provide features that make event logging traces very efficiently. Architectures such as the PowerPC include posted-write buffers for memory writes, so that occasional trace instructions writing bit-encoded event codes and timestamps to a memory buffer take no more than a single instruction. Given that most functions are on the order of hundreds to thousands of instructions in length (typically a line of C code generates multiple assembly instructions), a couple of additional instructions added at function entry and exit contribute little overhead to normal operation.

Event trace logs are invaluable for understanding operating system kernel and application code event timing. Although almost no hardware support is needed, an accurate timestamp clock makes the trace timing more useful. Without a hardware clock, you can still provide an event trace showing only the order of events, but the inclusion of microsecond-or-better–accuracy timestamps vastly improves the trace. System architects should carefully consider hardware support for these well-known and well-tested tracing and profiling methods, as well as scheduling time for software development.

When you implement performance-monitoring hardware and software on an embedded system, the capability to collect huge amounts of data is almost overwhelming. Effort put into data collection is of questionable value in the absence of a plan to analyze that data. Trace information is typically the easiest to analyze and is taken as needed for sequences of interest and mapped to code or to a timeline of

OS events. When traces are mapped to code, engineers can replay and step through code as it ran at full speed, noting branches taken and overall execution flow. For event traces mapped to OS events, engineers can analyze multithread context switches made by the scheduler, thread synchronizing events such as semaphore takes and gives, and application-specific events.

Profiles that collect event data and PC location down to the level of a 32-bit address take more analysis than simple mapping to be useful. Performance tuning effort can be focused well through the process of drilling down from the code module level, to the function level, and finally to the level of a specific line of code. Drilling down provides the engineer analyst with hotspots where more detailed information, such as traces, should be acquired. The drill-down process ensures that you won't spend time optimizing code that will have little impact on bottom-line performance improvement.

## PATH LENGTH, EFFICIENCY, AND CALLING FREQUENCY

Armed with nothing but hardware support to timestamp events, you can still determine code segment path length and execution efficiency. Ideally, performance counters would be used to automate the acquisition of these metrics. However, when performance counters aren't available, you can measure path length by hand in two different ways. First, by having the C compiler generate assembly code, you can then count the instructions by hand or by a word count utility. Second, if a single-step debugger is available (for example, a cross-debug agent or JTAG), then you can count instructions by stepping through assembly by hand. Although laborious, it is possible, as you'll see by looking at some example code.

The code in Listing 10.1 generates numbers in the Fibonacci sequence.

**LISTING 10.1**    Simple C Code to Compute the Fibonacci Sequence

```
typedef unsigned int UINT32;
#define FIB_LIMIT_FOR_32_BIT 47

UINT32 idx = 0, jdx = 1;
UINT32 seqCnt = FIB_LIMIT_FOR_32_BIT, iterCnt = 1;
UINT32 fib = 0, fib0 = 0, fib1 = 1;

void fib_wrapper(void)
{
   for(idx=0; idx < iterCnt; idx++)
   {
      fib = fib0 + fib1;
```

```
    while(jdx %lt; seqCnt)
    {
        fib0 = fib1; fib1 = fib; fib = fib0 + fib1;
        jdx++;
    }
  }
}
```

The easiest way to get an instruction count for a block of code such as the Fibonacci sequence-generating function in Listing 10.1 is to compile the C code into assembly. With the GCC C compiler, this is easily done with the following command line:

```
$ gcc fib.c -S -o fib.s
```

The resulting assembly is illustrated in Listing 10.2. Even with the automatic generation of the assembly from C, it's still no easy task to count instructions by hand. For a simple code block such as this example, hand counting can work, but the approach becomes time-consuming for real-world code blocks.

**LISTING 10.2**   GCC-Generated ASM for Fibonacci C Code

```
    .globl _fib_wrapper
.section __TEXT,__text,regular,pure_instructions
.align 2
_fib_wrapper:
stmw r30,-8(r1)
stwu r1,-48(r1)
mr r30,r1
mflr r0
bcl 20,31,"L00000000001$pb"
"L00000000001$pb":
mflr r10
mtlr r0
addis r2,r10,ha16(_idx-"L00000000001$pb")
la r2,lo16(_idx-"L00000000001$pb")(r2)
li r0,0
stw r0,0(r2)
L2:
addis r9,r10,ha16(_idx-"L00000000001$pb")
la r9,lo16(_idx-"L00000000001$pb")(r9)
addis r2,r10,ha16(_Iterations-"L00000000001$pb")
la r2,lo16(_Iterations-"L00000000001$pb")(r2)
lwz r9,0(r9)
```

```
lwz r0,0(r2)
cmplw cr7,r9,r0
blt cr7,L5
b L1
L5:
addis r11,r10,ha16(_fib-"L00000000001$pb")
la r11,lo16(_fib-"L00000000001$pb")(r11)
addis r9,r10,ha16(_fib0-"L00000000001$pb")
la r9,lo16(_fib0-"L00000000001$pb")(r9)
addis r2,r10,ha16(_fib1-"L00000000001$pb")
la r2,lo16(_fib1-"L00000000001$pb")(r2)
lwz r9,0(r9)
lwz r0,0(r2)
add r0,r9,r0
stw r0,0(r11)
L6:
addis r9,r10,ha16(_jdx-"L00000000001$pb")
la r9,lo16(_jdx-"L00000000001$pb")(r9)
addis r2,r10,ha16(_seqIterations-"L00000000001$pb")
la r2,lo16(_seqIterations-"L00000000001$pb")(r2)
lwz r9,0(r9)
lwz r0,0(r2)
cmplw cr7,r9,r0
blt cr7,L8
b L4
L8:
addis r9,r10,ha16(_fib0-"L00000000001$pb")
la r9,lo16(_fib0-"L00000000001$pb")(r9)
addis r2,r10,ha16(_fib1-"L00000000001$pb")
la r2,lo16(_fib1-"L00000000001$pb")(r2)
lwz r0,0(r2)
stw r0,0(r9)
addis r9,r10,ha16(_fib1-"L00000000001$pb")
la r9,lo16(_fib1-"L00000000001$pb")(r9)
addis r2,r10,ha16(_fib-"L00000000001$pb")
la r2,lo16(_fib-"L00000000001$pb")(r2)
lwz r0,0(r2)
stw r0,0(r9)
addis r11,r10,ha16(_fib-"L00000000001$pb")
la r11,lo16(_fib-"L00000000001$pb")(r11)
addis r9,r10,ha16(_fib0-"L00000000001$pb")
la r9,lo16(_fib0-"L00000000001$pb")(r9)
addis r2,r10,ha16(_fib1-"L00000000001$pb")
la r2,lo16(_fib1-"L00000000001$pb")(r2)
```

```
lwz r9,0(r9)
lwz r0,0(r2)
add r0,r9,r0
stw r0,0(r11)
addis r9,r10,ha16(_jdx-"L00000000001$pb")
la r9,lo16(_jdx-"L00000000001$pb")(r9)
addis r2,r10,ha16(_jdx-"L00000000001$pb")
la r2,lo16(_jdx-"L00000000001$pb")(r2)
lwz r2,0(r2)
addi r0,r2,1
stw r0,0(r9)
b L6
L4:
addis r9,r10,ha16(_idx-"L00000000001$pb")
la r9,lo16(_idx-"L00000000001$pb")(r9)
addis r2,r10,ha16(_idx-"L00000000001$pb")
la r2,lo16(_idx-"L00000000001$pb")(r2)
lwz r2,0(r2)
addi r0,r2,1
stw r0,0(r9)
b L2
L1:
lwz r1,0(r1)
lmw r30,-8(r1)
blr
```

If you're looking for a less tedious approach than counting instructions by hand from assembly source, you can use a single-step debugger and walk through a code segment in disassembled format. An interesting side effect of this approach for counting instructions is that the counter often learns quite a bit about the flow of the code in the process. Many single-step debugging tools, including JTAG (Joint Test Applications Group) hardware debuggers, can be extended or automated so that they can automatically step from one address to another, keeping count of instructions in between. Watching the debugger auto-step and count instructions between an entry point and exit point for code can even be an instructive experience that may spark ideas for path optimization.

Listing 10.3 provides a main program that can be compiled for G4- or G5-based Macintosh® computers running Mac OS® X. You can download the CHUD toolset for the Mac® and use it with the MONster instrumentation included in Listing 10.3 to measure the cycle and instruction counts using the hardware performance counters. The example code in Listing 10.3 takes the Fibonacci code from Listing 10.1 and adds sampling of the PowerPC G4 performance counters through the CHUD interface to the MONster analysis tool. The same type of cycle and event counters are found in the PowerPC performance counters in embedded IBM PowerPC cores.

**LISTING 10.3**   Simple C Code for PowerPC to Compute CPI for Fibonacci Code Block

```
#include "stdio.h"
#include "unistd.h"
// This code will work on the Macintosh G4 PowerPC with the Monster
// PowerPC Performance Counter acquisition and analysis tool.
// Simply pass in -DMONSTER_ANALYSIS when compiling the example.
// MONSTER provides a fully featured set of PMAPI counters and
// analysis along with the full suite of CHUD tools for the Macintosh
// G series of PowerPC processors.
//
// Alternatively on x86 Pentium machines which implement the Time Stamp
// Counter in the x86 version of Performance Counters called the PMU,
// pass in -DPMU_ANALYSIS. For the Pentium, only CPU cycles will be
// measured and CPI estimated based upon known instruction count.
//
// For the Macintosh G4, simply launch the main program from a Mac OS
// shell with the MONSTER analyzer set up for remote monitoring to
// follow along with the examples in the article.
//
// Leave the #define LONG_LONG_OK if your compiler and architecture
// support 64-bit unsigned integers, declared as unsigned long long in
// ANSI C.
//
// If not, please remove the #define below for 32-bit unsigned
// long declarations.
//

#define LONG_LONG_OK
#define FIB_LIMIT_FOR_32_BIT 47

typedef unsigned int UINT32;

#ifdef MONSTER_ANALYSIS
#include "CHUD/chud.h"
#include "mach/boolean.h"

#else
```

```
#ifdef LONG_LONG_OK
typedef unsigned long long int UINT64;

UINT64 startTSC = 0;
UINT64 stopTSC = 0;
UINT64 cycleCnt = 0;

UINT64 readTSC(void)
{
   UINT64 ts;

   __asm__ volatile(".byte 0x0f,0x31" : "=A" (ts));
   return ts;
}

UINT64 cyclesElapsed(UINT64 stopTS, UINT64 startTS)
{
   return (stopTS - startTS);
}

#else
typedef struct
{
   UINT32 low;
   UINT32 high;
} TS64;

TS64 startTSC = {0, 0};
TS64 stopTSC = {0, 0};
TS64 cycleCnt = 0;

TS64 readTSC(void)
{
   TS64 ts;
   __asm__ volatile(".byte 0x0f,0x31" : "=a" (ts.low), "=d" (ts.high));
   return ts;
}

TS64 cyclesElapsed(TS64 stopTS, TS64 startTS)
{
   UINT32 overFlowCnt;
   UINT32 cycleCnt;
   TS64 elapsedT;
```

```
      overFlowCnt = (stopTSC.high - startTSC.high);

      if(overFlowCnt && (stopTSC.low < startTSC.low))
      {
         overFlowCnt-;
         cycleCnt = (0xffffffff - startTSC.low) + stopTSC.low;
      }
      else
      {
         cycleCnt = stopTSC.low - startTSC.low;
      }

      elapsedT.low = cycleCnt;
      elapsedT.high = overFlowCnt;

      return elapsedT;
}
#endif
#endif

UINT32 idx = 0, jdx = 1;
UINT32 seqIterations = FIB_LIMIT_FOR_32_BIT;
UINT32 reqIterations = 1, Iterations = 1;
UINT32 fib = 0, fib0 = 0, fib1 = 1;

#define FIB_TEST(seqCnt, iterCnt) \
   for(idx=0; idx $lt; iterCnt; idx++) \
   { \
      fib = fib0 + fib1; \
      while(jdx < seqCnt) \
      { \
         fib0 = fib1; \
         fib1 = fib; \
         fib = fib0 + fib1; \
         jdx++; \
      } \
   } \

void fib_wrapper(void)
{
   FIB_TEST(seqIterations, Iterations);
}
```

```
#ifdef MONSTER_ANALYSIS
char label[]="Fibonacci Series";

int main( int argc, char *argv[])
{
   double tbegin, telapse;

   if(argc == 2)
   {
      sscanf(argv[1], "%ld", &reqIterations);

      seqIterations = reqIterations % FIB_LIMIT_FOR_32_BIT;
      Iterations = reqIterations / seqIterations;
   }
   else if(argc == 1)
      printf("Using defaults\n");
   else
      printf("Usage: fibtest [Num iterations]\n");

   chudInitialize();
   chudUmarkPID(getpid(), TRUE);
   chudAcquireRemoteAccess();
   tbegin=chudReadTimeBase(chudMicroSeconds);

   chudStartRemotePerfMonitor(label);
   FIB_TEST(seqIterations, Iterations);
   chudStopRemotePerfMonitor();

   telapse=chudReadTimeBase(chudMicroSeconds);

   printf("\nFibonacci(%lu)=%lu (0x%08lx) for %f usec\n",
          seqIterations, fib, fib, (telapse-tbegin));

   chudReleaseRemoteAccess();
   return 0;
}

#else
#define INST_CNT_FIB_INNER 15
#define INST_CNT_FIB_OUTTER 6
```

```
int main( int argc, char *argv[] )
{
   double clkRate = 0.0, fibCPI = 0.0;
   UINT32 instCnt = 0;

   if(argc == 2)
   {
      sscanf(argv[1], "%ld", &reqIterations);

      seqIterations = reqIterations % FIB_LIMIT_FOR_32_BIT;
      Iterations = reqIterations / seqIterations;
   }
   else if(argc == 1)
      printf("Using defaults\n");
   else
      printf("Usage: fibtest [Num iterations]\n");

   instCnt = (INST_CNT_FIB_INNER * seqIterations) +
             (INST_CNT_FIB_OUTTER * Iterations) + 1;

   // Estimate CPU clock rate
   startTSC = readTSC();
   usleep(1000000);
   stopTSC = readTSC();
   cycleCnt = cyclesElapsed(stopTSC, startTSC);

#ifdef LONG_LONG_OK
   printf("Cycle Count=%llu\n", cycleCnt);
   clkRate = ((double)cycleCnt)/1000000.0;
   printf("Based on usleep accuracy, CPU clk rate = %lu clks/sec,",
          cycleCnt);
   printf(" %7.1f Mhz\n", clkRate);
#else
   printf("Cycle Count=%lu\n", cycleCnt.low);
   printf("OverFlow Count=%lu\n", cycleCnt.high);
   clkRate = ((double)cycleCnt.low)/1000000.0;
   printf("Based on usleep accuracy, CPU clk rate = %lu clks/sec,",
          cycleCnt.low);
   printf(" %7.1f Mhz\n", clkRate);
#endif

   printf("\nRunning Fibonacci(%d) Test for %ld iterations\n",
          seqIterations, Iterations);
```

```
    // START Timed Fibonacci Test
    startTSC = readTSC();
    FIB_TEST(seqIterations, Iterations);
    stopTSC = readTSC();
    // END Timed Fibonacci Test

#ifdef LONG_LONG_OK
    printf("startTSC =0x%016x\n", startTSC);
    printf("stopTSC =0x%016x\n", stopTSC);

    cycleCnt = cyclesElapsed(stopTSC, startTSC);
    printf("\nFibonacci(%lu)=%lu (0x%08lx)\n", seqIterations, fib, fib);
    printf("\nCycle Count=%llu\n", cycleCnt);
    printf("\nInst Count=%lu\n", instCnt);
    fibCPI = ((double)cycleCnt) / ((double)instCnt);
    printf("\nCPI=%4.2f\n", fibCPI);

#else
    printf("startTSC high=0x%08x, startTSC low=0x%08x\n", startTSC.high,
startTSC.low);
    printf("stopTSC high=0x%08x, stopTSC low=0x%08x\n", stopTSC.high,
stopTSC.low);

    cycleCnt = cyclesElapsed(stopTSC, startTSC);
    printf("\nFibonacci(%lu)=%lu (0x%08lx)\n", seqIterations, fib, fib);
    printf("\nCycle Count=%lu\n", cycleCnt.low);
    printf("OverFlow Count=%lu\n", cycleCnt.high);
    fibCPI = ((double)cycleCnt.low) / ((double)instCnt);
    printf("\nCPI=%4.2f\n", fibCPI);
#endif

}
#endif
```

Running the code from Listing 10.3 built for the Macintosh G4, the MONster analysis tool determines the path length and execution efficiency for the Fibonacci sequence code block, as summarized in Listing 10.4.

The example analysis in Listing 10.4 was collected using the MONster configuration and source code easily compiled with GCC and downloadable from the CD-ROM.

**LISTING 10.4**  Sample Macintosh G4 MONster Analysis for Example Code

```
Processor 1: 1250 MHz PPC 7447A, 166 MHz CPU Bus, Branch Folding:
enabled, Threshold:
0, Multiplier: 2x
(tb1) P1 - Timebase results
(p1c1) PMC 1:   1 - CPU Cycles
(p1c2) PMC 2:   2 - Instr Completed
Config: 5 - CPI-simple
  1 - CPI (completed)
P1 Timebase (cpu cycles)  P1 pmc 1              P1 pmc 2
              SC res 1
Tb1: (cpu cycles)        (P1)  1-CPU Cycles:  (P1)
  2-Instr Completed:  CPI (completed)
8445302.308861008          8413160              1618307
          5.19874164790735
Tb1: (cpu cycles)        (P1)  1-CPU Cycles:  (P1)
  2-Instr Completed:  CPI (completed)
7374481.710107035          7346540              1360873
          5.398402349080333
Tb1: (cpu cycles)        (P1)  1-CPU Cycles:  (P1)
  2-Instr Completed:  CPI (completed)
7207497.309806291          7180243              1668938
          4.302282649205663
Tb1: (cpu cycles)        (P1)  1-CPU Cycles:  (P1)
  2-Instr Completed:  CPI (completed)
44985850.44768739          44808388            38595522
          1.160973752343601
Tb1: (cpu cycles)        (P1)  1-CPU Cycles:  (P1)
  2-Instr Completed:  CPI (completed)
472475463.2072901          470597098          458561558
          1.026246290797887
Tb1: (cpu cycles)        (P1)  1-CPU Cycles:  (P1)
  2-Instr Completed:  CPI (completed)
2149357027.379779          2140806560        2108619999
          1.015264277591631


Sam-Siewerts-Computer:~/TSC samsiewert$ ./perfmon 100
Fibonacci(6)=13 (0x0000000d) for 7545.213589 usec
Sam-Siewerts-Computer:~/TSC samsiewert$ ./perfmon 10000
Fibonacci(36)=24157817 (0x01709e79) for 5883.610250 usec
Sam-Siewerts-Computer:~/TSC samsiewert$ ./perfmon 1000000
Fibonacci(28)=514229 (0x0007d8b5) for 6008.113638 usec
Sam-Siewerts-Computer:~/TSC samsiewert$ ./perfmon 100000000
```

```
Fibonacci(27)=317811 (0x0004d973) for 36554.381943 usec
Sam-Siewerts-Computer:~/TSC samsiewert$ ./perfmon 10000000000
Fibonacci(31)=2178309 (0x00213d05) for 378554.531618 usec
Sam-Siewerts-Computer:~/TSC samsiewert$ ./perfmon 1000000000000
Fibonacci(17)=2584 (0x00000a18) for 1720178.701376 usec
Sam-Siewerts-Computer:~/TSC samsiewert$
```

Note that in the example runs, for larger numbers of iterations, the Fibonacci sequence code becomes cached and the CPI drops dramatically from 5 to 1. If the Fibonacci code were considered to be critical path code for performance, you might want to consider locking this code block into L1 instruction cache.

*ON THE CD*

If you don't have access to a PowerPC platform, an alternative Pentium TSC (TimeStamp Counter) build, which counts CPU core cycles and uses a hand-counted instruction count to derive CPI, is included on the CD-ROM. You can download and analyze this code on any Macintosh Mac OS X PC or Windows PC running Cygwin™ tools. On the Macintosh, if you use MONster with the Remote feature, the application will automatically upload counter data to the MONster analysis tool, including the cycle and instruction counts for the Fibonacci code block.

## FUNDAMENTAL OPTIMIZATIONS

Given analysis of code such as the example Fibonacci sequence code block, how do you take the information and start optimizing the code? The best approach is to make gains by following the low-hanging fruit model of optimization—apply optimizations that require the least effort and change to the code, but provide the biggest improvements first. Most often, this means simply ensuring that compiler optimizations that *can* be used *are* being used. After compiler optimizations are exhausted, then, simple code restructuring might be considered to eliminate cache miss hotspots. The optimization process is often architecture-specific. Most architectures include application programming notes with ideas for code optimization. Although the methods for optimizing go beyond the scope of this book, some of the most common are summarized here.

Following are some basic methods for optimizing code segments:

- Use compiler basic block optimizations (inline, loop unrolling, and so on).
- Simplify algorithm complexity and unnecessary instructions in code.
- Precompute commonly used expressions up front.
- Lock critical-path code into L1 instruction cache.
- Lock critical-path, high-frequency reference data into L1 data cache.

- Take advantage of memory prefetch—prefetch data to be read and modified into L1 or L2 cache.
- Use MMIO prefetch—start I/O for data used in algorithms early to avoid data dependency pipeline stalls.

After you've exhausted some of these optimization methods using profiling to support identification of the blocks most in need of optimization, you need to consider more complex optimization methods for additional improvement. Good functional regression testing should be included in the optimization process to ensure that functionality is not broken by optimizing code changes. This is especially true for more complex architecture-specific optimizations. Note that architecture-specific optimizations make code much less portable.

Some more advanced methods for optimizing code segments include the following:

- Use of compiler feedback optimization—profile provided as input to compiler.
- Hand-tune assembly to exploit features such as conditional execution.

## SUMMARY

After the current marriage of software, firmware, and hardware is optimized, how does the architect improve the performance of the next generation of the system? At some point, for every product, the cost of further code optimization will outweigh the gain of improved performance and marketability of the product. However, you can still use performance analysis features such as performance counters to characterize potential modifications that should go into next-generation products. For example, if a function is highly optimized, but remains as a high consumer of CPU resources, and the system is CPU-bound so that the CPU is the bottleneck, then hardware rearchitecting to address this is beneficial. That particular function might be considered for implementation in a hardware-accelerating state machine. Or perhaps a second processor core could be dedicated to that one function. The point is that performance counters are not only useful for coaxing maximum performance out of an existing hardware design, but can also be useful for guiding future hardware design.

## EXERCISES

1. Use the Pentium TSC code to count the cycles for a given code block. Then, in the single-step debugger, count the number of instructions for the same code block to compute the CPI for this code on your system. Provide evidence that your CPI calculation is accurate and explain why it's as high or low as you find it to be.

ON THE CD

2. Compare the accuracy for timing the execution of a common code block first using the CD-ROM time_stamp.c code and then using the Pentium TSC. Is there a significant difference? Why?
3. Download the Brink and Abyss Pentium-4 PMU profiling tools and profile the Fibonacci code running on a Linux system. Explain your results.

## CHAPTER REFERENCES

[Siewert] *http://www-128.ibm.com/developerworks/power/library/pa-bigiron3/*

# 11 High Availability and Reliability Design

## In This Chapter

- Introduction
- Reliability and Availability: Similarities and Differences
- Reliability
- Reliable Software
- Available Software
- Design Tradeoffs
- Hierarchical Approaches for Fail-Safe Design

## INTRODUCTION

High availability and high reliability (HA/HR) are measured differently, but both provide some indication of system robustness and quality expectations. Furthermore, because system failures can be dangerous, both also relate to system safety. Increasing availability and reliability of a system requires time and monetary investment, increasing cost, and increasing time-to-market for products. The worst thing that can come of engineering efforts to increase system availability and reliability is an unintentional decrease in overall availability and reliability. When design for HA/HR is not well tested or adds complexity, this unintentional reduction in HA/HR can often be the result. In this chapter, design methods for increasing HA/HR are introduced along with a review of exactly what HA and what HR really means. (Portions of the material on performance tuning presented in this chapter was first published on the IBM developerWorks Web site, © IBM developerWorks. Reprinted with permission.)

# RELIABILITY AND AVAILABILITY: SIMILARITIES AND DIFFERENCES

*Availability* is the percentage of time over a well-defined period that a system or service is available for users. So, for example, if a system is said to have 99.999%, or *five nines,* availability, this system must not be unavailable more than five minutes over the course of a year. Quick recovery and restoration of service after a fault greatly increases availability. The quicker the recovery, the more often the system or service can go down and still meet the five nines criteria. Five nines is a *high availability,* or HA metric.

In contrast, *high reliability* (HR) is perhaps best described by the old adage that a chain is only as strong as its weakest link. A system built from components that have very low probability of failure leads to high system reliability. The overall expected system reliability is the product of all subsystem reliabilities, and the sub-system reliability is a product of all component reliabilities. Based upon this mathematical fact, components are required to have very low probability of failure if the subsystems and system are to also have reasonably low probability of failure. For example, a system of 10 components, each with 99.999% reliability, is $(0.99999)^{10}$, or 99.99%, reliable. Any decrease in the reliability of a single component in this type of single-string design can greatly reduce overall reliability. For example, adding just one 95% reliable component in the previous example that was 99.99% reliable would drop the overall reliability to 94.99%. HR components are often constructed of higher quality raw materials, subjected to more rigorous testing, and often have more complex fabrication processes, all increasing component cost. There may be notable exceptions and advancements where lower cost components also have HR, making component choice obvious, but this is not typical.

The simple mathematical relationship between HA and HR is:

$$\text{Availability} = \text{MTBF} / (\text{MTBF} + \text{MTTR})$$

where MTBF = Mean Time Between Failures and MTTR = Mean Time to Recovery.

So, while an HR system has large MTBF, it can tolerate longer MTTR and still yield decent availability. Likewise a system with low reliability can provide decent availability if it has very fast recovery times. From this relation, you can see that one system with five nines HA might have low reliability and a very fast recovery (say 1 second) and therefore go down and recover 3,000 or more times in a year (10 times a day!). An HR system might go down once every two years and wait for operator intervention to safely and carefully recover operational state, taking on average 10 minutes every 2 years for the exact same HA metric of five nines. Clearly, most operators would not consider these systems to have the same quality.

## RELIABILITY

Theoretically, it's possible to build a system with low-quality, not-so-reliable components and subsystems, and still achieve HA. This type of system would have to include massive redundancy and complex switching logic to isolate frequently failing components and to bring spares online very quickly in place of those components that failed to prevent interruption to service. Most often, it's better to strike a balance and invest in more reliable components to minimize the interconnection and switching requirements. If you take a simple example of a system designed with redundant components that can be isolated or activated, it's clear that the interconnection and switching logic does not scale well to high levels of redundancy and sparing. Consider the simple, single-spare dual-string system shown in Figure 11.1.

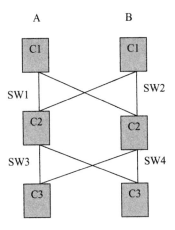

**FIGURE 11.1** Dual-string, cross-strapped subsystem interconnection.

The example system shown in Figure 11.1 has eight possible configurations that can be formed by activating and isolating components C1, C2, or C3 from side A or side B. The system must be able to positively detect failed components and track these failures to reconfigure with an operable switch state and new interconnection of activated components. Table 11.1 describes the eight possible configurations for this small-scale HA system example.

From the simple example shown in Figure 11.1, a trade-off can be made between the complexity of interconnecting components and redundancy management with the cost of including HR components. The cost of hardware components with HR is fairly well known and can be estimated based upon component testing, expected failure rates, MTBF, operational characteristics, packaging, and the overall physical features of the component.

**TABLE 11.1** Enumeration of Configurations for a Three Subsystem Dual-String Cross-Strapped System

| Configuration | Component C1 | Component C2 | Component C3 |
|:---:|:---:|:---:|:---:|
| 1 | A | A | A |
| 2 | A | A | B |
| 3 | A | B | A |
| 4 | A | B | B |
| 5 | B | A | A |
| 6 | B | A | B |
| 7 | B | B | A |
| 8 | B | B | B |

System architects should also consider three simple parameters before investing heavily in HA or HR for a system component or subsystem:

- Likelihood of unit failure
- Impact of failure on the system
- Cost of recovery versus cost of fail-safe isolation

Conceptually, architects should consider how levels of recovery are handled with varying degrees of automation, as depicted in Figure 11.2.

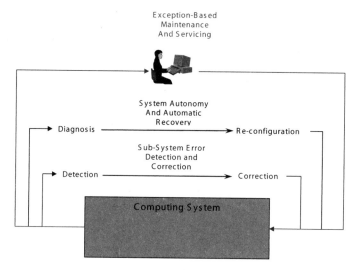

**FIGURE 11.2** Supporting multiple levels of recovery autonomy.

## RELIABLE SOFTWARE

Perhaps much harder to estimate is the cost of HR software. Clearly, reliable hardware running unreliable software will result in failure modes that are likely to cause service interruption. Complex software is often less reliable, and the best way to increase reliability is with testing. Testing takes time and ultimately adds to cost and time to market.

System architects have traditionally focused on designing HA and HR hardware with firmware to manage redundancy and to automate recovery. So, for example, firmware would reconfigure the components in the example in Table 11.1 to recover from a component failure. Traditionally, rigorous testing and verification have ensured that firmware has no flaws, but history has shown that defects can still wind up in the field and emerge due to subtle differences in timing or execution of data-driven algorithms.

Designing firmware and software for HR can be costly. The FAA requires rigorous documentation and testing to ensure that flight software on commercial aircraft is HR. The DO-178B class A standard requires software developers to maintain copious design, test, and process documentation. Furthermore, testing must include formal proof that code has been well tested with criteria such as multiple condition decision coverage (MCDC). This criteria ensures that all paths and all statements in the code have been exercised and shown to work. This laborious task greatly increases the cost of software components.

## AVAILABLE SOFTWARE

Real-time systems are composed of software services that provide service upon request. Normally these services block in-between requests. Due to coding or design error, it is possible that software sanity may be lost so that services will block indefinitely. To detect and recover from indefinite blocking, all services should be coded so that they will eventually time out if they do not unblock by some upper bound on an expected request period. When the service unblocks due to timeout or due to data available, the service should call `keep_alive(taskIdSelf())`, which will post the service's unique task ID to a software system sanity monitor. The sanity monitor is also a service. This service simply periodically checks to make sure all other services have checked in and are continuing to provide service. If a service has not checked in by a time limit, the sanity monitor can use `taskSuspend()` and `taskDelete()` in VxWorks along with an application-specific `shutdown()` to recover the wedged service and its resources so it can then be restarted. This begs the question, what happens if the sanity monitor itself loses sanity? In this case, a hardware watchdog timer will recover the system. The watchdog is a countdown timer, which if not reset by the sanity monitor, will start a full reboot recovery of the system. In rare circumstances, the recovery methods won't work and systems go into rolling reboot where the watchdog recovery results in loss of sanity over and over. With rigorous testing, including functional, stress, and soak time testing, this is very unlikely to happen. If it does, this will most likely require human intervention to fix the problem or will lead to system failure or lengthy unavailability.

## DESIGN TRADEOFFS

Designing for HR alone can be cost prohibitive, so most often a balance of design for HA and HR is better. HA at the hardware level is most often achieved through redundancy (sparing) and switching. A trade-off can be made between the cost of duplication and simply engineering HR into components to reduce the MTBF. Over time, designers have found a balance between HR and HA features to optimize cost and availability. Fundamental to duplication schemes is the recovery latency. When planning component or subsystem duplication for HA, architects must carefully consider the complexity and latency of the recovery scheme and how this will affect firmware and software layers. Trade-offs between working to simply increase reliability instead of increasing availability through sparing should be analyzed. A simple, well-proven methodology that is often employed by systems engineers is to consider the trade-off of probability of failure, impact of failure, and cost to mitigate impact or reduce likelihood of failure. This method is most often referred to as FMEA (Failure Modes and Effects Analysis).

Another, less formal process that system engineers often use is referred to as the *low-hanging fruit* process. This process involves ranking system design features under consideration by cost to implement, reliability improvement, availability improvement, and complexity. The point of low-hanging fruit analysis is to pick features that improve HA/HR the most for least cost and with least risk. Without existing products and field testing, the hardest part of FMEA or low-hanging fruit analysis is estimating the probability of failure for components and estimating improvement to HA/HR for specific features. For hardware, the tried and true method for estimating reliability is based upon component testing, system testing, environmental testing, accelerated testing, and field testing. The trade-offs between engineering reliability and availability into hardware are fairly obvious, but how does this work with firmware and software?

Designing and implementing HR firmware and software can be very costly. The main approach for ensuring that firmware/software is highly reliable is verification with formal coverage criteria along with unit tests, integration tests, system tests, and regression testing. Test coverage criteria include feature points; but for HR systems, much more rigorous criteria are necessary, including statement, path, and MCDC (Multiple Condition Decision Coverage).

You might wonder why designing test cases for path and statement coverage is not sufficient for HR software. The simple snippet of C code in Listing 11.1 shows why MCDC is required. The if test in main() has two expressions logically ordered together. Most C compilers generate code so that the second expression is short-circuited if the first evaluates to true. As a result, both paths in main() for the if blocks can be driven by a test without ever executing (testing) the OutsideLimits code. So, a test driver must drive the same path with the condition where recoveryRequired is false and where recoveryRequired is true and OutsideLimits is either true or false in combination with this. So, for simple path coverage in main there are only two paths noted by coverage of code on the line numbers: Path-A) 28, 30, 32 and Path-B) 28, 30, 13, 20, 36. However, by MCDC, you must ensure that main Path-A is covered in combination with the paths of the function OutsideLimits, which defines Path-C) 28, 30, 13, 15, 16, 32.

**LISTING 11.1**   Simple C Code with Two Paths and MCDC Testing Requirements

```
01: #define UPPER_LIMIT 100
02: #define TRUE 1
03: #define FALSE 0
04:
05: extern void logMessage(char *msg);
06: extern unsigned int MMIORead(unsigned int addr);
07: extern void StartRecovery(void);
08: extern void ContinueOperation(void);
09: extern int RecoveryRequired;
10:
11: int LimitTest(unsigned int val)
12: {
13:     if(val > UPPER_LIMIT)
14:     {
15:         logMessage("Limit Exceeded\n");
16:         return TRUE;
17:     }
18:     else
19:     {
20:         return FALSE;
21:     }
```

```
22: }
23:
24: main()
25: {
26:     unsigned int IOValue = 0;
27:
28:     IOValue = MMIORead(0xF0000100);
29:
30:     if(RecoveryRequired || OutsideLimits(IOValue))
31:     {
32:         StartRecovery();
33:     }
34:     else
35:     {
36:         ContinueOperation();
37:     }
38: }
```

## HIERARCHICAL APPROACHES FOR FAIL-SAFE DESIGN

Ideally, all system, subsystem, and component errors can be detected and corrected in a hierarchy so that component errors are detected and corrected without any action required by the containing subsystem. This hierarchical approach for fault detection and fault protection/correction can greatly simplify verification of a RAS (Reliability, Availability, and Serviceability) design. An ECC memory component provides for single-bit error detection and automatic correction. The incorporation of ECC memory provides a component level of RAS, which can increase RAS performance and reduce the complexity of supporting RAS at higher levels. HR systems often include design elements that ensure that nonrecoverable failures result in the system going out of service, along with safing to reduce risk of losing the asset, damaging property, or causing loss of life.

## SUMMARY

Systems designed for HA may not necessarily be designed for HR. HR systems tend to be HA although they often fail safe and wait for human intervention for recovery rather than risk automatic recovery. So, there is no clear correlation between the HA and HR other than the equation for availability in terms of MTBF and MTTR. As discussed, given that high MTBF and long MTTR compared to low

MTBF and rapid MTTR could yield the same availability, it appears that availability alone does not characterize the safeness or quality of a system very well.

## EXERCISES

1. How many configurations must a fault recovery system attempt for a dual string fully cross-strapped system with four subsystems?
2. Describe what you think a good fail-safe mode would be for an Earth-orbiting satellite that encounters a nonrecoverable multibit error when it passes through the high radiation zone known as the South Atlantic Anomaly. What should the satellite do? How should it eventually be recovered for continued operation?
3. If it takes 30 seconds for Windows to boot, how many times can this OS fail due to deadlock or loss of software sanity in a year for five nines HA ignoring detection time for each failure?
4. If the launch vehicle for satellites has an overall system reliability of 99.5% and has more than 2,000 components, what is the average reliability of each component?
5. Research the CodeTest software coverage analysis tool and describe how it provides test coverage criteria. Can it provide proof of MCDC coverage?

## CHAPTER REFERENCES

[ReliableLinux] Campbell, Iain, *Reliable Linux—Assuring High Availability*. Wiley, 2002.

# Part

# III

# Putting It All Together

# 12 System Lifecycle

## INTRODUCTION

Real-time embedded systems include at the very least mechanical, electrical, and software engineering to build a working and deliverable system. Some real-time embedded systems may involve chemical, biological, cryogenic, optical, or many other specialized subsystems and components as well that must be integrated and tested in addition to the more common mechanical, electrical, and software subsystems. For example, blood analysis machines provide real-time analysis of human blood samples using a robotic platform that can automate the biological testing of a large number of samples in much less time than manual laboratory testing. The NASA great observatory series of space telescopes all include spacecraft and instrumentation real-time embedded systems that include visible, X-ray, infrared, and ultra-violet detectors. The infrared instrumentation requires cryogenic cooling. Likewise, real-time embedded systems are often found in process control applications at chemical, nuclear, or biological production plants. Given the wide range and complexity of disciplines, types of components, and types of subsystems that must be integrated to field a successful real-time embedded system, it's imperative that a well-defined and disciplined process be followed during all stages of development. This chapter provides a framework for real-time embedded systems lifecycle planning, tips on tools that can help, and examples of methods used.

In this chapter, we'll walk through selected elements of a design for a stereo computer vision real-time tracking system. Completion of a project like this can be accomplished in 15 weeks if you want to engage in home-study practice to better understand the process of engineering a real-time embedded system.

## LIFECYCLE OVERVIEW

Having a good understanding of critical steps in the system-engineering process for real-time embedded systems long before a project is started can make projects go much more smoothly. Many in-depth texts describe the lifecycle phases and steps in much more detail than this book, but often don't provide the full context of engineering hardware, firmware, and software components and subsystems. Furthermore, we must learn how to ensure that all components and subsystems are integrated, debugged, and optimized to realize a quality system rather than just one aspect, such as software or hardware alone. Often trade-offs between hardware and software can be made with significant cost, risk, schedule, or quality impact if the process promotes periodic critical examination of the system as it evolves.

The spiral model for systems engineering (often presented as a software engineering process) is well suited for following a rigorous process, yet also ensuring that the system evolution is adaptive to ensure that optimizations can be made as lessons are learned during the process. Figure 12.1 shows a two phase spiral model for implementing a system starting from concept and resulting in delivery of the first functional system.

Figure 12.1 shows the process used by students at the University of Colorado to build computer vision, robotics, and real-time media applications in a 15-week time period. This may seem very short, but often in industry, a new product concept must be quickly demonstrated and an early version put in a customer's hands to generate demand and to define the market, sometimes in less than 15 weeks as well. The beauty of the spiral model is that it can include many phases (turns through analysis, design, development and unit testing, and regression testing) for

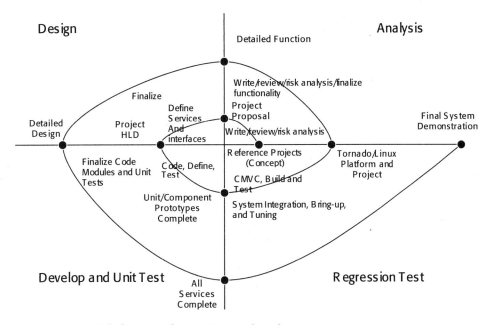

**FIGURE 12.1**  Spiral process for systems engineering.

more complex systems and fit a wide range of systems development schedules. The main concept behind the spiral is to mitigate risk by analyzing the system requirements and design every turn through the spiral. The theory behind this is that a better risk assessment can be made with some implementation and testing experience completed and that implementation and test can be developed through an evolutionary process. Furthermore, the spiral model should include increased time and monetary investment with each successive turn as risk is better understood and managed with better insight from previous phases of the spiral.

In theory, spirals can be as short or long as the participants choose, from one day to one year, but ideally they are short phases initially so that pitfalls in requirements, design, implementation, or testing can be discovered sooner rather than later. Experience at the University of Colorado has shown that this process works very well for students developing complicated systems with imperfect information, limited budgets, and very limited time. You can use the process in Figure 12.1 to guide development of a home or an academic system and can expand the process for use with an industrial project.

The starting point is a reference design. This reference design should be a system that is the closest known system to the one proposed. The reference system can be a resource for design, code, subsystem, component, and test reuse. In the first analysis phase, the new system can be defined in terms of functional, performance, and feature-level requirements (perhaps leveraging the reference system), along with an analysis of risk, often associated with new features, functions, or new levels of performance required. This first analysis phase involves writing requirements, reviewing them, and estimating risks and cost. The second phase, design, involves using design tools and methods to define the high-level system design, clearly identifying the subsystems and interfaces between them, but not yet defining all components. The third phase, development and unit test, involves implementing software stubs (basic interface and simplified behavior) and hardware prototypes (emulators) to discover how well high-level design concepts will work and to better estimate risk and cost. The fourth phase, regression, involves a preliminary integration (or practice integration) of subsystem emulators and stubs, and the establishment of software nightly builds and testing. This practice integration also allows for better definition of not only unit tests, but also how integrated subsystems and the system will be tested as the system is assembled.

The second turn of the spiral model repeats the same four phases, with the second analysis phase involving refinement of requirements and more accurate reestimation of risk and cost. For short development projects, such as a demonstration or academic development project, the second turn may be the final turn through the spiral process to deliver a working system. If this is the case, then detailed design must be completed down to the component level, with implementation and unit test at the same level, and a regression phase that concludes with full system integration and prerelease product testing. For a longer-term project, the second turn may not complete design and implementation. The evolutionary spiral can be designed so that a subset of features are implemented in the second turn and a third, fourth, or more turns are used to complete the features and to achieve desired performance and quality.

For the purpose of a class or self-study project, Figure 12.2 shows the same spiral development process fit to 15 weeks.

The time spent in each phase of the spiral is doubled or tripled in the second turn. This schedule also works well in an academic setting or for a rapid prototype development project where status must be provided by engineers (students) to management (teachers) for quick feedback during the first turn.

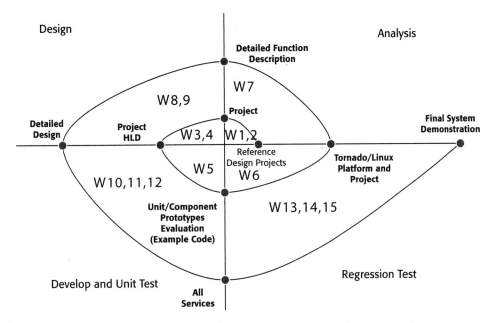

**FIGURE 12.2**  Fifteen-week spiral process for systems engineering.

# REQUIREMENTS

Defining requirements for a system during analysis is most often done by listing or enumerating functions, features, and performance metrics for the ultimate system. In the first turn of the spiral, requirements are defined in terms of subsystems and features with a few high-level performance metrics that will be evident to any user of the system. These are then refined to component level during subsequent turns through the spiral. One approach to define requirements and design with agility and quickness is to include the high-level requirements and design in one design document, making the tracing of requirements to design simple. This can also be done for detailed requirements definition and design, once again making trace simple. For large-scale projects, often an engineer will only work on requirements, and a design engineer will iterate with the requirements engineer to achieve a design that maps to all the requirements. For the purpose of the 15-week development project, some subset of system requirements might be developed by a team, and then subsystem requirements and design developed by each engineer.

## RISK ANALYSIS

As requirements are defined, the risk of each requirement should be reviewed. Risk can be analyzed by

- Probability of occurrence of a failure or process problem
- The impact of the same failure or process problem
- The cost of mitigating the risk item

This makes risk analysis simple. Risk can be reduced most significantly for the overall system design and development process by focusing on the most probable and highest-impact risk items first. These risks can then be further analyzed and mitigations proposed along with the cost of those mitigations to determine what goals are for the first or next spiral turn. For example, if development of a new driver for a new video encoder is properly realized as high risk for a 15-week project, this risk can be mitigated by investigating existing drivers and several off-the-shelf options for video encoder chips. This could be done quickly in the first spiral, and a recovery plan can be defined for the second turn. This is an example of a process risk. Likewise, a system risk can be handled in a similar way. For example, servos have limits in actuation quickness and accuracy. Characterization of a number of servos during the first turn of the spiral to determine limits for candidate servo components can help significantly reduce risk of not meeting performance requirements for a tilt/pan tracker in the end. Risk analysis should always accompany requirements analysis and should always follow each spiral turn.

## HIGH-LEVEL DESIGN

High-level design involves the enumeration and definition of all hardware and software interfaces and their characteristics as well as decomposition of the system into sub-systems. If components can be identified during this phase, this is ideal. High-level design methods should involve unified hardware/software design as well as individual design. A system design showing all system major elements should be agreed upon by the development team and be defined at a high enough level that it can fit on one page as shown in Figure 12.3.

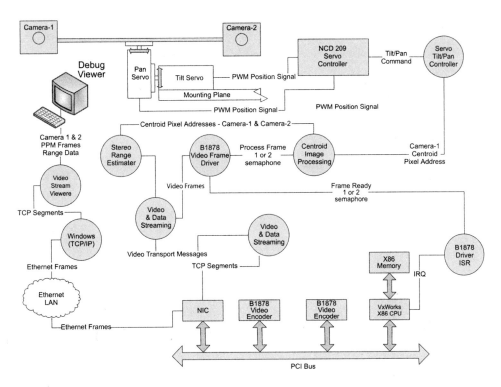

**FIGURE 12.3**    Stereo-vision example system design.

Although the single-page suggestion may be difficult and may lead to a busy block diagram, it provides a chance for the team or individual to look at all the major elements at once. The design can always be subdivided and cleaned up after this exercise, but the single-page view is often valuable throughout the project. A system view should show both hardware and software elements and the data flow between them with a high level of abstraction. The key for this design artifact is completeness and agreement by all involved that it is complete. To immediately clean up this busy view, the same diagram can be decomposed into a hardware-only view or software-only view. Figure 12.4 shows the hardware-only view for the Figure 12.3 system view.

Note that Figure 12.4 shows not only the electrical, but the mechanical hardware view. Once again, this can be broken down to show only mechanical views. In this way, subsystems are identified in a consistent manner and with a keystone (the system views) that allow a team to continually reevaluate the efficacy of the overall design.

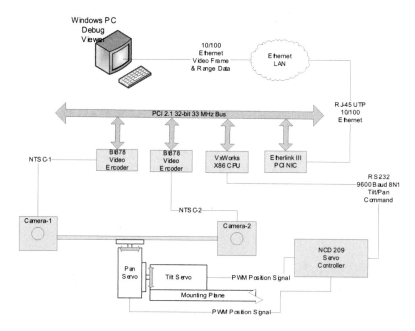

**FIGURE 12.4** Stereo-vision example hardware system view.

In high-level design, the fundamental concept is completeness rather than accuracy. For example, mechanical drawings might not include dimensions, software module and service sequence diagrams might not define all calling parameters or message attributes, and electrical schematics might not have all resistor values. The point is to fully define subsystems and their interfaces to set the stage for early testing and for detailed design in the next spiral. Methods used for design are specific to disciplines below the subsystem level (detailed design level), so the high-level design is the opportunity to ensure that the system can be integrated to meet system requirements, and a good system-level design mitigates risk considerably. Often it's advisable to design to a level lower than subsystems to ensure that the subsystem high-level design can be advanced with more confidence. This also allows for early identification of components and can support early component characterization and testing for systems that will be built from off-the-shelf components and subsystems.

Numerous methodologies support system-level design:

- Universal Modeling Language (UML)
- Specification and Description Language (SDL)

- Structured analysis
- Block diagrams
- Data flows

ON THE CD
The CD-ROM included with the text contains the start for a high-level system design for the stereo-vision project using UML with the Visio UML template.

This start on a system design can be completed to practice use of the UML methodology. Both UML and SDL are well-suited formalisms for system design. Structured analysis methods and block diagramming are less formal, but these methods can be used successfully if applied with rigor to ensure completeness as described in this chapter. Mostly, successful projects choose a methodology and stick to it, using the methodology framework to communicate design and to allow for team reviews and assessment of completeness.

## COMPONENT DETAILED DESIGN

Detailed design must go down to the component level and divide the system into design elements specific to hardware and software. Specific design methods are more appropriate for mechanical, electrical, or software components and subsystems. Figure 12.5 shows a dimensioned cut-away mechanical design for a two-servo tilt/pan camera tracking subsystem. The figure only shows the mechanical design for this subsystem, and during detailed design review, the electrical and software detailed design for this subsystem should likewise show similar detail.

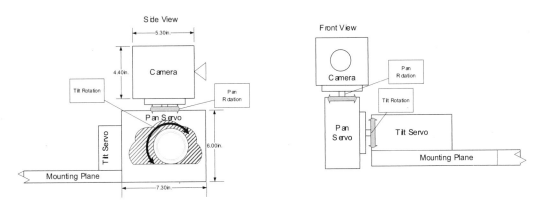

**FIGURE 12.5**  Detailed mechanical tilt/pan servo subsystem design.

Figure 12.5 should show sufficient detail so that the mechanical subsystem can be assembled from the design drawings and information. Clearly, even more detail would be needed, including all dimensions, material types, fasteners, adhesives, servo part numbers, and perhaps even assembly instructions. The less detail included, the more chance that some unspecified aspect of the subsystem design will lead to a design flaw. For example, not specifying the servo part number could cause a problem in the end with positioning accuracy requirements. Details such as multiple views, cut-aways, dimensions, and material specification are expected in a mechanical detailed design.

Figure 12.6 shows a similar level of detail for an electrical subsystem for the stereo-vision system.

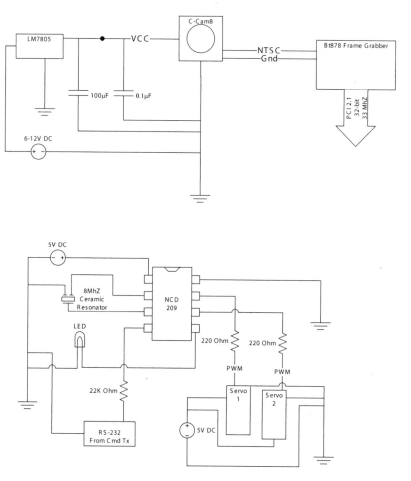

**FIGURE 12.6**    Detailed electrical design for tilt/pan camera subsystem.

Part numbers are shown along with all resistor values, voltage levels, and a schematic that is not yet laid out for a PCB (Printed Circuit Board), but which could be entered into a schematic capture tool such as OrCAD. All signal interfaces should be clearly labeled and described, such as the NTSC signal from the camera to the video encoder chip (Bt878). Parts should be specified well enough that they can be entered into a BOM (Bill of Material) database for order and assembly during implementation and test phases. Any simulation models of circuits completed, for example using SPICE (Simulation Program with Integrated Circuits Emphasis), should be included with this design as well.

Electrical design also should not only include circuit design, but logic design, which may often be captured in a mixed-signal circuit design, but logic elements often require additional explanation. Logic design should include all combinational and clocked state machine components and subsystems with schematic models or HDL (Hardware Design Language) models. Figure 12.7 shows logic diagram for a register component (JK flip-flop) and for an ALU (Arithmetic Logic Unit) for integer division.

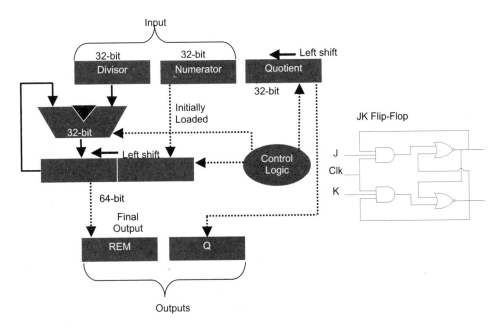

**FIGURE 12.7**   Detailed logic design block examples.

Most often, an HDL such as Verilog®, VHDL, or SystemC®, is used to implement logic designs and schematics to verify and simplify logic and to ensure that dynamic behavior is as required. This HDL design can be simulated for verification and built from discrete logic components, downloaded as a synthesized bit stream into an FPGA (Field Programmable Gate Array), or fabricated as an ASIC (Application Specific IC) for implementation. Detailed electrical logic design is aided by an EDA (Electronic Design Automation) tool chain that provides schematic capture, logic design using an HDL, simulation-based verification, synthesis, layout, and physical realization. For example, the following is a SystemC HDL specification for the integer divide logic design depicted in Figure 12.7:

```
// Division algorithm based upon "Computer Organization and Design:
// The Hardware/Software Interface, by D. Patterson and J. Hennessy
//
// SystemC implementation

#define MASK32 0x00000000FFFFFFFF

SC_MODULE(divide)
{
   sc_in_clk          CLOCK;
   sc_in<;bool>;       RESET;
   sc_in<;unsigned>;   DIV, NUM;
   sc_out<;unsigned>;  Q, REM;
   sc_out<;bool>;      ERROR;
   sc_out<;bool>;      READY;

   void compute();
   SC_CTOR(divide)
   {
     SC_THREAD(compute, CLOCK.pos());
     watching(RESET.delayed() == true);
   }
};


void divide::compute()
{
   // reset section
   signed lhr, rhr;
   unsigned i, q, r, d, n;
```

```
long long signed ir, save_ir;
bool err;

while(true)
{

    // IO cycle for completion with or without ERROR
    Q.write(q);
    REM.write(r);
    ERROR.write(err);
    READY.write(true);
    wait();

    // IO cycle for divide request
    d = DIV.read();
    n = NUM.read();
    READY.write(fales); // set busy state
    wait();

    // The divide computation
    if(d == 0)
        { q=0; r=0; err=true; }
    else if(n == 0)
        { q=0; r=0; err=false; }
    else
    {
        ir = n; q = 0; i = 0;

        while (i <; 32)
        {
            ir = ir <;<; 1;
            save_ir = ir;
            lhr = ((ir >;>; 32) &; MASK32);
            rhr = (ir &; MASK32);
            lhr = lhr - d;
            ir = (lrh <;<; 32) |
                    ((long long unsigned)rhr &; MASK32);

            if(ir <; 0)
            {
                ir = save_ir;
```

```
                        q = q <;<; 1;
                }
                else
                {
                    q = (q <;<; 1) + 1;
                }
                i++;
            }
        }
    }
}
```

This SystemC code can be executed on the SystemC simulator for verification.

One very important opportunity for early system-level design verification involves integrating software components with simulated or emulated hardware component and subsystem design. For example, boot code can be tested and run using an EDA co-simulation tool that provides an instruction set simulator that can run code on simulated hardware. The main issue with this is the immense processing power required to execute a cycle-accurate co-simulation model. Another option is to test software and hardware on an FPGA emulation platform that provides some level of the hardware/software interface defined in the system design, but may not implement the final physical form factor and may not implement all the required hardware interfaces. Likewise, some early testing between mechanical and electrical components may be possible. For example, the stereo-vision tracker servo subsystem could be tested with an FPGA-based servo controller interface to determine whether the hardware state machine for commanding the servo to set points using PWM is properly designed. Initial integrated testing of the servo subsystem might include a simplified single camera mono-vision test and simple command-line interface test software. The stereo servo mechanical subsystem would, of course, require a two-camera tilt/pan mounting system as shown in Figure 12.8.

Part of the final stages of detailed design should involve planning and status checks to ensure that the integration plans are on track as they were defined during the analysis stage of the second turn in the spiral. If not, the plans should be adjusted so that the second integration and regression phase goes smoothly. Numerous detailed design reviews should be held, often with much more limited audiences than high-level design so that hardware experts are reviewing hardware designs, mechanical experts are reviewing mechanical designs, and likewise for software designs. Design trade-offs, interface checks, and overall system efficacy should be determined during high-level design. High-level design reviews should include much more cross-discipline design review than detailed design. For real-

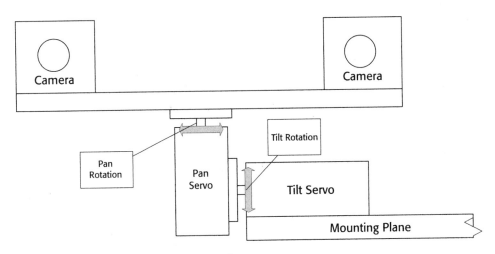

**FIGURE 12.8**    Two-camera stereo-vision mechanical design.

time embedded systems, deciding which real-time services are implemented with hardware state machines versus software is a key decision. Analyzing exactly what software services are required and how they will interact is a significant aspect of software high-level design and detailed design.

Real-time embedded system designs can benefit from design methods that specifically show software timing, service releases, and processing pipelines. Figure 12.9 shows a method for diagramming the services in a data processing pipeline where each pipeline stage must execute within a deadline.

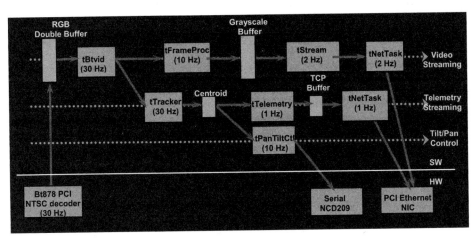

**FIGURE 12.9**    Stereo-vision processing pipeline sequence.

Design methods that can be directly compared to measurement or debug tools can vastly simplify verification. Figure 12.9 can fairly easily be compared to a WindView trace for a sequence of synchronously released services in a pipeline. Software and the interfaces and deployment of software on hardware can be well described within the UML framework. Figure 12.10 shows the overall deployment of software modules on hardware for the stereo-vision system.

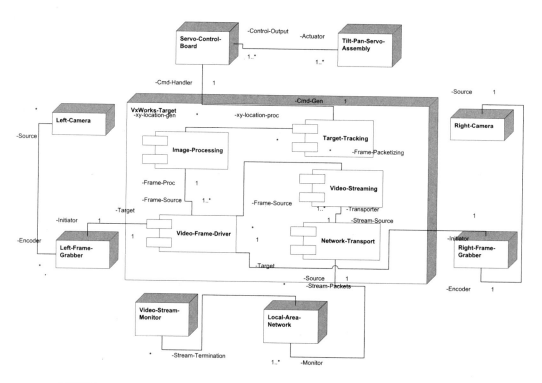

**FIGURE 12.10** Stereo-vision deployment diagram.

The deployment diagram in Figure 12.10 clearly shows the major software modules that must be developed. A given software component, for example the video driver, can now be designed with a class model that specifies functions, data, and a decomposition of a module into a class hierarchy. Figure 12.11 shows a possible class hierarchy for the video driver.

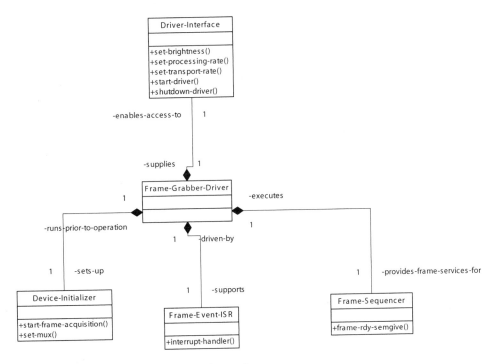

**FIGURE 12.11**    Stereo-vision video driver class.

The classes (and objects that instantiate them) can then be used in sequence or collaboration diagrams to show which modules call which class functions in each component and in what order. Figure 12.12 shows a sequence diagram for components in the stereo-vision system.

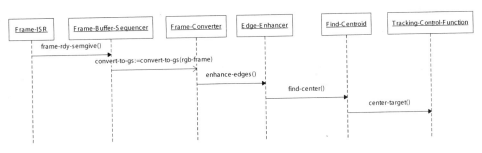

**FIGURE 12.12**    Stereo-vision sequence diagram.

Finally, to specify the design for the class functions (sometimes called methods), state machine design notation can be used to specify the function behavior now that it has been fully defined statically (class model) and in terms of the dynamic behavior at an interface level. Figure 12.13 shows a state machine design for the stereo-vision frame sequencing in the processing pipeline by the tBtvid driver.

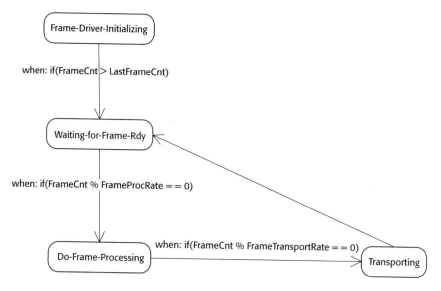

**FIGURE 12.13**    Stereo-vision sequencer state machine.

## COMPONENT UNIT TESTING

Component testing can be divided into these test types:

- Functional and interface tests
- Stress tests
- Soak tests
- Performance tests

Testing exit criteria should be defined for each of these types of tests ideally, both at the unit level and for system-level regression testing.

*Functional tests* verify that subsystems and components meet their interface and behavior requirements for those interfaces as specified by analysis phase requirements definition. Often it's impossible to fully test a functional interface due to the massive number of I/O combinations that might be required even for a simple software or hardware component. For example, a 64-switch interface has enough switch permutations that there is no way it can be fully tested. In this regard, functional tests should focus on input patterns and sequences that are expected and desired as well as those specifically not desired and which the system is expected to reject, handle, and prevent.

Because not all input combinations, timing patterns, and communication sequences can be tested between components and subsystems, *stress testing* provides important verification for unexpected inputs and timing. Stress testing is most often done with random input generation and with test harnesses that drive components harder than they are ever expected to be driven. So electrical subsystems are tested at higher voltage, higher temperatures, and higher speeds than the requirements. For example, a PCB layout designed for 100-MHz signal buses might be designed for gigahertz signaling and tested with signal rates 10 times the frequency of normal operation. Likewise, a software module might be tested with random inputs at higher-than-expected calling frequencies, and driven by service request workloads more demanding than those expected in actual operation.

*Soak testing* provides confidence in subsystem and component stability and lifetime estimates. For example, a software subsystem might be run for more than 48 hours with continuous workload to ensure that the software does not lose track of resources over time (a memory leak for a dynamic memory management service). Furthermore, soak time tests will uncover issues that are rare, such as unlikely combinations of events that might lead to timing problems, for example, a cache miss that causes very occasional software service deadline overruns. Similarly, for hardware, soak tests involve continuous runtime to verify component durability and lifetime expectations.

Finally, *performance tests* with units provide critical information for bottleneck analysis. If the performance of each unit can be tested in isolation, then the upper limits on the throughput, fidelity, or reliability of that unit can be determined apart from the system as a whole. Performance unit testing is fundamental to overall system risk analysis. The slowest and least reliable components can be identified from these unit tests and factored into a system-level performance and reliability analysis.

Software includes several types of unit tests that are specific to the nature of software modules:

- Black box test
- Glass box test

A *black box test* is a functional test or stress, stability, or performance test that is run without any knowledge of exactly what code is being exercised inside a software module. The danger of black box testing is that while rigorous functional, stress, stability, and performance tests might be defined, they may still only exercise a small percentage of the software in a module. A measure of the coverage of the software module for a given suite of tests indicates whether sufficient testing is being completed—this is a glass box test. A *glass box test* involves definition of test criteria:

- Number of execution paths driven out of total number in a module
- Number of statements or instructions covered out of total
- Number of decisions fully evaluated in a module

These conditions provide metrics for how complete the functional, stress, stability, or performance tests are in terms of fully exercising the software unit under test. More importantly, quantifying coverage allows the tester to know when they are done. Path coverage is simply all the instruction sequences that may be executed from every single branch point in code. Statement coverage refers to how many statements have been executed out of the sum of all unique instruction addresses. The decision coverage is less obvious.

Criteria called MCDC (Multiple Condition, Decision Coverage) evolved due to compiler and instruction set optimizations that allow for expressions or individual instructions to be executed conditionally. For example, the following C code includes two expressions with a logical OR test and two paths, one for a true outcome and another for the false outcome:

```
void control_update(void)
{
    if(inactive || (within_centroid_tolerance()
       && within_servo_deadbands()))
    {
        monitor_and_wait();
    }
    else
    {
        update_servo_control();
    }
}
```

In this code fragment, there are clearly only two paths. Both paths can be driven by evaluating inactive and the function within_centroid_tolerance(). For example, the monitor_and_wait() path is driven by a inactive=TRUE. The update_ servo_control() path can be driven by either inactive=FALSE and either one of the within_centroid_tolerance() or within_servo_deadbands() functions returning FALSE. Likewise the monitor_and_wait() path could also be driven by inactive= FALSE and both within_centroid_tolerance() or within_servo_deadbands() returning TRUE. So, there is a case where both paths are driven, but within_ servo_deadbands() is never called and evaluated. So, although path coverage for the function control_update() would indicate full coverage, code in within_ servo_deadbands() could execute and cause a failure in the field. If full path coverage criteria is measured on all functions, this might be caught, but if within_ servo_deadbands() is also called from another context, the function may appear covered, but was in fact never tested in the context of control_update(). The MCDC coverage criteria requires that all logical subexpressions be evaluated for full coverage.

## SYSTEM INTEGRATION AND TEST

As unit tests are completed, units can be assembled, including both hardware and software for integrated testing. Most often, it's best to take a building approach where components are integrated to form a single subsystem, which is tested. If the subsystem tests good, then two such subsystems are integrated into a partial system, and again tested. This is repeated until the whole system is integrated and tested good. Invariably, some unanticipated subsystem interaction results in two subsystems testing good, but when combined, the partial system does not test as expected. At this point, rerunning each subsystem test, a regression test, provides validation that the two sub-systems still are functional on their own. More complex still is a situation where two subsystems are integrated and test good, but when a third subsystem is added, the partial system does not test good. The ability to quickly isolate the problem is accelerated by quick unit regression test capability. Often a subsystem may fail when integrated due to integration error, a systemic interaction causing failure, or just random bad luck. Either way, the ability to test partial systems and regress component and subsystem units is fundamental to the integration-by-steps approach.

## CONFIGURATION MANAGEMENT AND VERSION CONTROL

Ideally, hardware and software will be developed on projects concurrently with integration tests using ISS (Instruction Set Simulation), TLM (Transaction Level Modes) for hardware, and with early testing of software on hardware emulation platforms. During this concurrent development, here are some tips on how to keep features and modules on track:

- Identify hardware and firmware module owners to take responsibility through entire lifecycle.
- Require tests to be developed in parallel with module development.
- Require early adoption of nightly testing using TLM simulation and/or RTL simulation.
- Adopt Configuration Management Version Control (CMVC) tools that allow for feature addition branches and version tagging.

Although these recommendations are followed in most projects, they often aren't implemented until the end of the process shown in Figure 12.14.

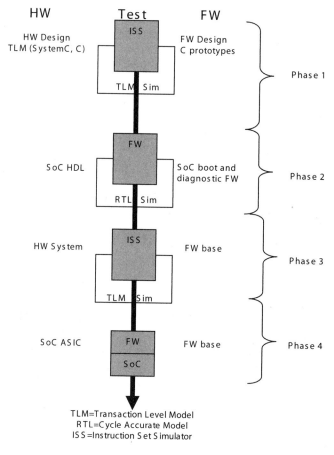

**FIGURE 12.14**    Concurrent HW and SW development timeline.

Starting early and automating tests for nightly regression is now possible with EDA and co-simulation tools available for hardware and software development. In the days before early verification tools were available, hardware and firmware development proceeded much more independently than they can now. A typical process included independent development of firmware on an emulator while hardware was designed and developed, with most of the cotesting done during the final post-silicon verification. Despite advances in verification tools, many developers still work along lines established in those days, and thus don't adopt testing and regression processes, or configuration and version control, to the extent that they should.

Because EDA and HDLs for hardware design make the hardware development process similar in nature to firmware development, both hardware and firmware can and should use configuration management tools—the same ones, if at all possible! This almost seems blasphemous to organizations that have grown accustomed to a silo model for hardware and software development, where a quick hand-off is made post-silicon, and interaction is otherwise minimal.

One difficulty when testing changing firmware on changing hardware is that stability often suffers: this can greatly impede the progress of both hardware and firmware development teams. This problem can be solved by having the hardware team make releases of simulators to the firmware team. Likewise, the firmware team should make releases of boot code and diagnostic code to the hardware team. Both teams need well-disciplined processes for maintaining versions and releases. One way to do this is to maintain a main line of C code or HDL that is guaranteed to be stable. As hardware or firmware developers add code, they do so on branches from the stable main line, and merge new features and bug fixes made on code branches back to the line. Figure 12.15 depicts this basic disciplined practice.

Figure 12.15 shows how a developer can take a stable baseline of C code or HDL, branch it for modification, add new features and test them on the branch, and then merge them with other potential changes on the main line. After the merge is completed, the new result must once again be tested, and then it can be put back on the main line, advancing the overall system and maintaining stability. The only place unstable code should be found with this process is on a branch. After a CVS repository has been set up and code checked into it, developers can create a working *sandbox* for their code; the sandbox is their own private copy from the repository. For simple modifications to the code base, a file can be modified and, after testing, put back into the base with a simple command:

```
cvs commit filename
```

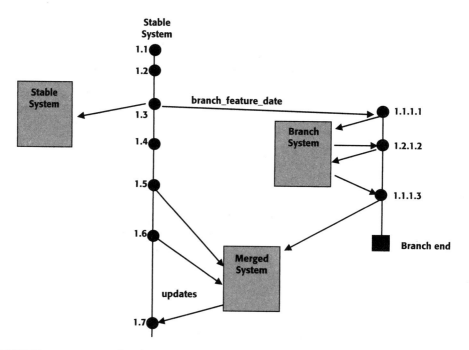

**FIGURE 12.15** Example of CVS module branching.

Branching is a more advanced method, which is useful when sets of files need to be modified, tested, and shared with other developers. A CVS branch has a tag, and therefore other developers can check out copies of a branch to their own branch sandbox, as Figure 12.15 shows. In Listing 12.1, the first set of commands does a checkout of the current code and then tags this revision of the code with a branch tag. *Tags* are simply sets of revisions of all files from the repository. The branch tag is a special tag that not only defines a set of file revisions, but also allows for modification to those files with a new revision that remains separate from the main repository revisions. This is shown in Figure 12.15 as the branch line that includes a main line revision and branch revision. The developer or developers working on the branch can share updates and test the branch revisions without affecting the main line of code.

The middle set of commands in Listing 12.1 provides an example of updates to the branch revision. When the developers are happy with the branch, the branched code set can be merged back to the main line of code with the final set of commands in Listing 12.1.

**LISTING 12.1**    CVS Commands for Branching

```
cd stable_directory
cvs checkout system
make system; test system
cvs tag -b -c branch_feature_date

cd branch_directory
cvs checkout -r branch_feature_date
modify files
make system; test system
cvs commit
modify files
make system; test system
cvs commit

cd merge_directory
cvs checkout system
cvs update -j branch_feature_date -kk system
make system; test system
cvs commit
```

Branches can be useful for almost any modification to a design maintained as a file set, but most often they are used for

- Complicated multifile bug fixes
- Addition of new features
- Performance optimization and tuning
- Special releases to external customers or internal users

Optimization is a great example of an area where branches combined with regression testing can allow for significant and aggressive performance improvements while minimizing risk to system stability. You may very well have optimized a system to improve performance, only to find after subsequent development of more sophisticated regression tests that the optimization has destabilized the system. Or, in some cases, it may take some soak time before the destabilization is noticed. For example, if the optimization introduces a new race condition, then that condition might not be hit for many days or weeks, long after the optimization has been initially tested and integrated back into the system. At this point, the optimization might be harder to back out.

Optimizations performed on branches can be tested and maintained on the branch and merged with a very clear change set. You can more readily back out of merging a destabilizing optimization back into the main line if you use tags on the branch.

## REGRESSION TESTING

Regression testing is not only critical for integration steps, but also for ensuring that a system configuration that worked yesterday still works today after incremental changes. If the system is broken due to incremental changes, this should be detected before such changes are made permanent to the working system. For example, a code change is suggested to a module to improve performance, but this change might break the functional specification. This should be caught by a nightly run system regression test.

## SUMMARY

A good understanding of system lifecycle and planning for spiral turns and phases can help minimize surprises, delays, and costly errors during the development of a project. The spiral lifecycle approach can also assist developers with risk maintenance and mitigation. More frequent reporting of progress to management also allows for better overall planning within an organization.

## EXERCISES

ON THE CD

1. Set up CVS or the Subversion CMVC tool for your work on a real-time project to be completed using this book.
2. Complete the example stereo vision UML Visio template design provided on the CD-ROM.
3. Write a SystemC model for a PWM generator state machine to control a hobby servo. Verify this design using the SystemC simulator and finally implement it on an FPGA ASIC such as the Virtex-II or Spartan.
4. Describe whether CVS is better than subversion or vice versa and why.

# 13 Continuous Media Applications

## In This Chapter

- Introduction
- Video
- Uncompressed Video Frame Formats
- Video Codecs
- Video Streaming
- Video Stream Analysis and Debug
- Audio Codecs and Streaming
- Audio Stream Analysis and Debug
- Voice Over Internet Protocol (VoIP)

## INTRODUCTION

Digital video processing is an excellent way to explore and learn more about real-time embedded systems. The camera or video stream frame rate provides a fundamental service frequency, typically at 30 Hz for NTSC, from which other services may run at the same frequency or a subperiod of this basic rate. Video processing services for a wide range of system projects include the following:

- Video stream compression and decompression (codec)
- Video stream transport over a network
- Image processing to detect edges of a target object and to determine its center in the XY plane
- Tracking a target object with tilt and pan servo control loop to keep the object center in the FOV (Field of View) center

- Two-camera stereo ranging to determine distance to a target object being tracked
- Digital video recording and playback
- Motion detection with video stream storage, motion stream playback
- Multiple video stream server (Video on Demand)
- Line following mobile robot with forward-looking obstacle detection
- Embedded camera in robotic arm for object and target recognition pick and place
- Fixed overhead camera-based navigation of a robotic arm for pick and place

The basic requirement for digital video processing is a video capture card/driver. The Video for Linux project maintains a number of drivers for Linux that can be used in an embedded Linux project; likewise, Linux drivers can be ported to VxWorks.

ON THE CD
The CD-ROM includes a VxWorks driver for the Bt878 NTSC capture chip, which provides rudimentary 320 x 240 RGB frame capture at 30 fps. This example driver was loosely based upon the original bttv Linux driver, but does not implement all the capture modes that the bttv driver does. This example driver was originally built from the chipset manuals, but when problems with documentation were encountered, the Linux bttv driver source helped immensely. One of the best ways to really learn about the video hardware/software interface is to port a driver to VxWorks from Linux or start with the chipset manuals and build one from the ground up.

From the basic capture, driver codec and/or image processing services can be run at the same 30-Hz rate or a subrate such as 15, 10, 6, 5, 3, 2, or 1 Hz easily derived from the basic 30-Hz interrupt rate from the frame encoder.

# VIDEO

The predominant video analog signal formats are NTSC (National Television Systems Committee) used in North America, Japan, and Korea; PAL (Phase Alteration by Line), used in South America, Africa, and Asia; and SECAM (Sequential Color with Memory), used in France and northern Asia. The NTSC standard used in North America was first defined in 1941 for black-and-white transmission and further refined in 1953 to include a color standard. The NTSC standard is used for television broadcast (HDTV, or High Definition Television is the emerging replacement with much higher resolution), for CCTV (Closed Circuit Television), and for numerous digital video-capture and video-editing devices. An NTSC camera input to a video encoder such as the Bt878 hosted on an x86 PC provides real-time digital video capture and can be used as a basic platform for real-time video projects.

The basic NTSC signal rasters a television CRT with odd and even lines (interlacing) so that there's a retrace between the odd and even raster traces from the lower-right corner back to the upper-left corner of the screen. The interlacing was designed into NTSC to control flicker between frames for early television systems. The odd and even lines are updated at 59.94 Hz with 486 lines out of a total of 525 used to display the image, and the remaining lines used for signal sync, vertical retrace, and the vertical blank lines that used to carry closed caption data. This basic signal was modified to carry color with two chrominance signals at 3.57955 MHz that are 90 degrees out of phase. A luminance signal took the place of the black-and-white signal in color NTSC. Video-capture chips, such as the Bt878, encode this color NTSC signal into luminance and chrominance digital data by sampling the signal and using ADCs (Analog-to-Digital converters) to generate a digital measurement of the luminance and chrominance signals. The video-capture chip must maintain PLL (Phase Locked Loop) with the NTSC signal to properly sample the NTSC signal at the right points in time. The NTSC signal lock is obtained during sync and retrace periods where the signal has a flat output known as the *front and back porch* [Luther99].

The digitized NTSC data is initially in the form of luminance and chrominance samples that can be converted to RGB data. For digital processing, RGB data is the most easily processed and the most common standard for display using a computer graphics adapter. Figure 13.1 shows the conceptual color cube representation of RGB where the basic Red, Green, and Blue outputs can be additively combined to derive all other common colors as a 24-bit pixel composite of the 8-bit R, G, and B values.

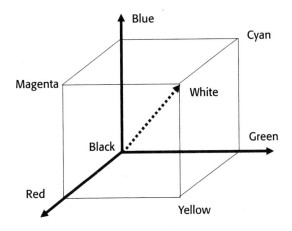

**FIGURE 13.1**  RGB color cube.

A standard digital conversion among luminance, chrominance, and RGB defines a method for deriving RGB from NTSC sampling:

- YUV (Where Y is luminance, and U, V are the chrominance) to RGB Conversion
  - $B = 1.164(Y - 16) + 2.018(U - 128)$
  - $G = 1.164(Y - 16) - 0.813(V - 128) - 0.391(U - 128)$
  - $R = 1.164(Y - 16) + 1.596(V - 128)$

To convert back from RGB to YUV, the following is used:

- RGB to YUV Conversion (for computers with RGB [0-255])
  - $Y = (0.257 \times R) + (0.504 \times G) + (0.098 \times B) + 16$
  - $Cr = V = (0.439 \times R) - (0.368 \times G) - (0.071 \times B) + 128$
  - $Cb = U = -(0.148 \times R) - (0.291 \times G) + (0.439 \times B) + 128$

In both cases, all computed outputs should be clamped to a range of 0 to 255. The Bt878 video encoder performs this digital conversion with a hardware state machine so that RGB data can be captured from NTSC and pushed by DMA into the host PC memory.

Often grayscale or monochrome digital video is sufficient for basic computer vision applications or video-monitoring applications such as motion-detection security camera systems. Acquisition of NTSC into RGB digital data provides a very flexible approach because monochrome can be derived from it and the RGB data can be displayed locally in full 24-bit color but stored in a grayscale or in a compressed 16-bit luminance chrominance format. Grayscale monochrome frames can be derived from RGB by two methods:

- Selecting one color band from the three
- Converting the three colors to grayscale with a summing linear relationship

Figure 13.2 compares both methods showing grayscale derived by selection of R, G, or B bands alone and comparing this to the standard mixing conversion (based upon characteristics of human vision), which is defined as

$$Y = 0.3R + 0.59G + 0.11B$$

From Figure 13.2, the balance does appear most pleasing to the eye, however, for computer vision, it's not clear that a balance provides better image processing for functions such as segmenting a scene with edge detection.

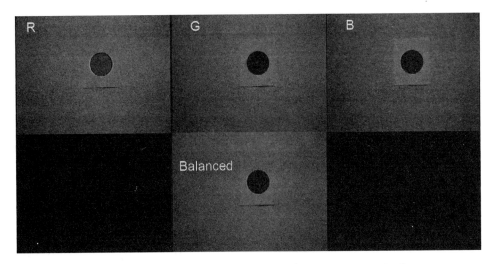

**FIGURE 13.2**   Grayscale monochrome derived from RGB by three methods.

Color is one dimension of streaming video that also can be thought of as having a time and space dimension. Codec engines can take advantage of color, time, and space dimensions to compress a stream of video frames for storage or transport over a network to reduce required capacity and bandwidth. Conversion from color RGB to grayscale is a 3 to 1 compression, converting each pixel (picture element) into an 8-bit data value from 24 bits. Similarly, a 24-bit pixel RGB frame can be converted into a smaller luminance/chrominance (YCrCb) 16-bit pixel frame, providing a 3 to 2 compression with some color loss. The most commonly used YCrCb format is YCrCb 4:2:2, where four luminance samples are stored for every 2 Cr and Cb chrominance samples as depicted in Figure 13.3.

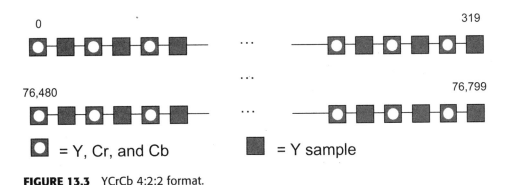

**FIGURE 13.3**   YCrCb 4:2:2 format.

Figure 13.3 shows YCrCb samples for a 320 × 240 frame size. The Bt878 encoder actually encodes RGB as αRGB, where an 8-bit alpha luminance is combined with the 24-bit RGB values for a 32-bit pixel. The alpha can be used as the Y sample and the Cr and Cb can be derived from RGB using the YUV to RGB conversion. If alpha is not available, Y can be computed from RGB as well [Jack96]. In YCrCb 4:2:2, each Y, Cr, and Cb sample is 8 bits. The 2 RGB pixels require 48 bits, whereas 2 YCrCb pixels require 32 bits total (or 16 bits per pixel compared to 24 bits per pixel for RGB), yielding a one-third smaller frame size overall. The sample to pixel map format for YCrCb is

- Pixel-0 = $Y7:Y0_0$, $Cb7:Cb0_0$; Pixel-1 = $Y7:Y0_1$, $Cr7:Cr0_0$
- Pixel-2 = $Y7:Y0_2$, $Cb7:Cb0_1$; Pixel-3 = $Y7:Y0_3$, $Cr7:Cr0_1$

So, for YCrCb, for every 4 Y samples, there are 2 Cr and 2 Cb samples packed into 4 total pixels. The frame size of 76,800 total pixels in a 320 x 240 frame is divisible by 4, so YCrCb works for any NxM frame where N and M are divisible by 2.

## UNCOMPRESSED VIDEO FRAME FORMATS

ON THE CD

Before diving into how to compress, transport, and decompress a video stream, you should understand basic uncompressed video formats that can be used for debug and early testing. The two simplest single frame formats are PPM (Portable Pixmap) and PGM (Portable Grey Map). These two single-frame formats can be displayed by tools included with the CD-ROM and commonly available viewers such as the Irfan viewer. Both simply require a header describing the data pixel and frame format along with the raw binary data in the format specified. For example, a PPM file might have the following header:

```
P6
#test
320 240
255
```

The header is followed by 76,800 24-bit RGB pixels arranged into 320 columns and 240 rows with each color band ranging from 0 to 255 in value. The PPM and PGM headers are always in plain ASCII text, and the data is in binary form. The # character is used to add comment lines in the header. The P6 indicates this is a PPM file and not some other Netpbm format such as PGM. The PGM header is almost identical, for example:

```
P5
# grayscale
320 240
255
```

This header indicates PGM with the P5 and again specifies that 76,800 8-bit monochrome pixels will follow the header with a value range from 0 to 255. Several example PPM and PGM files are included on the CD-ROM.

ON THE CD

## VIDEO CODECS

The compression from RGB to YCrCb is lossy in the color dimension. Codecs can provide compression of video streams in three dimensions:

- Color space
- X, Y frame space
- Time

Compression in X, Y frame space can be lossless or lossy with varying degrees of compression performance. Methods typically applied to strings of information such as RLE (Run Length Encoding) or Huffman encoding can be used on frame data within a single frame. Pixels, like any string of symbols, can be compressed by encoding repeating patterns. The RLE encoding simply replaces all repeating symbol (pixel) sequences with a count and value. A simple approach like this can provide lossless compression in images. Huffman encoding can likewise provide string compression for repeating pixel sequences. Often the compression provided by string oriented lossless compression is not significant because video data, unlike text, often has random variations even in mostly flat backgrounds. For significant compression within a frame, lossy methods must be applied that use transforms or pixel averaging to combine neighboring pixels. The neighboring pixels can be regenerated during decompression with an inverse transform or interpolation. Information is lost, but compression can be 4 to 1 or higher compared to RLE or Huffman, which might provide a 10% smaller frame size reduction.

Compression over multiple frames can be significant. The most basic method is to transmit change-only data. Change-only data is determined by computing a difference frame for every stream frame pair. Pixel differences above a threshold (zero threshold for lossless) are transmitted as pixel address and pixel change, and all other pixels are considered unchanged. This leads to high compression rates for streams where the scene is not changing quickly. The thresholding helps eliminate changes due to small background noise in lighting, the detector itself, the atmosphere, and other perturbations to an otherwise static scene. In the extreme cases, a totally static scene yields infinite compression, and a totally changing scene actually inflates the frame size. For each change-only pixel, the address plus the change must be encoded. For an 8-bit grayscale pixel, this requires 8 bits for the change pixel and 17 bits for the pixel address for a $320 \times 240$ frame size. Most often, change-only compression includes evaluation of the number of changes; if there are so many that the change-only frame provides no compression (or worse yet inflation), then the raw data frame is sent instead. This is an adaptive form of compression.

Optimal codecs apply a series of lossless and lossy compression schemes for maximum performance. For example, a stream could first be compressed in the color space by transforming RGB to YCrCb (a 33% decrease in frame size), followed by difference imaging with a threshold, and finally compressed further by a lossless method such as RLE. Lossy methods followed by lossless can vastly improve the performance of the lossless compression; in cases where change-only compression won't help, the color space and lossless compression will still decrease frame size. Adaptive change-only compression requires a compression header describing the compression applied so that the decompression can correctly treat each frame as a difference frame or not and so the decompression can be applied in the reverse order of compression.

Codec standards such as M-JPEG (Motion-Joint Photographic Expert's Group), MPEG (Moving Picture Expert's Group), DivX, and Theora can be used, but building your own codec is the best way to learn about and appreciate how codecs work. The MPEG standard uses lossy image transforms, including frequency space and entropy encoding [Solari97]. The most current extensions, such as MPEG-4, also include prediction and difference-image encoding over time. In contrast, M-JPEG does not employ compression over time (multiple frames), which has the advantage of being independent of motion in the video stream and allowing video editing to include cuts on any frame boundary. The DivX codec is a proprietary codec that uses MPEG-4, and Theora is an open source codec designed to be competitive with MPEG-4. Aside from building your own codec, integrating an open source codec such as Theora is the next best way to learn about video codec technology. The codec can be combined with a transport protocol for streaming such as RTP (Real-Time Transport Protocol) built on top of UDP (User Datagram Protocol) and most often used in conjunction with RTSP (Real-Time Streaming Protocol) and RTCP (Real-Time Control Protocol).

## VIDEO STREAMING

RTSP such as RTP avoid the overhead of reliable connection-oriented transport methods such as TCP (Transmission Control Protocol) and the complication of retransmission because video and audio streams can and do allow occasional data drop-outs. For a real-time isochronal stream of video or audio, retransmission not only adds overhead but can also be detrimental to QoS. A frame or audio sound bite drop-out is preferable to guaranteed delivery of data long after the deadline for continuous decompression and playback of a media bit stream. In general, the smaller the buffering of playback data the better for streaming protocols because buffering and holding data adds latency. For example, in audio, data buffer induced latency makes a two-way conversation feel like you're talking on a satellite link. Likewise, buffering video streams makes stream control difficult and inaccurate. The ideal transport would provide constant bit rate with minimal buffering and latency. Streaming protocols such as RTP provide this type of performance on top of simple datagram transport with the added features of packet reordering, timestamping, and delivery monitoring, but without any form of retransmission [Topic02].

## VIDEO STREAM ANALYSIS AND DEBUG

 The VxWorks Bt878 video encoder driver included on the CD-ROM can be used to capture video streams for compression, transport, decompression, image processing, and computer vision. The Linux Video for Linux project version of this driver can likewise by used to build similar applications on Linux or Real-Time Linux. With either frame capture driver, basic debug methods include the following:

- Dumping single frames for analysis
- Streaming frames to a viewer for observation
- Frame metadata derived from stream or image processing

Dumping a single frame with the VxWorks driver can be done by calling a function, `write_save_buffer()`, to dump the current frame over the Tornado TSFS (Target-Server Filesystem). Be sure the byte ordering is correct between the target and host if they are different architectures (e.g., an x86 target and a Sun Solaris host) and if the pixel size is larger than a single byte. Figure 13.4 shows an image dumped by TSFS and viewed with the freely available Irfan viewer for Windows.

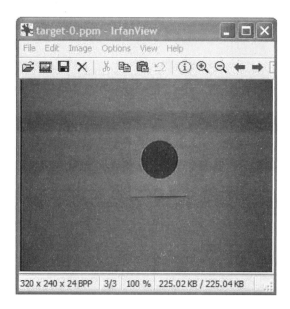

ON THE CD

**FIGURE 13.4**  Bt878 driver frame dump example.
(see CD-ROM for color image)

Frame dumps provide basic analysis of lighting, focus, field of view, truth data for edge detection and object centroid calculation, and rudimentary debug to ensure that NTSC encoding is properly configured so that frames are being captured. The Irfan viewer provides point-and-click pixel address information. So a dumped image can be analyzed to determine the centroid of the target, the red circle in Figure 13.4, by reading the pixel address and comparing to the address calculated by target-based image processing. Lighting can be adjusted in the room or by setting ADC sensitivity using set_brightness(). The impact of calling set_brightness() can be observed with frame dumps. You can focus a camera using frame dumps, but it's difficult and slow given the latency in feedback. Debugging can be greatly enhanced by providing an uncompressed debug stream and by using analog equipment such as a television to ensure that camera hardware is functional and focused well.

Debug streaming should be done with a simple uncompressed frame stream unless a reliable and lossless codec is available. The point of frame dumps and debug streaming is to view the raw data or to introduce image processing or compression after the raw data stream has been verified.

ON THE CD

The CD-ROM includes a basic PPM (Portable Pixmap) stream viewer, which can be used to view uncompressed video streams at low frame rates. This viewer was built using the Python high-level programming language so that it's easy to modify and portable to almost any platform (any platform that runs Python). Figure 13.5 shows the vpipe_display.py python application displaying the host based stream that can be generated with frametx_test.py.

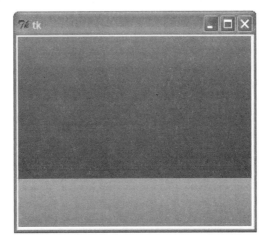

**FIGURE 13.5**  vpipe display test stream.

The point of this test stream generator is to ensure that the vpipe display tool is working and the frametx_test.py provides an example of a TCP/IP frame source client that can connect to the vpipe display server for streaming debug. The streaming rainbow pattern shown provides a quick and easy way to make sure no bugs are in the debug tool itself.

The following VxWorks target code can be spawned as a task (debug streaming service) and connects to the vpipe display server and sends PPM format frames once a second based upon a semaphore given in the driver main loop:

```
void stream_client(void)
{
  /* opens client socket and connects to server */
  init_frametx();

  enable_streaming=1;
```

```
while(!streamShutdown)
{
    semTake(streamRdy, WAIT_FOREVER);
    frame_to_net(rgb_buffer);
}
}
```

The init_frametx() function requires that the vpipe display server is already up and running and in the listen state for a TCP/IP socket. This utility is included with the video driver source code for VxWorks. The VxWorks video driver main loop is released by the encoder end of frame interrupt, and this loop gives the semaphore streamRdy so that a frame is written out over TCP to the vpipe display server once every 30th frame, or once a second. This results in streaming to the vpipe display tool as shown in Figure 13.6.

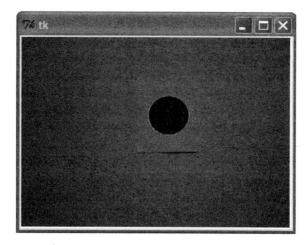

**FIGURE 13.6** vpipe display debug video stream.

The debug streaming rate can be increased by simply increasing the frequency of the semaphore give in the driver main loop up to a maximum of 30 fps. However, be sure that the target has sufficient processing capability and that the Ethernet link has sufficient bandwidth to keep up with this rate.

Image processing on the video capture target can compute frame metadata that can be very useful for debug, for example, frame difference sums, target centroid pixel address, or current frame compression ratio achieved. This data derived during image processing, compression, and decompression can assist immensely with performance analysis as well as debugging. The data can be dumped on com-

mand with a VxWorks function call made in the windshell or can be sent for remote monitoring over a TCP/IP connection.

## AUDIO CODECS AND STREAMING

Most any sound card can be used to encode audio data into a digital format suitable for compression, transport, and decompression. The Linux ALSA (Advanced
Linux Sound Architecture) provides drivers for numerous audio cards, including
the Cirrus® Crystal™ 4281. This driver was adapted for VxWorks and can be
found on the CD-ROM.

ON THE CD

The Crystal 4281 includes the Cirrus 4297 codec, which can encode an analog
audio source into 8-bit mono or 16-bit stereo digital data and can play back data in
the same format. The 4281 also includes a controller that is used to coordinate data
transfer from the codec FIFOs (First In First Out hardware buffer) to processor
memory and vice versa. Recorded data is pushed into the host processor's memory
by the 4281 DMA. Likewise, the 4281 DMA pulls data for playback from the host
processor's memory. The 4281 encodes the incoming audio signal with ADC sampling at a selectable rate and DMA buffering that can be specified. The example driver code programs 11,025 samples per second and sets up DMA for recorded data
to a 512-byte buffer so that a DMA completion interrupt is raised approximately 21
times every second (11,025/512 times a second) for 8-bit mono encoding. Likewise,
the playback is interrupt driven by the 4281 DMA so that at the same rate as record,
an interrupt indicates that new data should be moved into the playback buffer. The
driver uses double buffers so that one half of the record buffer is being written into
by the DMA while the other half is being copied out for audio transport, and one
half of the playback buffer is being read by DMA into the DAC playback channel
while the other half is being written by software with data to be played back.

The 4297/4281 does no compression, but does provide digital encoding suitable
for software compression or encryption. The DMA interrupt-based synchronization
with software also allows for easy coordination of audio stream transport from
record to playback services. Some of the most tricky aspects of this driver are the
4297 gain and attenuation settings, properly tuning the timing to avoid playback and
record data drop-outs, and selecting the proper 4297 PCM channels for playback.

## AUDIO STREAM ANALYSIS AND DEBUG

One of the simplest ways to debug an audio driver is to examine the record and
playback buffer data with memory dumps. The data in each should be a PCM
waveform. Zero data in the record or playback buffer indicates a codec or DMA

misconfiguration and will cause noisy pops and clicks in the playback audio. Most often, the Crystal 4281 is used to implement two-way Voice over Internet (VoIP) transport. To make initial debugging simpler, use headphones and a constant audio stream source such as a CD player or MP3 player to pipe in music. Initially, the record function can be tested and record DMA buffer update verified with record buffer memory dumps. This can be done in VxWorks using the windshell d command, which will dump data from any address. The record data can be looped back through transport for local playback and verification. Again, the playback buffer should be dumped to verify that the data is being updated. The audio cards often include analog loop-back features, so it's important to verify that data in the playback buffer is truly being updated to avoid being fooled by analog loop back and mistaking this as a working digital transport loop back.

## VOICE OVER INTERNET PROTOCOL (VOIP)

After a basic record and playback audio driver has been debugged and is working, this can be combined with session and transport services along with a codec or encryption engine for VoIP. Figure 13.7 shows one end of a VoIP digital terminal.

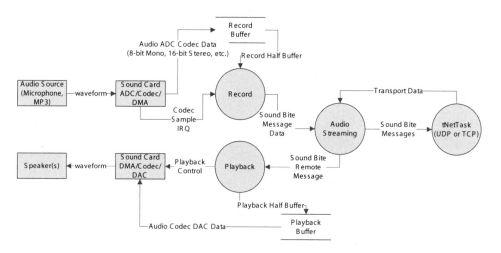

**FIGURE 13.7** VoIP data flow for one end.

Each terminal must have record and playback services interfacing to streaming and transport services. The basic sound-bite record, transport, and playback rates are driven by the sampling rate, the audio format, and the buffer size for a sound bite. Ideally, this process should emulate a constant bit-rate encoding, transport, and decoding between the record and playback channels. Figure 13.8 shows how two of these digital terminals can be combined to provide full-duplex VoIP.

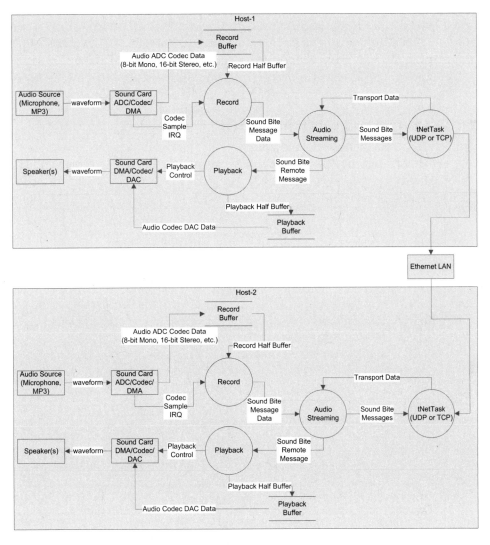

**FIGURE 13.8**    Full-duplex VoIP data flow.

The basic full-duplex VoIP implementation still does not define how calls are initiated or any common voice services such as voice mail, call waiting, conference calling, and hold. These features can be added fairly easily, however, after the basic full-duplex capability is implemented and debugged.

## SUMMARY

Continuous media applications include any media source and usage where periodic frames must be processed and transported in real time. This could be a broad range of media and multimedia applications, including video, audio, digital teleconferencing, virtual reality, video monitoring, video editing, video-on-demand streaming servers, and many more emergent soft real-time media applications. In the future, the complexity of emergent TV standards such as HDTV (High Definition TV) and DLP (Digital Light Projection) will require significantly more real-time embedded control [Poynton03].

## EXERCISES

ON THE CD

1. Use the Bt878 btvid.c driver included on the CD-ROM or the Linux equivalent bttv driver to capture NTSC frames using a Hauppauge WinTV frame grabber. Prove that you got the driver working by streaming output to the Python vpipe_display.py viewing tool.

ON THE CD

2. Use the image-processing sharpen.c program on the CD-ROM to provide edge enhancement to a PPM 320 × 240 image of your choice.
3. Write a program to detect the edges of the example target-0.ppm image and to produce an output that shows only red lines outlining the edges of the target object with an otherwise white background.
4. Download the ALSA driver for the Cirrus 4281 or a similar audio card and write a Linux application to record analog audio input into files for later playback through the same driver.

## CHAPTER REFERENCES

[Jack96] Jack, Keith, *Video Demystified—A Handbook for the Digital Engineer.* High Text Publications, 1996.
[Luther99] Luther, Arch, and Andrew Inglis, *Video Engineering,* 3rd ed. McGraw-Hill, 1999.

[Poynton03] Poynton, Charles, *Digital Video and HDTV: Algorithms and Interfaces.* Morgan Kaufmann Publishers, Elsevier Science (USA), 2003.

[Solari97] Solari, Stephen J., *Digital Video and Audio Compression.* McGraw-Hill, 1997.

[Topic02] Topic, Michael, *Streaming Media Demystified.* McGraw-Hill, 2002.

# 14 Robotic Applications

## INTRODUCTION

Robotic applications are great examples of real-time embedded systems because they clearly use sensing and actuators to affect objects in the real world within the real-time physical constraints of environments that humans often operate in as well. Figure 14.1 shows the NASA robonaut riding a segway, a typical human activity requiring real-time coordination.

Real-time applications also might have deadlines that are beyond human ability. A real-time system must simply operate within an environment to monitor and/or control a physical process at a rate required by the physics of the process. In the case of robotics, this is a distinct advantage that robotics have over human labor, the capability to keep up with a process that requires faster response and more accuracy than is humanly possible. Furthermore, robots can perform repetitive tasks for long hours without tiring. Figure 14.2 shows an industrial robotic assembly line.

Image created by NASA. Public domain.

**FIGURE 14.1** NASA robonaut riding a segway—a common human real-time activity.

**FIGURE 14.2** Industrial robots on an assembly line.

Robotics are often deployed in controlled environments such as assembly lines rather than in uncontrolled environments where humans often operate better, at least presently.

This chapter reviews basic concepts that are important to the design and implementation of basic real-time robotic systems.

## ROBOTIC ARM

The *robotic arm* approximates the dexterity of the human arm with a minimum of five degrees of rotational freedom, including base rotation, shoulder, elbow, wrist, and a gripper. The gripper can be a simple claw or approximate the dexterity of a human hand with individual fingers. In general, the gripper is often called an end *effector* to describe the broad range of devices that might be used to manipulate objects or tools. These basic arms are available as low-cost hobby kits and can be fit with custom controllers and sensors for fairly advanced robotics projects. The main limitations of low-cost hobby arms are that they are unable to grip and move any significant mass, offer less accurate and repeatable positioning, and are less dexterous than industrial or research robotic arms. Most industrial or research robotic arms have six or more degrees of freedom (additional wrist motion and complex end effectors) and can manipulate masses from one to hundreds of kilograms. Robotic arms are often combined with computer vision with cameras either fixed in the arm or with views of the arm from fixed locations. A basic five-degree-of-freedom arm with end effector vision can be used to implement interesting tasks, including search, target recognition, grappling, and target relocation. Figure 14.3 shows the OWI-7 robotic trainer arm with a reference coordinate system.

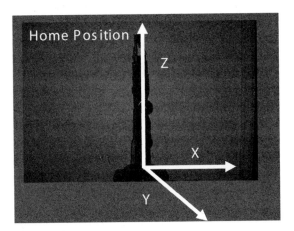

**FIGURE 14.3**   Robotic arm coordinates and home position.

With a reference coordinate system with an origin at the fixed base for the arm, the reach capability of an arm can be defined based upon the arm mechanical design and kinematics. Figure 14.4 shows the OWI arm with elbow rotation so that the forearm is held parallel to the base surface. In this position, the base can be rotated to move the end effector over a circular trace around the arm base.

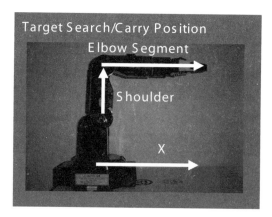

**FIGURE 14.4**   Robotic elbow rotation only.

The five-degree of freedom arm is capable of tracing out reachable circles around its base between an inner and outer ring. Figure 14.5 shows the innermost ring of reach capability for the OWI arm.

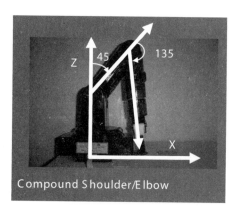 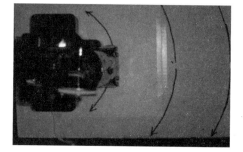

**FIGURE 14.5**   Innermost surface ring reach capability.

Combined rotation of the shoulder and elbow allows the OWI arm end effector to reach locations on circular arcs around the base at various radii from the innermost ring. Figure 14.6 shows an intermediate ring of reach capability.

**FIGURE 14.6**   Intermediate surface ring reach capability.

Finally, the outermost ring of reach capability for the OWI arm is defined by arm length with no elbow rotation and shoulder rotation so that the end effector reaches the surface. Figure 14.7 shows the limit of outermost reach capability.

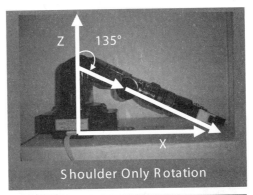

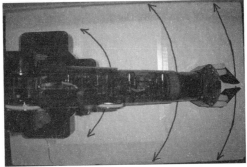

**FIGURE 14.7**   Outermost surface ring reach capability.

This basic analysis only considers the surface reach capability of the OWI arm on its X-Y base plane. More sophisticated tasks might require three-dimensional reach capability analysis. After the kinematics and reach capability analysis has been completed so that the joint rotations are known for moving the end effector to and from desired target locations, now an actuation and control interface must be designed.

## ACTUATION

Actuation and end effector control is greatly simplified when the target object masses that the end effector must work with are negligible. Significant target mass requires more complex active joint motor torque control. Moving significant mass requires geared motor controllers with torque controlling DAC output. Another option for actuation is the use of stepper motors with active feedback control channels for each degree of freedom. For the OWI arm and negligible payload mass, the actuation can be designed using relays or simple H-bridge motor controllers. The motors must be reversible. The simplest circuit for reversing a motor can be implemented with switches to change the polarity across the motor leads as shown in Figure 14.8.

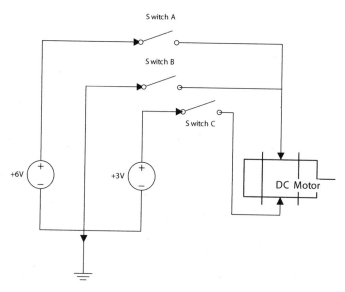

**FIGURE 14.8**    Three-switch reversible motor.

The possible switch states are enumerated in Table 14.1 along with the motor actuation provided.

**TABLE 14.1**  Three-Switch Reversible Motor Control

| SW-A | SW-B | SW-C | MOTOR |
|------|------|------|-------|
| Off  | X    | Off  | Off   |
| Off  | On   | On   | Forward |
| On   | Off  | On   | Reverse |

Setting 3 switches is not very practical because this requires 3 relays and therefore 15 total for a five-degree-of-freedom arm. Figure 14.9 shows how 2 relays can be used to implement the 3-switch reversible motor circuit by using relays that include normally open and normally closed poles.

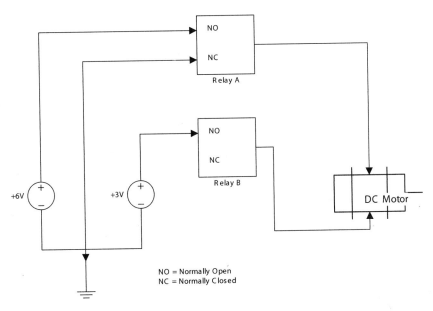

**FIGURE 14.9**  Two-relay reversible motor.

This simplifies the relay reversible motor actuation to 10 relays required for a five-degree-of-freedom arm. Table 14.2 summarizes the motor actuation as a function of the relay setting for this design.

**TABLE 14.2**    Two-Relay Reversible Motor Control

| RLY-A | RLY-B | MOTOR |
|-------|-------|-------|
| Off | Off | Off |
| Off | On | Forward |
| On | Off | Off |
| On | On | Reverse |

This is scaled to actuate a five-degree-of-freedom arm using ten relays as shown in Figure 14.10.

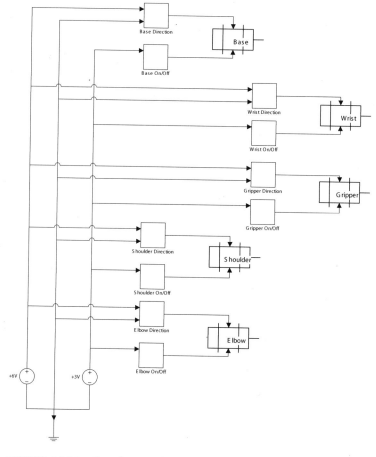

**FIGURE 14.10**    Five-degree of freedom robotic arm relay circuit.

Actuation of a robotic arm can lead to mechanical arm failure if the motors are allowed to over drive the joint rotations beyond mechanical limits of rotation for each joint. To avoid gear damage, a mechanical clutch or slip system can be employed, which is a feature of the OWI arm; however, reliance upon a clutch or slip system is still not ideal. Joints designed with mechanical slip or clutches can slip under the weight of the arm and cause positioning errors if they are too loose, and if they are too tight, over driving a joint will still cause gear damage. A better approach is to integrate hard- and soft-limit switches so that electrical and software protection mechanisms prevent over rotation of joints. Figure 14.11 shows a circuit design for hard-limit switches.

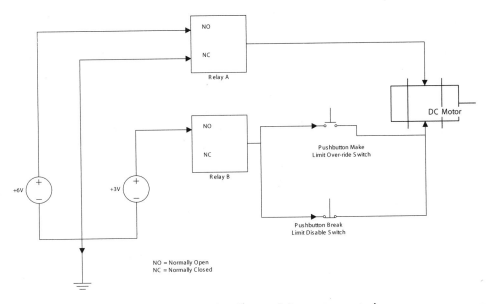

**FIGURE 14.11**   Use of hard-limit switches for arm joint motor control.

The limit switches shown in Figure 14.11 must be mounted on the arm so that the joints cause the switch to be activated at each limit of mechanical motion. The downside to this circuit is that the arm joint that hits a limit remains inoperable until it is manually reset.

A better approach is to use soft-limits monitoring with a software service that periodically, or on an interrupt basis, samples the output of a switched circuit through an ADC so that software can disable motors that hit a limit. This design is shown in Figure 14.12.

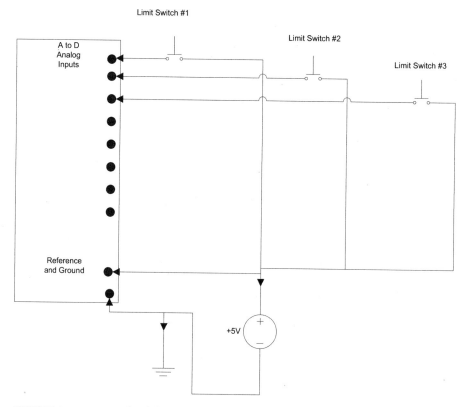

**FIGURE 14.12** Use of soft-limit switches for motor control safing.

Each of the soft-limit switches can be mechanically integrated so they will trigger before the hard-limit switches, allowing software to safe (disable) a potentially over-rotated joint, decide whether a limit override for recovery is feasible, and then recover by commanding rotation back to the operable range. If software-limits monitoring fails or the software controller is not sane, the hardware limits will continue to protect the arm from damage. The relay actuation design with hard- and soft-limit switches provides basic arm actuation, but only with binary on/off motor control.

The concept of reversible motor poles can be generalized using relays in an H-bridge, providing more motor control states than the two-relay design. The H-bridge relay circuit is shown in Figure 14.13.

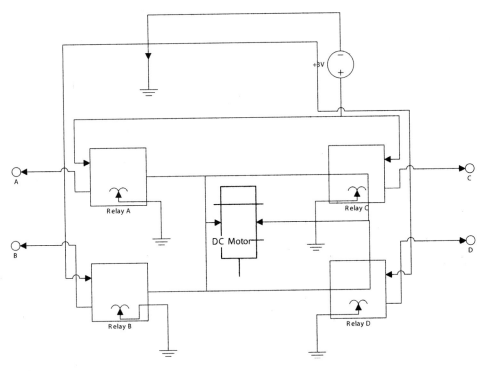

**FIGURE 14.13**   Relay H-bridge motor control.

Inspection of the relay H-bridge states shows that the H-bridge also provides additional control features as listed in Table 14.3.

**TABLE 14.3**   Relay H-Bridge Motor Control States

| A | B | C | D | MOTOR |
|---|---|---|---|-------|
| 0 | 0 | 0 | 0 | Off |
| 0 | 0 | 1 | 1 | Brake |
| 0 | 1 | 0 | 1 | Fuse Test |
| 0 | 1 | 1 | 0 | Reverse |
| 1 | 0 | 0 | 1 | Forward |
| 1 | 0 | 1 | 0 | Fuse Test |
| 1 | 1 | 0 | 0 | Brake |

The braking features of an H-bridge can provide the basis for torque and over-shoot control so that the motor controller can ramp up torque and ramp it down while positioning. The ramp up can be provided by a DAC, and the ramp down braking can be provided by the H-bridge braking states. The short-circuit states of the H-bridge, *fuse tests*, must specifically be avoided by H-bridge controller logic.

Relay actuation provides only on and off motor control and requires the use of electro-mechanical relay coils, which create noise, dissipate significant power, and take up significant space even for compact reed relays. Figure 14.14 shows the same H-bridge controller design as Figure 14.13, but using solid state MOSFETs (Metal Oxide Substrate Field Effect Transistors).

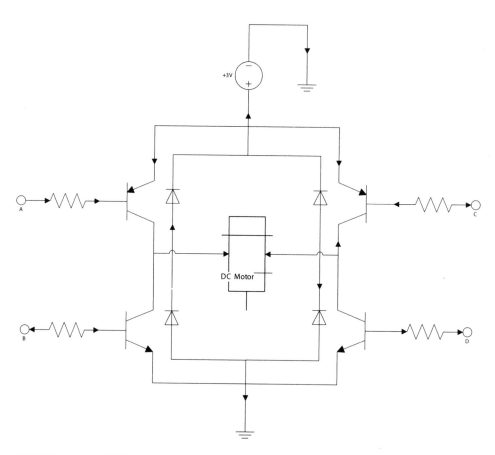

**FIGURE 14.14**   MOSFET H-bridge motor control.

The MOSFET design provides the same states and control as the four-relay H-bridge, but much more efficiently with less power required compared to electro-magnetic coil actuation.

## END EFFECTOR PATH

The ability to actuate an arm still does not provide the ability to navigate the arm's end effector to and from specific reachable locations. This must be done by path planning software and by end effector guidance. The simplest path planning and end effector guidance function implements arm motion dead reckoning and single-joint rotation sequences. *Dead reckoning* turns on a joint motor for a period of time based upon a rotation rate that is assumed constant, perhaps calibrated during an arm initialization sequence between joint limits. Using a dead reckoning estimation for joint rotation leads to significant positioning error, but can work for positioning tasks where significant error is tolerable. Moving one joint at a time is also tolerable for paths that do not need to optimize the time, energy, or distance for the motion between two targets. Many more optimal paths between two targets can be implemented using position feedback and multiple concurrent joint rotation. Concurrent joint rotation is simple to do with a relay or H-bridge controller, although the kinematics describing the path taken are more complex. Motion feedback requires active sensing during joint rotation.

## SENSING

Joint rotation sensing can be provided by joint position encoders and/or computer vision feedback. Position encoders include the following:

- Electrical (multiturn potentiometer)
- Optical (LED and photodiode with light-path occlusion and counting)
- Mechanical switch (with a momentary switch counter)

Position encoders provide direct feedback during arm positioning. This feedback can be used to drive the feedback in a control loop when the arm is moved to a desired target position. This assumes the desired target is known, either preprogrammed or known through additional sensing such as computer vision. Figure 14.15 shows the basic feedback control design for a position-encoded controlled process to move an arm from one target position to another.

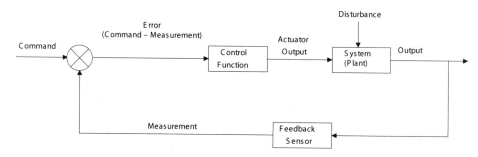

**FIGURE 14.15**   Basic feedback control arm positioning.

Figure 14.15 can be further refined to specifically show an actuation with feedback design using relays and a potentiometer position encoder feedback channel. The main disturbance to constant rotation will come from stick/slip friction in the joint rotation and motor ramp up and ramp down characteristics in the motor/arm plant. Figure 14.16 shows this specific feedback control design.

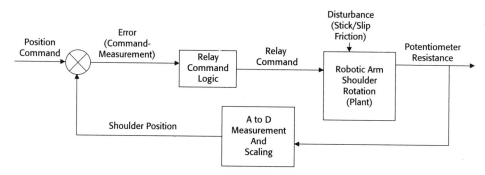

**FIGURE 14.16**   Relay control with position encoder feedback through an ADC.

Closer inspection of the design in Figure 14.16 reveals that the control loop has an analog and a digital domain as shown in Figure 14.17.

This mixed-signal control loop design requires sampling of the feedback sensors and a digital control law. The control law can be implemented for each joint on an individual basis as a basic PID (Proportional, Integral, Differential) process control problem. For the PID approach, a proportional gain, an integral gain, and a differential gain are used in the control transfer function in Equation 14.1:

$$G_c(s) = K_p + \frac{K_i}{s} + K_d s = \frac{K_p s + K_i + K_d s^2}{s} \qquad (14.1)$$

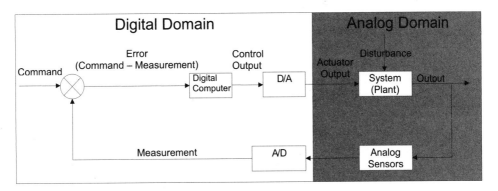

**FIGURE 14.17** Arm positioning with feedback digital and analog domains.

The transfer function defined by a Laplace transform is depicted as a control loop block diagram in Figure 14.18.

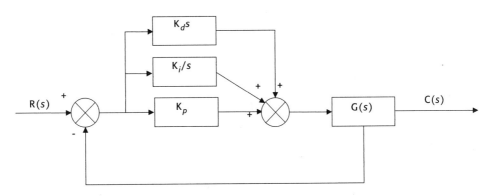

**FIGURE 14.18** PID control loop.

The Laplace transform for the PID control law makes traditional stability analysis simple; however, to implement a PID control law on a digital computer, a state space or time domain formulation for the PID control law must be understood. Furthermore, a relationship between the measured error and the control function output must be known in terms of discrete samples. This time domain relationship is shown in Equation 14.2.

$$u(t) = K_p y(t) + K_i \sum y(t) + K_d \frac{\Delta y}{\Delta t} \qquad (14.2)$$

This equation can then be used to design the control loop as shown in Figure 14.19.

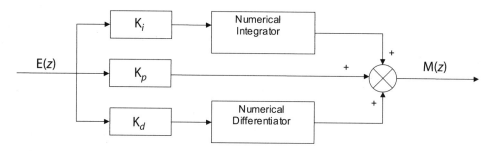

**FIGURE 14.19** PID digital control loop.

The numerical integration can be done using an algorithm such as forward integration, trapezoidal, or Runge-Kutta over a series of time samples. Likewise, differentiation over time samples can be approximated as a simple difference. The proportional, integral, and differential gains must then be applied to the integrated and differentiated functions and summed with the proportional for the next control output. Applying these three components of the digital control law with appropriately tuned gains leads to quick rise time, minimum overshoot, and quick settling time as shown in Figure 14.20.

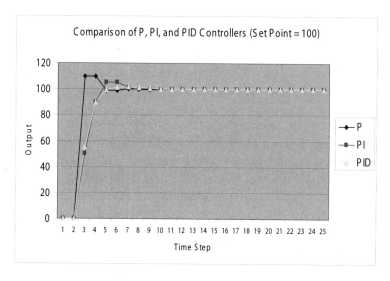

**FIGURE 14.20** PID time response.

Figure 14.20 shows proportional control alone, proportional with integral, and finally the full PID. Tuning the gains for a PID control law can be accomplished as summarized by Table 14.4.

**TABLE 14.4**  PID Gain Tuning Rules

| Parameter | Rise Time | Overshoot | Settling Time |
|---|---|---|---|
| $K_p$ gain increase | Decreases | Increases | Small Change |
| $K_i$ gain increase | Decreases | Increases | Increases |
| $K_d$ gain increase | Small Change | Decreases | Decreases |

The PID controller provides a framework for basic single-input, single-output control law development. More advanced control can be designed using the modern control state space methods for multiple inputs and outputs. State space control provides a generalized method to analyze and design a control function for a set of differential equations based upon the kinematics and mechanics of a robotic system as shown in Equation 14.3.

$$A = system - matrix, B = input - matrix$$
$$y = Cx + Du$$
$$y = output - vector, u = input - vector$$
$$C = ouput - matrix, D = feed - forward - matrix \qquad (14.3)$$

Figure 14.21 shows the feedback control block diagram for the generalized set of state space control system of differential equations.

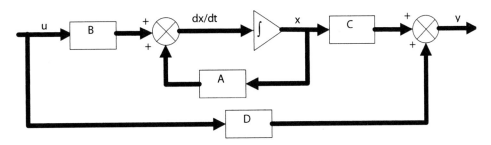

**FIGURE 14.21**  State space feedback control.

A detailed coverage of state space control analysis and design methods is be-yond the scope of this book, but many excellent resources are available for further study [Nise03].

## TASKING

The robotic arm must be commanded and controlled at a higher level than actua-tion and feedback control to provide these basic capabilities:

- Searching, identifying and acquiring a visual target for pick up
- Path planning and execution to pick up a target
- Object grappling and grapple feedback
- Carry path planning and execution to relocate the object to a new target location

These tasks compose the larger task of pick and place. The OWI arm command and control software and hardware actuation and feedback control system can be de-signed so that a single high-level command can initiate pick and place tasks within the arm reach capability space. The target search, identification, and acquisition task is a fundamental computer vision task that requires an overhead, side, or front/back fixed camera system or a simpler embedded camera in the end effector. With an em-bedded camera, the arm can start a search sequence to sweep the camera field of view (FOV) over the concentric reach capability rings shown earlier in Figures 14.5, 14.6, and 14.7. While the camera is being swept over the rings, frame acquisition of NTSC frames at 30 fps or less can format the digital camera data into a digital frame stream. The digital frame stream images can be processed so that each frame is enhanced to better define edges and to segment objects for comparison matching with a target object description. The target object description can include target geometry and color (invariants) as well as target size (variant). After the target is seen (matched with a segmented object in the FOV) then the arm can start to track and close in on the target.

Closing in on a visual target in the reach capability space of the OWI requires constant video to visual object centering based upon computation of the object's centroid in the FOV. The arm can use the centroid visual feedback to rotate the base to control XY plane errors to keep the object centered as the arm is lowered toward the XY plane. The kinematics require that the arm shoulder and elbow be lowered to approach a target on the XY plane and to control the X translation of the end effector and embedded camera. Simultaneously, the base rotation can be controlled to coordinate the target Y translation to keep the target centered as the arm is lowered. This basic task requires actuation and control of three degrees of freedom at a minimum. The OWI wrist only has a single degree of freedom, which rotates about the forearm. More sophisticated robotic arms also include rotation about the other two axes of the wrist joint. So, a fixed camera embedded in the OWI arm may need independent tilt/pan control so that the camera angle can be maintained perpendicular to the XY plane as the arm is lowered. More sophisticated wrist degrees of freedom would also provide this fine camera pointing.

Target pick up requires the arm to use position and limits feedback so that the arm knows when it has intersected the XY plane and acquired the XY plane located target object. Furthermore, the grappler should be in the fully open position at this time. After this ready to grapple position has been achieved with feedback computer vision and positioning, the grappler can be closed around the target object. Positive indication of successful target grappling can be provided by sensing switches built-in to the end effector fingers. Most often, brass contacts separated by a semiconducting foam (IC packing foam) or microswitches with interface plates on each finger provide good feedback for grappling.

After the target has been successfully grappled, the arm can switch to a carry path planning task to guide it to the drop-off target location. This drop-off path planning might again involve search or a predetermined target position at a relative offset from the target acquisition location. Either way, this is essentially identical to the acquire path planning and execution except that the arm is raised to a carry height at a desired reach capability ring, and then carried with base translation. The raise and carry sequence can be concurrent for a more optimal path in terms of time and distance traveled. The arm is again lowered to the drop-off target, and the target object is released using the grappler feedback to ensure that the fingers no longer sense a grip on the object.

This overall sequence is a high-level automation using tasking. The operator still commands the sequence, but the robotic arm performs the subtasks composing the overall task autonomously. Two major architectural concepts in the field of robotics have emerged that provide a framework for robot tasking and planning interfaced to lower level controls with or without human interaction. Two of the most important concepts are shared control and the degree of autonomy that a robotic system has along with the Rodney Brook's subsumption architecture [Brooks86]. In the next section, these architectural concepts are briefly introduced.

## AUTOMATION AND AUTONOMY

Figure 14.22 shows command and control loops for a robotic system that range from fully autonomous to telerobotic. Telerobotic operation is commonly known as "joy stick" operation where all robotic motion mimics operator inputs.

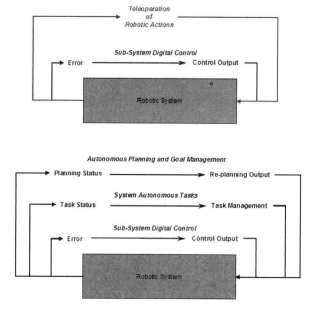

**FIGURE 14.22**   Teleoperated and fully autonomous robotic task control loops.

An intermediate level of control between fully autonomous and telerobotic is called *shared control*. In shared control, some aspects of robotic tasking are autonomous, some are telerobotic, and others are automated but require operator concurrence to approve the action or initiated the action. The concept of shared control is shown in Figure 14.23.

Telerobotic systems may still have closed-loop digital control, but all tasking and decision-making comes from the operator; in the extreme case, literally every movement of the robot is an extension of the user's movements, and no actuation is initiated autonomously. After the robotic action is commanded by the user, controlled motion may be maintained by closed-loop digital control. This is similar to concepts in virtual reality, where a user's input is directly replicated in the virtual model, and the concept of remotely piloting aircraft. For example, you could set up an OWI interface so that the OWI arm attempts to match the movement and position of the human arm based upon operator arm acceleration and flexure measurements.

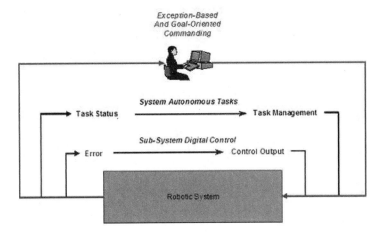

**FIGURE 14.23** Shared control of a robotic system.

## SUMMARY

Robotics requires a hierarchy of automation, the subsumption architecture, where low-level component actuation and sensing is interfaced to higher level subsystem control. Subsytems in turn are tasked with goals and configured with behaviors. For example, a rolling robot may be tasked with exploring and mapping a room, but is also configured to have a collision avoidance behavior. This control, behavior, and tasking must be coordinated by an intelligent human operator or by artificially intelligent goal-based planning. This chapter introduced robotic system architecture and design from a bottom-up viewpoint providing practical examples for how to control and task a five-degree-of-freedom robotic arm.

## EXERCISES

1. Develop a kinematics model for the reach capability of the OWI five-degree-of-freedom robotic arm using a C program or MATLAB model.
2. Build a simple single change relay or MOSFET H-bridge reversible motor controller and design a serial or parallel port command interface for it.
3. Implement a PID control C function with tunable gains that can be used to control a robotic arm joint rotation or similar actuator.

## CHAPTER REFERENCES

[Brooks86] Brooks, R.A., "A Robust Layered Control System for a Mobile Robot." *IEEE Journal of Robotics and Automation*, RA-2, (April, 1986): pp. 14-23.

[Nise03] Nise, Norman S., *Control Systems Engineering with CD*, 4th ed. Wiley, John & Sons, 2003.

## CHAPTER WEB REFERENCES

- The OWI-7 five-degree-of-freedom arm comes from OWI Robotics and offers a great way to learn about basic robotics, *http://owirobots.com/*.
- Lynxmotion offers the Lynx 5 and 6 servo-controlled robotic arm kits with good repeatability and precision, *http://www.lynxmotion.com/*.
- Garage Technologies Inc. also offers a six-degree-of-freedom arm, *http://www.garage-technologies.com/index.html*.
- NeuroRobotics Ltd., offers a research grade robotic arm, *http://www.neurorobotics.co.uk/*.
- Robotics Research manufactures seven-degree-of-freedom highly dexterous arms with torque control, *http://www.robotics-research.com/*.
- Honda's ASIMO robot, *http://world.honda.com/ASIMO/*.
- Toyota partner robot, *http://www.toyota.co.jp/en/special/robot/*.
- Sony entertainment robotics, *http://www.sony.net/Products/aibo/*.
- RobotWorx industrial robotics integration, *http://www.robots.com/*.
- Motoman industrial robotics, *http://motoman.com/*.
- ABB industrial robotics, *http://www.abb.com/robotics*.
- NASA Johnson Space Center Robonaut, *http://vesuvius.jsc.nasa.gov/er_er/html/robonaut/robonaut.html*.

# 15 Computer Vision Applications

## In This Chapter

- Introduction
- Object Tracking
- Image Processing for Object Recognition
- Characterizing Cameras
- Pixel and Servo Coordinates
- Stereo-Vision

## INTRODUCTION

Computer vision requires video frame acquisition, digital video processing, and the use of information extracted from the image stream to control a process or provide information. For example, a stereo mapping vision system can move a laser pointer to positions and measure distance to the reflected spot over and over to create a three-dimensional model of a room. Or, computer vision might be used by a robotic platform to navigate a vehicle or end effector to a visual target. Processing video streams is inherently a real-time process because the processing must keep pace with a periodic video frame rate. Furthermore, when video processing is embedded in a digital control loop where the digital video is used as feedback sensing, the overall digital control loop must meet real-time requirements for control stability. Computer vision is an excellent application for studying real-time concepts due to clear and obvious real-time processing requirements.

## OBJECT TRACKING

Object tracking with computer vision is a basic vision feedback control problem used in many automation and instrumentation applications. For example, telescopes automatically track celestial targets and can scan the sky to find them initially and to center objects of interest in the telescope field of view (FOV). Assembly-line robotics that spot weld structures can use position feedback for coarse alignment, but often use computer vision for fine positioning and position verification before applying a weld. Space probes often use optical navigation in deep space where radio tracking and navigation may be difficult due to light time latencies at great distances. A basic bright object or shape/color target tracking camera system can be constructed from two servos and a camera. Figure 15.1 shows a front and side view of a tilt/pan camera tracking subsystem.

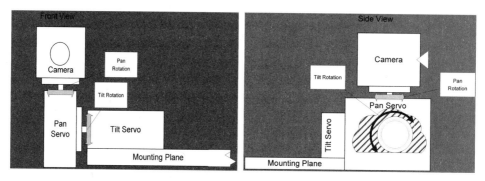

**FIGURE 15.1**    Tilt/pan computer vision tracking subsystem.

In this design, the camera FOV is moved to track an object in motion or is moved to scan a larger FOV to find an object. Alternatively, a fixed camera with a large FOV might observe a target illuminator such as a laser pointer, which is tilted and panned instead of the camera. This can be useful for stereo ranging or simply tracking the motion of an object. An observer can judge how well the fixed camera is able to locate a given object by seeing how well the laser spot is able to track the object, providing a tracker debug method.

Figure 15.2 shows a stereo-vision tracking subsystem. This subsystem can be used to track not only the XY location of an object in a FOV, but also the distance to it from the camera baseline.

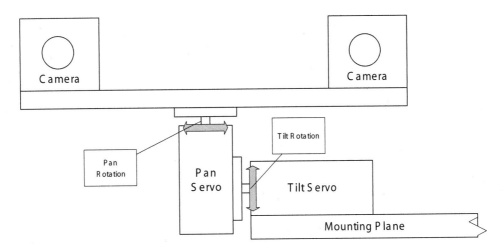

**FIGURE 15.2**   Stereo tilt/pan computer vision tracking subsystem.

The tracking problem can be handled in almost the same fashion as the mono-vision tracker; however, either one camera can drive the tilt/pan control to keep the target centered, or a scheme to use information from both can be used. If just one camera is used, right or left side, then the parallax of the object as seen by one camera will not be the same as the other. For more accurate stereo-vision systems, each camera, separated by a common baseline, can be independently tilted and panned on the baseline to keep the object centered as human vision systems do. Most stereo tracking and ranging systems simply tilt and pan the entire baseline and either favor one camera or take an average from the two to split the difference on centering the object in each camera's FOV.

The tracking performance for a tilt/pan subsystem is based on the following:

- Vision frame rate
- Servo actuation limits
- Digital control processing latency

Ideally, the frame rate is high enough and the processing latency low enough that the system is servo limited. The processing must be completed before the next observation frame is available (deadline is the same as service request period). As discussed in Chapter 14, "Robotic Applications," a PID control loop can be designed to optimize tracking control for quick rise time, minimal overshoot, and quick settling. With a mono-vision tracker, it's easy to observe tracking control issues such as latency, overshoot, and settling with system testing. Tracking not only requires that the image processing recognize the object to be tracked, but also that the edges can be detected and the geometrical center of the object computed. With this information from image processing, the tilt/pan error can be calculated in terms of pixel distances between the center of the image and the center of the object to be tracked. The center of an object is called the *centroid*. The next section presents methods for finding a centroid.

## IMAGE PROCESSING FOR OBJECT RECOGNITION

Visual objects can be recognized based upon shape, size, and color. Color is the most invariant property because it only changes with changes in lighting. If lighting can be controlled or if the system can provide illumination, this is a huge advantage for a computer vision system. Shape is also mostly invariant, changing only when an object orientation is changed for nonsymmetric objects. Symmetric objects such as spheres are always easier to detect and track. A highly focused last spot is also fairly easy to track, but any defocusing or beam spread can create problems. Finally, size is the most variant because it changes with distance to the object in the Z plane. Size can be ignored, or if the actual size of an object is known, it can actually be used to judge distance even with mono-vision. Tracking color and shape is most often used. Colors can be detected based upon luminance and chrominance levels or RGB levels for each pixel. Shape is best determined by enhancing and detecting object edges in a scene.

A simple PSF (Point Spread Function) can be applied to a digital luminance (grayscale) or RGB image to enhance object edges. For example, Table 15.1 provides a commonly used PSF for edge enhancement:

**TABLE 15.1** Edge Enhancement Kernel

| | | |
|---|---|---|
| $-k/8$ | $-k/8$ | $-k/8$ |
| $-k/8$ | $k+1$ | $-k/8$ |
| $-k/8$ | $-k/8$ | $-k/8$ |

This matrix is applied to an image array so that each pixel is replaced by the sum of $-k/8$ times each neighboring pixel and $k+1$ times itself.

The CD-ROM contains C functions and examples for applying this kernel to 320 × 240 RGB and grayscale images. To apply the kernel to a 320 × 240 pixel image, it is applied to pixel address 1,1 through 1,318 for the first row, and likewise for each row through pixel address 238,318 for the last row. Figure 15.3 shows the standard convention for image pixel addressing starting with 0,0 in the upper-left corner down to 319,239 in the lower-left corner.

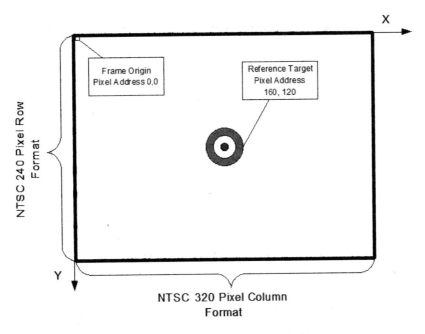

**FIGURE 15.3**    Image coordinates for a 320 x 240 pixel frame.

Applying this kernel as described previously along with a threshold filter yields the following image enhancement for a red circular target as shown in Figure 15.4 in both color and grayscale (color available on the CD-ROM).

Edge enhancement alone finds edges that are not necessarily of interest. The threshold filter eliminates background edges based on color thresholds so that only edges matching color criteria remain in the final enhanced and filtered image. Now that the target image has been segmented from other objects in the scene, the centroid of the target can be found by walking through each row of the image and recording the X and Y location of object entry and exit based upon color or intensity threshold. The X, Y locations define the object boundary, and the centroid can

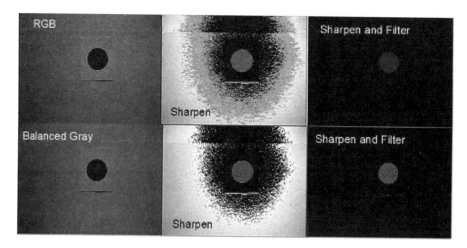

**FIGURE 15.4**    Edge enhancement and filtering for common color and grayscale image.

be computed by finding the center of the greatest X extent and the center of the greatest Y extent for a symmetrical object such as a circle.

ON THE CD

Example code for centroid location is included with the CD-ROM. Figure 15.5 shows the centroid found by rastering with the location indicated by adding green lines to the image array.

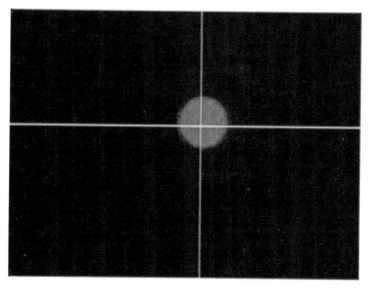

**FIGURE 15.5**    Centroid found by rastering an enhanced target image.

This basic process must be tuned for the lighting conditions, the target shape and color, and the camera characteristics. It's often simpler to segment scenes, detect objects, and find extents and centroids in grayscale or one-color band rather than RGB color space. To better understand how to tune target recognition and analysis, it's best to start with camera characterization and to control lighting.

## CHARACTERIZING CAMERAS

Cameras have FOVs (extents that can be seen through the camera lens at a given distance) that are determined by the camera optics. Furthermore, opto-electrical cameras such as NTSC CCTV cameras have detectors with arrays of charge sensitive devices, most often a CCD (Charge Coupled Device). The pixel detectors most often charge up when exposed to light, and the charge voltage can be read out from the array of pixel detector devices through an ADC interface to digitize data. An NTSC camera actually produces an analog signal (described more fully in Chapter 13, "Continuous Media Applications") from the CCD readout, which in turn is sampled and digitized by a frame grabber. Given the overall system, the images can be affected by camera optics, detector physics, and video signal sampling and digital conversion in the frame grabber. Lighting can saturate pixel detectors or ADC in the frame acquisition interface. Controlled lighting and well matched ADC sensitivity should be used to ensure that an image is not washed out or dark. Washed out images have average intensity that is way above the mid-level output of 128 for an 8-bit pixel. Dark images, of course, have average intensity that is way below a low-level output of say 10, for example. Robotic systems often employ target illumination. They carry their own lighting and calibrate the illumination to ensure that images are neither washed out or dark.

Basic characterization of the camera optics and NTSC output can be achieved by simply hooking the camera up to a television and taking FOV measurements. A tape measure can be placed in the FOV, and the camera distance can be varied to determine the physical extents observable by the camera optics and detector as a function of distance. Figure 15.6 shows this relationship for a CCTV NTSC camera for X extents measured with optical observations of a rule.

For this camera, the relationship is very linear; however, optical affects often cause nonlinear variation in extents. For example, many lower cost optical systems cause optical aberrations such as *fish-eye*, where the extents of an object are exaggerated in the center of the FOV. So, a square object appears to bulge in the middle. The camera should be carefully characterized so that any nonlinear effects can be corrected by curve fitting if they are significant.

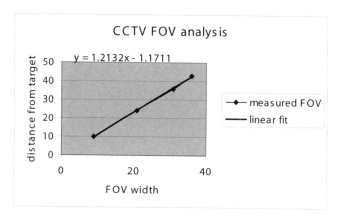

**FIGURE 15.6** Physical Extents visible in camera FOV as a function of distance.

For the same CCTV NTSC camera, the detector is larger than the NTSC sampled digital output. The number of detector pixels in the C-Cam8 NTSC thumbnail camera is $510 \times 492$; however, the Bt878 frame grabber can convert this into a $320 \times 240$ pixel image. The FOV can be characterized further in this sample space by calculating the sample pixels per physical inch as a function of camera distance from target. Figure 15.7 shows that this is a nonlinear relationship for the same CCTV NTSC camera optical/NTSC characteristics shown in Figure 15.6. The nonlinearity is therefore introduced in the NTSC sampling and digitization by the Bt878 encoder for the $320 \times 240$ RGB format.

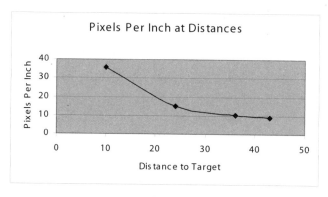

**FIGURE 15.7** Physical extent relationship to sampled pixels for a CCTV camera.

It's important that the camera and overall image acquisition system be characterized to identify and model the mapping from physical space to sample pixel coordinates because all image processing will be done with the sample pixels.

## PIXEL AND SERVO COORDINATES

As shown earlier in Figure 15.3, pixel coordinates are addresses ranging from 0,0 to $n,m$ for an $n$ by $m$ image. Servo coordinates are defined by the X extent traversed at a distance by the smallest unit of pan rotation the servo can provide. The Y extents are likewise defined in servo coordinates for a given distance. This is easy to see if a laser pointer is attached to the tilt/pan platform so that the smallest tilt/pan servo motions can be charted on a wall by noting locations of the laser spot and physically measuring the distance between spots. Knowing the relationship between one unit of servo tilt or pan in terms of overall camera system FOV pixel translation can be very helpful for calibration of a tilt/pan system. Figure 15.8 shows an automatable process for determining the servo to pixel coordinate function on the X and Y axis for a given distance.

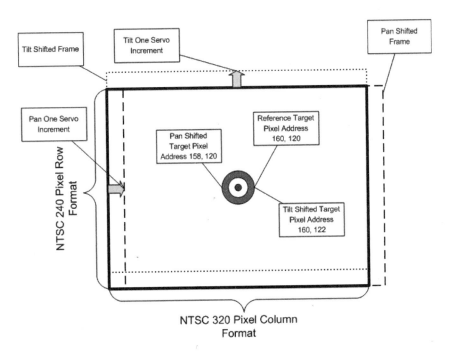

**FIGURE 15.8**  Pixel to servo coordinate calibration.

This information can be used to compute the servo rotation required to center an object in the FOV. So, for an optical tracker set up where a single servo increment causes a 2-pixel FOV change, then when a target is 10 pixels right of the center, the servo must be panned 5 servo increments right. This relationship is linear near the center of the camera tilt/pan and becomes increasingly nonlinear at maximum tilt/pan. So be sure to characterize the relationship over target range extents observable at maximum tilt/pan corners of the effective tilt/pan FOV.

## STEREO-VISION

Stereo-vision is based upon the phenomena of parallax, where an observation at two locations along a baseline of a common object appears to cause an offset of the object. This can be observed by holding one finger out, closing the right eye and observing, and then closing the left and opening the right causing the finger to apparently change position. In fact, the observation is due to the change in eye observation angle for the object. The apparent shift of the object therefore is based upon its distance from the observation baseline. Distances to stars are measured using parallax by observing a star one half-year apart as the earth orbits the sun and defines the unit in distance called a *parsec*. Likewise, two cameras on a common baseline can be used to observe a common object, and the apparent shift of the object in the right camera's FOV compared to the left camera can be used to compute the distance from the baseline to the target. The geometry for a stereo observation is illustrated in Figure 15.9.

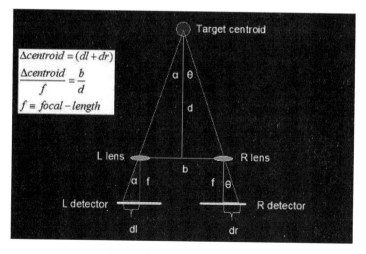

**FIGURE 15.9** Stereo-vision observation geometry.

Note that the triangle formed by the target, left lens, and baseline center is similar to the triangle formed by the left lens, detector center, and the image offset dl. The triangle on the right side formed by the target, right lens, and baseline center is similar to the triangle formed by the right lens, detector center, and the image offset dr. By the property of similar triangles, (dl + dr)/f = b/d. The baseline b is known, the focal length f is known for a given camera (or can be found by characterization of the camera), and dl and dr can be computed from the offsets of the target centroid from each camera FOV center. This leaves d, the distance to the target as the only unknown.

## SUMMARY

Stereo-vision systems emulate human vision systems and can track and judge distances in real-time much like we can. Many tasks that we intuitively would call real-time are tasks that we complete using vision, audio, body kinematics and kinetics, and that are governed by real-world physics. Many real-time embedded tasks are also similar to human real-time tasks. This is one reason that studying robotics, vision systems, video/audio recording, transport, playback, and digital control are all excellent applications for understanding real-time theory. Note, however, that a real-time system is not fast, slow, or necessarily constrained by the same physics or timescales that humans are. Real-time systems must simply complete requests for service prior to a deadline relative to the service request time. Furthermore, embedding places real-time computing into specific service requirements and requires observation and response for process control. Often the most useful real-time embedded systems operate in dangerous environments and must complete tasks much faster, more accurately, and with less fatigue than a human ever could. An industrial welding robot on an automobile assembly line provides exactly this type of invaluable real-time service. Similarly, an earthquake fault-line monitoring system might only need to detect land mass movement over very long periods of time with slow yet highly accurate measurements completed within a deadline. So, while the intuitive real-time tasks are very helpful for understanding real-time embedded systems and applications, the fundamental theory and broader applications should also be studied and appreciated.

## EXERCISES

1. Implement a C function with tunable gains for a PID control law that can be used for a tilt/pan tracking subsystem. Build a tilt/pan subsystem, integrate the btvid.c or Linux bttv driver, and track a moving object using image processing to follow the object centroid.
2. Implement a stereo range finder for a known target and show that it can correctly read the distance.
3. Implement a stereo range finder that can also tilt/pan track a moving object.
4. Implement a stereo imaging system that uses a laser pointer to paint a three-dimensional scene and create a three-dimensional map of the area.

# Appendix

# A   Glossary

## A

**actuator:** Electro-mechanical device that converts analog or digital electrical inputs into mechanical energy interacting with the physical world.

**ADC:** Analog-to-Digital Converter, encodes analog signals into digital values.

**Amdahl's Law:** If F is the sequential portio of a calculation, and $((1 - F)$ is the portion that can be executed concurrently (in parallel), then the maximum speedup that can be achieved by using N processors is $1/(F + ((1 - F)/N))$. EQ. IF $F = 0$, THEN WITH $N = 4$, SPEEDUP IS 4.

**API:** Application Program Interface, provides function call interface to lower-level software and/or hardware functionality.

**Application Executive:** Also known as a Cyclic Executive, a main loop program that calls functions on a periodic subrate of the main loop period.

**asynchronous:** An event or stimulus that occurs at any point in time rather than at known predictable points in time; for example, an external interrupt may occur at any time and will immediately change the thread of execution on a CPU.

**asynchronous logic:** Digital logic that is not globally clocked, but rather changes state based on edge triggering in a combinational logic circuit or edge triggering by multiple independent clocks.

**atomic operation:** A noninterruptable CPU instruction; that is, any instruction that can be fetched and completed before the CPU can be interrupted.

## B

**bandwidth:** Data transfer per unit time, for example, bytes/second.

**BDM:** Background Debug Mode, a variant of JTAG that allows data and instructions to be clocked into and out of a 10-pin interface to a processor.

**best effort:** Scheduling policy that does not guarantee any particular response time for a service request, but attempts to make progress on all such requests and maximize total throughput.

**binary semaphore:** A semaphore that has only two states: full and empty; a take on an empty binary semaphore will block the calling thread and a take on a full binary semaphore will change the state to empty; a give on an empty binary semaphore will change the state to full and a give on a full semaphore has no effect.

**black-box test:** A set of test vectors and driver that operate only on the functional interface of a subsystem or system with no knowledge of the internal workings or execution paths in the case of software.

**block transfer:** Transfer of data (typically contiguous, but may be a scatter/gather list) that includes multiple memory words/bytes on a bus with automatic addressing of each element in the block, rather than addressing and performing a full bus cycle to transfer each word.

**blocking:** When a thread of execution has been dispatched on the CPU for execution, but it needs some other resource such as memory access, an I/O interface, or some other external condition to be true so that it must give up the CPU and wait, the thread is said to be blocked.

**block-oriented driver:** A software I/O device interface that enables memory blocks to be transferred to and from the I/O device, rather than transferring just one memory word at a time.

**boot code:** Software that is the very first to execute after a processor is reset and hardware sets the program counter to an initial address for execution; boot normally completes after initializing fundamental resources such as memory, cache, and memory mapped devices; installing interrupt vector handlers; initializing basic critical I/O devices and disabling others; finally loading a higher level program or RTOS kernel image, and then jumping to its entry point.

**bottom half:** Software interfacing to I/O device hardware that services interrupts related to the device, provides basic configuration and control, monitors status, and buffers I/O data. The top half makes a bottom half usable for application software.

**BSP:** Board Support Package, the boot code and basic I/O interface initialization code needed by an RTOS to boot and cycle on an embedded system board.

**BSS:** Block Started by Symbol, the name for sections of uninitialized global program data used by compilers and linkers such as C program globals without static initializers: because the data is not initialized, this data need not take up space in nonvolatile memory, but must be allocated a data segment in working main memory.

**Bt878:** Brooktree Video/Audio encoder that can digitize an NTSC input.

**burst transfer:** A bus transaction that involves an initial address cycle followed by many data read/write cycles terminated by the bus master (similar to block transfer, but of unlimited length).

**bus:** A parallel interface for reading/writing data words from/to addresses. A bus includes digital data lines, address lines, and control lines. Note that address and data lines may be multiplexed rather than separate lines.

**bus analyzer:** A passive device that snoops on a bus to capture a record of all bus cycles. It typically acts like a specialized Logic Analyzer and can be set up to trigger and start collecting a bus cycle trace when a particular address, data, or control bit pattern is active on the bus.

**bus master:** A device that can initiate bus cycles to address a large device and then read/write data to the target device that supplies data or receives data.

**byte-oriented driver:** A device interface that provides the ability to read/write single words/bytes to and from the I/O device one at a time.

## C

**C (in RMA):** The execution time required by a service to provide a response not including any time spent blocking (only time where the CPU was in fact being used to compute a response output).

**cache:** High-speed access memory that typically can be read or written in a single CPU cycle, but due to high cost per storable word, is used as an efficient copy of a much larger main memory device. Hardware functionality is typically included to aid with cache memory management, including maintenance of cache/memory coherency, mapping of main memory addresses to cache lines (direct mapped, set associative, fully associative), and loading/write-back of data between cache and main memory.

**cache coherency:** A cached copy of data at a given address will be different than the data at the same address in main memory after a cached write to this address. When this happens, the cache control hardware/software must restore agreement between the data in cache and main memory sometime before data would otherwise be corrupted. Two main policies are used to maintain coherency: write-back and write-through. When memory addresses are cached and also used for DMA or other types of I/O, however, special care must also be taken by application code to ensure that data is not corrupted by intelligently performing write-backs and re-loads of cache lines as needed.

**cache hit:** A read or write is performed by an application on data cached at the address accessed/updated.

**cache line eviction:** A system event where data is written back to memory, freeing up a cache line.

**cache line invalidation:** A system event where a cache line is marked, typically with a status bit called "dirty," which indicates that the cache line must be reloaded from memory before data is read from it.

**cache line locking:** Many caches have control features allowing a program to lock a particular address into a line of cache preventing this line from being replaced when other addresses are loaded (makes most sense for set associative caches rather than direct mapped). Cache line size varies, but is often 16-64 bytes.

**cache line prefetch:** Many caches have a feature allowing a program to request the cache to load a cache line despite the fact that the associated address has not been accessed yet. The idea is that this address will eventually be accessed in the future, and rather than stalling the CPU pipeline at the time it is accessed, intelligent applications can plan ahead.

**cache miss:** A read or write is performed by an application on data that is not presently in cache and therefore the CPU must first load the data at the address being accessed/modified.

**cache miss penalty:** The number of CPU core cycles that the CPU pipeline must be stalled when a cache line must be loaded after a cache miss for a thread of execution to continue.

**call-back:** A programming technique where a pointer to a function is passed to a different function (registered) so that the function, which obtains this pointer, can call the function passed to it by reference later on. A technique commonly used in user interfaces so that an event such as a mouse click can be handled generically by code, which will call any number of user application callbacks when the mouse click event is detected.

**canonical service:** A coding style template used for a real-time service provided by an RTOS task or thread. This style may vary, but at a minimum includes a main loop, which executes as long as the service is "in service" and has a code section that either polls for input or synchronously or asynchronously waits for a service request.

**CCTV:** Closed Circuit Television, a common term used to describe a camera that outputs an NTSC signal.

**ceiling:** The ceiling is a mathematical operation that can be performed on a real number (floating point). The ceiling($n$) is the closest integer whole number greater than or equal to $n$, for example, ceiling($1.1$) = 2. Floor($1.0$) = ceiling($1.0$) assuming that the significance is 1, which is the typical definition of floor and ceiling unless otherwise noted.

**CFD:** Control Flow Diagram, a diagram used in Structured Analysis/Design that indicates where control signals in the system originate, where they terminate, and how they change the flow of data and/or the processing of data in a DFD. (Note that a CFD is typically a subset of a DFD, which shows both data flow and control flow).

**Chaining Interrupt Service Routine:** A chaining ISR, calls more than one handler for the very same interrupt source and priority, which is a technique often used in software when a hardware interrupt line is shared by multiple devices. (Note that most chaining ISRs also perform ISR polling).

**check-stop:** When an error condition on a CPU that cannot be handled and further execution by the CPU is considered either dangerous or impossible, then the CPU hardware may enter a state known as check-stop, where it ceases to fetch and execute instructions and can only leave this state via a reset. For example, a detectable memory error that cannot be corrected normally causes the CPU to enter check-stop.

**circuit-switched I/O:** An I/O channel that is dedicated to one and only one data source and sink. Often the channel may be point to point, but may be switched before the circuit is established.

**Cirrus Crystal 4281:** An audio encoder/decoder used in ECEN 4623/5623.

**CLI:** Command Line Interface, a simple ASCII terminal type interface that can operate over serial or any other byte-stream I/O interface to provide the ability to command a device and obtain basic status information.

**codec:** Compression and decompression protocol such as MPEG-4 that is used in streaming to compress video frames prior to transport and to decompress them after transport to be displayed. Video and audio codecs are often implemented in hardware or software and inherently operate on continuous media streams rather than files.

**completion test:** This necessary and sufficient scheduling feasibility test is based upon the Sha, Lehoczky, and Ding theorem that is documented in the Briand and Roy reference book used in ECEN 4623/5623.

**computational complexity:** The mathematical magnitude of operations required to successfully execute a given algorithm; for example, searching a data set can take $N$ operations for $N$ items linearly searched or $\log(N)$ operations for a balanced tree search of $N$ items, or even constant $C$ operations for $N$ items with a perfect hashing function.

**context switch:** When a CPU is multiplexed (shared) by more than one thread of execution and the scheduler provides preemption, the scheduler does preempt a thread to dispatch another; it must save state information associated with the currently executing thread (e.g., register values, including program counters) so that this thread can later be dispatched again to restore its thread of execution without a state error.

**context switch overhead:** The number of machine code instructions (and clock cycles) that an RTOS scheduler must execute to perform a context switch.

**continuous media:** I/O stream that requires isochronal delivery of data between a source and sink, for example, video stream, audio stream, and possibly a telemetry stream.

**control flow:** A CFD unidirectional association between two processes and/or external entities that indicates an asynchronous mechanism used to control a process or data source/sink.

**coverage criteria:** When unit tests and/or system tests are completed on software, coverage criteria define the completeness of the testing by specifying the percentage of execution paths, statements, conditions, and decisions that must be covered.

**CPI:** Clocks Per Instruction, a measure of CPU efficiency with the idea that a CPU pipeline should have a CPI of 1.0 or less if the pipeline can retire an instruction every clock. If the pipeline is also superscalar so that multiple instruction pipelines may execute, then this type of microparallelism can theoretically yield a CPI less than 1.0.

**CPU:** Central Processing Unit, a processor core providing arithmetic and logic operations, possibly floating point arithmetic, and basic register and memory operations.

**CPU bound:** When an application program is unable to execute any faster due to the clock rate of the CPU and the CPI.

**CPU pipeline:** The use of microparallelism in the CPU core to provide a stage of instruction processing every clock so that after the parallel pipeline is started, an instruction is completed every clock. Stages typically include fetch, decode, execution, and write-back as a minimum. The key to pipelining is that it is possible for the pipeline to fetch, decode, execute, and write-back all at the same time for four instructions at various stages. Each instruction will actually take multiple cycles to complete, but in the aggregate, one instruction is completed every clock. (Note that pipelines may also be superscalar so that whole pipelines may be run in parallel as well.)

**critical instant:** This assumption made by Liu and Layland when they formalized fixed-priority RM describes a worst-case scenario where all services in a system would be released simultaneously.

**critical section:** When two independent threads of execution share a resource, such as a shared memory location, the section of code that accesses and possibly updates this shared resource in each thread is called a critical section. To ensure correctness, both threads will employ a synchronization mechanism such as a mutex semaphore to protect the critical section.

**cross compiler:** A compiler that can generate code for a target processor that may be different from the host system that it runs on.

**cross debugger:** A debugger that can single step through code executing on a target processor different from the host system the debugger interface is running on. Most often, this works with a host debugger that communicates with and controls a target agent debugger.

**CSMA/CD:** Carrier Sense Multi-Access/Collision Detection, a protocol used in Ethernet to detect when a node is already transmitting on the shared link and to back off and attempt to use the network later.

**cycle-based profiling:** Profiling code executing on a processor by periodically saving off the current PC in a trace buffer. This is most often implemented by an interrupt generating counter that counts cycles and can be programmed to raise an interrupt every N cycles. The ISR associated can then service the interrupt and save off the program counter each time into a trace buffer.

**cyclic executive:** An embedded software architecture composed of one or more main loop application(s) and ISRs. The main loop(s) execute on a periodic basis. In some cases, the cyclic executive may be an extension of Main+ISR so that several loops run concurrently or are multiplexed on a single CPU and provide different rates of execution, for example, a high-, medium-, and low-frequency executive.

**D**

**D (in RMA):** The deadline for a service that is relative to a request for the service.

**DAC:** Digital-to-Analog Conversion, most often used to provide analog output to an actuator from a digital I/O interface, for example, a motor or speaker.

**data segment:** A memory region reserved for global variables and constants in a C program thread. Most often, each thread has its own data segment. (Note that most programs include a Stack, Data, and Text segment as a minimum.)

**datagram transport:** Transmission of packets on a link so that errors in transmission can be detected, but are not automatically corrected nor is there automatic retransmission of lost data. Furthermore, there is no concept of a connection (real or virtual) so that multiple messages are unrelated and if fragmented will not be reordered or reassembled automatically.

**DDR:** Double Data Rate, a bus data encoding technique where read or write data is transferred on both edges of a reference clock rather than just one (rising edge and falling edge); this doubles the data rate.

**dead reckoning:** A technique used in robotics and vehicle navigation whereby a direction, motion, or rotation is selected and executed at a constant rate for a calculated period of time to produce a desired amount of translation or rotation to reach a target; for example, a vehicle might be pointed north and drive at 5 feet per second for 1 hour to get to a target city due north of a starting point south of this target. The major disadvantages of dead reckoning is that no mid-course correction is possible, and overshoot and undershoot are also likely.

**deadline:** A time relative to a request for service when the service must be completed to realize full utility of the service.

**deadlock:** A multithread condition where two or more threads of execution are waiting on resources held by another, and the graph of wait-for associations is circular. For example, if A is waiting on resource R1 to produce resource R2, and B is waiting on resource R2 to produce resource R1, this is a deadlock.

**decoder:** A digital device that takes a bit-encoded input and produces an analog actuator output, for example, an audio playback decoder that drives a speaker.

**delayed task:** The state of a VxWorks task that has been programmed arbitrarily to yield the CPU for a period of time before replacing itself back on the ready queue, for example, taskDelay is called.

**DFD:** Data Flow Diagram, a diagram used in Structured Analysis/Design that indicates where data in the system originates, how it is processed, and where it terminates (from data source to data sink).

**digital control:** Feedback control where the control law is driven by discrete periodic sensor samples and based upon a Z-transform (rather than a Laplace transform in analog control).

**direct-mapped cache:** A cache memory that has cache lines directly mapped to main memory locations so that a given main memory address can be loaded into one and only one cache line, yet a set/range of main memory locations may be loaded into that particular line.

**dispatch:** When an RTOS scheduler selects a thread ready to run, restores state associated with the thread, and transfers execution control back to the thread's last PC if it was preempted earlier (or to its entry point if the thread is ready to run for the first time).

**DM:** Deadline Monotonic, a real-time theory directly related to RM, but with a policy that the shortest deadline receives the highest priority (rather than shortest period) and a feasibility test based on deadlines rather than periods.

**DMA:** Direct Memory Access, a hardware state machine independent of the CPU core that is able to transfer data in or out of memory without directly executing core instructions, thus allowing the core to continue execution while regions of memory are copied, updated by an I/O device, or read out to an I/O device.

**DOF:** Degree of Freedom, a rotational or translational dimension that a mechanical device can move in. For example, a typical robotic arm has five rotating joints:

base, shoulder, elbow, wrist, and gripper; the robot is therefore said to have five degrees of freedom.

**double-buffering:** A technique often used in continuous media applications to allow for data acquisition into one buffer while another is being read out and processed. When the acquisition buffer is full, the buffer pointers are swapped so that the newly acquired data is processed and the already processed buffer can now be used for acquisition.

**driver:** A driver is software composed of code that interfaces to a hardware device and provides buffering, control, and status and which also interfaces to RTOS threads/applications and provides controlled access to the hardware device for I/O.

**DSP:** Digital Signal Processing, a specialized embedded processor core that includes parallel mixed analog and digital processing for typical signal processing functions, for example, for a Fourier transform.

**dynamic linking:** A technique where PIC software compiled into an object file format such as ELF can be loaded and linked into existing software on an RTOS platform on the fly after the RTOS has already been booted and is up and running.

**dynamic priority:** Thread or interrupt processing priorities are changed during run time by code.

## E

**Earliest Deadline First:** A dynamic priority scheme for scheduling where services are assigned priority dynamically every time the ready queue is updated, with highest priority given to the service with the earliest impending deadline. The scheme requires not only dynamic priority, but also preemption to work.

**ECC:** Error Correcting Circuitry, a digital circuit that automatically corrects an SBE using an error detection and correction encoding such as the Hamming code. Normally the data read out of memory is corrected before the final value is placed in the read buffer, but not necessarily also corrected in main memory. A write-back may be required to correct the actual memory location.

**EDAC:** Error Detection and Correction, an information-encoding scheme that not only allows for detection of errors, but correction of those errors, for example, the Hamming code.

**EDTV:** Enhanced Definition Television, refers to 480 or 576-line 60-frame/sec digital television transmission (compared to 60 interlaced frames/sec for NTSC), commonly known as 480p or 576p, which implies progressivity. NTSC, on the other hand, is commonly known as 480i or 576i, which implies interlaced. EDTV most often has 720 horizontal pixels with a 16:9 aspect ratio and is considered DVD quality.

**EEPROM:** Electronically Erasable Programmable Read Only Memory, a non-volatile memory device that can be erased and rewritten in circuit if so desired.

**EFSM:** Extended Finite State Machine, a formal method based upon state machines that extends the basic state transition on I/O to include side effects on transitions such as global data update and data processing.

**ELF:** Executable and Linking Format, an object file format that includes significant annotation and is PIC so that these files can be dynamically loaded and linked and they can support debug and trace analysis to map addresses back to source code.

**embedded system:** A digital and analog computer system that provides a specific set of services, driven by sensor inputs, and produces sensor outputs to provide services, for example, digital control in an anti-lock braking system or call switching and billing management for a telecommunications main trunk. (Note that the scale of the services provided and of the hardware itself does not matter.)

**encoder:** A circuit that takes analog signal inputs, uses an ADC to convert them to digital, and then bit encodes them, for example, an audio recorder that takes analog microphone input and encodes the input signal into 255 different tones.

**entry point:** An address in a text segment that is the first instruction in a function and serves as the starting point for a thread so that a scheduler can simply set the program counter to this address to start execution of this thread.

**EPROM:** Erasable Programmable Read Only Memory, a nonvolatile memory device that typically can be erased by a UV light source and electrically reprogrammed, but not in circuit, rather by pulling the device from a socket, exposing it to UV, and then placing it in an external programmer.

**event-based profiling:** A profiling technique where the program counter is saved into a trace buffer whenever events of a specific type exceed a threshold; for example, when data cache misses exceed $N$ misses, the program counter is saved into a trace buffer.

**exception (NMI):** An exception is normally a nonmaskable interrupt because it signifies a serious error condition that must be handled before any program should continue execution, for example, a bus error.

**execution jitter:** When a service is dispatched and the number of cycles and/or instructions required to complete the service varies on each release.

**Extended Finite State Machine:** An FSM (Finite State Machine) with more features than just states and I/O transitions so that the Von Neumann architecture and general programs may be modeled formally; for example, on a state transition, a procedural function may be called and/or global memory updated.

**external fragmentation:** When blocks of a resource such as memory are allowed to be arbitrarily sized, small sections of the resource between used sections may evolve from successive allocations and frees so that significant resource exists, but is unusable unless allocations are moved to provide larger contiguous free spaces from small many noncontiguous spaces (fragmentation outside of blocks).

**F**

**FCFS:** First Come, First Served, the policy often used by an RTOS when services/threads are at the same priority level, that is, the first service ready is the first one dispatched.

**feasibility test:** An algorithmic or formulaic operation that takes a set of services and their RM characteristics and provides a binary output indicating whether this service set can be scheduled given resources available and resources required by the service set.

**FEC:** Forward Error Correction, an EDAC method provided inline so that bit errors are handled at the link layer, for example, Reed Solomon encoding (in contrast to EDAC memory).

**feedback:** A signal used in control systems that provides sensor inputs to compute the difference between desired and actual plant state so that a control law can drive the plant to a desired target control point.

**FIFO:** First In, First Out, a policy for queues (e.g., a dispatch queue) where the first element queued is always the first element dequeued.

**firmware:** The first code to execute on a processor and therefore must initially execute out of an NV-RAM device, although it may load itself into memory and continue execution to complete a boot process before an RTOS is initialized and run. Less specifically, firmware is usually thought of as any software that directly interfaces to hardware to make the hardware usable by higher levels of software.

**fixed-priority scheduling:** A scheduling policy whereby threads on the ready queue are dispatched in priority order, and the priority of any given thread is not modified over time (except by the application itself).

**flash memory:** A nonvolatile memory technology that can be erased and reprogrammed in circuit like EEPROM, but has much higher density for a given cost.

**floor:** A mathematical operation that can be performed on a real number (floating point). The floor($n$) is the closest integer whole number less than or equal to $n$, for example, floor(1.1) = 1. (Note that floor(1.0) = ceiling(1.0) assuming that the significance is 1, which is the typical definition of floor and ceiling unless otherwise noted.)

**FLOPS:** Floating-point Operations per Second.

**flow control:** Signals between a data transmitter and receiver used to indicate buffer capabilities on each side so that a transmitter does not overdrive a receiver resulting in data loss when the receiver is unable to buffer incoming data.

**form factor:** The physical dimensions of an electronic device that may be independent of the electrical characteristics; for example, the PCI bus electrical specification and protocol is implemented as compact PCI, stackable PC/104+, and PMC (PCI Mezzanine).

**FPGA:** Field Programmable Gate Array, an array of generic transistors that can be programmed once or on power-up to provide combinational logic and state machines for digital processing.

**fully associative cache:** A cache that allows main memory addresses to be loaded to any cache line. This is the ideal cache because replacement is not constrained at all, but associative memory is complex and expensive. By comparison, a direct-mapped cache is completely constrained and a set-associative cache is a compromise.

## G

**gather read list:** A list of not necessarily contiguous addresses in memory that are to be read into a contiguous buffer. For example, a host memory may have multiple blocks scattered through memory space that are to be read by an I/O device, which will gather all these blocks into a single contiguous buffer before an I/O operation.

**GPIO:** General Purpose I/O, digital inputs and outputs at TTL logic levels, which can be used as a generic interface to digital devices such as LEDs.

## H

**HA:** High Availability, a system that guarantees it will be ready to provide services with a quantifiable reliability; for example, a system is said to provide five nines availability if it's ready to provide service upon request 99.999% of a given year (that is, is only unavailable for a total of about 5 minutes per year). HA systems can crash, but they can't be out of service very long if they do.

**Hamming code:** A bit encoding used to detect and correct SBEs and to detect MBEs for memory devices, which may be subject to SEUs.

**hard real time:** A service or set of services required to meet their deadlines relative to request frequency; if such deadlines are missed, there is not only no utility in continuing the service, but also the consequences to the system are considered fatal or critical.

**harmonic:** When the relative periods of services are all common multiples of each other; this characteristic can yield cases where the CPU resource can be deterministically scheduled to full utility.

**Harvard architecture:** A core CPU architecture that splits the memory hierarchy into separate instruction and data streams, typically including an L1 instruction cache that is independent of an L1 data cache.

**HDTV:** High Definition Television, HDTV is defined in ITU-R BT.709 as 1080 active scanning lines, 1920 pixels per line, with a 16:9 aspect ratio. HDTV also supports high-quality audio with Dolby Digital (AC-3) surround sound.

**heap:** A memory space used for dynamic buffer management and/or dynamic allocation of memory as requested by an application. Heap space is memory outside the data, text, and stack segments and is most often reserved by the boot or RTOS during initialization.

**host:** Desktop development computing system used in IDE for cross compilation, cross debugging, connection to the target agent, trace tools, and any number of other tools that connect to a target server on the host to communicate with target agent software resident on the embedded system.

**H-Reset:** Hardware Reset, either from a power-on reset state transition or from assertion of an external signal to drive a hardware reset.

**HR:** High Reliability, a system that has been designed to have a very low probability of failure to provide services. Typically, measures such as redundancy, cross strapping, and fail-safe modes are designed to ensure that critical services have an extremely low likelihood of failure.

**HSTL:** High Speed Transceiver Logic, a 0.0-1.5v logic level standard used for high-speed, single-ended digital I/O, most often for memory I/O (speeds of 180 MHz and greater).

**HWIC:** Hardware In Circuit, a concept whereby debug and trace tools have hardware probes in circuit with a CPU by interfacing to signals coming from the CPU/SoC ASIC to the rest of the system board for the purpose of snoop tracing and/or control, for example, JTAG debug emulator, Vision ICE Event Trace, RISCWatch trace port probe, and CodeTEST Universal trace probe.

**I**

**ICE:** In-Circuit Emulator, a debug and trace device that monitors all I/O pins on a CPU/SoC ASIC and provides memory trace, external interrupt trace, JTAG, and I/O pin trace, and emulates the state of the system, including all registers, cache, and addressing to aid in firmware development and board verification.

**IDE:** Integrated Development Environment, a software development system for an embedded system that includes a cross and native compiler, cross and native debugger, and many target tools interfaced through a host-based target server and a target-based target agent.

**importance:** In real-time systems theory, services with low priority based upon RM policy may still be critical to system operation; they are important despite being low priority.

**interference:** When a higher priority thread preempts a lower one in a fixed-priority preemptive system, the time that the CPU is unavailable to lower priority threads is referred to as interference time.

**internal fragmentation:** When a resource such as memory is made available in minimum sized blocks, this can help reduce external fragmentation, but when a user of the resource requires less than a full block, this causes internal fragmentation.

**interrupt handler:** During the normal CPU pipeline processing (fetch, decode, execute, write-back), an external device may assert a signal input, or an internal subblock may also assert a signal input to the CPU core, which causes it to asynchronously branch to an interrupt vector (a memory location) where basic code, called the *handler*, acknowledges and services the hardware and then calls application ISRs.

**interrupt latency:** The delay between assertion of an interrupt signal by a device and the time at which the program counter is vectored to an interrupt handler.

**interrupt vector:** An address in memory where the CPU sets the program counter after an interrupt signal is asserted, causing the CPU to asynchronously branch to this location and to execute the instruction there. Normally a CPU will have a number of interrupt inputs (e.g., x86 IRQ0-15), and each signal asserted causes the CPU to vector to a different address so that different handlers can be associated with each interrupt signal.

**interval timer:** A double-buffered state machine in a CPU core that allows software to set a value in a register that is loaded into a separate count-down register. The register asserts an interrupt at zero (or perhaps all F's if it counts up) and automatically is reloaded with the interval register value to repeat the process over and over. This hardware can therefore be used for basic timer services in an RTOS.

**I/O bound:** A condition where an application does not have sufficient I/O bandwidth to meet throughput goals or real-time deadlines.

**IOPs:** I/OS per second.

**ISA Legacy Interrupt:** Industry Standard Architecture Legacy Interrupt, specifically refers to x86 architecture IRQ 0-15, which have been part of the x86 architecture from the beginning (8086) and support a number of well-known PC devices and services such as booting from a hard drive.

**isochronal:** Literally *the same in time,* which in real-time systems means that a service is required to produce a response at a precise time relative to a service request—not too early and not too late. This is important to continuous media applications and digital control, which are sensitive to jitter. Most often, isochronal services hold a response computed ahead of deadline that is delivered to an interface within a narrow band around the optimal time.

**ISR:** Interrupt Service Routine, the application level of an interrupt handler, which is often a call-back function registered with an RTOS that installs the interrupt handler at an interrupt vector.

## J

**Jiffy:** A Linux term for the tick of an interval timer—the smallest unit of time that the OS can track. For example, on x86 architecture, the standard interval timer ticks about every 0.45 microseconds, but the Linux OS typically loads an interval timer count so that it can control processes on a 10-millisecond software tick.

**jitter:** When latency and/or timing of an operation or process changes with each iteration, that is, when latency/timing is not constant. Jitter as a term can be used to describe many different types of operations or processes: execution jitter, period jitter, and response jitter.

**JTAG:** Joint Test Applications Group, an IEEE committee that standardized the concept of boundary scan and the TAP (Test Access Port), which is used to verify integration of ASICS in a system (boundary scan), but is now also typically used in firmware development to control and single step a CPU by loading data and commands through the TAP with JTAG. JTAG includes the following signals: TDI (Test Data In), TDO (Test Data Out), TRST (Test Reset), Clock, and Test Mode Set.

## K

**keep-alive:** An indication from a thread/process/task on a system that it is functioning normally or perhaps similar indication from a subsystem in a larger system. The keep-alive is most often a simple ID and count indicating that the subsystem/thread/process/task is advancing through its service loop. Keep-alive is often referred to as a heartbeat as well.

**kernel:** The software in an RTOS that directly controls all critical resources such as CPU, memory, and device I/O. The kernel is typically interfaced to by applications through an API or device driver.

**kernel image:** The binary machine code text segment, data segment, stack, and BSS used for the RTOS kernel software.

**kernel instrumentation:** Tools such as WindView and CodeTest, which provide active tracing of C code and/or RTOS events require that code, often specifically kernel code, to be instrumented with trace instructions that provide efficient update of a trace buffer with a trace token to track progress of the code and to mark events for later timeline analysis.

## L

**L1 cache:** Level-1 Cache, a high-speed memory integrated on-chip with a CPU core—on the same ASIC for data access that can most often be completed in a single clock.

**L2 cache:** Level-2 Cache, a high-speed memory off-chip that can be accessed in several clocks.

**LA:** Logic Analyzer, a hardware-, firmware-, or software-analysis tool that provides generic acquisition of digitally clocked signals (or arbitrary digital signals that are clocked by the analyzer internally).

**latch-up:** A nonrecoverable bit error due to permanent transistor logic damage to a memory device or register.

**latency:** Delay in an operation or process due to physical limitations such as electronic propagation delay, the speed of light, the number of clock cycles required to execute instructions, or time to modify a physical memory device.

**laxity:** Laxity = (Time-to-Deadline: Time-to-Completion), but the time to the completion of a service can be difficult to determine, so most often an estimate of the Time-to-Completion is used, which is derived from (WCET: Computation-Time-So-Far).

**layered driver:** A layered driver includes a top half and bottom half. The top half provides an interface to application code wanting to use a hardware resource, and the bottom half provides an interface to a hardware device.

**LCM:** Least Common Multiple, the LCM is the smallest number that is also a multiple of 2 different numbers; for example, given $x=3$, $y=5$, the LCM$(x,y)=15$. This concept is key to periodic service analysis in real-time theory because it's necessary to diagram service times over the LCM of all periods to fully analyze timing demands upon a resource.

**Least Laxity First (LLF):** A dynamic priority policy where services on the ready queue are assigned higher priority if their laxity is the least (where laxity is the time difference between their deadline and remaining computation time). This requires the scheduler to know all outstanding service request times, their deadlines, the current time, and remaining computation time for all services, and to reassign priorities to all services on every preemption. Estimating remaining computation time for each service can be difficult and typically requires a worst-case approximation.

**LED:** Light Emitting Diode, a device typically used to provide visual I/O and status for an embedded system.

**Lehoczky, Sha, and Ding Theorem:** If a set of services can be scheduled over the period of the longest period service after a critical instant, then the system is feasible (that is, guaranteed not to miss a deadline in the future).

**limit sensor:** A sensor that detects when hardware has reached a physical limit, for example, when a robotic arm has driven a joint through full rotation after which continued motor drive will break the joint.

**linking (dynamic or static):** The process by which an executable image is assigned addresses for all function entry points, all global variables, and all constants that may be referenced by other software modules. These addresses can be statically assigned once and for all at a predetermined offset in physical memory (static linking) or may be position independent so that only relative addresses are assigned until the module is loaded, at which time physical addresses are derived from the relative (dynamic linking).

**livelock:** Related to deadlock, this situation arises when a circular wait for resources evolves and an attempt to break the deadlock is made by having each requester drop their requests and then request them again. If the requests are well synchronized, then the system may cycle between deadlock and dropping requests over and over.

**LSP:** Linux Support Package, an embedded Linux term, much like a BSP, which refers to code required to boot Linux on a given architecture and platform, such as the PowerPC 750 LSP.

**LVDS:** Low Voltage Differential Serial, an electrical standard for transmission of high-rate serial signals on wire pairs that carry differential signals to encode data.

**M**

**Main+ISR:** This is essentially the same software architecture as a cyclic executive, however, Main+ISR may be much simpler in that it normally has just one main loop and a small number of ISRs compared to a cyclic executive, which may have multiple loops operating at different frequencies.

**MBE:** Multi-Bit Error, a condition when more than one bit in a word is in error, which typically cannot be corrected.

**memory hierarchy:** The whole memory system design from the fastest and typically smallest devices to the slowest and typically largest devices, for example, L1/L2 cache, main memory, and flash.

**memory protection:** An MMU feature that allows address ranges on page boundaries (a minimum size memory block) to be specified as read-only; if an update to such a range is attempted, the MMU will assert an NMI exception.

**message queue:** An RTOS software mechanism that abstracts shared memory data into atomic enqueue and dequeue operations on a buffer controlled by the RTOS and known only to applications by an ID, accessible to them only through RTOS message queue operations. Operations are atomic with respect to threads only (not interrupts), and so most often only a message queue send is allowed in interrupt context, never a message queue receive.

**Message Sequence Chart:** A diagramming method used in SDL (Specification and Design Language) as well as UML (Universal Modeling Language) that shows threads of execution and all messages (or function call interfaces), which associate the threads in a protocol.

**microcode:** Machine code that executes on a state machine internal to a processor or on a simple state machine device that is independent of the main execution pipeline. For example, the Bt878 RISC processor executes code fetched from the x86 processor's memory over the PCI bus; this code is microcode from the viewpoint of the x86 system.

**microparallelism:** Parallel processing inside the CPU core.

**MIPS:** Millions of Instructions per Second.

**MMIO:** Memory Mapped I/O, I/O devices that can be read or written can be mapped into the address space of a processor allowing software to simply update an address to write to the device or read an address to read from the device. The device must respond to the addressing by the CPU, that is decode it and then read/write data on a bus that both the device and CPU interface with.

**MMU:** Memory Management Unit, a block in most CPU cores that provides virtual-to-physical address mapping, performs address range checking, and protects read-only address ranges from unintentional update.

**module loading:** When an ELF module is transferred to an embedded target and dynamically linked into the kernel and other application code on the fly.

**MTD:** Mapping to Device, a term used to describe bottom half code used in a flash filesystem driver.

**multiaccess network:** A network such as Ethernet where more than one device can use the physical and link layers of the network, thus requiring a CSMA/CD protocol for shared use.

**multitasking:** When a CPU is shared and multiplexed by a scheduler so that multiple threads with state information may execute on a single CPU or may be mapped onto a set of CPUs dynamically. Tasks include state information that goes beyond the minimal requirements of register state, stack, and program counter for a thread, for example, task variables, a task error indicator, name, and many other elements of a VxWorks TCB.

**multithreaded:** When a CPU is shared and multiplexed by a scheduler with the minimal management of execution state for each thread of execution (register state, stack, and program counter).

**mutex semaphore:** A specialized semaphore (compared to a binary semaphore) that is specifically used to protect critical sections of code for multithread safety. This semaphore is used to guarantee mutually exclusive access to a shared resource so that only one thread may access a common resource at a time. With shared memory, this prevents data corruption that could be caused by multiple readers/writers; for example, if a writer has partially updated a shared data structure, is preempted/interrupted, and then a reader accessed the partially updated data, the data may be completely inconsistent.

**N**

**N&S:** Necessary and Sufficient, a feasibility test in real-time theory that passes all service sets that can be scheduled and never fails a set that can be scheduled (more precise than a sufficient test, which may falsely reject some service sets, but will never falsely okay a service set than cannot be safely scheduled).

**Nand flash:** A flash memory device that is normally erased to all F's, and writes are bitwise masked in with an AND operation. Nand flash is most often used for storing quantities of data (for example, flash filesystems) due to high density, low cost, and long erase/re-write lifetimes.

**NCD SCAM chip:** A preburned microchip PIC that includes code to generate PWM signals for hobby servos (two channels) based upon an RS-232 command.

**nesting:** When a construct is used inside the same sort of construct—one inside the other. For example, if a critical section encloses another critical section, the critical sections are nested.

**nonblocking:** When a request for a resource cannot be met immediately, the RTOS can either block the calling thread until it is available or return an error code indicating why the request cannot be met and let the thread go on—the latter is non-blocking.

**Nor flash:** A flash memory device most often used to store small amounts of execute in place ROM resident embedded boot code due to reliability and fast random access operation.

**NTSC:** National Television Systems Council, the standard for analog color television transmission with $640 \times 480$ pixels. The standard defines up to 525 scan lines, but only 480 are used for an NTSC display frame with the remaining used for sync, vertical retrace, and closed caption data (sometimes referred to as vertical blanking lines). The NTSC signal interlaces scan lines, drawing odd-numbered scan lines in odd-numbered fields and even-numbered scan lines in even-numbered fields to produce a nonflickering image at approximately 60 Hz refresh frequency (the frequency was adjusted for color to 59.94 Hz). This yields approximately 30 interlaced video frames per second. For color, NTSC carries luminance and chrominance signals where luminance carries the normal monochromatic NTSC signal. The chrominance signal is carried at 3.579545 MHz and can either be ignored or recovered using a color burst reference signal that is output on the back porch of each horizontal scan line. Due to some of the quality issues with the color subcarrier scheme, NTSC is sometimes referred to as "Never Twice the Same Color." Newer higher definition standards for television have since emerged, including EDTV and HDTV, but for embedded computer vision projects, NTSC is still an affordable and readily available camera and frame capture standard that is in wide usage.

**NVRAM:** Non-Volatile Random Access Memory, memory that persistently holds data whether or not a system is powered, for example, a battery backed-up DRAM, a flash memory device, EEPROM, or EPROM.

### O

**object code:** Machine code annotated with symbol information (variable and function names and addresses) and information to support debugging (source file names and locations).

**OCD:** On-Chip Debugging, a type of JTAG frontend that allows a typical line debugger to single step code through the JTAG protocol.

**offloading:** The concept of taking a software service and reallocating it to a hardware implementation on a parallel processing unit to free the main CPU of loading. For example, a NIC may perform functions basic to TCP/IP such as checksums to offload those operations from the host CPU.

**OnCE:** On-Chip Emulation, a type of JTAG frontend that allows for not only debug through JTAG, but additional control such as register viewing and setting.

**online admission:** When a system can run a feasibility test while currently providing other services to determine whether new services can safely be added to the current safe set.

**on-off control:** The use of relays to turn on and off motors to control a mechanical device.

**optical navigation:** Using computer vision images of a scene to determine ranges to targets and to plan paths to navigate to a target using only video data.

**optimal policy:** A fixed priority assignment policy that will successfully schedule any set of services that can be scheduled by any other fixed-priority policy.

**overrun policy:** How a system handles a service that attempts to continue execution beyond its advertised deadline, for example, the scheduler could terminate the service.

**P**

**packet switched:** A network protocol that allows links to be shared by multiple datagram or virtual circuit protocols and routes packets between end-points based upon their header information.

**PCI:** Peripheral Component Interconnect is an industry standard bus architecture that initially provided a 32-bit parallel multiplexed address and data bus originally at 33 MHz with sideband control signals, revised to include 64 bits at 66 MHz. The standard was later extended as PCI-X to include more sophisticated nonblocking split transactions and rates for a 64-bit bus to a theoretical maximum of 533 MHz. PCI was extended once again to include a differential serial version, known as PCI-Express, which provides 2.5-Gbps byte lane links that can be combined in widths from x1 to x32. For all versions, the same basic configuration mechanism and plug and play features for the interconnect have been maintained.

**PCI bus probing:** A process that allows a BIOS or OS software to find all PCI devices and functions on a given PCI bus using configuration space registers.

**PCI configuration space:** A well-known port address on x86 architecture where a PCI bus master can read/write registers to find other PCI devices and their functions and configure them as far as memory mapping and interrupts as a minimum.

**PCI-Express:** Previously known as 3GIO, this standard is a scalable differential serial bus architecture for 2.5 Gbps mainboard interconnection and peripheral connection.

**PCI interrupt routing:** PCI interrupts A-D can be routed onto x86 legacy interrupts IRQ0-15 to allow PCI devices to interrupt an x86 core.

**peak-up:** A computer vision algorithm that finds a bright spot or the center of an object by segmenting an image and finding the centroid of a target within the image.

**pending task:** A VxWorks task state that indicates the task is blocking on a resource not presently available.

**period jitter:** When the period of a service request is not constant.

**period transform:** A real-time theory adjustment to a service's characteristics to simplify analysis or to elevate importance of a service whereby the service's period is assumed to be shorter than it really is.

**pessimistic assumption:** RM is full of assumptions that are worst case and therefore make it a very safe form of analysis, but also may lead to excessive resource margin to guarantee deadlines, for example, WCET.

**PID controller:** Proportional Integral Differential controller, a controller that sets outputs proportional to error; integrates sensor inputs to find, for example, velocity from acceleration; and uses derivatives such as velocity from position measurements to control a system and obtain a target operational state. For example, a cruise control provides acceleration proportional to the difference between current and target speed and integrates to determine when the target will be achieved and when to decelerate.

**pipeline hazard:** A condition in a CPU pipeline that forces it to stall, for example, a cache miss.

**pipeline stall:** When a CPU pipeline must stop until a resource is made available.

**pixel:** A picture element—an array of picture elements forms an N × M image where each pixel encodes the XY position, brightness, and RGB color mix for the picture element in the image.

**point to point:** A network topology that connects nodes one-to-one.

**polling:** When status is checked periodically (synchronously) by a looping construct.

**Polling Interrupt Service Routine:** An ISR that must determine the source of an interrupt by reading status registers when a hardware interrupt is shared by multiple devices (note that most polling ISRs also provide ISR chaining).

**position independent code:** Code that is base-address independent so that it can be mapped in at any base address, and all other entry points, jumps, and memory locations are set relative to the dynamically determined base address.

**POSIX:** Portable Operating Systems Interface, a standard for OS mechanisms and APIs. POSIX includes a number of substandards, such as 1003.1b, which covers basic real-time mechanisms.

**power-on reset:** A CPU state after initial power-on, which most often causes the CPU to branch to a known address and perform basic operations such as resetting the memory controller, bus, and other basic interfaces.

**preemption:** When the current thread executing on a CPU is placed back on the ready queue by the scheduler, and state information is saved so that a different thread can be allocated the CPU.

**priority:** An encoding that controls the order of dispatch for threads by a scheduler when more than one is ready to use the CPU resource.

**priority ceiling:** A priority is defined that is the highest priority a thread can have that may lock a resource; this priority level is stored as the resource's priority ceiling (see Briand and Roy, p. 67 for more information). A thread that has locked the resource is given priority as high as the highest-priority thread blocking on the resource up to the ceiling value; that is, the thread holding the resource always has a priority higher than or equal to all threads waiting to obtain the resource, but amplification is limited to the ceiling value.

**priority inheritance:** If a thread is holding a resource and another thread of higher priority is blocking on the same resource, the thread holding the resource inherits the blocked thread's priority for the duration of the critical section. There is no limit on the priority level that may be inherited. (For more information, see Briand and Roy, p. 66.)

**priority inversion (unbounded):** When a thread is unable to obtain the CPU and a thread of lower priority is holding it. The condition is most often caused by a secondary resource needed by a thread such as a shared memory critical section. In a simple two-thread case, if a lower-priority thread is in a critical section, then a higher-priority thread experiences priority inversion for the duration of the critical section; however, if the low priority thread suffers interference from a medium-priority thread, the high-priority thread could potentially be blocked for an indeterminate amount of time, which is an unbounded priority inversion.

**Priority Preemptive Run-to-Completion:** A scheduling mechanism that dispatches any thread ready to run based on priority as soon as the set of ready threads is updated (preemptive) and allows a dispatched thread to run indefinitely unless another higher-priority thread is added to the ready set (via an interrupt or a call to the RTOS by the currently running thread). One danger of this type of system is that a high-priority nonterminating thread will take over the CPU resource completely.

**priority queue:** A mechanism for implementing a FIFO policy, but with $N$ levels of priority so that all items at the highest priority level are dequeued first FIFO before all items at the next lower priority level.

**process:** A thread of execution with stack, register state, program counter state, and significant additional software state, such as copies of all I/O descriptors (much more than a task TCB for example), including a protected memory data segment (protected from writes by other processes).

**program counter:** The program counter is normally a register used by a CPU to track the current or next address of main memory that contains a machine instruction to execute. (Note that a trace of the program counter over time provides the definition of the thread of execution until a context switch occurs, if it does at all.)

**programmed I/O:** A technique where software reads and writes each word to and from a device interface involving the CPU in each and every transfer.

**protocol stack:** A layered driver that includes data processing between the bottom half and top half layers. Each layer can be separated and has a distinct interface, for example, TCP/IP.

**PWM:** Pulse Width Modulation, a technique to control a motor or other normally analog device by creating a pulse train of digital TTL output to simulate an analog output.

## Q

**QoS:** Quality of Service, definition of service levels based upon guarantees of resource availability for each service. For example, processor capacity can be reserved for each service in advance (say 10%), and the system guarantees that this capacity will be available in a worst-case period of time, however, the system may not guarantee all services will meet their deadlines.

## R

**reachability space:** The points in space where a robotic device can place an end effector, for example, places in space where a robotic arm can grapple an object.

**ready:** The VxWorks task state where a task is ready to running and waiting only on the CPU to be granted by the scheduler.

**real-time (system):** A system driven by external events (typically sensors that provide input through ADCs) for which services provide computation to produce a response (typically actuators that are interfaced to DACs) before a deadline relative to the event-driven request for service. A hard real-time system must never miss a deadline, but a soft real-time system or best-effort system may.

**real-time clock:** A hardware clock circuit that maintains an absolute date and time (e.g., Gregorian or Julian date), often employing a battery-backed clock circuit and/or a method to synchronize with an external time source such as Universal Coordinated Time.

**real-time correctness:** A real-time service must produce functionally correct outputs and also provide the outputs prior to a relative deadline to be real-time correct.

**reboot:** When a system is commanded to, or as a part of a recovery mode, reenter the boot code entry point causing reinitialization of memory and I/O interfaces, and restart of all services.

**recovery:** A key feature of an HA system; this is the mechanism by which a system that is experiencing system failures restarts those services. A system may need to start a recovery process for a number of reasons, such as deadlock, priority inversion, livelock, or resource exhaustion. Often recovery is achieved by the hardware watch-dog, which reboots the system.

**regression test:** Rerunning a test to verify that features previously verified still work after bug fixes or feature additions. This is intended to prevent unintentional interactions between software modifications that might introduce new problems.

**relay:** A mechanical or solid-state device that provides a simple switch, for example, double pole double throw or single pole single throw.

**reliable transport:** A data transport protocol on a network that includes error detection/correction and retransmission, and supports diverse routing so that overall data is delivered if at all possible.

**resource arbiter:** A subsystem that implements a resource grant policy; for example, a bus arbiter coordinates bus grants for bus requests from multiple masters and targets.

**response time:** The latency between a request for service (typically by an ISR) and the generation of a response output.

**ring buffer:** A data structure that provides multiple serially reusable buffers most often to buffer incoming data from a device interface before it can be processed and likewise for output data before it can be transmitted.

**RISC:** Reduced Instruction Set Computer, an architecture that simplifies computer instruction set architecture to use fixed-length instructions with load/store instructions to access memory and memory mapped devices, often simplifying instruction pipelines compared to more complex instruction set architectures.

**RM:** Rate Monotonic, the basic theory formulated by Liu and Layland for fixed-priority multiplexing of a single CPU that is intended to provide multiple services over time.

**RMA:** Rate Monotonic Analysis, the process of analyzing the C, T, and D characteristics of a set of services to be executed on a CPU and determination of priorities according to RM policy and feasibility according to a sufficient, or better yet, necessary and sufficient test.

**RM LUB:** Rate Monotonic Least Upper Bound, the equation first introduced by Liu and Layland, which provides a sufficient, but not necessary and sufficient, feasibility test for a set of services based upon utility demands and the closed form bound for utility derived in this text.

**RM policy:** Services with shorter period are assigned higher priority.

**ROM based:**  A boot or kernel image that is PIC and initially runs out of a non-volatile device, but tests and initializes memory, then copies itself to working memory, and continues execution there.

**ROM resident:**  A boot or kernel image that executes out of nonvolatile memory and sets up a data and stack segment in working memory, but the text segment remains always in the nonvolatile memory.

**round robin:**  A best-effort scheme with preemptive time-slicing in which the scheduler assigns threads a slice in a fair fashion so that all ready threads are given a slice of CPU and put back on the end of the queue if needed.

## S

**sanity monitor (software):**  A service that periodically resets the hardware watch-dog timer and also monitors keep-alive messages from other critical services in the system. If a critical service fails to post a keep-alive, then the sanity monitor provides error handling and attempts to recover that service. If the sanity monitor itself fails to function, then the hardware watch-dog timer times out and the whole system reboots and starts a system-level recovery process.

**SBE:**  Single Bit Error, when an SEU causes a bit flip or other form of unintended bit flip occurs in a memory word.

**scatter write list:**  A list of not necessarily contiguous addresses in memory that are to be written from a contiguous buffer. For example, a host memory may have multiple blocks in memory scattered through memory space that are updated by an I/O device that contains all the data to be updated in a single contiguous buffer.

**scheduling point:**  A necessary and sufficient test based upon the Sha, Lehoczky, and Ding theorem that determines whether all services can be scheduled within the longest period.

**SDRAM:**  Synchronous Dynamic Random Access Memory, a DRAM memory that provides a synchronous interface for control inputs so that it synchonizes with the system memory bus and processor allowing incoming memory commands to be pipelined.

**semaphore:**  An RTOS mechanism that can be used for synchronization of otherwise asynchronous tasks to coordinate resource usage, such as shared memory, or to simply indicate a condition, such as data is available on an interface.

**semaphore give:**  A semaphore operation that allows a thread to indicate that a resource is available; if another thread is blocking on this resource, then this will unblock that thread.

**semaphore take:** A semaphore operation that allows a thread to check and see if a resource is available; if not, the RTOS can either block the calling thread until it is or simply return an error code.

**sensor:** A transducer device that indicates physical status of a system or the environment in which it operates with an electrical signal to encode the system/ environment characteristic it is designed to measure, for example, a thermistor, a position encoder, limit switch, stress/strain gauge, pressure transducer, and so on.

**service:** A specific computation (provided based on inputs) that produces a required output to meet a system requirement.

**service release:** When an external event sensed by an embedded system indicates a request for service, the thread that provides the service is released; for example, an ISR can do a semaphore give to indicate sensor data is available for processing.

**set-associative cache:** A cache that allows main memory addresses to be loaded in $N$ different cache lines. A set-associative cache is said to be $N$ ways, where each way is a different cache line in which the same address data may be loaded, for example, 32-way set-associative cache.

**SEU:** Single Event Upset, a phenomena where a memory bit is flipped due to an environmental influence such as electromagnetic radiation. The bit's original value may be restored if the SEU can be detected and corrected by a system-monitoring technique.

**shared interrupt:** When an interrupt can be asserted by multiple devices, it is shared and requires the interrupt handler to poll status; that is, the handler must read the status of every device that may have asserted the interrupt to figure out which device did.

**shared memory:** When more than one thread on a single CPU or on multiple CPUs can access the same memory locations, this memory is shared. Shared memory must be protected by a synchronization mechanism if reads and writes are allowed.

**signal (software):** A software signal is often also called a software interrupt and in fact functions much like a hardware interrupt but at the scheduler/thread level. When a signal is thrown by one thread to another, the throw call causes the RTOS to potentially dispatch the catching thread's handler instead of the code it is currently executing after the catch kernel code is executed. So, a signal can be used to asynchronously interrupt a running thread.

**Signal Block Diagram:** A systems design method used in SDL (Specification and Description Language) where hardware and software elements can be modeled as blocks with signal list inputs and outputs; inside the blocks at a lower level, all signals are ultimately consumed or generated by EFSMs.

**signal catch:** When a signal is received by a thread by the RTOS scheduler on behalf of the thread. The catch modifies the catching thread's state so that the program counters, registers, and stack are saved, and when the thread is dispatched next, the scheduler dispatches the thread's registered signal handler rather than where it was last preempted.

**signal throw:** When a thread wants to asynchronously interrupt the normal flow of execution of another thread, it can call an RTOS mechanism to throw a signal to the other thread instructing the RTOS to dispatch the other thread's signal handler rather than its last context.

**SJN (Shortest Job Next):** A scheduling policy where the job with the shortest estimated or known run-time is dispatched to run to completion from the job queue.

**slack time:** On a real-time system, when no real-time services are requesting CPU time (that is, waiting on the ready queue or actively running), this unused CPU time is called slack time and often can be used for nonreal-time best-effort processing. Slack time is often created by service releases where the actual execution time taken is much shorter than WCET due to execution jitter.

**SoC:** System On-a-Chip, an ASIC that includes one or more CPU cores, a bus, and I/O interfaces so that it essentially places devices previously on a board in earlier products on a single ASIC.

**soft real time:** When a service can occasionally miss a deadline and overrun it or terminate and drop a service release without system failure, these services are considered soft. For example, a video encoder compression and transport service might occasionally drop a frame when compression takes too long. As long as the video stream is not critical and an occasional drop-out is within acceptable w.r.t. system requirements, this service can be considered a soft real-time service.

**software profiling:** Periodically tracing the cycle count and the current program counter or actively tracing it by instrumenting all function entry and exit points to save cycle count to a trace buffer allows for determination of where most of the execution time is spent and how many cycles basic blocks of code such as functions require. This type of tracing provides a profile of the software. Profiles can be at a function level, basic code block level (bounded by branches), or at a C statement level. Overhead is higher for lower level profiling.

**software sanity:** Software is said to be sane when embedded services check in with a sanity monitor by posting a keep-alive; the sanity monitor itself is known to be sane (functioning correctly) if it resets the hardware watch-dog timer.

**SRAM:** Static Random Access Memory, a memory device that retains its contents as long as power remains applied, unlike dynamic RAM (DRAM) that needs to be periodically refreshed.

**S-Reset:** Soft Reset, a reset state for a CPU that can be commanded by an application program.

**stack segment:** A segment of memory allocated for a thread that provides buffer space for function arguments and local variables. Each application thread, the kernel thread, ISRs, and signal handlers typically all have their own stack space for parameter passing and local variable instantiation.

**state machine:** A formal design notation that includes a start state, state transitions driven by inputs made while in a specific state, and outputs on transitions.

**static priority stereo-vision:** The use of two cameras separated by a known constant distance to judge distances to objects of unknown physical dimensions through the use of triangulation.

**stress testing:** Test vectors designed to stress the system by going beyond the requirements-based specification for limits, for example, commanding at high rate, exposure to high voltage ESD, shock testing, and thermal cycling.

**superscalar:** A CPU pipeline feature that employs parallel hardware within a single CPU core to allow for two or more instructions to be fetched, executed, and retired concurrently. Note that this feature of a CPU pipeline can yield a CPI less than 1.0 for the CPU core.

**suspended task:** A VxWorks task state entered when an exception (NMI) is generated by a task. The RTOS handles the exception and suspends the task to protect the system.

**SWIC:** Software In Circuit, a technique where software instrumentation is used to trace execution, for example, logging messages to a file from an application.

**switch-hook:** A VxWorks call-back mechanism where the kernel calls a user function on each and every context switch.

**symbol table:** An array of function and global variable names and addresses where they are stored in their text and data segments, respectively.

**synchronous:** An event or stimulus that occurs at a specific point in time relative to other events in the system rather than at any time. For example, a thread of execution can perform a semaphore take to synchronize with an ISR; the ISR will execute asynchronously, but the processing provided by the thread performing the semaphore take will be synchronous because this processing will only be provided after the semaphore take *and* the semaphore give performed by the ISR.

**synchronous bus:** A bus that has clocked address, data, and control cycles.

**syndrome:** The encoded bits in an error-detection and correction scheme that indicate SBE or MBE and contain the code for correction of SBEs.

**system lifecycle:** The process of turning an embedded system concept into a working maintained system. The steps potentially include concept, requirements, high-level design, detailed design, implementation of units and subsystems, unit/subsystem test, integration, system test, acceptance testing, fielding, maintenance, and unit/system regression testing.

**system test:** End-to-end and feature tests performed after the units and subsystems in a larger system have been unit tested and are integrated for the first time.

### T

**T (in RMA):** The period of a service request type. In many cases, this will be based upon the worst-case frequency of the event(s) that cause a service to be released.

**target:** The embedded computing system, including the processor complex and all I/O devices.

**target agent:** An embedded service that provides development, debug, and performance analysis features such as cross debugging, code loading and linking, and RTOS event traces.

**target server:** A service on the host development system that provides an interface to host tools and translates user inputs into target agent commands and target agent responses into application data.

**task:** A thread with normal thread state, including stack, registers, and program counters, but also signal handlers, task variables, task ID and name, priority, entry point, and a number of state and inter-task communication data contained in a TCB.

**task spinning:** When a task loops where it is expected to block and wait for a resource before proceeding.

**task wedging:** When a task blocks on a resource indefinitely, is suspended, or fails to loop and post a keep-alive periodically.

**TCB:** Task Control Block, the data structure associated with a VxWorks task, which contains all task data in addition to task stack and context.

**text segment (code segment):** A segment of memory used for storing the machine code associated with an application, kernel image, or boot image.

**TFTP:** Trivial File Transfer Protocol, a simplified FTP (File Transfer Protocol) that allows a client to download files from one known directory in a filesystem.

**thread (of execution):** The trace of a CPU's program counter over time, not including context-switch code execution by an RTOS. State information may or may not be associated with a thread of execution, but the value of the program counter before a context switch is the minimum state that must be maintained on a system that includes preemption.

**throughput:** An aggregate measure of speed and efficiency for a device. For example, for a processor, the measure is MIPS (millions of instructions per second), and for an I/O device the measure is Mbps or Gbps (megabits/sec or gigabits/sec).

**tick:** A counter that counts interval timer interrupts and is used by an RTOS for basic timer services, such as to provide the minimum resolution for timeouts on blocking calls (the RTOS will unblock a call made with a timeout specified within tick accuracy).

**timeout:** When making a blocking call to avoid "wedging." Where a thread is blocked indefinitely, it is most often advisable to specify a timeout for any blocking call at which time the thread will be asynchronously awoken and will continue execution; this can be done by setting up a timer to throw a signal to a timeout handler prior to making a blocking call if the API does not directly support a timeout option.

**timer services:** An interrupt handler set up by the RTOS that counts ticks on each interval timer interrupt and signals any threads that have reached a timeout threshold.

**time-slice:** A unit of CPU called a quantum, which can be allocated to a thread in a preemptable best effort system. In these systems, timer services often make a call into the scheduler on each system tick to provide quantum preemption. Therefore, the tick, a quantum, and timeout resolution are often all the same in many operating systems.

**top half:** The interface presented to calling threads/tasks/processes by a driver. The top half includes thread control features such as blocking (using a semTake most often) and policy such as how many threads it will allow to read/write a device at once.

**trace:** A linear buffer with records that include time (cycle count) and state information for a processor core and/or application code.

**TTL:** Transistor-to-Transistor Logic, traditional 5v digital logic levels. Also, Time-To-Live, which is a counter in a datagram that is decremented on each node-to-node hop so that the packet is discarded when TTL=0; this prevents a packet from hopping around the network indefinitely and creating a problem.

**U**

**unbounded:** When a condition can persist for a nondeterministic amount of time, for example, unbounded priority inversion where the set of middle-level priority interference tasks may cause the inversion to persist for an arbitrary time.

**unit test:** A test designed to validate and verify a software and/or hardware unit that is a building block for a larger system in isolation.

**utility curve:** An XY graph that shows time on the X axis between a service release and relative deadline and shows utility or damage caused to the system by service response generation.

## V

**virtual timer:** A timer that is not directly supported by a hardware interval timer, but rather is a software tick counter that can generate a signal after the passing of $N$ software ticks.

**VoIP:** Voice over IP, a protocol for transporting voice duplex audio over the Internet protocol.

## W

**watch-dog timer:** A hardware-based interval timer that counts down (or up) and when it reaches zero (or all F's), it generates an H-reset signal causing the system to reboot. Critical software services are expected to post keep-alives to a system sanity monitor, which normally in turn resets the watch-dog timer before it expires. If the software loses sanity, that is, the sanity monitor fails to reset the watch-dog timer (if a deadlock were to occur), then the idea is that the system will be able to recover by rebooting.

**WCET:** Worst Case Execution Time, the longest number of CPU cycles required by a service release ever observed and/or theoretically possible given the hardware architecture and algorithm for data processing used in the service.

**wear leveling:** A flash filesystem method to ensure that maximum capacity and operational longevity is maintained in a flash device hat hosts a filesystem. Because flash is divided into sectors, with each sector having a maximum expected number of erase/write cycles, this method attempts to keep erase counts for all sectors approximately the same so no one sector wears out early.

**white-box test:** A set of test vectors that drives specific execution paths in a software unit by design so that the software unit test meets specific path, statement, condition, and/or decision coverage criteria. Such tests require intimate knowledge of the software unit such as API return codes, error conditions, and I/O ranges.

**write-back:** When a processor updates memory from registers or cache.

**write-through:** When a processor maintains cache/memory coherency by always writing cache and the corresponding memory location on all writes to locations that are cached.

# Appendix

# B   About the CD-ROM

This CD-ROM includes the following code:

- **VxWorks-Examples:** VxWorks example C code demonstrating RTOS features and mechanisms, including the POSIX 1003.1b real-time API extensions
- **VxWorks-Drivers:** Bt878 video frame grabber driver and Cirrus 4281 example driver C code for VxWorks RTOS
- **Image-Processing:** Image-processing C code examples that can be built as applications for Linux or VxWorks
- **Linux-Examples:** Linux Pthread example C code and usage of Linux POSIX features
- **PMAPI:** Performance-monitoring API code for PowerPC Darwin OS and for x86 PCs
- **Contributed:** Contributed code implementing projects in computer vision, VoIP, and robotics

The CD-ROM also contains the following resources:

- **Figures:** All figures contained in the book
- **Lecture-Notes:** All lecture notes used for teaching ECEN 5623, Real-Time Embedded Systems at the University of Colorado
- **Visio-Design-Examples:** A partially completed Visio UML design template for a stereo-vision system designed for an x86 VxWorks platform
- **Pictures:** JPEG, MPEG, and AVI photos and streaming video of example project demonstrations completed at the University of Colorado

All VxWorks C code has been tested using Tornado 2.0.2 and VxWorks 5.4. Much newer versions of Tornado and VxWorks are available, and the code is expected to compile and work on these new revisions, but has not been tested for them. VxWorks C code should be imported into a Tornado workspace and project that is a "loadable project" and built within the Tornado build framework.

All Linux C code has been tested using Linux 2.4.x with a Red Hat 9.x distribution. Make files are included with the Linux code.

## SYSTEM REQUIREMENTS

Requirements include the following:

- VxWorks 5.4 or newer running on a Pentium, Pentium II, III, or IV x86 microprocessor
- A host development system running Windows 2000 or XP
- Ethernet network to interconnect the host and target system
- For Linux, an x86 Pentium or better system running a 2.4.x or newer kernel and Red Hat 9 or newer Linux distribution.

# Appendix C

# Real-Time Linux Distributions and Resources

- Concurrent Computer, *http://www.ccur.com/isd_solutions_redhawklinux.asp*
- Blue Cat Linux, *http://www.lynuxworks.com/embedded-linux/embedded-linux.php*
- FSM Labs RT Linux, *http://www.fsmlabs.com/index.php*
- Wind River Systems RT Linux, *http://www.windriver.com/linux*
- Monta Vista Linux, *http://www.mvista.com/*
- The small footprint embeddable PeeWee Linux, *http://peeweelinux.com/*
- TimeSys Linux, *http://www.timesys.com/*
- Real-Time Linux Foundation, *http://www.realtimelinuxfoundation.org*
- Real-Time Linux Foundation list of RT Linux variants, *http://www.realtimelinuxfoundation.org/variants/variants.html*

# RTOS Resources

- eCos RTOS, *http://www.ecoscentric.com/index.shtml*
- LynxOS RTOS, *http://www.lynuxworks.com/rtos/rtos.php*
- MicroC/OSII, *http://www.rabbitsemiconductor.com/etc/microc.shtml*
- OSE RTOS, *http://www.enea.com/*
- QNX RTOS, *http://www.qnx.com/*
- RTEMS RTOS, *http://www.rtems.com/*
- Accelerated Technology Nucleus RTOS, *http://www.acceleratedtechnology.com/*
- Green Hills ThreadX RTOS, *http://www.ghs.com/products/rtos/threadx.html*

# Appendix

# E References

[Abbott03] Abbott, Doug, Linux for Embedded and Real-Time Applications. Elsevier Science (USA), 2003.

[Anderson99] Anderson, Don, *Firewire System Architecture*, 2nd ed. Addison-Wesley, 1999.

[Anderson01] Anderson, Don, and Dave Dzatko, *Universal Serial Bus System Architecture*, 2nd ed. Addison-Wesley, 2001.

[Barr99] Barr, Michael, *Programming Embedded Systems in C and C++*. O'Reilly & Associates, 1999.

[Bovet03] Bovet, Daniel P., and Marco Cesati, *Understanding the Linux Kernel*, 2nd ed. O'Reilly Media, 2003.

[Briand99] Briand, Loïc P., and Daniel M. Roy, *Meeting Deadlines in Hard Real-Time Systems: The Rate Monotonic Approach*. IEEE Computer Society, 1999.

[Brooks86] Brooks, R. A., "A Robust Layered Control System for a Mobile Robot." *IEEE Journal of Robotics and Automation*, RA-2, (April 1986): pp. 14-23.

[Budruk04] Budruk, Ravi, Don Anderson, and Tom Shanley, *PCI Express System Architecture*. Addison-Wesley, 2004.

[Buttazzo02] Buttazzo, Giorgio C., *Hard Real-Time Computing Systems: Predictable Scheduling Algorithms and Applications*. Kluwer Academic Publishers, 2002.

[Campbell02] Campbell, Iain, *Reliable Linux: Assuring High Availability*. John Wiley & Sons, 2002.

[Ciletti03] Ciletti, Michael D., *Advanced Digital Design with the Verilog HDL*, Prentice-Hall, Pearson Education, 2003.

[Cook02] Cook, David, *Robot Building for Beginners*. Springer-Verlag, 2002.

[Cook04] Cook, David, *Intermediate Robot Building*. Springer-Verlag, 2004.

[Corbet03] Corbet, Karim, *Building Embedded Linux Systems*. O'Reilly Media, 2003.

[Corbet05] Corbet, Jonathan, Alessandro Rubini, and Greg Kroah-Hartmen, *Linux Device Drivers*, 3rd ed. O'Reilly Media, 2005.

[Di Steffano67] Di Steffano III, Joseph J., Allen J. Stubberud, and Ivan J. Williams, *Feedback and Control Systems*, Schaum's Outline Series. McGraw-Hill, 1967.

[Douglas04] Douglas, Bruce P., *Real Time UML Third Edition: Advances in the UML for Real-Time Systems.* Addison-Wesley, 2004.

[Gallmeister95] Gallmeister, Bill O., *POSIX.4: Programming for the Real World.* O'Reilly & Associates, 1995.

[Ghezzi91] Ghezzi, Carlo, Mehdi Jazayeri, and Dino Mandrioli, *Fundamentals of Software Engineering.* Prentice-Hall, 1991.

[Gomaa00] Gomaa, Hassan, *Designing Concurrent, Distributed, and Real-Time Applications with UML.* Addison-Wesley, 2000.

[Goody00] Goody, Roy W., *OrCAD PSpice for Windows.* Vol. 1 *DC and AC Circuits,* 3rd ed. Pearson Education, 2000.

[Grötker02] Grötker, Thorsten, Stan Liao, Grant Martin, and Stuart Swan, *System Design with SystemC.* Kluwer Academic Publishers, 2002.

[Hennessy90] Hennessy, John L., and David A. Patterson, *Computer Architecture: A Quantitative Approach,* Morgan Kaufmann Publishers, 1990.

[Hennessy03] Hennessy, John L., and David A. Patterson, *Computer Architecture: A Quantitative Approach.* 3rd ed. Morgan Kaufmann Publishers, 2003.

[Herbert04] Herbert, Thomas F., *The Linux TCP/IP Stack: Networking for Embedded Systems.* Charles River Media, 2004.

[IBM00] IBM Corporation, *PowerPC Microprocessor Family: The Programming Environments for 32-Bit Microprocessors,* G522-0290-01. IBM Corporation, 2000.

[Intel02a] Intel Corporation, *IA-32 Intel Architecture Software Developer's Manual.* Vol. 1, *Basic Architecture.* Intel Corporation, 2002.

[Intel02b] Intel Corporation, *IA-32 Intel Architecture Software Developer's Manual.* Vol. 2, *Instruction Set Reference.* Intel Corporation, 2002.

[Intel02c] Intel Corporation, *IA-32 Intel Architecture Software Developer's Manual.* Vol. 3, *System Programming Guide.* Intel Corporation, 2002.

[Intel02d] Intel Corporation, *Intel Pentium 4 and Intel Xeon Processor Optimization Reference Manual.* Intel Corporation, 2002.

[Jack96] Jack, Keith, *Video Demystified,* 2nd ed. HighText Interactive, 1996.

[Kernighan88] Kernighan, Brian W., and Dennis M. Ritchie, *The C Programming Language,* 2nd ed. Prentice-Hall, Inc., 1988.

[Labrosse02] Labrosse, Jean J., *MicroC/OS-II, The Real-Time Kernel,* 2nd ed. CMP Books, 2002.

[LaPlante04] LaPlante, Phillip A., *Real-Time Systems Design and Analysis,* 3rd ed. Wiley, 2004.

[Lewis02] Lewis, Daniel W., *Fundamentals of Embedded Software: Where C and Assembly Meet.* Prentice-Hall, 2002.

[Li03] Li, Qing, and Caroline Yao, *Real-Time Concepts for Embedded Systems.* CMP Books, 2003.

[Luther99] Luther, Arch, and Andrew Inglis, *Video Engineering,* 3rd ed. McGraw-Hill, 1999.

[Mano91] Mano, M. Morris, *Digital Design,* 2nd ed. Prentice Hall, 1991.

[Motorola97] Motorola Inc., *PowerPC Microprocessor Family: The Programming Environments for 32-Bit Microprocessors,* MPCFPE32B/AD REV. 1. Motorola, 1997.

[Nichols96] Nichols, Bradford, Dick Buttlar, and Jacqueline Proulx Farrell, *Pthreads Programming.* O'Reilly & Associates, 1996.

[Nise03] Nise, Norman S., *Control Systems Engineering with CD,* 4th ed. Wiley, John & Sons., 2003.

[Noergaard05] Noergaard, Tammy, *Embedded Systems Architecture: A Comprehensive Guide for Engineers and Programmers.* Elsevier, 2005.

[Patterson94] Patterson, David A., and John L. Hennessy, *Computer Organization and Design: The Hardware/Software Interface.* Morgan Kaufmann Publishers, 1994.

[Phillips94] Phillips, Charles L., and Troy Nagle, *Digital Control System Analysis and Design,* 3rd ed. Pearson Education, 1994.

[Powel03] Douglass, Bruce Powel, *Real-Time Design Patterns: Robust Scalable Architecture for Real-Time Systems,* Addison-Wesley, 2003.

[Poynton03] Poynton, Charles, *Digital Video and HDTV: Algorithms and Interfaces.* Morgan Kaufmann Publishers, Elsevier Science (USA), 2003.

[Pressman92] Pressman, Roger S., *Software Engineering: A Practitioner's Approach,* 3rd ed. McGraw-Hill, 1992.

[Schroeder98] Schroeder, Chris, *Inside OrCAD Capture for Windows.* Elsevier Science and Technology Books, 1998.

[Shanley95] Shanley, Tom, and Don Anderson, *ISA System Architecture,* 3rd ed. Addison-Wesley, 1995.

[Shanley99] Shanley, Tom, and Don Anderson, *PCI System Architecture,* 4th ed. Addison-Wesley, 1999.

[Shanley01] Shanley, Tom, *PCI-X System Architecture.* Addison-Wesley, 2001.

[Shaw01] Shaw, Alan C., *Real-Time Systems and Software.* John Wiley & Sons, 2001.

[Simon99] Simon, David E., *An Embedded Software Primer.* Addison-Wesley, 1999.

[Smith97] Smith, Steven, *The Scientist and Engineer's Guide to Digital Signal Processing.* California Technical Publishing, 1997.

[Solari97] Solari, Stephen J. *Digital Video and Audio Compression,* McGraw-Hill, 1997.

[Stevens98] Stevens, W. Richard, *Unix Network Programming, Networking APIs: Sockets and XTI,* 2nd ed., Vol. 1. Prentice-Hall, 1998.

[Stevens99] Stevens, W. Richard, *Unix Network Programming, Interprocess Communications,* 2nd ed., Vol. 2. Prentice-Hall, 1999.

[Topic02] Topic, Michael, *Streaming Media Demystified.* McGraw-Hill, 2002.

[Wind River99] Wind River Systems, Inc., *VxWorks Programmer's Guide, 5.4,* Edition 1, Wind River Systems, 1999.

# WEB REFERENCES

[ABB] ABB industrial robotics, *http://www.abb.com/robotics*.

[AcroRob] Acroname Robotics, *http://acroname.com/*.

[ALSA] Advanced Linux Sound Architecture, *http://www.alsa-project.org/*.

[CIMG] CIMG Library with C++ image processing templates, *http://cimg.source forge.net/*.

[Concurrent] The Concurrent Versions System, CVS, can be very helpful for managing source code bases for real-time embedded development projects, *http://www.nongnu.org/cvs/*.

[DocumentPC] Documentation for the PowerPC from IBM can be found on the main Technical Documentation site, *http://www-306.ibm.com/chips/techlib*.

[eCos RTOS] The eCos RTOS is available through the Free Software Foundation with GPL licensing, *http://ecos.sourceware.org/*.

[FSMLabs] FSMLabs provides a University program for use of their RT Linux distributions, *http://www.fsmlabs.com/universities.html*.

[GarageTech] Garage Technologies Inc. also offers a six-degree-of-freedom arm, *http://www.garage-technologies.com/index.html*.

[Hitec] Hitec offers a wide range of servos suitable for simple robotics projects, *http://www.hitecrcd.com/homepage/product_fs.htm*.

[Honda ASIMO] Honda's ASIMO robot, *http://world.honda.com/ASIMO/*.

[IBM] IBM provides a download for PowerPC 4xx processor core models for use with Open SystemC design tools, *http://www-128.ibm.com/developerworks/power/pek/*.

[IETF RTP] IETF RTP, *http://www.ietf.org/rfc/rfc3550.txt*.

[IETF RTSP] IETF RTSP, *http://www.ietf.org/rfc/rfc2326.txt*.

[Intel Dual-Core] Intel Dual-Core Pentium documentation, *http://www.intel.com/design/pentiumd/documentation.htm*.

[Intel Mobile] Intel Mobile Pentium documentation, *http://www.intel.com/design/mobile/pentiumm/documentation.htm*.

[Intel Pentium] Intel Pentium (IA32) documentation, *http://www.intel.com/design/pentium4/documentation.htm*.

[Irfanview] Irfanview provides viewing of PPM and PGM formats and many more, *http://www.irfanview.com/*.

[Latest Python] The latest version of the Python programming language used for video stream display in examples, *http://python.org/*.

[Lynxmotion] Lynxmotion offers the Lynx 5 and 6 servo-controlled robotic arm kits, *http://www.lynxmotion.com/*.

[Microc] The Microc RTOS (along with a book describing it) can be purchased for a very reasonable cost for academic or personal use, *http://www.rabbitsemiconductor.com/etc/microc.shtml*.

[Miscrosoft Vis] Microsoft Visio can be used for UML design, basic circuit, mechanical, and system level design. The tool can be downloaded for free trial from Microsoft, *http://www.microsoft.com/office/visio/prodinfo/trial.mspx*.

[Motoman] Motoman industrial robotics, *http://motoman.com/*.

[NASA] NASA Johnson Space Center Robonaut, *http://vesuvius.jsc.nasa.gov/er_er/html/robonaut/robonaut.html*.

[NCD] National Control Devices, source for NCD209 Microchip PIC Hobby Servo Controller, *http://www.controlanything.com/*.

[NeuroRob] NeuroRobotics Ltd. offers a research-grade robotic arm, *http://www.neurorobotics.co.uk/*.

[OpenCD] Open Source Computer Vision Library project, *http://sourceforge.net/projects/opencvlibrary/*.

[OpenSystemC] The Open SystemC Initiative provides tools and a simulation environment for SystemC design automation, *http://www.systemc.org/*.

[OrCAD] OrCAD has a number of free downloads for lightweight versions of their products for schematic capture and simulation, *http://orcad.com/downloads.aspx*.

[OWI-7] The OWI-7 five-degree-of-freedom arm comes from OWI Robotics, *http://owirobots.com/*.

[PeeWee] PeeWee Linux is an enhanced 2.2 Linux kernel with a small footprint for embedding, *http://peeweelinux.com/*.

[Real-Time Java] The Real-Time Java specification, *https://rtsj.dev.java.net/*.

[Real-TimeLin] The Real-Time Linux Foundation has many resources for configuring your own RT Linux platform, *http://www.realtimelinuxfoundation.org/*.

[RivaTV] The RivaTV project is developing drivers to support NTSC frame capture, like Video for Linux, but specifically for nVidia, *http://rivatv.sourceforge.net/*.

[RobotWorx] RobotWorx industrial robotics integration, *http://www.robots.com/*.

[RobResearch] Robotics Research manufactures seven-degree-of-freedom highly dexterous arms with torque control, *http://www.robotics-research.com/*.

[RTEMS] RTEMS is an open source or free licensed RTOS, *http://www.rtems.com/*.

[Sony Ent] Sony entertainment robotics, *http://www.sony.net/Products/aibo/*.

[Subversion] The Subversion source code control system offers an alternative to CVS, *http://subversion.tigris.org/*.

[TAO] TAO Real-Time CORBA, *http://www.cs.wustl.edu/~schmidt/TAO.html*.

[Toyota Partner] Toyota partner robot, *http://www.toyota.co.jp/en/special/robot/*.

[UML Visio] The UML Visio stencils used are available for download, *http://www.phruby.com/stencildownload.html*.

[VidLinux] Video for Linux, *http://www.exploits.org/v4l/*.

[Weeder] Weeder Technologies has a wide range of serial multi-drop data acquisition and control boards, *http://www.weedtech.com/*.

[Wind River] Join the Wind River University program to obtain RT Linux and VxWorks for use in classroom instruction, *http://www.windriver.com/*.

[Xilinx] The Xilinx University Program offers access to many reconfigurable computing resources for embedded systems design, *http://www.xilinx.com/univ/*.

# Index

thread safe re-entrancy functions, 50–52. *See also* reentrant code
ThreadX, 43
Tightly Coupled Memory, 21, 93, 102–103, 205
timeouts, 10
timestamping, 209, 210
TLM. *See* Transaction Level Modes
trace ports, 188–189, 207
tracing, 206–208, 209
Transaction Level Modes, 257, 258
trapezoidal algorithm, 296
tuning performance to workload, 202–206

**U**
Universal Serial Bus, 143, 147–148
USB. *See* Universal Serial Bus

**V**
Verilog, 248
Versa Module Extension bus, 144–145
VHDL, 248

Virtex Chip-Scope, 207
Virtex II-Pro (Xilinx), 207
VME bus. *See* Versa Module Extension bus
VxWorks, 37, 43, 45, 50, 51–52, 104, 116, 118, 119, 155–157, 161, 166–169, 172, 174–175, 180, 182, 185, 187, 194, 229, 264, 271, 273–275

**W**
Walking 1's test, 190
WCET. *See* Worst-Case Execution Time
Windows, 154, 271
Wind River Systems, 43, 181
WindView, 154, 155
workload, definition of, 202
Worst-Case Execution Time, 20, 24–25, 86–91, 102, 104, 116, 119, 202
write latency. *See* I/O resources

**Z**
zero wait-state memory, 87, 88